D1877287

Labor, Employment, and Social Policies in the EU Enlargement Process

Changing Perspectives and Policy Options

Bernard Funck and Lodovico Pizzati
Editors

THE WORLD BANK
Washington, D.C.

1818 H Street, NW
Washington, DC 20433

1 2 3 4 04 03 02

ISBN 0-8213-5008-0

Library of Congress Cataloging-in-Publication Data

Labor, employment, and social policies in the EU enlargement process : changing perspectives and policy options / edited by Bernard Funck, Lodovico Pizzati.

p. cm.

"Papers presented at the conference held in Baden, Austria in June 2001"—Introd.

Includes bibliographical references and index.

ISBN 0-8213-5008-0

1. Labor market—Europe, Eastern—Congresses. 2. Labor market—Europe, Central—Congresses. 3. European Union—Europe, Eastern—Congresses. 4. European Union—Europe, Central—Congresses. 5. Europe—Economic integration—Congresses. I. Pizzati, Lodovico. II. Funck, Bernard, 1959–

HD5764.7.A6 L275 2001
331.12'042'0947—dc21

2001046678

Contents

BOXES

TABLES

FIGURES

MAPS

Foreword

Adapting to structural changes in the global economy, raising employment levels and competitiveness, preventing social exclusion—the challenges are common to all European countries. In their search for effective ways to meet these challenges, European countries have been increasingly willing to reassess old habits and dogma. The European Union enlargement is adding a new dimension to these challenges, as well as new opportunities for member and candidate countries to overcome them together. Clearly, the prospect of a more broadly integrated and a more competitive Europe should contribute to greater European and global prosperity. Still, given unemployment levels prevailing across Europe, it is hardly surprising that the prospect of heightened competition in product, services, capital, and labor markets would have many worried about their jobs and living standards. Indeed, there is a risk that such emotion-laden questions might cloud the policy debate and distract the public and policymakers from the facts and policy options at hand. It was time, we felt, to talk it over.

This was the purpose of the conference "Labor, Employment, and Social Policies in the EU Enlargement Process: Changing Perspectives and Policy Options," which took place in Baden and Vienna on June 28–30, 2001. The discussions sought to develop a common understanding of actual labor, employment, and social developments on the ground, as well as of the nature of the challenges ahead; to share concerns and lessons from policy initiatives; to draw on previous experiences of European integration and on the most recent research in the field; and to communicate the results of these exchanges to the public.

In keeping with these objectives, the conference was jointly organized by a broad array of institutions engaged in shaping public policies and opinion in Europe, including the Bertelsmann Foundation, the Institute for Public Affairs (Bratislava), the European Forum Alpbach, the Bruno Kreisky Forum for International Dialogue, the World Bank, and the Central and Eastern European research institutes and think tanks that are members of the Towards European Integration network led by the Bertelsmann Foundation and the World Bank. The European Commission, the Federal Ministry of Economic Affairs and Labor of Austria, the Federation of Austrian Industries, the Austrian National Bank, the Province of Lower Austria, Wiener Städtische Versicherung, and Bank Austria also supported the conference. The conference was attended by senior policymakers, academics, and social partners from western, central, and eastern Europe, as well as key observers from other OECD countries. The present volume brings together the papers that were presented on that occasion as well as some of the comments they elicited from participants.

In addition to the papers presented in this volume, the conference also drew inspiration from the speeches and remarks made by:

Edit Bauer
State Secretary, Ministry of Labor, Social Affairs and Family, Bratislava, Slovak Republic

Martin Bruncko
Director, Foreign Policy Studies, Institute for Public Affairs, Bratislava, Slovak Republic

Richard Freeman
Professor, London School of Economics, London, United Kingdom

Friedrich Gleissner
Vice-President, European Forum Alpbach, Vienna, Austria

Robert Holzmann
Director, Social Protection, World Bank, Washington, D.C., United States

Ferdinand Lacina
Former Minister of Finance
Chairman of the Board, Vienna Institute for International Economic Studies (WIIW)
Member of the Board, Bruno Kreisky Forum for International Dialogue, Vienna, Austria

Klaus Liebscher
Governor, Austrian National Bank, Vienna, Austria

Josef Mayer
Vice-Minister, Foreign Economic Policy and European Integration, Ministry of Economic Affairs and Labor, Vienna, Austria

Cornelius Ochmann
Director, Central and Eastern Europe, Bertelsmann Foundation, Gütersloh, Germany

Remigijus Simasius
Lithuanian Free Market Institute, Vilnius, Lithuania

Jan Svejnar
Executive Director, William Davidson Institute, Ann Arbor, Michigan, United States
Everett E. Berg Professor of Business Administration, Ann Arbor, Michigan, United States

Much of the success of the conference is due to the effective session chairmanship provided by:

Erhard Busek
Special Representative of the Austrian Government for EU Enlargement
President, European Forum Alpbach, Vienna, Austria

Bernard Funck
Lead Economist, World Bank, Washington, D.C., United States

Roger Grawe
Country Director for Hungary, Czech Republic, Slovak Republic, Slovenia and Moldova, World Bank, Budapest, Hungary

Annette Heuser
Director, Bertelsmann Foundation Brussels Office, Brussels, Belgium

András Inotai
Director-General, Institute for World Economics, Academy of Sciences, Budapest, Hungary

Cornelius Ochmann
Director, Central and Eastern Europe, Bertelsmann Foundation, Gütersloh, Germany

Finally, we would like to acknowledge especially the contributions of Erhard Busek and Franz Kaps in bringing us all together in this important undertaking; of Gabriele Schroers, Margit Schmidt, and Michael Fazekas in making it happen; and of the World Bank Publications team in managing the production of this volume.

Erhard Busek
President, European Forum Alpbach, Austria

Ferdinand Lacina
Member of the Board, Bruno Kreisky Forum for International Dialogue, Austria

Johannes Linn
Vice President, Europe and Central Asia, World Bank

Grigorij Meseznikov
President, Institute for Public Affairs, Slovak Republic

Werner Weidenfeld
Member of the Board, Bertelsmann Foundation
Director, Center for Applied Policy Research, Germany

Contributors

Maria Helena André
Confederal Secretary, European Trade Union Confederation, Brussels, Belgium

Eva Belabed
Rapporteur, Economic and Social Committee of the European Union, Brussels
Director, European Policy, Chamber for Workers and Employees for Upper Austria (AKOÖ), Vienna, Austria

Michał Boni
Chief of the Advisory Team to Deputy Prime Minister, Minister of Labor and Social Policy
Former Minister of Labor, Warsaw, Poland

Janis A. Emmanouilidis
Senior Researcher, Bertelsmann Group for Policy Research, Center for Applied Policy Research, Munich, Germany

Károly Fazekas
Deputy Director, Institute of Economics, Hungarian Academy of Sciences, Budapest, Hungary

Georg Fischer
Head of Employment Analysis, Directorate General for Employment and Social Affairs, European Commission, Brussels, Belgium

Bernard Funck
Lead Economist, World Bank, Washington, D.C., United States

Ion Giurescu
Secretary of State, Ministry of Labor and Social Solidarity, Bucharest, Romania

Jennifer Hunt
Associate Professor, Yale University, New Haven, Connecticut, United States

Elena Iankova
Research Fellow, Institute for European Studies, Cornell University, Ithaca, New York, United States
Visiting Fellow, Johnson Graduate School of Management, Cornell University, Syracuse, New York, United States

Juan Jimeno
FEDEA and Universidad de Alcala, Madrid, Spain

Rimantas Kairelis
Vice Minister, Ministry of Social Security and Labor, Vilnius, Lithuania

Zdenka Kovac
Director, Small Business Development Centre, Lubljana, Slovenia

Arvo Kuddo
Senior Labor Economist, World Bank, Washington, D.C., United States
Former Minister of Labor and Social Affairs, Tallinn, Estonia

Mária Ladó
Research Director, National Labor Center, Budapest, Hungary

Michael Landesmann
Director of Research, Vienna Institute for International Economic Studies, Vienna, Austria

Johannes F. Linn
Vice President, Europe and Central Asia, World Bank, Washington, D.C., United States

Tom Mulherin
Assistant Secretary-General, Department of Social, Community & Family Affairs, Dublin, Ireland
Vice-Chairman, EU Social Protection Committee, Brussels, Belgium

Lodovico Pizzati
Economist, World Bank, Washington, D.C., United States

Marcin Przybyla
Economist, World Bank, Warsaw, Poland

Iveta Radičová
Head, Center for Social Policy Analysis, Comenius University, Bratislava, Slovak Republic

Ana Revenga
Lead Economist, World Bank, Washington, D.C., United States

Michelle Riboud
Manager, Human Development Group, World Bank Institute, Washington, D.C., United States

Jan Rutkowski
Senior Labor Economist, World Bank, Washington, D.C., United States

Michal Rutkowski
Sector Manager, Social Protection, World Bank, Washington, D.C., United States

Carolina Sánchez-Páramo
Economist, World Bank, Washington, D.C., United States

Christof Schremmer
Managing Director, Austrian Institute for Regional Development and Spatial Planning, Vienna, Austria

Werner Sengenberger
International Labour Organization, Vienna, Austria

Carlos Silva-Jauregui
Senior Economist, World Bank, Washington, D.C., United States

Prof. Dr. Viktor Steiner
University of Munich and Cesifo, Munich, Germany

Rita Suessmuth
Former President of the German Parliament
Member of the German Parliament
Chairperson of the Independent Commission on Migration to Germany

Peter Tempel
Deputy Chief of Cabinet of EU Commissioner Verheugen, European Commission, Brussels, Belgium

Katherine Terrell
Professor of Economics, University of Michigan Business School and Ford School of Public Policy, Ann Arbor, Michigan, United States

Michal Vašečka
Sociologist, Institute for Public Affairs, Bratislava, Slovak Republic

Hermine Vidovic
Staff Economist, Vienna Institute for International Economic Studies, Vienna, Austria

Andreas Woergoetter
Head of Division, Economics Department, Organisation for Economic Co-operation and Development, Paris, France

Ruta Zilvere
Undersecretary of State, Ministry of Welfare, Riga, Latvia

CHAPTER 1

Overview

Bernard Funck and Lodovico Pizzati

Transition has been a wrenching process for the labor markets of Central and Eastern European countries (CEECs), and the prospect of joining the European Union gives rise to both hopes and misgivings among their population. Similarly, among member countries, a new resolve to shake off a legacy of high unemployment and to build "the most competitive economy in the world" (to use the words of the Lisbon European Council meeting of March 2000) mixes in some quarters with lingering apprehension that EU enlargement disrupts already strained labor markets.

This volume contains the papers presented at the conference held in Baden, Austria, in June 2001 to investigate these questions. The content of this research work captures the thoughts and analysis of the senior policymakers, academics, and social partners who participated in this series of seminars. This digest of research work seeks to present the latest factual trends on labor issues in accession countries, reviews existing labor market policies and social protection mechanisms, and discusses alternative strategies for employment creation in Central and Eastern Europe.

Johannes Linn and Georg Fischer start off the discussions and lay out many of the issues that will run through the entire volume. Linn's intervention highlights how much the issues faced by EU members and candidates have in common. These are (1) the underemployment of the working-age population and how it can be minimized; (2) whether a policy tradeoff exists between full employment, on the one hand, and high wages and productivity levels, on the other; (3) how the employment impact of structural shifts in the economic structure can be appropriately mitigated; (4) how to deal with the growing concentrations of unemployment and underemployment in certain age, regional, ethnic, and gender groups; (5) how to address the causes of low labor mobility as well as the fears that labor migration evokes; and, more generally, (6) how to balance the objectives of high employment, job security, and poverty reduction.

Linn stresses that there are no single, technically simple, or politically easy solutions to these questions. Designing effective policy responses will require bringing into play not just one but a whole range of policy instruments, including (1) good macroeconomics; (2) targeted interventions to restructure old industries, supplemented by complementary measures to reduce transitional costs for workers; (3) an appropriate investment climate for new firms; and, of course, (4) specific employment and labor market policies designed to lower labor taxation and increase the flexibility of labor markets.

These issues are common to candidate and member countries, and candidate countries have been invited to formulate a common overall policy response to them with the European Union. Is that a source of sclerosis or strength? Fischer believes the latter is the case. At any rate, it is the ambition of the EU's "Lisbon Strategy" that liberalization of markets, more adaptable and flexible labor markets, more modern welfare systems, and the social model go hand in hand as a comprehensive reform package in the pursuit of full employment in a highly competitive EU economy.

Labor Markets in the CEECs: Trends and Issues

Before getting into the heart of the policy issues, participants in the conference agreed that it was important to take stock of recent labor market trends in accession countries as they emerge from transition and explore how they are transforming their labor market policies to cope with the shifting reality of economic opening, enterprise restructuring, and integration within the enlarging European Union. Therefore, Part I of this volume begins with a bird's eye view of labor market developments and challenges at the regional level before zooming down to case studies of how these issues play at the national level in Poland, Lithuania, Romania, and Slovenia.

Hermine Vidovic paints a picture of soaring open unemployment, a massive exit from the labor market, and only moderate job creation across the region. In her overview the dramatic fall of gross domestic product (GDP) at the beginning of the transition was accompanied by sharp employment declines. The economic recovery that started in most countries in 1993 and 1994 led only to slight or temporary employment increases, increases which could be sustained only in Hungary and Slovenia. In general, huge job losses in industry and agriculture have been offset only to a small extent by new jobs in the services sector. In total, close to 10 million jobs were lost on a net basis between 1990 and 2000 in the ten CEECs. A parallel drop in labor force participation (to levels that generally remain higher, however, than the EU average) was not sufficient to prevent the spread of mass unemployment. The latter has several common features: (1) its incidence varies widely across regions; (2) it affects women, youth, low-skilled persons, ethnic minorities, and other socially disadvantaged groups the most; and (3) the proportion of long-term unemployment has been steadily rising.

After a decade of transition, the polarization between CEECs and countries in the former Soviet Union (FSU) in terms of economic and social performance has become striking. Katherine Terrell asks why employment in relative terms has not declined as much in the FSU countries in response to the decline in GDP as it has in the CEECs. The answer, she finds, has to do with the design of social policies, namely, with the fact that a higher level of benefits in the CEECs would have set a floor below the wage distribution and prevented as sharp a decline in wages as in the FSU. This would have led to greater quantity—than price—adjustment in the CEECs than in the FSU.

This would explain why the CEEC model would have yielded much more unemployment. But at the same time, Terrell points out, it would have allowed for more structural change and for less income inequality. With higher wage floors in the CEECs, not only were old firms forced to shed least productive labor, but the same people had longer spells of unemployment because they were "priced out" of potential new jobs. Higher social benefits would have smoothed the transition and provided start-up capital to finance the spread of new small-scale private activities in Central and Eastern Europe.

Each candidate has struggled (is still struggling) in its own way to define effective policy responses to the structural change and unemployment. While recognizing that only sustained growth can provide a lasting solution, they have sought to implement supporting packages that directly address existing labor market bottlenecks. The overall thrust of the strategies that countries are trying to put in place revolves around four broad themes (the four "pillars" of the policy framework proposed by the EU): improved employability, increased adaptability of enterprises and employees to new terms of economic competitiveness, development of entrepreneurship, and elimination of inequalities in the labor market.

Reflecting differences in country circumstances, however, the details and specific emphasis of the policy packages vary. The first difference is one of mindset. Following what Zdenka Kovac, Franci Kluzer, and Alenka Kaizer call "a period of romantic expectation" that the newly adopted market orientation would solve all problems, a consensus is now emerging in Slovenia in favor of taking a more proactive stance. Conversely, Ion Giurescu calls on Romania to break with the myth of a protective state capable of supporting its population on a permanent basis. The sources of labor market pressure also differ from one country to the next.

While agricultural employment has dropped by two-thirds in Hungary and Estonia (as noted in Vidovic's paper), it has increased in absolute and relative terms in Romania and Lithuania, notes Rimantas Kairelis, as impoverished segments of the population in those countries drifted back to small-scale subsistence farming. Agricultural employment remains high in Poland, too. Michał Boni notes the progress Poland has made in retrenching workers from sunset industries; the same, however, could not be said of Romania.

Transcending those differences is a growing consensus on the following priority: developing human resources (for instance, the "second chance" given in Slovenia to the unemployed to attain higher education levels) while activating labor markets. Witness the current debates on making the labor code more flexible in Poland and Slovenia, and the planned or proposed revamping of social safety nets in a bid to reduce "unemployment traps" (a serious problem in Romania where, according to Ion Giurescu, unemployment benefits are about at par with the minimum wage).

In his comments Michał Rutkowski underlines the importance for candidate countries to forge ahead with labor market reforms. Relaxing minimum wage regulations, where they are binding, and bringing down labor taxes, he explains, are needed to help improve low-skilled job prospects and the candidate countries' growth potential. Eva Belabed, for her part, emphasizes the necessity of involving social partners in policy formulation and the importance of that social dialogue to make the enlargement process sustainable.

Lessons from Previous Enlargements

The challenges facing the Central and Eastern European countries are similar, in nature if not in intensity, to the challenges that confronted previous adherents to the European Union. The second part reviews the experiences of Spain, another country that joined the EU at an income level lower than the EU average. It also describes the experience of the Laenders of the former East Germany, the only precedent of a transition economy joining the Union. The contributors to Part II tease out the lessons these countries might bring for the next wave of candidate countries.

Striking similarities exist between the accession of Spain and the CEECs. In both cases, notes Juan Jimeno, integration meant a substantial labor market reallocation from resource-intensive to labor-intensive activities, and from agriculture and manufacturing to services. In addition, in both cases labor productivity was the main driver of growth; initially, at least, growth generated little employment and left Spain saddled with extraordinarily high unemployment levels. Restrictive employment protection legislation did not prevent intense labor shedding caused by industrial restructuring and changes in the sectoral composition of employment. In Spain this high level of protection, combined with generous and long-lasting unemployment benefits, undoubtedly exacerbated the hysteretic features of the labor market. More flexible labor markets are needed to accommodate the labor reallocation required by shifts to different specialization patterns, modernization, and technological upgrading. Eventually, labor market reforms to ease employment protection legislation became unavoidable. From this experience, argues Jimeno, one should not infer that "one policy size fits all." To the contrary, the effects of institutions on labor market performance are country specific and time specific, and it might be counterproductive to harmonize too quickly the institutions and policies of the CEECs with those of Western Europe.

The manner in which labor markets in East Germany have coped with unification presents an even more telling precedent for the candidate countries. At the beginning of German unification, politicians and economists alike thought that the transition to a market economy and convergence to West German living standards would be much less painful than they turned out to be. Instead, employment contracted markedly (from 9 million to 6 million people), and unemployment soared to even higher levels than observed in other transition countries. Viktor Steiner shows that while average real wages in East Germany converged quickly toward 80 percent of West German levels, East German labor productivity languished at only about 60 percent of the West German level. Given the implied cost disadvantage, it is not surprising that employment would have continued to decline even as the economy recovered.

One important factor behind the observed wage rigidity in the face of mass unemployment is the high level of income support for the unemployed relative to average wages in East Germany. Another factor is the widespread availability of active labor market programs, especially public works and publicly funded training programs that often provide more generous income support than regular employment in the low-wage sector. This experience highlights the risk that a well-intentioned social program, rather than improving employment prospects, can entrap segments of the population in persistent unemployment.

Spatial Disparities and Labor Mobility

The fact that close to 15 percent of the population of the Eastern German Laenders decided to migrate in the aftermath of the unification of Germany could not fail to draw attention to the potential consequences of a further eastern enlargement of the European Union. This touches on one of the paradoxes the conference attempted to come to terms with: the fears sometimes expressed within member countries that enlargement may open the floodgates to a human wave of migrants in search of a better life. Strangely enough, candidate countries worry about the opposite: their concern is that low labor mobility is exacerbating regional disparities. The papers in Part III examine the facts involved on both sides of this puzzle (too much mobility? not enough?) and explore the policy options available to the candidate and member countries.

The first paper, by Jan Rutkowski and Marcin Przybyla, returns to an issue raised by Michał Boni in Part I—the gaping disparities in Poland (and in many EU members) in the incidence of unemployment across regions. The authors examine the determinants of regional differences in creating jobs. Key among them are the degree of urbanization, the importance of service activities, the level of wages relative to productivity, the density of infrastructure, and, last but not least, the flexibility of the wage structure. The authors find that a relatively high and uniform minimum wage at the national level does reduce the employment chances of low productivity workers. They conclude that a lower minimum wage at the national level or differentiation of the wage by regions would help reduce the level of unemployment as well as its dispersion across regions. In their comments Michael Landesmann and Werner Sengenberger question how robust this conclusion is, and just how effective such policy measures might be.

Why, then, are regional disparities so persistent? Károly Fazekas investigates this question in great detail in the case of Hungary, a country where, in contrast to Poland, employment has been growing (and unemployment dropping) in recent years, and where the minimum wage had been, until recently, relatively low. Differences in unemployment rates, although not particularly wide across regions (by international standards), are not only high but widening at the subregional level. Contrary to popular wisdom, these differences relate less to the spatial pattern of job destruction (the collapse of old industries)—which has been relatively uniform—than to that of job creation—which has not.

The uneven distribution of foreign direct investment appears to have played a major role in this. Fazekas considers why prevailing labor cost differentials did not sufficiently motivate investors to move to the depressed, high unemployment regions. What seems to be happening is that skill-intensive technologies look for an educated work force and the region-specific external economies and agglomeration effects of more developed areas, where they then concentrate. Low-skill technologies, on the other hand, may well reach the less developed regions (foreign direct investment [FDI] in low-skill industries like food, clothing, and mining has reached some of the remote, poorly educated eastern parts of Hungary), but expansion of low-skill technologies is constrained by transport cost considerations. The phenomenon can become self-sustaining if labor costs start to decrease in the most favored regions as a result of the productivity improvements brought about by foreign investment (as observed in Budapest and in the central agglomeration relative to the peripheries, or in large cities relative to small towns). This erodes whatever competitive advantage less favored regions may have had initially. The high cost of commuting relative to earning prospects leads to a segregation of local markets that particularly affects unskilled workers. Indeed, education appears to have a very strong impact on the chances of finding a job by commuting.

These findings suggest that labor market policies alone may not be sufficient to address unemployment disparities across regions. Other policy instruments (education, public transportation, road investments) will also need to come into play.

What was so different in the former East Germany that caused so many people to move? Jennifer Hunt uses detailed interview data from the German socio-economic panel to investigate this question. Perhaps half of the cumulative outflows from East Germany were spurred by political, not economic, reasons. Indeed, until the parliamentary elections in East Germany in March 1990, the main motivation for emigration was political, with family reunification coming second. It was only later (when it became clear that unification was imminent) that economic reasons (particularly the wage gap between Eastern and Western Laenders) became dominant. Such motivations concerned a smaller absolute number of people because emigration from the East fell quickly after 1990. From then on commuting became more prevalent, allowing workers (a third of whom had recently been laid off) to double their previous salaries while still benefiting from the low consumption prices and housing costs in the East by commuting to the West.

The flows from new EU members are likely to be smaller by comparison, Hunt observes. First, workers from Central and Eastern Europe may feel less of a spur to move than did their East German counterparts: the political impetus that played such a role in the latter's case is now absent in the accession countries, and the worst mass layoffs may be behind us. Clearly, language and culture are less similar than in the German case, and family ties between the source and destination region play less of a role. Also, for much of the population in the accession countries, the distances involved in commuting are much greater, although the phenomenon might be important along the Bavarian and Austrian borders, and along the Italian border with Slovenia.

Indeed, commuting may pose a greater challenge for Austria than outright migration, Christof Schremmer finds. About two-thirds of Austria's jobs are located within 60 kilometers of areas in the candidate countries where wages are up to six or seven times lower (at the current exchange rates). Many fear those jobs might be seriously at risk once borders open up. The available evidence does not support the view that migration would displace local workers, notes Schremmer. Today peripheral regions in Austria with the highest proportion of foreign workers are also the ones with the lowest unemployment rates. There is little doubt in his mind that in the long run the economic impact of opening up Austrian markets (including labor markets) to competition will be positive. But there may be painful frictions along the way, political or otherwise. The slower the accession takes place, the less positive the economic impacts will be. But the political frictions may be less as well. Schremmer suggests that a gradual opening of the labor markets along the Austrian border over the next five to seven years could strike the right balance between the two considerations. In the interval, a real appreciation of the CEEC currencies might help close the current wage gap.

In a paper that sets out the issue in the broader context of the EU enlargement strategy, Peter Tempel joins Michael Landesmann in noting that the numerous studies about the potential for migration into the Union from the candidate countries seem to concur that the total numbers involved may be small or even insignificant on the whole—although perhaps not for border regions where such flows might concentrate (as the two previous papers had indicated). Rather than ignoring the fears that the prospect of free movement of labor between the CEECs and the current members of the EU ignites, the author argues it is better to respond to these fears, be they justified or not. The proposed flexible transitional period of up to seven years, with reviews after two and five years, is meant to do just that. The solution found offers, the author feels, adequate protection for those Member States that need it for a certain period and at the same time opens up the possibility of immediate liberalization for those that want it. Indeed, some Member States have already announced their intention to permit unrestricted free movement of persons from the point of accession. A limited period of transition, Tempel stresses, is much easier to cope with than the risk that, at the end of the day, the political support necessary for the endorsement of the outcome of the negotiations may be lacking.

Rita Suessmuth's paper indicates that mentalities may be evolving on this question within the European Union itself. Germany has recently set up an "Independent Commission on Migration" (which she chaired). Its work is based on the explicit assumption that the country has a vital need for migrants. But this attitude coexists with fears that EU enlargement could be detrimental to current members and candidate countries. These risks, she notes, should not be overestimated. Nor should the positive side of the balance sheet be ignored. Migration flows might help Western European countries counteract the effects of declining birth rates and an aging population on their growth potential and innovation capacity, on pension systems and national budgets.

In this context, she argues, new attitudes and approaches are in order. It will be particularly important for a country like Germany to attract highly qualified migrants whose innovative abilities and technological knowledge make a decisive contribution to future prosperity. For this to happen, migrants coming to the EU must be allowed to participate on equal terms in the host country's economic, cultural, and political life while respecting cultural diversity. It will take decades, Suessmuth concludes, to change the understanding of migration in Western European societies, but this is an effort that should be undertaken sooner rather than later. The Europeans' approach to migration will help determine the competitiveness of the enlarged EU in a globalized world.

Arvo Kuddo highlights the potential displacement effects that the opening of labor markets will cause, not within member countries but in applicant countries. Like Juan Jimeno, he stresses the need for more flexible labor market institutions. Kuddo favors giving collective industrial relations rather than government regulation a greater role (a point already made by Zdenka Kovac and her colleagues in their case study of Slovenia).

Eurosclerosis or European Social Model?

To what extent are the accession countries' labor markets actually rigid? Is the prospect of joining the European Union a force for progress in this area, or will Central and Eastern European countries inherit its syndrome of labor market rigidities and persistently high unemployment, a syndrome sometime labeled "Eurosclerosis"? Is there such a thing as a European Social Model and, if so, what is it? These are some of the questions addressed in Part IV.

Michelle Riboud, Carlos Silva-Jauregui, and Carolina Sánchez-Páramo point out that it is impossible to talk about "the accession countries" as if they were a uniform group in this respect. Despite their common recent history and the steps they have all taken to evolve toward EU standards, the labor policies they have adopted differ in fundamental ways. Taken together, however, the labor markets of the CEECs do not appear excessively rigid when compared to those of EU and Organisation for Economic Co-operation and Development (OECD) members. In terms of employment protection, for instance, they tend to rank in the middle of the "labor market flexibility scale" (with the exception of Slovenia). Employment protection legislation in the CEECs is definitely less flexible than in the United States or the United Kingdom but certainly not as rigid as in Southern Europe. Although they have adopted—again with some variation—the set of policies (passive and active) common to all EU and OECD countries, the Central and Eastern European countries are devoting modest amounts of budgetary resources to the unemployed and, in this respect, are closer to the United States, the United Kingdom, and Southern Europe than to the rest of Western Europe. Finally, candidate countries have moved away from centralized wage bargaining toward a more liberal system of wage negotiation. Where the CEECs really stand out is in terms of the tax burden on labor: theirs is the highest in Europe.

How much do prevailing rigidities matter? Certainly, they cannot on their own, the authors find, account for the dramatic labor market developments that have occurred as part of the transition process. But they may play a more crucial role in the future in determining candidate countries' ability to engineer a recovery of employment and a decline in long-term unemployment. In this respect there is evidence that those countries that have undertaken the most far-reaching liberal reforms are also enjoying the most dynamic markets, with larger job and worker flows.

Is there such a thing as a European Social Model to guide them in this reform process? Maria Helena André thinks there is. This model may have taken different forms from country to country, but it reflects the same set of values: a vision of the European Member States as "welfare states," a recognition of social rights and of the role of social partners, and an awareness of the need for public services and social protection systems. André emphasizes that this model, for all the criticism leveled at it, is the reason Europe has become one of the most advanced societies in the world during the past fifty years. Economic and social progress went hand in hand and thus mutually reinforced each other. That this model needs to be revitalized in the light of the deep changes taking place in European economies and societies is well recognized.

The Lisbon Council on Employment, Economic Reform and Social Cohesion, held in March 2000, represented, in André's view, a new start in this respect. It emphasized the objective of full employment based on stronger and sustainable growth, social cohesion, the creation of the knowledge-based society, and access to lifelong learning. The implementation of the European Employment Strategy, she recommends, should now become an integral part of the enlargement process of the European Union and involve the full participation of the candidate countries' social partners.

The European Social Model should not be seen as a fixed blueprint but as a set of values that countries adapt to different and changing societal circumstances, notes Georg Fischer in his paper in Part IV. Change is indeed essential. It is at the heart of the European Council's announcements on Europe becoming the most competitive economy, on modernizing the European Social Model, on restoring the conditions for full employment. The social partners, argues Fischer, must take the lead to bring about the necessary changes (including more modern workplace organization, more flexible work-time arrangements, and broader access to training in enterprises and to lifelong learning).

Is it reasonable to expect this to happen? Mária Ladó remarks on the current weakness of the social dialogue in candidate countries, while Elena Iankova deplores the lack of civil society involvement in the overall accession process. For his part, Andreas Woergoetter sounds a cautionary note on the replicability of the social partnership in candidate countries. Social partnership has worked best in Western Europe (including Austria) in times of relative stability. When restructuring was needed, this model has often resulted in an externalization and socialization of adjustment costs, which the governments in candidate countries can ill afford.

When Markets Fail: The Risk of Poverty and Social Exclusion

The levels of unemployment (particularly long-term unemployment) that accompany economic restructuring are worrisome not only because they waste productive resources. Ana Revenga documents the very strong link observed in empirical studies on Central and Eastern Europe between long-term unemployment, poverty, and social exclusion. With the rise in long-term unemployment, a trend can clearly be observed toward the emergence of more persistent poverty, that is, toward the formation of a class of "structurally" poor households—an underclass. Some groups appear more vulnerable than others: minorities, rural households, especially in isolated areas and depressed regions, and children. In contrast, the same studies show that safety nets have been relatively effective in protecting the elderly from poverty.

The problem, Revenga points out, is that safety nets are generally designed to protect households from shocks that are *temporary*, but are often inadequate for dealing with the problem of *permanent* poverty or *long-term* unemployment. When poverty becomes permanent, traditional safety nets can create a vicious circle of growing dependency, degrading skills, and diminished ability to integrate into the labor market. Ultimately, this leads to social exclusion. Some of these problems can be tackled by redesigning systems and making the transition from welfare to work easier, as a number of OECD countries have been trying to do. However, for such supply-side measures to pay off, greater labor demand for people with relatively low skills must be fostered. This, in turn, requires strong, stable growth and reduced tax wedges on labor.

Despite efforts to reform the welfare system in Latvia, poverty in that country has not only been expanding but also deepening. Ruta Zilvere notes, in addition to the growing income poverty, an increase in social polarization, a higher incidence of unnatural and violent deaths, and the marginalization of individuals, families, and social groups, as evidenced by the increased number of beggars, homeless people, and street children and the spread of substance abuse as an escape from social hardship. Long-term unemployment, along with its correlate—a low level of education, is one of the main sources of vulnerability. Social safety nets do exist, but clearly they have not been effective enough. Recognizing the problem, the Latvian government is now exploring new approaches, including support and counseling targeted to the long-term unemployed. A Guaranteed Minimum Income Benefit, which already exists in a number of candidate countries such as the Czech Republic and Slovak Republic, has been proposed.

In contrast to what Ruta Zilvere observed in Latvia, ethnicity has become a major dimension of poverty in other candidate countries, particularly in those with large Roma minorities. Michal Vašečka and Iveta Radičová explore the dimensions of the problem in the Slovak Republic, one of the countries where the proportion of Roma is believed to be highest (although reliable statistics on this topic are lacking). The end of communism ended the policy of forcible integration of the ethnic Roma into the mainstream of society, causing large numbers of them to experience, in the authors' words, *double marginalization* (to impoverished regions and to communities with low social capital). Furthermore, a heavy reliance on a system of social assistance would have trapped many beneficiaries in situations of passivity and welfare dependency. The demise of the Roma is regularly flagged in the reports of the European Commission that assess progress in meeting the Copenhagen membership criteria.

This is not to say that the European Union has ready-made solutions to offer. To the contrary, insists Tom Mulherin, the issues presented by Ruta Zilvere, Michal Vašečka, and Iveta Radičová echo the current concerns of Member States. What the EU has in place is a process of open coordination designed to enable members to learn from each other's efforts in the field. Following the Lisbon Council's invitation that the Union "promote a better understanding of social exclusion through continuous dialogue and exchanges of information and best practices on the basis of commonly agreed indicators," current efforts are going in two directions: the definition of commonly accepted indicators of social inclusion and the formulation by the member countries of National Action Plans for inclusion for peer review within the Union.

From the perspective of the candidate countries, Janis Emmanouilidis notes, the role of the European Union does not stop there. The European Union is imposing broader conditionality linked to the accession negotiation process. It is providing financial aid and technical assistance to support the adoption of the Union's social policy *acquis* (for strengthening social protection systems and improving the social dialogue between governments, social partners, nongovernmental organizations [NGOs], and the general public). It is pressing candidate countries to adhere to international legal norms that promote social inclusion (for example, the European Social Charter, the Framework Convention for National Minorities, the Convention on the Elimination of All Forms of Racial Discrimination, and the Convention on the Elimination of All Forms of Discrimination against Women). As already noted, it is taking up matters of ethnic and other forms of discrimination in the context of accession negotiations.

How will the EU's role evolve in the context of enlargement? So far member countries' attitude toward social standards has been dominated by concerns about maintaining a level playing field in their economic competition, Emmanouilidis argues. As a result, the process has primarily aimed at defining the lowest common denominator of social policy among them. This approach leaves ample room for the principle of subsidiarity to operate, as well as for poorer countries to compete on the basis of lower wage costs. The risk is that the European Union would be perceived as indifferent to the plight of some of its current or future citizens (including those who might feel victimized by the implementation of the *acquis communautaire*), and that such a perception would undermine political support for the Union. For the sustainability of the European integration process, Emmanouilidis suggests that it would be preferable to abandon the current quest for a lowest-common-denominator social policy and strive instead toward more ambitious common standards backed by sufficient financial transfers—that is, toward what the author calls a vision of the EU as a "development community."

Conclusions

It would not do justice to the diversity of views expressed in this volume to reduce them to a common denominator, either. Clearly, no one recipe or consensus exists. What does exist, as the conference made apparent, is a common awareness of the need for change and a willingness to examine without prejudices the facts, proposals, ideas, and experiences that may help bring it about. Given the current starting point, something will indeed need to change if the enlarged Europe is to become by 2010 the most competitive economy in the world with full employment of 70 percent of its adult population (Resolution of the Lisbon European Council of March 2000). This will require a new balance between flexibility and job security; between social protection and labor taxation; between social solidarity and incentives to join the labor force; between the roles of the state regulation, collective industrial relations, and individual contracts; between active and passive labor market policies; and between initial education and lifelong learning.

This search for a balance is common to member and candidate countries. All of them are struggling to define new ways to reconcile and promote employability, flexibility, and equity. In Central and Eastern Europe the transition shattered the old model and forced change. While labor market developments in candidate countries have perhaps been dominated so far by the fallout from the opening of other markets (for goods, capital) in the process of transition, the quality of labor market policies will increasingly matter going forward, now that firms are more frontally exposed to global competition. A similar process has taken place in Western Europe, where frustration with persistently high unemployment combined with a need to adjust to the liberalization of other markets in the context of the Single Market has led member countries to reconsider old dogmas and try new ways.

Rather than seeking to formulate a new cannon applicable to all, this volume explores the diversity of experience and allows its readers to draw lessons that are useful to their particular concerns and circumstances. It is our hope that this volume and the Baden conference that preceded it will make a significant contribution to the public debate on this matter.

Introduction

CHAPTER 2

Introductory Remarks

Johannes F. Linn

Employment and labor market issues are obviously key challenges for European countries, as I was able to witness in observing the vigorous policy debates during recent visits to Warsaw and to Berlin. Unemployment, labor market policies, and migration issues are at the center of the policy debate about structural reforms in European countries and about the EU enlargement process.

Let me share with you some personal thoughts about these issues, not as an expert, but as an informed observer who might raise some helpful questions to carry forward the research and policy debate. I deliberately do not distinguish between EU Members and EU accession countries in the subsequent discussion, since I believe the issues and options they face are quite comparable.

What Are the Key Employment and Labor Market Issues?

To begin, let us consider the key issues and questions that arise as we deal with labor market and employment issues in Europe. Obviously, the issues do not apply with equal force across countries, and as part of the policy analysis and debate it is important to identify which are most prevalent and relevant for each particular country concerned.

1. Many European countries face high unemployment, low labor force participation, and hence underemployment of the available labor force. This

raises a question: What are the causes of this underemployment, and how can it be minimized?

2. Unemployment and underemployment are high in many European countries, but some argue that this has prevented the prevalence of low wage jobs and has been associated with high labor productivity. The question therefore arises whether there is a tradeoff between full employment on the one hand and wage and productivity levels on the other.

3. Underemployment is in part the result of structural shifts in the economies, as old industries shut down, agriculture is rationalized, and regional shifts in production and employment occur. The question is how the employment impacts of such structural shifts can be appropriately mitigated.

4. Unemployment and underemployment are also concentrated in certain age, regional, ethnic, and gender groups. How does policy best deal with such concentrations?

5. There are barriers to labor mobility, in the sense that people could move, but do not move, from low to high employment areas or sectors, or from low productivity to high productivity jobs. This could be attributable to subsidy and tax distortions or regulatory rigidities, or to cultural aspects. Determining the sources of low labor mobility is an important issue for labor market research.

6. Labor migration raises two types of concerns: for the regions that lose labor, the question is whether this leads to depopulation and brain drain, and hence long-term backwardness; for the receiving regions, there are concerns about the potentially negative impact on employment, wages, and social services that immigration may cause. Are these real or only imagined problems?

7. High unemployment and underemployment may result in poverty, especially in the absence of adequate social safety nets, but high employment regimes (as in the United States) may also be associated with job insecurity and hence vulnerability, if employees can readily be fired, and there is high labor turnover.

Are There Simple Solutions?

- Since there are many important employment and labor market issues and tradeoffs, there is no single solution.

- Since employment and labor market issues and their causes are complex, there are no simple technical solutions.

- Since there are many tradeoffs across different groups of winners and losers, there are no easy political solutions.

In sum, there are no single, technically simple, or politically easy solutions to the many complex and politically demanding employment and labor market issues that European countries face.

What Are the Key Policy Instruments and Lessons?

In spite of the complexity of the employment and labor market issues, there are important policy instruments and lessons. First, good macroeconomic policies are essential for long-term economic stability, investment, and growth, including growth of employment. In practice, however, governments often end up with a combination of tight monetary policy and loose fiscal policy. This is clearly bad since such a policy mix results in high interest rates and an overvalued exchange rate, which in turn weaken investment and growth, discourage the growth of small and medium enterprises (SMEs), and hence result in low employment growth. However, fixing poor macro policies, and especially poor fiscal policy, is not easy, since tax rates are generally too high already, and public expenditures are often inflexible downward, in support of entrenched interests.

Policies toward old industries represent the second type of instrument available. Here the choice is between protecting jobs in old industries or freeing up the resources, including labor, tied up in low productivity industries and facilitating their move to more productive uses. It is now generally recognized that protecting old industries as a way to save or create jobs is not a long-term option. But as one permits or encourages the downsizing of old industries, the social costs of transformation must be appropriately addressed (as, for example, in the current programs of coal sector restructuring in Central and Eastern Europe, supported by the World Bank) and an effort must be made to explain the approach to the affected population groups.

Third, policies are available in support of new enterprises. It is essential to create an appropriate investment climate for new firms, SMEs, and self-employment, and for foreign direct investment. The regulatory framework for entry, registration of new firms, investment permits, the tax system, the rules covering exit (including bankruptcy), and the condition of the financial sector and hence access to credit are key determining features of new industrial and service enterprise growth. Research has shown that those countries that have had favorable conditions and hence rapid growth of new firms and SMEs have done better in terms of overall economic growth as well as in employment creation.

Fourth, I would like to mention specific employment and labor market policies. I begin with labor taxation. Income taxes, pension contributions, unemployment and health insurance contributions, and often other tax or tax-like contributions frequently add to the cost of employment, discourage job growth, and foster the informal or shadow economy and low labor force participation. Lowering the marginal tax rates on labor and exploring alternative forms of cost recovery or taxation (user charges and/or consumption taxes) are important ways to enhance the employment creation effect of economic growth. In addition, traditional social expenditure programs will frequently have to be restructured to reduce the aggregate revenue requirement, by targeting the programs on real social needs and increasing efficiency of delivery.

Employment policies can reduce the costs to employers of adding additional labor and hence will help create employment. Allowing for increased flexibility and differentiation of labor contracts, of part-time and overtime regulations, and of minimum wages is beneficial. Other options include reducing the protection against layoffs and adapting practices of collective bargaining to the changing economic landscape. (Employment is shifting toward smaller scale enterprises and the tertiary sectors, where activities can be more informal and atomistic and where forms and terms of employment are necessarily more diverse.) However, there are difficult and unavoidable tradeoffs here between job creation on the one hand and job security, equity, and fairness in the treatment of employees on the other, which need to be weighed explicitly. Finally, active labor market policies are available. Training and education (focused narrowly on specific vocational skills or broadly on cognitive capacities), transitional funding, and credits for laid-off workers, and specific programs for small entrepreneurs are among the instruments that can help unemployed workers, especially those affected by the restructuring of sectors and enterprises, find new, more productive and better paying jobs or occupations. It remains uncertain to what extent these types of active labor market policies help to create jobs, and there are risks of discriminatory treatment in the way they are being implemented to help particular strata of the population. However, these instruments should be explored as complementary tools in an effort to reduce the transitional costs of economic restructuring.

Conclusion

Employment and labor market issues and policies are clearly important aspects of overall economic and social policies in the European countries. They have important efficiency, growth, and social dimensions and play a very important role in the political sustainability of economic reforms.

In designing specific packages of employment and labor market policies, policymakers should:

- Match policy instruments with policy issues. For example, active labor market policies will not help avoid the difficulties created by a bad macro policy mix, but they are well suited to addressing the transitional costs of sectoral restructuring.

- Be clear about who the winners and the losers are and be clear about the possible conflict between efficiency and social goals. Avoiding disappointment by not meeting (unrealistic) expectations is an important aspect of sustainable policy.

- Bear in mind that long-term and short-term policy impacts may differ. For example, the long-term effects of restructuring may well be win-win for all, but in the short term some groups of the population may face substantial costs. Helping the losers minimize these costs and making sure that winners are actually aware of the benefits they receive will provide for fewer social disruptions and stronger political support for reforms.

The traditional dividing line between employers and employees and their respective interests may be less important now than in the past, as self-employment, profit sharing, and stock option programs become more common in the new economy.

CHAPTER 3

Introductory Remarks

Georg Fischer

This seminar focuses on the two issues at the center of the political debate in Europe—transition and accession, two closely related processes, a twofold challenge.

The European Council of Copenhagen clearly linked the two processes. It proposed that successful preparation for membership in the European Union included transition to a market economy, successful adjustment to the Single Market, and more generally, participation in EU-wide economic and social policies. The European Councils of Amsterdam, Luxembourg, and Lisbon have clarified the economic, social, and employment-related challenges for the European Union and further developed the policy approaches.

I know that there is a debate about how to perceive the employment and social policy approaches, including the legal provisions ("social acquis") that the European Union developed. Some will argue that these are additional burdens on economies that already must undergo difficult changes. This is a view that is not shared by the European Community, its institutions, and the Member States. They see these policies as part of a comprehensive package that makes Europe adaptable and competitive in a global economy.

This does not mean that the European Union is unaware of the need for change. Subsequent European Councils have stressed that Europe has to improve its competitiveness and its economic and employment performance. The Lisbon Council has put full employment back on the European agenda. Economic, employment, and social policies should restore the conditions for reaching full employment within the most competitive economy in the world. The European Council asks the EU to make progress in this direction while sustaining and modernizing the European Social Model. Essentially, what the EU has embarked upon is an agenda for reform and for achieving a number of important and related objectives concerning economic performance, social cohesion, employment, and competitiveness.

Particularly in the field of employment, quantitative and therefore measurable objectives have been specified. They are to reach by the year 2010 substantially higher levels of employment: a 70 percent employment rate for the adult population, more than 60 percent for the female working-age population, and 50 percent for the elderly work force. Europe is closer to some of these targets than others and far away from the target on employment of the elderly. Some Member States have already reached one or even all the quantitative targets.

The employment target for the elderly illustrates one more element of the European strategy: the relationship between quantitative targets, job creation, and quality in work. One of the major obstacles for maintaining and increasing employment of the elderly lies in the way they participate in employment: low skill levels and very low participation in further training. Working conditions and working time arrangements badly suit the needs of aging workers. Europe will need to learn to manage the aging of the workforce at the level of enterprises in order to allow workers to stay longer in employment. Without fundamental changes in this respect, changing economic incentives through tax and social security reform, as important as the latter is, will not induce the necessary rise in participation of the elderly. Tax-benefit reforms must be hand in hand with measures to enhance job availability and to make existing jobs more accessible and attractive for workers.

Liberalization of markets, more adaptable and flexible labor markets, modernized welfare systems, and the social model need to go together as a comprehensive reform package. This is often called the "Lisbon Strategy."

Very recently, the Goeteborg European Council extended this Lisbon Strategy to candidate countries by inviting them to adopt and to implement under their specific national circumstances the overall economic, social, and sustainable development approaches of the European Union.

The enlargement perspective imposes on the EU a new thinking on the interdependence between the old and new Members, and the Goeteborg European Council reflects this clearly. The ambitious objectives of full employment and of a modernized social model in a highly competitive EU economy require that the economies and societies of the present and future Member States make their contributions in a coordinated manner.

In the light of the broader economic and social agenda for the European Union, now extended to candidate countries, this conference is very timely indeed. Its agenda, topics, and speakers promise an interesting—sometimes controversial—event that should contribute to the debate on modernizing the European economy and social model and how this relates to candidate countries.

PART I

Labor Markets in the CEECs: Trends and Issues

CHAPTER 4

Labor Market Trends in Central and Eastern European Countries

Hermine Vidovic

Since the start of the transition, labor markets have changed significantly in Central and Eastern European countries (CEECs). In contrast to the pretransition period, when the centrally planned economies enjoyed full employment coupled with hidden unemployment, the labor force has contracted sharply in almost all CEECs. The whole process has been accompanied by soaring open unemployment—previously existing only in former Yugoslavia—a massive exit from the labor market, and only moderate job creation. This chapter gives a brief overview of the recent economic developments in the ten candidate countries—Bulgaria, the Czech Republic, Estonia, Hungary, Latvia, Lithuania, Poland, Romania, the Slovak Republic, and Slovenia—and examines the main labor market features based on available data.

Output

Almost all Central and Eastern European candidate countries suffered from huge output contractions in the initial period of transition. Output recovery started unevenly in the subsequent years, with Poland enjoying the fastest recovery (from 1992 onward), while growth in Lithuania and Latvia resumed only in 1996 (table 4.1A). In the year 2000 four countries—Poland, Slovenia, Hungary, and the Slovak Republic—already exceeded their pretransition output level to a considerable extent, while the Czech Republic reached just the 1990 level. Estonia reached 87 percent of the 1990 level; Romania and Bulgaria, about 80 percent. GDP recovery has so far been slowest in Lithuania and Latvia. These significant disparities among the transition countries in their economic performance are clearly reflected in the different levels of the GDP per capita (table 4.1B). Measured in terms of purchasing power standards, GDP per head is highest in Slovenia, reaching slightly over 70 percent of the EU average in 2000, thus surpassing the level of Greece and being close to Portugal. The Czech Republic and Hungary come next (61 percent and 53 percent, respectively). The Slovak Republic reported about half the EU level. Poland and Estonia reported 41 percent each. There is a remarkable gap between these countries and Latvia and Lithuania (30 percent each), Romania (27 percent), and Bulgaria (25 percent).

Labor Market

The total population of the candidate countries stood at 104.4 million in 2000, which is about 1.7 million less than in 1990 (table 4.2). Poland and Romania account for about 60 percent of the total population in the region. The sharpest decline in population over the 1990–2000 period occurred in Estonia and Latvia, by 13 percent and 11 percent respectively, followed by Bulgaria (–6 percent) and Romania and Hungary where it declined by about 3 percent each. Population increases were registered only in the Slovak Republic and Poland, while in the Czech Republic the population remained almost stagnant. The main reason for the drop was outward migration, particularly in the initial period of transition, which came to a halt in 1993; the continued decline in the subsequent years was mainly due to a natural decrease but also resulted from economic hardship, especially in Bulgaria and Romania.

The share of the working-age population (15 to 64 years) has been on the increase in all countries since 1993, accounting for roughly two-thirds of the total population. As in most Western countries, the population in the CEECs is aging. The share of people older than 65 is generally on the rise. Aging of the population is most pronounced in Bulgaria, followed by the Czech Republic and Hungary. In accordance with the increasing shares of the productive and postproductive age groups, the share of young people up to the age of 14 years has been on the decline. The proportion of the preproductive age group is highest in Poland and the Slovak Republic, while it accounts for only 17 percent in Bulgaria.

Employment losses went along with falling activity and employment rates in all candidate countries. In Hungary the activity rate in 1997 was almost 12 percentage points lower than in 1989 and the female rate dropped 17 percentage points during this period.[1] The reasons for the decrease in activity rates are manifold: the increase in early retirements and disability pensions, the reduction of working pensioners,[2] the "discouraged worker" effect (jobless persons no longer actively seeking new employment opportunities), the return of unemployed people to education, and employment in the informal sector (ECE 1995).

TABLE 4.1A GROSS DOMESTIC PRODUCT
(annual percentage change, constant prices)

Country	*1990*	*1991*	*1992*	*1993*	*1994*	*1995*	*1996*	*1997*	*1998*	*1999*	*2000*[a]	*Index 1990 = 100* *2000*
Czech Republic	–1.2	–11.6	–0.5	0.1	2.2	5.9	4.3	–0.8	–1.2	–0.4	2.9	99.9
Hungary	–3.5	–11.9	–3.1	–0.6	2.9	1.5	1.3	4.6	4.9	4.2	5.2	108.0
Poland	–11.6	–7.0	2.6	3.8	5.2	7.0	6.0	6.8	4.8	4.1	4.0	143.1
Slovak Republic	–2.5	–14.6	–6.5	–3.7	4.9	6.7	6.2	6.2	4.1	1.9	2.2	105.3
Slovenia	–4.7	–8.9	–5.5	2.8	5.3	4.1	3.5	4.6	3.8	5.2	4.6	120.1
Bulgaria	–9.1	–11.7	–7.3	–1.5	1.8	2.9	–10.1	–7.0	3.5	2.4	5.8	79.2
Romania	–5.6	–12.9	–8.8	1.5	3.9	7.1	3.9	–6.1	–5.4	–3.2	1.6	81.5
Estonia	–8.1	–13.6	–14.2	–9.0	–2.0	4.3	3.9	10.6	4.7	–1.1	6.4	87.3
Latvia	2.9	–10.4	–34.9	–14.9	0.6	–0.8	3.3	8.6	3.9	1.1	6.6	62.2
Lithuania	–3.3	–5.7	–21.3	–16.2	–9.8	3.3	4.7	7.3	5.1	–3.9	3.3	67.9

a. Preliminary.
Source: Vienna Institute for International Economic Studies (WIIW) database incorporating national statistics.

TABLE 4.1B GDP PER CAPITA AT PURCHASING POWER PARITY (ECU/EURO)

Country	*1990*	*1993*	*1994*	*1995*	*1996*	*1997*	*1998*	*1999*	*2000*	*2005*	*2010*	*2015*
										Projection assuming 4% per annum GDP growth and zero population growth per annum		
Czech Republic	10,063	9,786	10,226	11,286	11,984	11,973	12,045	12,277	12,538	15,108	18,381	22,363
Hungary	7,229	7,370	7,783	8,330	8,613	9,086	9,735	10,417	11,245	13,919	16,934	20,603
Poland	4,577	4,952	5,319	6,299	6,783	7,278	7,756	8,258	8,779	10,476	12,745	15,507
Slovak Republic	7,500	6,319	7,143	7,914	8,529	9,091	9,615	10,002	10,433	12,571	15,295	18,609
Slovenia	10,131	9,924	10,703	11,607	12,192	12,847	13,589	14,591	15,562	19,116	23,257	28,296
Bulgaria	4,871	4,455	4,652	5,007	4,600	4,378	4,583	4,823	5,237	6,372	7,752	9,431
Romania	5,349	4,847	5,160	5,768	6,113	5,785	5,576	5,526	5,741	6,783	8,253	10,041
Estonia	—	5,164	5,244	5,742	6,128	6,990	7,491	7,605	8,713	10,909	13,272	16,147
Latvia	—	4,019	4,198	4,392	4,659	5,131	5,465	5,738	6,348	7,760	9,441	11,487
Lithuania	—	4,991	4,617	4,974	5,301	5,725	6,124	6,022	6,362	7,666	9,327	11,348
Croatia	5,992	4,355	4,709	5,214	5,833	6,155	6,518	6,558	7,033	8,312	10,113	12,304
Macedonia	3,658	3,471	3,701	3,770	3,845	3,891	4,053	4,231	4,514	5,331	6,487	7,892
Russia	8,433	6,894	6,160	6,164	6,074	6,177	5,991	6,518	7,230	8,711	10,599	12,895
Ukraine	5,881	4,559	3,623	3,337	3,080	3,026	3,044	3,123	3,413	4,233	5,150	6,266
										Projection assuming 2% per annum GDP growth and zero population growth per annum		
Austria	16,074	18,144	18,938	19,974	20,679	21,079	22,021	22,931	23,733	26,204	28,931	31,942
Germany	15,081	17,576	18,681	19,890	19,927	20,416	21,202	21,906	22,585	24,936	27,532	30,397
Greece	8,838	10,379	11,012	11,920	12,322	12,444	13,049	13,788	14,353	15,847	17,496	19,317
Portugal	9,291	11,087	11,902	12,774	13,180	13,998	14,643	15,368	15,829	17,477	19,296	21,304
Spain	11,603	12,908	13,208	14,141	14,671	15,090	15,973	16,870	17,561	19,389	21,407	23,635
Turkey	4,424	5,158	4,895	5,239	5,534	5,844	6,024	5,740	5,993	6,616	7,305	8,065
Japan	16,810	19,187	19,687	21,043	22,141	22,450	22,182	22,619	22,936	25,323	27,958	30,868
USA	21,941	23,900	25,123	26,172	27,179	28,500	29,964	31,540	33,149	36,599	40,408	44,614
EU (15) average	14,782	16,248	17,020	18,117	18,536	18,944	19,744	20,554	21,253	23,465	25,907	28,604

	European Union (15) average = 100											
Czech Republic	68	60	60	62	65	63	61	60	59	64	71	78
Hungary	49	45	46	46	46	48	49	51	53	59	65	72
Poland	31	30	31	35	37	38	39	40	41	45	49	54
Slovak Republic	51	39	42	44	46	48	49	49	49	54	59	65
Slovenia	69	61	63	64	66	68	69	71	73	81	90	99
Bulgaria	33	27	27	28	25	23	23	23	25	27	30	33
Romania	36	30	30	32	33	31	28	27	27	29	32	35
Estonia	—	32	31	32	33	37	38	37	41	46	51	56
Latvia	—	25	25	24	25	27	28	28	30	33	36	40
Lithuania	—	31	27	27	29	30	31	29	30	33	36	40
Croatia	41	27	28	29	31	32	33	32	33	35	39	43
Macedonia	25	21	22	21	21	21	21	21	21	23	25	28
Russia	57	42	36	34	33	33	30	32	34	37	41	45
Ukraine	40	28	21	18	17	16	15	15	16	18	20	22
Austria	109	112	111	110	112	111	112	112	112	112	112	112
Germany	102	108	110	110	107	108	107	107	106	106	106	106
Greece	60	64	65	66	66	66	66	67	68	68	68	68
Portugal	63	68	70	71	71	74	74	75	74	74	74	74
Spain	78	79	78	78	79	80	81	82	83	83	83	83
Turkey	30	32	29	29	30	31	31	28	28	28	28	28
Japan	114	118	116	116	119	119	112	110	108	108	108	108
USA	148	147	148	144	147	150	152	153	156	156	156	156
EU (15) average	100	100	100	100	100	100	100	100	100	100	100	100

— Not applicable.

Note: Current PPP from 1990 to 1999, constant purchasing power parity (PPP) in projections. Benchmark PPPs for 1996 were estimated from purchasing power standards for OECD (28) average and extrapolated with GDP price deflators. GDP per capita for OECD countries according to OECD *National Account* statistics converted into European currency units (ECU).

Sources: Organisation for Economic Co-operation and Development (OECD) 1999a; national statistics; Austrian Institute of Economic Research (WIFO); WIIW estimates.

TABLE 4.2 POPULATION, 1990–2000
(thousands)

Country	*1990*	*1993*	*1994*	*1995*	*1996*	*1997*	*1998*	*1999*	*2000*	*1991–2000 Cumulative growth in %*
Czech Republic	10,363	10,331	10,336	10,331	10,315	10,304	10,295	10,283	10,273	–0.9
Hungary	10,355	10,277	10,246	10,212	10,174	10,135	10,092	10,043	10,005	–3.4
Poland	38,183	38,505	38,581	38,609	38,639	38,660	38,667	38,654	38,644	1.2
Slovak Republic	5,298	5,325	5,347	5,364	5,374	5,383	5,391	5,395	5,401	1.9
Slovenia	1,998	1,991	1,989	1,988	1,991	1,987	1,983	1,986	1,990	–0.4
Bulgaria	8,718	8,472	8,444	8,406	8,363	8,212	8,257	8,211	8,170	–6.3
Romania	23,207	22,755	22,731	22,681	22,608	22,546	22,503	22,458	22,443	–3.3
Estonia	1,571	1,517	1,499	1,484	1,469	1,458	1,450	1,442	1,369	–12.8
Latvia	2,670	2,586	2,548	2,516	2,491	2,469	2,449	2,410	2,373	–11.1
Lithuania	3,722	3,730	3,721	3,715	3,710	3,706	3,702	3,700	3,696	–0.7
CEEC (10)	106,085	105,488	105,441	105,305	105,134	104,860	104,788	104,581	104,363	–1.6

Note: Midyear population except for Hungary and Poland, which show population in December.
Source: WIIW database incorporating national statistics.

Activity rates available from Labour Force Surveys (LFS) based on the working-age population 15 years and older fell in all countries over the 1993 to 2000 period, most pronouncedly in Bulgaria, Hungary, and Poland. In the Czech Republic and in Hungary female activity rates shrank faster than those for males. In Bulgaria men and women were equally affected by the fall in activity rates. In 2000 activity rates based on the working-age population 15 to 64 years were highest in Romania (74.8 percent). In the Czech Republic, the Slovak Republic, and the Baltic States they were close to 70 percent. A comparison between the CEECs and the EU-15 shows that, despite considerable falls in the initial period of transition, activity rates are higher than the EU average (69 percent in 1999) in all but three countries—Hungary, Bulgaria, and Poland (table 4.3).

Available LFS data indicate a decline in employment rates (total number of employed relative to the population 15 to 64 years) in all countries except Hungary, Slovenia, and Latvia (table 4.4). In Hungary, where employment (rates) resumed growth in 1998, the upward trend continued in the two subsequent years. Poland, which reported increasing employment rates in the 1996–98 period, saw a slowdown starting in 1999. Slovenia, the Czech Republic, and Romania are still recording higher employment rates than the EU average (63.1 percent). By the year 2000, employment rates ranged from close to 70 percent in Romania to 50 percent in Bulgaria. The male employment rate exceeds the female rate in all countries. However, the gender gap in employment remained smaller in the CEECs than in most countries of the European Union. With the exception of Bulgaria and Hungary, female employment rates in the countries under consideration were higher than in the EU Member States.

TABLE 4.3 ECONOMIC ACTIVITY RATES IN THE CEECs, 1996–2000
(labor force as a percentage of the working-age population)

Country	*1996*	*1997*	*1998*	*1999*	*2000*
Czech Republic	73.2	73.1	73.0	72.3	71.7
Hungary	58.9	58.1	58.7	59.7	59.5
Poland	68.9	68.4	68.0	—	67.5
Slovak Republic	70.0	69.7	69.8	69.9	71.1
Slovenia	67.9	70.1	71.0	69.2	69.1
Bulgaria	63.9	63.9	63.1	61.3	61.0
Romania	76.4	76.6	75.6	75.5	74.8
Estonia	72.1	72.5	71.9	70.6	70.8
Latvia	72.1	72.3	71.5	—	69.2
Lithuania	78.8	74.2	74.7	75.3	72.2
EU (15)	68.4	68.6	68.9	69.2	—

— Not available.
Note: Ages 15 to 64.
Source: Eurostat, European Commission 2000, national LFS of respective country.

TABLE 4.4 EMPLOYMENT RATES IN THE CEECs, 1996–2000
(employed as a percentage of the working-age population)

Country	*1996*	*1997*	*1998*	*1999*	*2000*
Czech Republic	69.5	68.9	67.6	66.0	65.1
Hungary	53.0	53.0	54.2	55.6	55.6
Poland	60.4	60.7	60.8	—	56.3
Slovak Republic	62.1	61.0	60.3	57.9	57.6
Slovenia	63.0	65.7	65.1	63.9	64.1
Bulgaria	55.3	54.7	54.2	51.7	50.4
Romania	71.3	72.0	70.8	70.4	69.1
Estonia	64.2	64.9	65.3	62.0	—
Latvia	55.9	58.5	58.7	59.5	—
Lithuania	60.3	63.1	62.9	65.0	—
EU(15)	60.3	60.7	61.0	62.1	63.1
France	59.4	59.4	59.9	60.4	61.7
Greece	53.6	53.6	55.6	55.4	55.9
Germany	65.0	64.6	63.7	64.8	65.3
Portugal	64.0	64.8	66.8	67.4	68.1
Spain	47.2	48.6	49.7	52.3	54.7
United Kingdom	69.0	70.1	70.2	70.6	71.2

— Not available.
Note: Ages 15 to 64.
Source: Eurostat, European Commission 2000, national LFS of respective country.

Employment

The dramatic fall of the GDP at the beginning of the transition was accompanied by strong employment declines. Bulgaria, Estonia, Latvia, and Hungary were affected most by job losses, while employment dropped less pronouncedly in Poland, the Czech Republic, and in Lithuania. In the majority of Eastern European countries, the bulk of job losses occurred in the initial stage of the transition. Economic recovery, starting in most countries in 1993 and 1994, has led only to slight or temporary employment increases that could not be sustained.

Recent developments show that despite the continuation and strengthening of economic growth in 2000, there was little improvement in the labor market in most countries of the region. Employment continued to grow only in Hungary and Slovenia, in both countries for the third consecutive year. In Bulgaria and Romania the rates of employment decline even accelerated, while they were somewhat lower than a year earlier in the Czech Republic, the Slovak Republic, and Poland. Successful in creating new jobs in the mid-1990s, Poland has been suffering from painful employment cuts since 1999 despite permanent GDP growth. The main reasons are the expiration of job guarantees and mass layoffs in the steel and textile industries as a consequence of restructuring (ECE 2001). As for the Baltic States hit hard by the Russian crisis, the employment decline slowed down in Estonia, while it accelerated in Lithuania and remained stationary in Latvia.

A comparison between employment and GDP growth shows that most countries achieved productivity gains over the past decade. Exceptions are Lithuania and Latvia, where the employment drop was at times much smaller than the fall in output, implying a considerable decline in productivity. Productivity gains were most pronounced in Poland, Hungary, and Slovenia over that period. So far, productivity gains were reached first of all through the shedding of labor (table 4.5).

Employment Patterns

The past decade witnessed significant changes in the economic structure and consequently in the sectoral composition of GDP and employment. In most countries a reallocation of labor occurred from agriculture and industry to the services sector. Contrary to that trend, Romania is an extreme case where agricultural employment has been growing in both relative and absolute terms and the proportion of employed in agriculture accounts for 43 percent of the total. Similar trends were observed in Bulgaria and Lithuania, with the respective shares reaching 26 percent and 20 percent in 2000. These developments are partly caused by the emergence of numerous small private farm units after the ownership transformation of huge agricultural enterprises, but they also can be attributed to economic hardship that has forced people to return to self-employed farming (Burda 1996). Also in Poland the proportion of those employed in agriculture is still very high, though LFS data show a steady decline. In 2000 it was 19 percent, down from 23 percent in 1995 (registration data put the share even at 26 percent). According to Polish estimates, hidden unemployment in the country's agricultural sector comprises about 1 million persons. Labor shedding in agriculture was highest in Estonia and in Hungary, where the number of employed in 1999 contracted to less than one-third of the 1989 level. The transformation or liquidation of agricultural cooperatives alone accounted in Hungary for the elimination of almost 400,000 jobs in agriculture after 1989 (Fazekas 1997).

Employment in industry (including construction) has declined in all countries since 1989, reflecting the high overemployment prevailing under the previous system. Most affected were Bulgaria and Latvia, where in 1999 industrial employment was less than half of what it was in 1989; in Slovenia and Estonia employment was cut by about one-third and in the Slovak Republic and in the Czech Republic by about one-quarter compared to 1989. Despite these huge employment losses, the share of employed in that sector is still high compared with Western countries: in Hungary and Estonia industrial employment accounts for about one-third of the total; Slovenia and the Czech Republic—the most advanced countries under review in terms of GDP per capita—and the Slovak Republic report still the highest share of employment in industry, reaching close to 40 percent. In Latvia and Lithuania the proportion is lowest: only about one-quarter of the employed work in industry.

TABLE 4.5 GDP AND EMPLOYMENT GROWTH, 1990–2000

Country	GDP (cumulative growth in percent)			Employment (cumulative growth in percent)			Employment Growth (1,000 persons)		
	1990–92	*1993–2000*	*1990–2000*	*1990–92*	*1993–2000*	*1990–2000*	*1989–92*	*1992–2000*	*1989–2000*
Czech Republic	–13.2	13.7	–1.3	–8.8	–6.9	–15.1	–475.9	–340.1	–816.0
Hungary	–17.6	26.5	4.2	–21.9	–5.7	–26.4	–1,144.5	–233.6	–1,378.1
Poland	–15.6	50.2	26.7	–13.7	2.9	–11.2	–2,325.2	423.4	–1,901.8
Slovak Republic	–22.1	31.8	2.6	–13.7	–2.8	–16.2	–344.0	–61.4	–405.3
Slovenia	–17.9	39.5	14.5	–17.1	–2.0	–18.8	–162.2	–15.9	–178.1
Bulgaria	–25.6	–3.3	–28.1	–25.0	–10.1	–32.6	–1,091.4	–330.3	–1,421.7
Romania	–25.0	2.6	–23.0	–4.5	–19.7	–23.3	–487.7	–2,058.0	–2,545.7
Estonia	–31.9	17.8	–19.8	–8.6	–20.5	–27.4	–72.2	–157.1	–229.3
Latvia[a]	–40.0	6.7	–36.0	–8.1	–19.8	–26.3	–114.5	–256.2	–370.7
Lithuania[a]	–28.2	–8.5	–34.3	0.1	–14.5	–14.4	2.5	–269.2	–266.7

a. Employment data start from 1990.
Source: WIIW database incorporating national statistics.

In the more advanced transition countries, services sector employment has gained momentum from 1992 onwards, in Romania from 1994 and in Bulgaria from 1995. Estonia, Latvia, and Hungary report the highest levels of services sector employment (close to 60 percent) and display a similar pattern as the southern EU countries. With the exception of Romania, services employment accounted for the largest share of total employment in 1999. In Poland and Bulgaria the proportion of those employed in the services sector was about 45 percent of the total; in Romania, less than one-third. In the Czech Republic, the Slovak Republic, and Slovenia employment in services accounted for slightly more than one-half of the total in 1999.

However, compared with the huge job losses in industry and agriculture, employment increases in absolute terms in the services sector were rather modest in most of the countries. The most outstanding growth rate was reported for Slovenia, which showed a 15 percent increase over the 1989–99 period, followed by Poland and the Czech Republic. If one looks at the increase in the absolute number of persons employed in the services sector, Poland is in the lead. (During the 1989–99 period, 820,000 new services jobs were created there.) Next comes the Czech Republic, reporting an increase in services jobs by 270,000 persons over the same period. Combined with other factors, this increase might also have contributed to the low unemployment rate in the Czech Republic in the past. Romania, conversely, reported 230,000 services job losses over the same period. Most of service-sector employment has been created in trade, real estate activities, and financial intermediation, as well as public administration. In contrast, in all countries under review, transport and telecommunications reported job losses over the 1989–99 period.

Following the privatization of huge state-owned enterprises and the establishment of new firms, employment in the private sector rose significantly during the transition period. However, a comparison of private sector shares is rather difficult because of divergent definitions of the public sector across the respective countries. In 1999 the private sector's share in total employment reached 70 percent in most countries, slightly over 60 percent in the Czech Republic and the Slovak Republic, and more than half in Bulgaria, Romania, and Slovenia. In most countries agriculture accounts for the highest share of private sector employment.

Unemployment

Unemployment, believed to be of a temporary nature at the beginning of the transition, has become a long-lasting phenomenon. In all countries but the Czech Republic (at least until the mid-1990s), the number of registered unemployed increased rapidly during the past decade (table 4.6). The year 1993 witnessed a record level, followed by a slowdown until 1997 caused by the exit from the labor market of a huge number of persons rather than by new job creation. In 1998 unemployment started to accelerate again in all countries except Hungary and Slovenia.

By the end of 2000, registered unemployment reached the highest level since the beginning of the transition in Bulgaria, Estonia, and Lithuania and decreased somewhat elsewhere. Unemployment rates ranged from 8 percent in Latvia to almost 18 percent in both Bulgaria and the Slovak Republic. In Poland, where unemployment fell in the mid-1990s, the number of jobless has been rising again since 1998. The sharp increase in the number of jobless is due to several factors (ECE 2001): (1) mass layoffs in coal mining and in the steel and textile industries, (2) the expiration of employment guarantees in privatized firms, and (3) the entrance of the baby boom generation into the labor market. Data obtained from the Labour Force Surveys reveal a different picture: according to that measure only Hungary and Slovenia report declining unemployment rates, while in the Czech Republic and Latvia unemployment remained stagnant and continued to increase in the remaining countries.

Although there are substantial intercountry differences, several common features of unemployment can be identified: (1) unemployment varies significantly across regions, while at the same time there is low mobility of labor; (2) the proportion of long-term unemployment is steadily on the increase; (3) in most countries women are more affected by unemployment than men; (4) youth unemployment is increasing rapidly; (5) the lowest skill and educational groups are disproportionately affected; and (6) unemployment levels among ethnic minorities and other socially disadvantaged groups are many times higher than the average rate.

Regional Differences in Unemployment

In Central and Eastern European countries, like in Western countries, there are large regional disparities in labor markets. Imbalances are largely attributable to the regional industrial structures prevailing under the previous system. For instance, monostructured regions—especially regions that concentrated on armament, mining, steel, and textile industries in the past—are more affected by unemployment than others; often the entire social and economic infrastructure had focused on a single industry. In general, unemployment in the CEECs tends to be lowest in big cities with a developed services sector, regions with a diversified industrial structure, regions offering good opportunities for tourism and leisure, and areas bordering more developed countries where people can commute for work (Keune 1998b). In most countries under review, there is a low incidence of unemployment in the capital cities, which is also true with respect to youth and female unemployment. Unemployment rates recorded for the Hungarian and Slovak regions bordering Austria and for the Slovenian regions bordering Italy are lowest or among the lowest rates of the respective countries. In contrast, Polish regions adjacent to the German border display higher unemployment rates than average (Behrens 2001). Like in the European Union, in the CEECs the internal mobility of labor is low; it is aggravated by the lack of housing and high rents, high transport costs, and the cutting of public transport services (Köllö 1999).

TABLE 4.6 UNEMPLOYMENT RATES BASED ON REGISTRATION DATA
(percentage of labor force, end of period)

Country	*1991*	*1992*	*1993*	*1994*	*1995*	*1996*	*1997*	*1998*	*1999*	*2000*
Czech Republic	4.1	2.6	3.5	3.2	2.9	3.5	5.2	7.5	9.4	8.8
Hungary	8.2	13.9	14.0	12.0	11.7	11.4	11.0	9.6	9.6	8.9
Poland	11.8	13.6	16.4	16.0	14.9	13.2	10.3	10.4	13.0	15.0
Slovak Republic	11.8	10.4	14.4	14.6	13.1	12.8	12.5	15.6	19.2	17.9
Slovenia	10.1	13.4	15.4	14.2	14.5	14.4	14.8	14.6	13.0	12.0
Bulgaria	11.1	15.2	16.4	12.8	11.1	12.5	13.7	12.2	16.0	17.9
Romania	3.0	8.2	10.4	10.9	9.5	6.6	8.9	10.4	11.8	10.5
Estonia	—	—	—	4.6	4.7	5.2	4.3	4.9	—	—
Latvia	—	2.3	5.8	6.5	6.6	7.2	7.0	9.2	9.1	7.8
Lithuania	—	—	3.6	4.5	7.3	6.2	6.7	6.9	—	—

— Not available.
Source: WIIW database incorporating national statistics.

In Poland the regions most heavily affected by unemployment are in the North and West, where there was a large decline in industry. The splitting up of large state-owned farms contributed to the decline. The lowest rates are reported for the South and parts of the East, which are still dominated by agricultural employment. In the Czech Republic labor market differences at the regional level are less pronounced than in the other CEECs. However, larger regional disparities can be observed for regional unemployment rates at the level of districts. The highest jobless rates are reported for northern Bohemia and northern Moravia, which are characterized by heavy industry, coal mining, and the steel industry. In southern Moravia labor market problems are found mainly in the agriculture sector. Hungarian regional unemployment is lowest in the more advanced western counties (apart from Budapest) bordering Austria and highest in northern Hungary and the northern Great Plain. The Slovak Republic displays the widest gaps of regional unemployment rates among all candidate countries. There is a large mismatch between the density of economic activities and the concentration of the unemployed. The Bratislava region is booming—over 60 percent of all foreign direct investment is concentrated in the Bratislava agglomeration—and high unemployment rates persist in the eastern and southern regions of the country. The eastern and southern regions are still suffering from huge layoffs in the armament industries and from the impact of agricultural reforms (OECD 1999b).

In contrast, Romania shows the smallest variations in regional unemployment, from 3.4 percent in the Bucharest region to 7.3 percent in the Sud-Est region. In Bulgaria the regions Montana, Plovdiv, and Russe report higher unemployment than most others. This is closely related to the respective employment structures. (Montana has a high share of agricultural employment, while in Plovdiv and Russe there is a high share of industrial employment in declining sectors of heavy industries.) In Slovenia the northern part of the country—the regions of Podravska, Pomurska, and Zasavska—is affected most by unemployment. Based on data obtained from the Labour Force Surveys, regional disparities in unemployment are generally not as pronounced in the Baltic States as in the other CEECs. Differences occur mainly between rural and urban areas. Regions reporting high unemployment are in southeastern Estonia, eastern and southeastern Latvia, and some southern areas of Lithuania (OECD 2000).

Long-Term Unemployment

Long-term unemployment, a stubborn problem also in the European Union (46 percent of total unemployed), has become a major feature of unemployment in the CEECs, though available data show an uneven picture (table 4.7). The highest value is reported for Slovenia, where more than 60 percent of total unemployment is long term, followed by Bulgaria, the Slovak Republic, Romania, and Latvia with more than half of the total. In the Czech Republic, where long-term unemployment constitutes slightly less than half of the total, this share has been growing rapidly

TABLE 4.7 LONG-TERM UNEMPLOYMENT IN THE CEECs, 1996–2000
(percentage of total unemployed)

Country	*1996*	*1997*	*1998*	*1999*	*2000*
Czech Republic	28.2	28.1	29.5	36.0	48.3
Hungary	48.3	43.8	41.6	44.6	44.0
Poland	39.1	37.9	37.5	32.9	37.9
Slovak Republic	51.6	50.3	50.7	46.9	53.9
Slovenia[a]	52.2	56.7	57.7	57.7	62.4
Bulgaria[a]	—	60.4	59.1	56.8	58.2
Romania[a]	51.3	47.7	41.9	44.3	51.5
Estonia	55.3	45.8	47.0	45.8	44.4
Latvia[a]	—	47.1	33.6	—	56.0
Lithuania	—	—	29.7	—	—

— Not available.
a. More than 11 months.
Source: Eurostat, national LFS of respective country.

over recent years. On the other hand, the incidence of long-term unemployment is less severe in Poland and probably in Lithuania. Like in the European Union, in Central and Eastern Europe long-term unemployment tends to be proportionately higher in high unemployment countries (European Commission 1999c).

Unemployment by Gender

The decline in employment has disproportionately hit women. For example, in Hungary female employment fell by 40 percent over the 1985–97 period, while about 30 percent of male jobs got lost; the respective figures in Estonia were 31 percent and 11 percent, and even the smallest cut in female employment recorded for the Czech Republic was ten times higher than for males (ECE 1999). The strong employment drop is not necessarily reflected in the unemployment figures since many employed females decided to leave the labor force altogether. Thus the unemployment rates of women are not much higher than those of men, and in some countries they are even lower. Across the region female unemployment rates range from about 6 percent in Hungary and Romania to almost 19 percent in the Slovak Republic (table 4.8). Four of the countries report lower unemployment rates for women than for men and a lower-than-average rate (Bulgaria, Romania, Estonia, Hungary). In the case of Hungary this development can be explained by the drastic cut of female employment over the transition period, which was higher than in any other country. In the Slovak Republic both genders were similarly affected by unemployment. Poland and the Czech Republic report female unemployment rates that are 3 to 4 percentage points higher than the male rates; in Slovenia the female rate is only slightly higher.

TABLE 4.8 UNEMPLOYMENT RATES BY GENDER, 1996–2000
(percentage of labor force)

Country	*1996*	*1997*	*1998*	*1999*	*2000*
Czech Republic					
Total	3.9	4.8	6.5	8.7	8.7
Male	3.4	3.9	5.0	7.3	7.3
Female	4.7	5.9	8.2	10.5	10.6
Hungary					
Total	9.9	8.7	7.8	7	6.4
Male	10.7	9.5	8.5	7.5	7.0
Female	8.8	7.8	7	6.3	5.6
Poland					
Total	12.3	11.2	10.6	—	16.1
Male	11.0	9.6	9.1	—	14.4
Female	13.9	13.2	12.3	—	18.1
Slovak Republic					
Total	11.3	11.8	12.5	16.2	18.6
Male	10.2	10.9	11.9	16.0	18.6
Female	12.7	12.8	13.2	16.4	18.6
Slovenia					
Total	7.3	7.4	7.9	7.6	7.0
Male	7.5	7.1	7.7	7.3	6.8
Female	7.0	7.6	8.1	7.9	7.3
Bulgaria					
Total	14.2	14.4	14.1	15.7	16.9
Male	14.2	14.3	14.4	15.8	17.1
Female	14.1	14.4	13.9	15.5	16.6
Romania					
Total	6.7	6.0	6.3	6.8	7.1
Male	6.3	5.7	6.5	7.4	7.7
Female	7.3	6.4	6.1	6.2	6.4
Estonia					
Total	10.0	9.7	9.9	12.3	13.7
Male	10.7	10.1	10.8	13.6	14.6
Female	9.2	9.2	8.9	11.0	12.7
Latvia					
Total	18.3	14.4	13.8	14.5	14.5
Male	18.9	14.3	13.4	—	—
Female	17.7	14.6	14.1	—	—
Lithuania					
Total	16.4	14.1	13.3	14.1	15.4
Male	—	14.2	14.3	15.6	—
Female	—	13.9	12.2	12.6	—

— Not available.
Source: Eurostat 2000, CESTAT 2001, national LFS of respective country.

Youth Unemployment

Unemployment disproportionately hits young people and those with a low level of education. The sharp employment decline over the transition period has made entering the very tight labor market extremely difficult for young people. In addition, demographic developments have aggravated the situation; the number of young entrants (especially in Poland) has been steadily on the increase (Keune 1998a). In most countries of the region, the LFS unemployment rate among people younger than 25 years is twice as high as the total unemployment rate, and in Romania it is even three times higher (table 4.9). The high rate of 35 percent in Bulgaria, the Slovak Republic, and Poland indicates a quite critical situation for young people in the labor market of the respective countries. The lowest values can be found in Hungary (12 percent) and in the Czech Republic and Slovenia (about 17 percent).

The youth unemployment rate across EU members also varies significantly: it is particularly high in Italy and Greece, where more than 30 percent of young people in the labor force are unemployed (European Commission 1999b).

TABLE 4.9 YOUTH UNEMPLOYMENT RATES IN THE CEECs, 1994–2000
(percentage of labor force)

Country	*1994*	*1995*	*1996*	*1997*	*1998*	*1999*	*2000*
Czech Republic	8.7	7.8	7.2	8.6	12.4	17.0	17.0
Hungary	19.4	18.6	18.0	15.9	13.5	12.4	12.1
Poland	32.5	31.2	28.5	24.8	23.2	—	35.1
Slovak Republic	27.3	24.8	20.9	21.7	23.6	32.1	35.2
Slovenia	22.2	18.8	18.8	17.6	18.6	18.1	16.8
Bulgaria	44.9	37.7	33.5	36.0	36.0	33.8	35.3
Romania	22.5	20.6	20.2	18.0	18.3	18.8	18.6
Estonia	11.6	14.1	16.0	14.4	15.7	19.8	23.9
Latvia	—	30.1	29.0	24.9	25.5	—	—
Lithuania	32.1	31.6	27.4	25.2	22.2	26.5	—

— Not available.
Note: Youth are persons younger than 25 years old.
Source: Eurostat 2000, CESTAT 2001, national LFS statistics.

Conclusions

The results obtained are mixed: even in the economically most advanced transition countries, labor market developments are far from uniform but rather reflect the diversity of the respective macroeconomic situations. Only Hungary and Slovenia have succeeded in increasing employment and combating unemployment, and these trends are likely to continue. In general, huge job losses in industry and agriculture have been offset only to a very small extent by new jobs in the services sector; the latter is still underdeveloped by Western standards in most countries. Job creation in the private sector is still too weak to contribute to a noteworthy improvement in the labor market. More than 8 million jobs were lost over the past decade, resulting in a decline of activity rates all over the region. A huge number of people, primarily women, exited from the labor market. The high proportion of long-term unemployed indicates that many of them will leave the labor force. This implies a further decline in activity rates but more so an increase in poverty. In order to overcome these deficiencies, individual countries must focus on their budgetary situation and give priority to economic and social policies.

Notes

1. Based on the Labour Force Balance, available up to 1997 only (Hungarian Central Statistical Office 1998). The given figures may serve only as a guideline. Caution is warranted in comparing pre- and post-transition employment figures due to considerable conceptual and measurement differences. Available statistics do not provide consistent time series covering the whole transition period (for example, for total employment, activity rates but also for the sectoral composition of employment for most of the countries).

2. In Hungary the reduction of working pensioners started already in the second half of the eighties, declining from 479,000 in 1987 to 112,000 in 1997; in the Czech Republic working pensioners totaled 270,000 in 1997 compared with 570,000 in 1989. For Poland it is estimated that 1.2 million to 1.3 million took early retirement until 1994 (Kabaj 1996). Data for the most recent years are not available.

References

The word *processed* describes informally reproduced works that may not be commonly available through libraries.

Behrens, A. 2001. "Regional Unemployment Rates in the Central European Candidate Countries 1999." *Statistics in Focus*. Luxembourg: Eurostat.

Burda, M. C. 1996. "Unemployment in Central and Eastern Europe: East Meets West." In H. Giersch, ed., *Fighting Europe's Unemployment in the 1990s.* Berlin, Heidelberg, and New York: Springer-Verlag.

CESTAT. 2001. *Statistical Bulletin 2000/4.* Ljubljana: Statistical Office of the Republic of Slovenia.

ECE (Economic Commission for Europe). 1995. *Economic Survey of Europe, 1994–1995.* New York and Geneva.

———. 1999. *Economic Survey of Europe No. 1.* New York and Geneva.

———. 2001. *Economic Survey of Europe No. 1.* New York and Geneva.

European Commission. 1999a. *Central European Countries Employment and Labor Market Review.* Luxembourg: Eurostat.

———. 1999b. *Employment in Europe.* Luxembourg: Office for Official Publications of the European Communities.

———. 1999c. *Regional Policy and Cohesion: Sixth Periodic Report on the Social and Economic Situation and Development of the Regions of the European Union.* Luxembourg: Eurostat.

———. 2000. *Employment in Europe.* Luxembourg: Office for Official Publications of the European Communities.

Eurostat. 2000. *Statistical Yearbook on Candidate and South-East European Countries.* Luxembourg.

Fazekas, K. 1997. *Hungary: Employment and Sustainable Livelihoods.* Budapest: International Labour Office, Central and Eastern European Team.

Hungarian Central Statistical Office. 1998. *Statistical Yearbook of Hungary 1997.* Budapest.

Kabaj, M. 1996. "Programmes and Strategies for Counteracting Unemployment and the Promotion of Productive Employment in Poland." ILO–CEET Working Paper 15. International Labour Organization, Budapest.

Keune, M. 1998a. *Youth Unemployment in Hungary and Poland: Action Programme on Youth Unemployment.* Employment and Training Papers 20. Geneva: International Labour Organization.

Keune, M., ed. 1998b. *Regional Development and Employment Policy: Lessons from Central and Eastern Europe.* Budapest: International Labour Organization.

Köllö, J. 1999. "Regional Inequalities in Central and Eastern Europe: Implication for the Eastern Enlargement of the EU." Hungarian Academy of Science. Processed.

Nesporova, A. 1999. *Employment and Labour Market Policies in Transition Economies*. Geneva: International Labour Organization.

OECD (Organisation for Economic Co-operation and Development). 1999a. *Benchmark Results of the 1996 Eurostat-OECD Comparison by Analytical Categories*. Paris.

———. 1999b. *Slovak Republic*. OECD Economic Surveys. Paris.

———. 2000. *Baltic States: A Regional Economic Assessment.* OECD Economic Surveys. Paris.

CHAPTER 5

The Role of Social Policies and the EU in Labor Reallocation in Transition Economies

Katherine Terrell and Tito Boeri

This paper takes a big-picture approach. We feel that we can learn a lot by examining the differences in the adjustment trajectories of the countries of the former Soviet Union (FSU) and those of the Central and Eastern European countries (the CEECs). And as you can see in figure 5.1, there has been a far greater decline in the GDP of the FSU countries than in the GDP of the CEECs. The CEECs started rebounding after the fourth year of their transition, whereas the FSU countries began to rebound only recently. What is also remarkable is the fact that employment has not declined as much in the FSU countries relative to the CEECs, given this tremendous fall in output. This is an interesting puzzle that we want to examine and see if we can solve.

One of the answers is that real wages have been allowed to decline tremendously in the FSU compared to the CEECs. As you can see in figure 5.2, on average the CEECs' wages in 1997 are about 85 percent of their real level in 1989, whereas in the FSU countries real wages are still at about half of their 1989 level. Larger price adjustments allow for smaller quantity adjustments, so this explains part of the difference in the levels of employment and output over time. Obviously, these averages mask a great deal of variation. But the overall pattern of two different trajectories in terms of output employment and wages is fascinating.

To what extent does the transition experience in these two regions differ in terms of structural change and labor reallocation? Here we define reallocation from the old to the new sectors along three different dimensions: (1) economic activity

FIGURE 5.1 EMPLOYMENT AND OUTPUT ADJUSTMENT
(start of transition = 100)

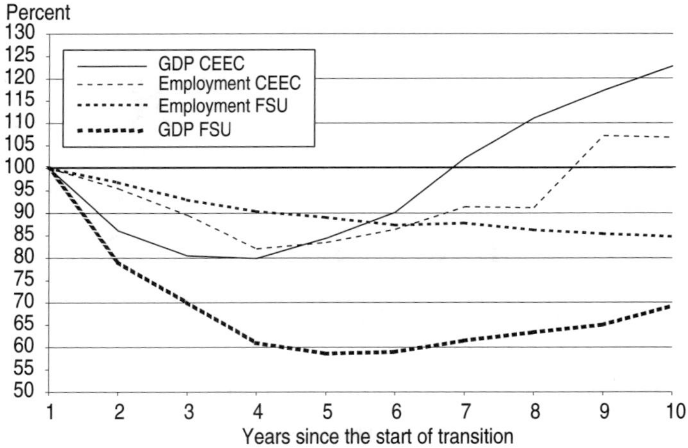

Note: Unweighted Average, 1989 = 100 for Poland; 1990 = 100 for other CEECs (Central and Eastern European countries); 1991 = 100 for the FSU .
Source: EBRD 2000 and 2001.

FIGURE 5.2 REAL WAGES IN CENTRAL AND EASTERN EUROPE AND THE FORMER SOVIET UNION, 1989–97
(1989 = 100)

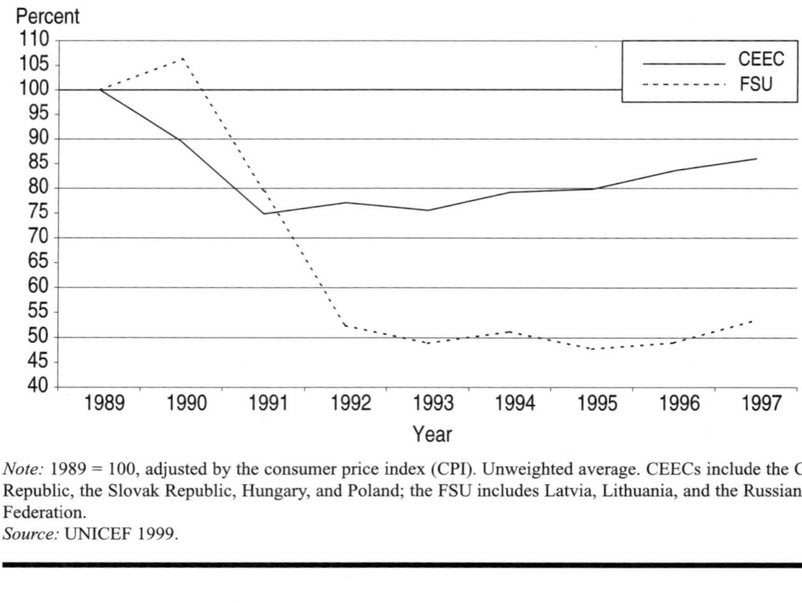

Note: 1989 = 100, adjusted by the consumer price index (CPI). Unweighted average. CEECs include the Czech Republic, the Slovak Republic, Hungary, and Poland; the FSU includes Latvia, Lithuania, and the Russian Federation.
Source: UNICEF 1999.

(we believe there was too much labor dedicated to industrial activity and not enough to services in the old system); (2) the size of the firm (we believe firms were too large, and a new small-scale sector was needed); and (3) the type of ownership (private versus public).

The first three columns in table 5.1 indicate that there has been a great deal of labor reallocation, as everybody has been mentioning. In all countries the share of employment in the industrial sectors declined, and the percentage decline was not so dissimilar in the CEECs and the FSU countries. However, there is a difference in the pattern of reallocation. In the FSU countries labor is moving from industry to agriculture; the share in agriculture has grown by 5.9 percentage points. Small plots are offering subsistence for many poor households in these countries. And whereas the service sector has grown in all of these countries, the share in the CEECs has grown by almost three times that in the FSU. If we look at market-oriented services—in other words, if we exclude health, education, and public administration—these differences would be even larger.

All of the countries have done very well in terms of privatization. Over half of the employed are now working in the private sector. However, the creation of the new private sector is another matter, and here, again, you see big differences between the CEECs and the FSU countries. Essentially you have twice as many people who are self-employed in the CEECs as in the FSU and three times larger share of employment in firms with fewer than 100 employees.

With all this reallocation there is obviously friction, which means the creation of unemployment. Unemployment was rising much faster in the CEECs and started much earlier, so the rates peaked within two to four years from the start of transition (table 5.1). The outlier in Central and Eastern Europe is the Czech Republic, whose unemployment remained low. On the other hand, unemployment has been growing in the other FSU countries and only recently reached high levels. Therefore, the problem of long-term unemployment has been around longer in the CEECs than in the FSU countries.

Microeconomic analysis of transition probabilities across the different states in the labor market (for example, from employment to unemployment) helps us better understand the sources of the unemployment problem. Comparing the probabilities that an employed person becomes unemployed in the transition economies (both FSUs and CEECs) to the probability in the United States, you find the flows into unemployment were not all that much higher in the transition countries. You would expect them to be a great deal higher since the United States was not undergoing unusually high structural adjustment in this period. Similarly, the flows out of the labor force are on the order of those for the United States as well. They are not extremely high.

What, then, was contributing to long-term unemployment in these countries? It was the inability of people to leave unemployment for employment. These probabilities are relatively low in the transition economies compared to the United

TABLE 5.1 STRUCTURAL CHANGE AND UNEMPLOYMENT DYNAMICS
(percent, except where noted)

Country	*Change in the employment share from 1990 to 1997*			*Private sector employment share in 1997*	*Employment share in firms with fewer than 100 employees in 1996*	*Nonagricultural self-employment (percentage of employed) in 1998*	*First peak in unemployment rate (years from the start of transition)*[e]	*Mean share in long-term unemployment*[f] *(1994–98)*
	Agriculture[a] *(1)*	*Industry*[b] *(2)*	*Services*[c] *(3)*	*(4)*	*(5)*	*(6)*	*(7)*	*(8)*
CEECs	–0.04	–10.0	10.1	64.7	41.7	—	—	43.9
Czech Republic	–6.2	–5.9	12.1	59.7	46.9	13.2	9.4 (9)	26.8
Hungary	–9.1	–6.0	15.1	80.0	40.7	13.1	13.9 (2)	47.6
Poland	0.6	–7.9	7.4	64.0	50.3	16.0	16.4 (4)	39.0
Romania	12.1	–14.2	2.1	55.0	—	—	9.2 (3)	46.6
Slovenia	3.0	–12.5	9.5	—	31.4[d]	9.2	15.4 (3)	54.1
Slovak Republic	–6.0	–10.6	16.6	64.6	44.8	—	14.6 (4)	49.5
FSUs	6.9	–11.6	4.5	—	—	—	—	—
Russian Federation	0.04	–10.5	11.1	65.0	13.0	6.3	13.3 (7)	32.0
Ukraine	2.3	–12.9	10.6	52.0	—	1.4	4.3 (8)	—
Belarus	–2.1	–7.3	9.1	—	—	—	3.9 (5)	—
Kazakhstan	3.1	–12.9	10.8	—	—	—	14.0 (7)	—

— Not available.

a. Agriculture, hunting, forestry, and fishing.

b. Manufacturing; mining and quarrying; electricity, gas, and water; and construction.

c. Finance, insurance, real estate, and business services; community, social, and personal services; wholesale; and transport.

d. For 1997.

e. Poland (1989), other CEECs (1990), FSU (1991).

f. "Long-term unemployment" is defined as unemployed for 12 or more months.

Sources: Boeri 2000; EBRD 1999 and 2000; World Bank Institute's Window into Economic Policy; OECD various issues; OECD 1999; Statistical Office of the Republic of Slovenia 1998; and the World Bank Privatization and Restructuring Database.

States. However, in the FSU countries these probabilities are relatively high compared to those for the CEECs, which explains the FSU's lower levels and durations of unemployment in this period.

What explains these asymmetries in the trajectories? As economists, we want to turn to theory and see to what extent it can help us understand what is happening. Although the main theory in this area, the optimal speed of transition models, can help us on many levels, it does not help us understand the differences in the trajectories that we see here.

There are important weaknesses in this theory for explaining the different adjustment experiences. First, differences in paces at which the reform was undertaken cannot explain differences in adjustment. The Russian Federation and Ukraine had very quick privatization policies, much faster than Slovenia and Poland, for example, and yet employment and GDP have grown much faster in Slovenia and Poland than in those countries.

Second, it was thought that governments would engineer destruction of jobs in the old sector, but in fact this did not happen. On average about 23 percent of the separations were layoffs in the CEECs during this time, and in the OECD countries the average is about 60 percent. So layoffs are much higher in the OECD countries than in the CEECs.

Third, the optimal speed of transition models are unable to characterize the reallocation process, in part because they assume a homogeneous labor market, and we have seen from a number of studies that there are clearly defined winners and losers in this transition process. If we define winners as individuals whose wage gains were higher or whose probability of becoming unemployed is lower or whose probability of getting a job if they are unemployed is higher, we know that the winners are men, educated persons, the young, and those living in urban areas.

Perhaps the most important flaw in the theory is its depiction of the role of wages. In all of the models, wages play a secondary role (determined by level of unemployment) and are not used to explain the level of employment. Yet we know from labor demand theory that wages are extremely important in determining employment levels and the reallocation of labor from one sector to another. The fact that wages adjusted less in the CEECs than in the FSU countries largely explains why employment declines are so much higher in the CEECs. Because the CEECs kept wages higher, the old sector was not able to keep labor and they had to let employees go.[1]

The question, then, is what policies and institutions were used to keep wages from falling more in one region than in the other? I would argue that we do not have sufficient evidence on any of these institutions to identify with certainty the ones that have had a strong or a modest role, but I will try to summarize what is known. The evidence to date on unions seems to indicate that none of these countries (except perhaps Poland) have formed new unions that are the voice of workers in the workplace. Unions are still disorganized, and unionization rates are still quite low. I believe only about 30 percent of workers in many of these countries are unionized today; virtually all workers belonged to a union before transition began. In Lithuania only about 13 percent are unionized today. On the other hand, unionization rates are high in Russia; but obviously, if you have wage arrears and contracts that are not being honored, as you do there, unions could not be all that strong.

The other policies that were put in place at the beginning of transition that you might think would have reduced wage growth and had an impact on this process were the tax-based income policies. Again, there has not been that much research, but the fact that they were put on intermittently allowed for periods of wage catch-up. Moreover, the fact that they were instituted in the old sector and not the new sector would also suggest that these institutions did not play an important role.

New labor laws came into existence in many of these countries. Many have described the labor market in these countries as very inflexible, and I am rather surprised. The Institute for Management Development (IMD) in Geneva surveyed 4,000 business executives in 1998, and they gave scores for how flexible they thought the labor markets were. The range in the CEECs is from 5.2 to 7.2, the higher being more flexible. The score for the United States is 6.9. So the labor markets in the CEECs are considered as flexible as the labor market in the United States, which is relatively flexible. Italy's score is 2.3. So I am little surprised by the prevalent view that these markets are terribly inflexible.

The other thing that surprised me is the belief that minimum wages were having such a tremendous impact. My statistics show that in Hungary, for example, only 10 percent of the employees were earning the minimum wage in 1991. In 1995 it had fallen to 2 percent. Similar statistics exist for the Czech Republic.

My understanding is that minimum wages have not been all that binding, and if you look at the trend over time in figure 5.3 in the CEECs, the minimum wages started at about 45 percent of the average wage, which is comparable to the EU countries, maybe even a little lower. It has fallen over the years to about 30 percent of the average wage, which is comparable to U.S. levels. And in the United States no studies have shown that the minimum wage has had a tremendous impact on employment or other factors. But as you can see in figure 5.3, the minimum wage in FSU countries is far lower. It is about 10 percent of the average wage, so it is clearly not binding there.

What about nonemployment benefits? Numerous studies have looked at the impact of unemployment benefits on unemployment duration and the probability of finding a job. And these studies, at least for all the Central and Eastern European countries, have not found any strong negative impact in terms of work disincentives for these schemes.

In fact, a whole barrage of nonemployment benefits—active labor market policies, social assistance, and unemployment benefits—played the role of a wage floor, given the weakness of the other institutions that we have mentioned. We

FIGURE 5.3 MINIMUM WAGE AS A PERCENTAGE OF REAL WAGE, 1990–96

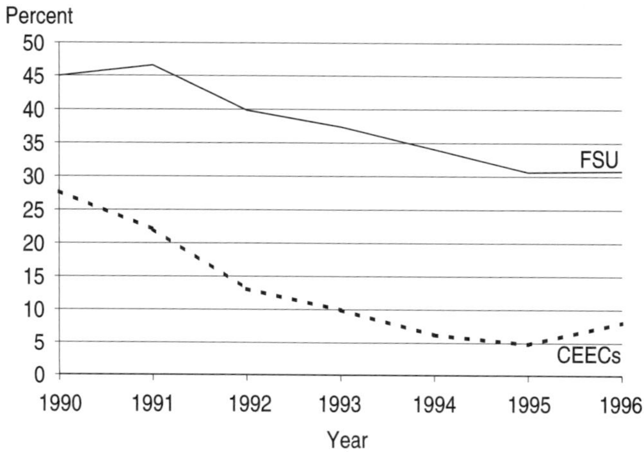

Note: Unweighted average; CEECs include Bulgaria, the Czech Republic, Hungary, Poland, Romania, and the Slovak Republic; the FSU includes the Russian Federation and Ukraine.
Source: Vaughan-Whitehead 1998.

argue in this paper that the differences in the way the nonemployment benefits are structured in the CEECs versus the FSU countries help explain differences in their wage level and, hence, in their employment trajectories.

As you can see in the first column of table 5.2, the percentage of GDP that is spent on nonemployment benefits is far higher in the Central and Eastern European countries than in Russia and Ukraine. And we note that the level of these social expenditures as a share of GDP is lower in the CEECs than in the EU countries.

Not only does an unemployed individual in the CEECs get more in benefits on average, but individuals in the low end of the wage distribution get relatively more unemployment benefits than people in the high-wage distribution in the CEECs compared to the FSU countries. As columns 3 and 4 in table 5.2 show, the CEECs are redistributing income to the lower end of the wage distribution. This level is high enough that these benefits are acting as a wage floor. And we believe they have contributed to the different patterns and changes in earnings inequality. As shown in columns 5 and 6 of the table, earnings inequality in Russia and Ukraine and in the FSU countries has grown tremendously compared to earnings inequality in the CEECs. The reason is that the bottom fell out of the income distribution in the former Soviet Union, whereas the bottom was kept up in the Central and Eastern European countries (Garner and Terrell 1998; Commander and Lee 1998).

TABLE 5.2 EARNINGS INEQUALITY AND NONEMPLOYMENT BENEFITS IN SELECTED TRANSITION ECONOMIES

	Nonemployment benefit system				*Earnings inequality*		*Income inequality*	
	1991–95 expenditure		*Replacement rate*[a]		*Gini coefficients*[b]		*Share of income (percent)*[d]	
Region and country	*Percent of GDP (1)*	*Percent of social expenditures (2)*	*At two times the average wage (3)*	*At 2/3 of the average wage (4)*	*1987–89 (5)*	*1997 (6)*	*At the bottom (10th) decile (7)*	*At the top (90th) decile (8)*
Central and Eastern Europe								
Bulgaria	1.6	17.2	18	47	21.0	29.1[c]	3.4	22.5
Czech Republic	3.6	32.7	21	52	20.0	25.9	4.3	22.4
Hungary	2.4	32.3	18	50	27.0	34.8	3.9	24.8
Poland	5.0	31.8	14	46	21.0	30.0	3.0	26.3
Romania	1.9	27.5	16	40	19.0	42.2	3.7	22.7
Newly Independent States Federation								
Russia	0.6	10.9	8	11	27.0	48.3[c]	1.7	38.7
Ukraine	0.3	3.3	—	—	24.0	41.3[c]	3.9	26.4

— Not available.
a. The average of gross replacement rates in 1992–93, inclusive of social assistance for one person in the first two years of employment, adjusted for inflation where indexing was applicable.
b. Calculated using monthly earnings data as reported by employers. Small employers are often excluded.
c. 1996 data.
d. 1995 for Bulgaria, 1994 for Romania, 1998 for the Russian Federation, and 1996 for the rest of the countries.
Sources: Boeri 2000; Atkinson and Micklewright 1992; EBRD 2001; World Bank 2001.

The difference in the growth in earnings inequality in the FSU compared with the CEECs during transition is not driven by different rates of increase in the income of those at the top of the distribution, but by the relative size of the safety net for those at the bottom of the distribution.

In conclusion, why was labor market adjustment in the Central and Eastern European countries so different from in the former Soviet Union? We argue that the answer has largely to do with the way these social policies were designed and that a higher level of benefits in the CEECs implied floors to wage distribution and prevented further decline in wages. This allowed for more quantity than price adjustment in the CEECs vis-à-vis the former Soviet Union.

Why was the CEEC model more conducive to structural change than the FSU model? With higher floors, the old firms were forced to shed the least productive labor. On the other hand, the new private sector had to pay higher wages. Therefore, people in the low end of the wage distribution, low-productivity workers, had longer spells of unemployment because they could not get these jobs. But the higher nonemployment benefits also made possible implicit, if not explicit, start-up loans. So the CEEC model may have helped create the new private sector as well in countries like the Czech Republic and Poland.

Which model is preferable? Well, there is a tradeoff. The CEEC model clearly yielded much more unemployment, but at the same time it allowed for more structural change and for less income inequality. So it depends on what weights you put on these things.

What are the implications of EU enlargement? Until now these higher benefits have allowed for structural change. What we worry about is if accession countries spend even more. If they raise these benefits to the levels of the EU, such benefit levels may become detrimental and lower the level of structural adjustment in these countries. But that is something for discussion.

Note

1. Basu, Estrin, and Svejnar (1999) and other studies document differences in the wage-employment elasticities.

References

Atkinson, Anthony B., and John Micklewright. 1992. *Economic Transformation in Eastern Europe and the Distribution of Income*. Cambridge: Cambridge University Press.

Basu, Swati, Saul Estrin, and Jan Svejnar. 1999. "Employment and Wage Behavior of Enterprises under Communism and in Transition: Evidence from Central Europe and Russia." Davidson Institute Working Paper 114. William Davidson Institute, Ann Arbor.

Boeri, Tito. 2000. *Structural Change, Welfare Systems and Labour Reallocation.* Oxford: Oxford University Press.

Commander, Simon, and Une Lee. 1998. *How Does Public Policy Affect the Income Distribution? Evidence from Russia, 1992–1996*. European Bank for Reconstruction and Development and the World Bank.

EBRD (European Bank for Reconstruction and Development). Various years. *Transition Report*. London.

———. 1999. *Transition Report*. London.

———. 2000. *Transition Report*. London.

———. 2001. *Transition Report Update 2001.* London.

Garner, Thesia, and Katherine Terrell. 1998. "A Gini Decompositon Analysis of Inequality in the Czech and Slovak Republics during the Transition." *The Economics of Transition* 1 (6): 23–46.

OECD (Organisation for Economic Co-operation and Development). Various issues. *Main Economic Indicators*. Paris.

———. 1999. *Slovak Republic.* OECD Economic Surveys. Paris.

Statistical Office of the Republic of Slovenia. 1998. *Statistical Yearbook of Slovenia.* Ljubljana.

UNICEF (United Nations Children's Fund). 1999. "Women in Transition." *Regional Monitoring Report*. The Monee Project No. 6. Florence.

Vaughan-Whitehead, Daniel. 1998. "Wage Policy Reforms in Central and Eastern Europe: A First Assessment." Chapter 2 in D. Vaughan-Whitehead, ed., *Paying the Price: The Wage Crisis in Central and Eastern Europe.* London: Macmillen Press.

World Bank. 2001. *World Development Report 2000/2001.* Washington, D.C.

CHAPTER 6

The Labor Market in Poland: Current Trends and Challenges

Michał Boni

Characterization of the Polish Labor Market

During the past twelve years of Polish transition, every aspect of life has been subjected to changes. The foundations were set for a market system with a radically increased role of private ownership, both in the privatized sector of the economy and in the newly formed private enterprises. Currently, 63 percent of Poland's GDP is generated by the private sector, which accounts for 70 percent of total employment. (See figures 6.1 and 6.2 for trends in the past decade.) There was a clear shift in the structure of employment (figure 6.3). The service sector now accounts for more than 50 percent of total employment, the industrial sector for 31 percent, and agriculture for 19 percent (which in no way changes the still excessive unemployment in agriculture and hidden employment in agriculture, estimated to concern some 900,000 people).

Structural changes in the economy, which lift the reins on entrepreneurship and prepare Polish enterprises for global competition and guarantee lower inflation and macroeconomic stability, have resulted in marked economic growth running for several years at the rate of more than 5 percent GDP annually (figure 6.4). This has situated Poland at the top of the league among the transforming countries of Eastern and Central Europe.

The data indicate the major impact of economic growth on the Polish employment market. Some people claim that only growth above a 5 percent rate reflects positively on the employment index.

FIGURE 6.1 EMPLOYMENT IN PRIVATE AND PUBLIC SECTORS, 1990 AND 1999
(percentage of total employment)

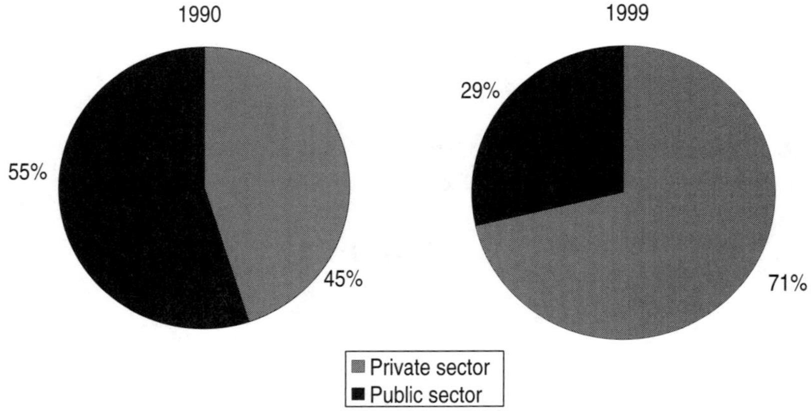

Source: Central Statistical Office.

In this transition period, there was a dramatic jump in the presence of small and medium enterprises, generating some 45 percent of GDP and accounting for nearly 60 percent of total employment. The sunset and traditional sectors (mining, steel, armaments, railways) slashed employment by nearly 700,000 people during the years of transformation, including 200,000 in the past two years.

All social policy institutions have been revamped. A system of assistance to the unemployed was set up, and there is a Labor Fund built up of transfers from the state budget and contributions from employers equal to 2.5 percent of their payrolls. A network of welfare assistance has been developed. Fundamental changes have been made in the pension system, with future retirement benefits paid from two sources: the traditional fund based on the "pay-as-you-go" system and a modern fund in which the contributions are capitalized. In effect, social policy relies more heavily on individual savings and personal prudence.

Social policy has now been anchored in a merger between government responsibilities and the very initiatives taken by local communities. Nonetheless, in addition to beneficiaries of change and development, the transformations have led to the emergence of social groups on the brink of exclusion. One of the most important distinctions of social status was having or not having a job. This factor became the key determinant of Polish poverty. These were also years of consolidating the backbone of democracy—developing a civil society and nongovernmental organizations. Poland entered NATO structures and embarked on an intensive process of negotiations to gain accession to the European Union.

FIGURE 6.2 GROSS DOMESTIC PRODUCT IN PUBLIC AND PRIVATE SECTORS, SELECTED YEARS 1990–98

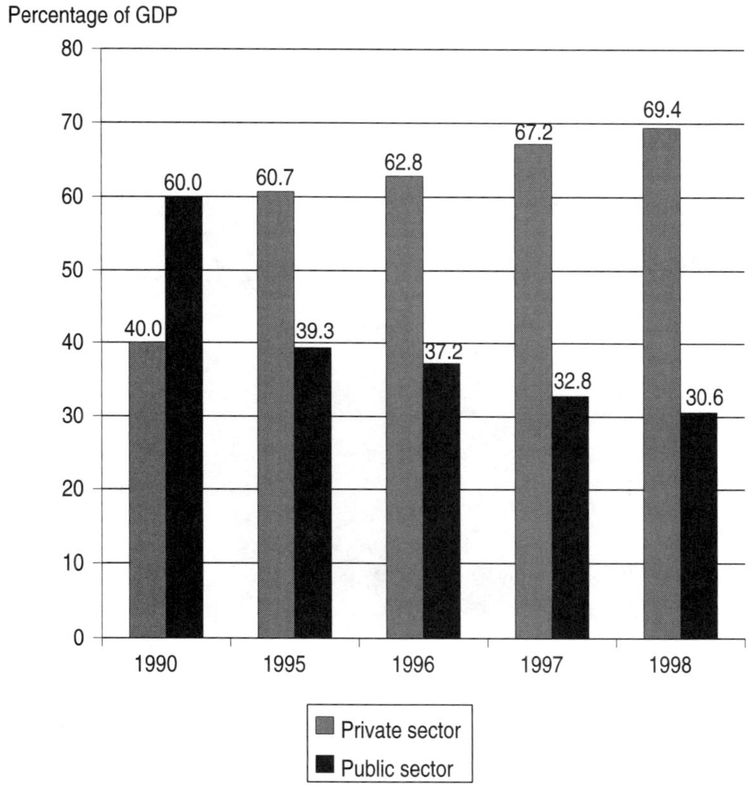

Source: Central Statistical Office.

The processes of transformation left a very clear imprint on the labor market in Poland. In the early months unemployment increased (figure 6.5), and the employment numbers declined (with unemployment growing to nearly 16 percent or 3 million people in 1993). This initial phase was followed by a period of increasing employment, when unemployment declined to about 10 percent by the end of 1998. Since then unemployment has been climbing again and, according to registration data, it is now reaching 16 percent.

FIGURE 6.3 EMPLOYMENT BY MAIN SECTORS, 1989, 1993, AND 1999
(percentage of total)

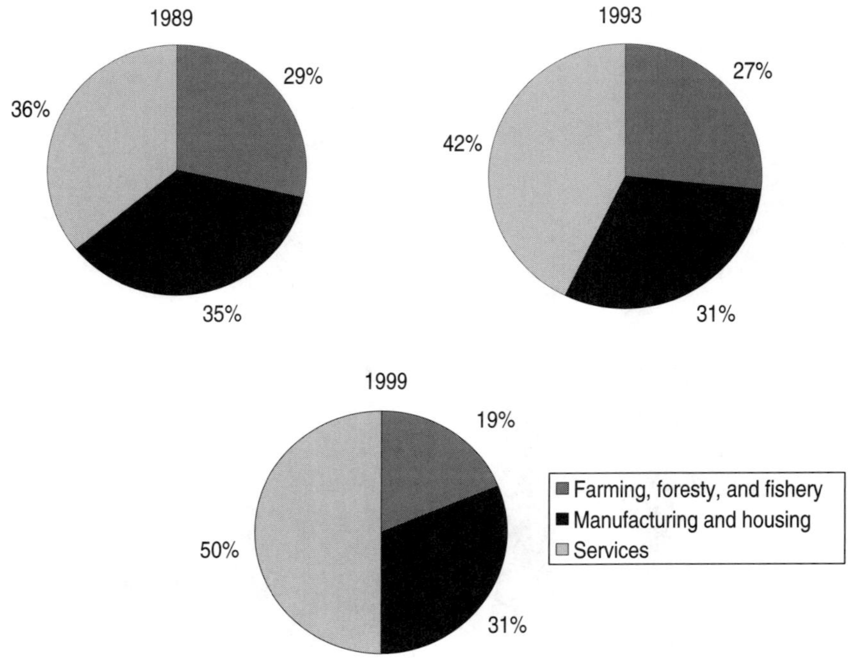

Source: Central Statistical Office.

One can therefore speak of a second wave of unemployment growth. This is a disquieting development with highly complex causes. It also gives rise to numerous challenges that have to be faced through drafting and executing appropriate strategies. On the one hand, these strategies should represent a combination of economic and social approaches to employment-stimulating policy and, on the other hand, given the accession process, they should be in line with the methodology applied in EU member countries.

Starting with these premises, a *National Strategy of Employment and Development of Human Resources for 2000–2006* was drafted and adopted in the year 2000, and on its basis operational plans are being drawn up. The consistency of the Polish employment-promotion program strategy with EU directives was reviewed in the *Joint Assessment Paper* discussed in Warsaw late in May 2000.

In order to more fully assess the employment strategy and instruments designed to counter growing unemployment, the picture and characterization of the

FIGURE 6.4 GDP GROWTH AND THE RATE OF UNEMPLOYMENT, 1992–2000

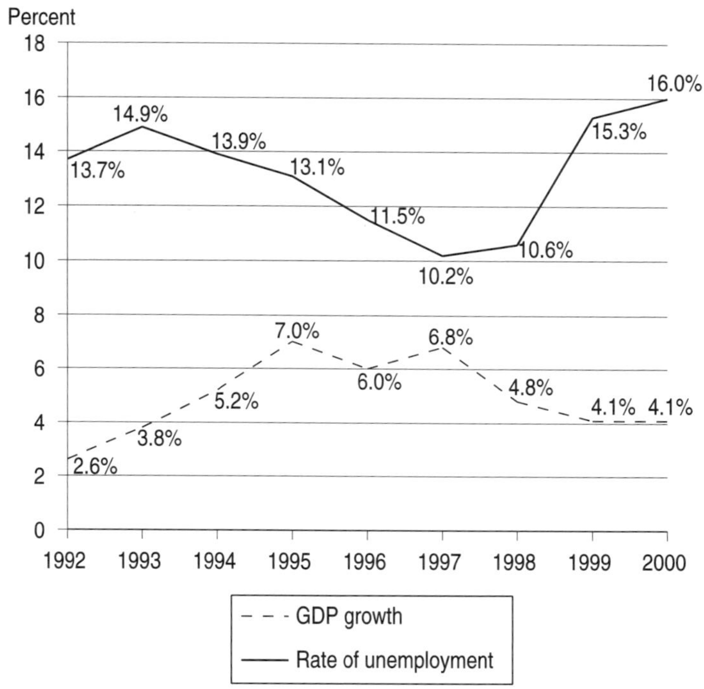

Source: Central Statistical Office.

Polish labor market need to be presented in greater detail. A disquieting development is the relatively low employment ratio (figure 6.6) and the disparity (about 14 percent) between the male and female employment rates (figure 6.7). True, in the EU countries this spread is higher, in the range of 20 percent. In the unemployed population there are more women than men (currently about 54 percent as shown in figure 6.8). But during the years of declining unemployment, the share of women among those without jobs was higher, growing to 60 percent. This means that even in an economic growth environment, the employment of women encountered greater resistance. A similar situation may be observed concerning duration of unemployment. Nearly 53 percent of women cannot find a job during more than 12 months (figure 6.9).

FIGURE 6.5 REGISTERED UNEMPLOYMENT, 1990–2000

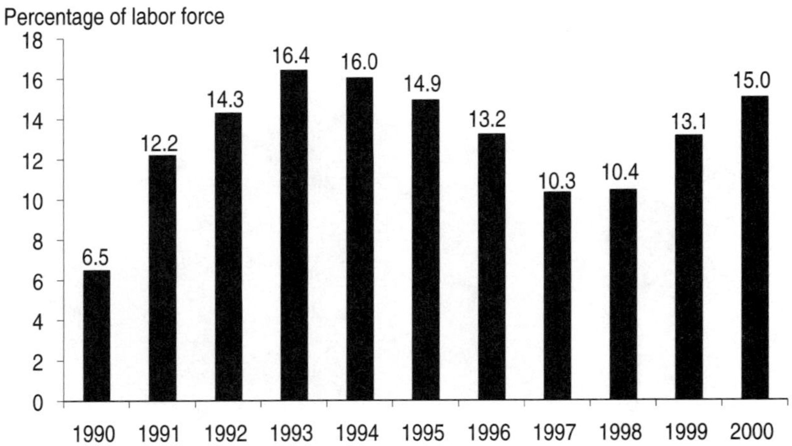

Source: Central Statistical Office.

FIGURE 6.6 EMPLOYMENT RATE, 1992–2000

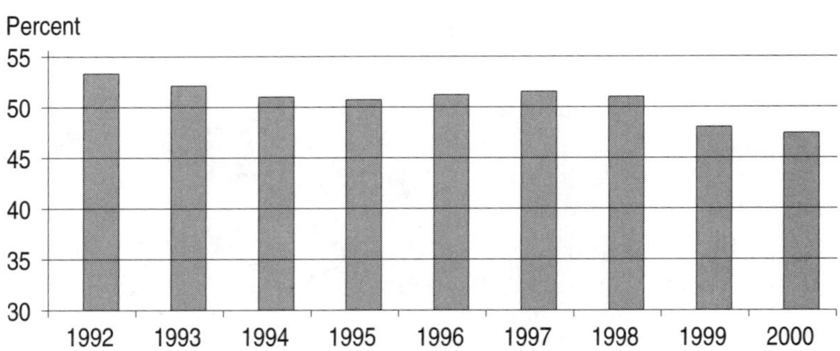

Source: Central Statistical Office.

FIGURE 6.7 EMPLOYMENT RATE BY GENDER, 1992–2000

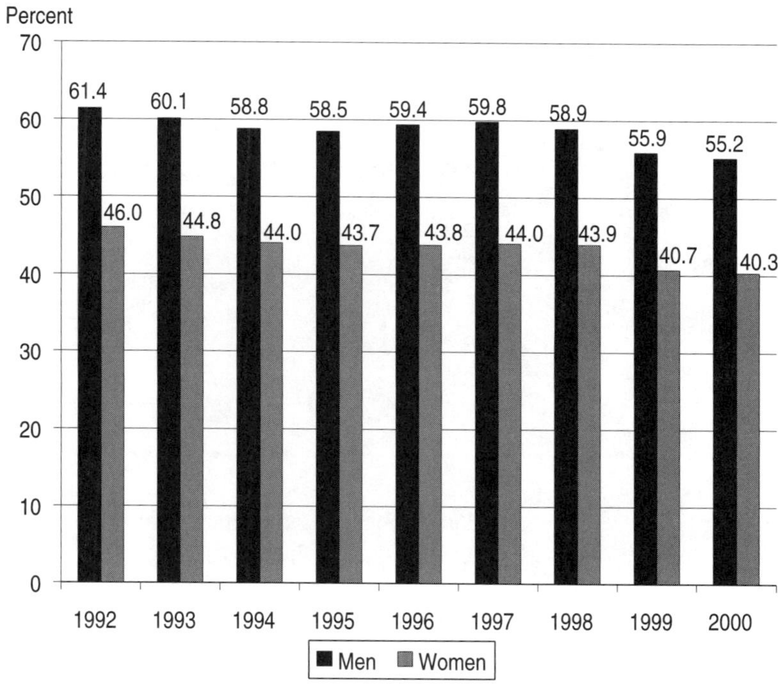

Source: Central Statistical Office.

FIGURE 6.8 UNEMPLOYMENT BY GENDER, 2001
(percentage of labor force)

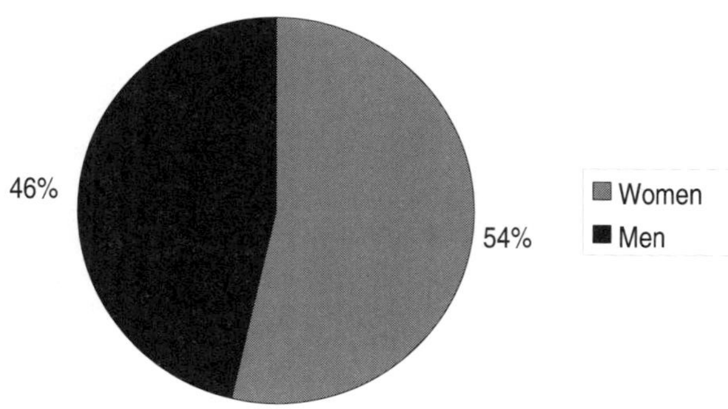

Source: Central Statistical Office.

FIGURE 6.9 UNEMPLOYED WOMEN BY DURATION OF JOB SEARCH, 2001
(percent)

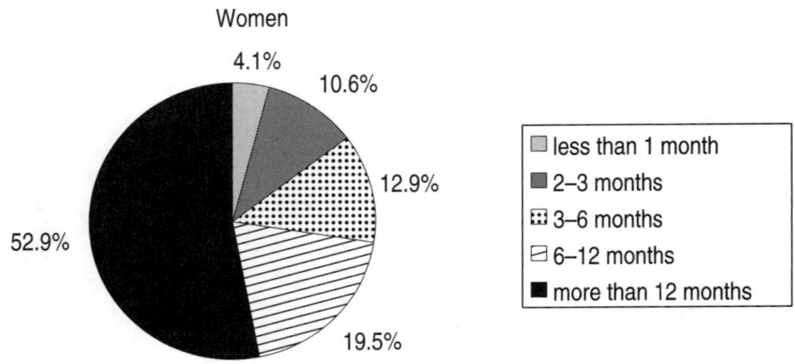

Source: Central Statistical Office.

Among the more than 1.5 million unemployed women, nearly 65 percent have less than full primary education, and 30 percent have just primary education or basic vocational schooling. More than 700,000 women have no work experience, or their experience is less than 12 months. Their employment activation, considering short employment experience, poor qualifications, and long unemployment, will be an extremely difficult task. It would require tri-modular efforts, rooted in developing mobility and occupational reintegration.

The lack of a net addition of new jobs in the service sector, observed in 2000, is a disquieting development since this sector generated over 750,000 new jobs in the years 1994 to 1999.

One of the more significant characteristics of the Polish labor market is the geographic differentiation of unemployment. This has been evident from the very beginning of the 1990s, and even economic development made little dent in such disparities. The situation in large metropolitan areas, particularly in Warsaw, is much better than in rural regions and the small towns of northern and eastern Poland. In these Polish regions the unemployment rate is 2.5 times higher. For example, Mazowieckie (Warsaw and environs) Voivodship is 11.8 percent, while Warmińsko-Mazurskie Voivodship is 25.6 percent (figure 6.10). In the local labor market there can be as much as a twelvefold spread in employment opportunities. The rigid structure of geographic differentiation reveals the scale of the development gap and economic potential of Poland's different regions and is a major determinant of the regional opportunity-equalizing policies. By mobilizing partners and local authorities, these policies should skillfully deploy European funds during the current pre-accession phase.

FIGURE 6.10 UNEMPLOYMENT RATE BY VOIVODSHIP, 2001

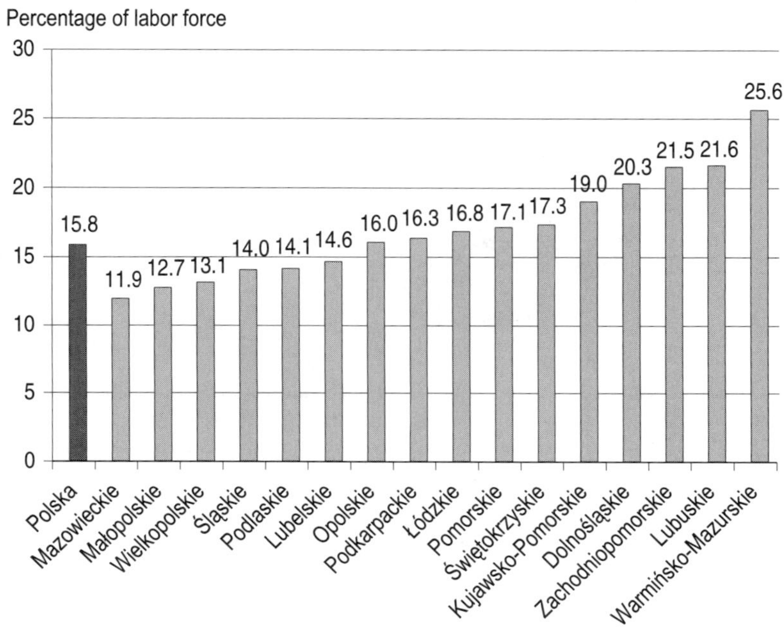

Source: Central Statistical Office.

These regional employment discrepancies are bonded to one of the gravest problems for the Polish economy and labor market—the situation of Polish agriculture and employment of rural inhabitants. Some 52 percent of women in rural areas are unemployed, but rural inhabitants represent 43 percent of the country's total unemployed population (figure 6.11). It will be an immense problem to create new jobs for them, partly because of their poor qualifications.

Another worrisome development (next to the fixed overall structure and geographic structure of unemployment over the past ten years) is the delineation of the unemployment structure according to educational status (figures 6.12 and 6.13). More than 70 percent of the unemployed have only complete or incomplete primary education (34 percent) or basic vocational schooling (37 percent). The only variable element during the past decade was the share of unemployed with primary or incomplete primary education in the total population of the unemployed. It is currently significantly higher than in the early days of transformation, which indicates not only the declining demand in the economy for labor

FIGURE 6.11 RURAL AND URBAN UNEMPLOYMENT, 2001
(percentage of total unemployment)

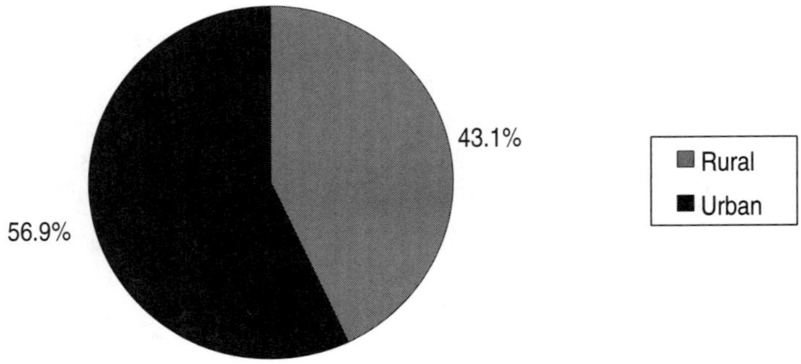

Source: Central Statistical Office.

with poor qualifications but also that the unemployed population contains a growing group of people with limited opportunities for occupational reactivation. These are people with poor qualifications, they have been unemployed a long time, and they are more often women than men, more often rural than urban inhabitants. On the other hand, it should be noted that unemployed women are on the average better educated than unemployed men (figure 6.14).

An important parameter in assessing the labor market is an analysis of unemployment by age (figure 6.15). There is clearly an immense scale of unemployment among the young and relatively young (up to age 34)—nearly 60 percent of the total. The scale of unemployment among people up to the age of 24, just starting their working life, is highly disquieting (figure 6.16). In that population every third person is unemployed. Such a phenomenon is a dangerous one indeed. The said baby boom will be responsible for a 1.2- million-person increase in the labor force by 2006. Add to this the people who have postponed their workforce entry in the years 1995 to 1999 by extending their education (some 600,000 people). Consequently, the pressure on the labor market in coming years will be immense.

Another phenomenon relating to the age of the unemployed is worth noting. Comparing unemployment by age and gender indicates that unemployment among men above 35, and particularly above 45, is particularly high and disquieting (figure 6.17).This is indicative of large-scale occupational deactivation, during the restructuring process, of men in these age groups, who most frequently found themselves redundant (because of their low qualifications). In Poland, as in many other countries, long-term unemployment is significant for assessment of the labor market. It is higher for women than for men (more than 50 percent compared with about 36 percent), but is high in any case (nearly 45 percent).

FIGURE 6.12 UNEMPLOYMENT BY EDUCATIONAL STATUS, 2001
(percentage of total unemployment)

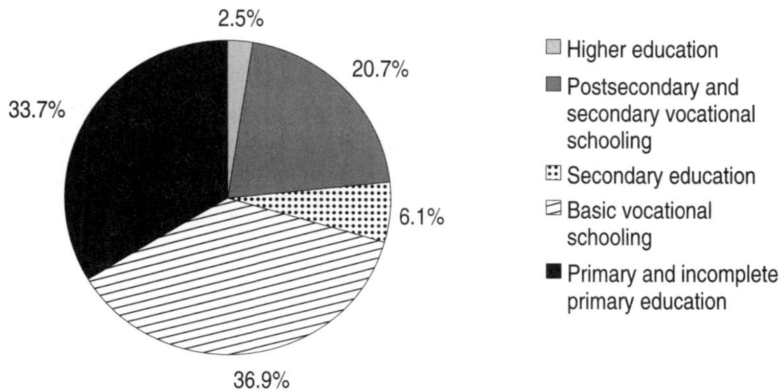

Source: Central Statistical Office.

FIGURE 6.13 UNEMPLOYMENT BY EDUCATIONAL STATUS, 1992 AND 2001

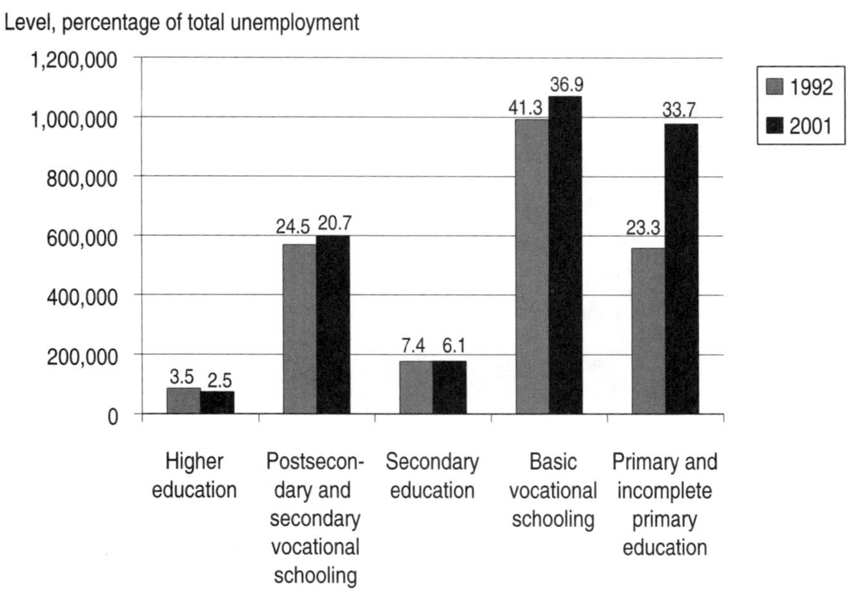

Source: Central Statistical Office.

FIGURE 6.14 UNEMPLOYMENT BY EDUCATIONAL STATUS AND GENDER, 2001
(percentage of total unemployment)

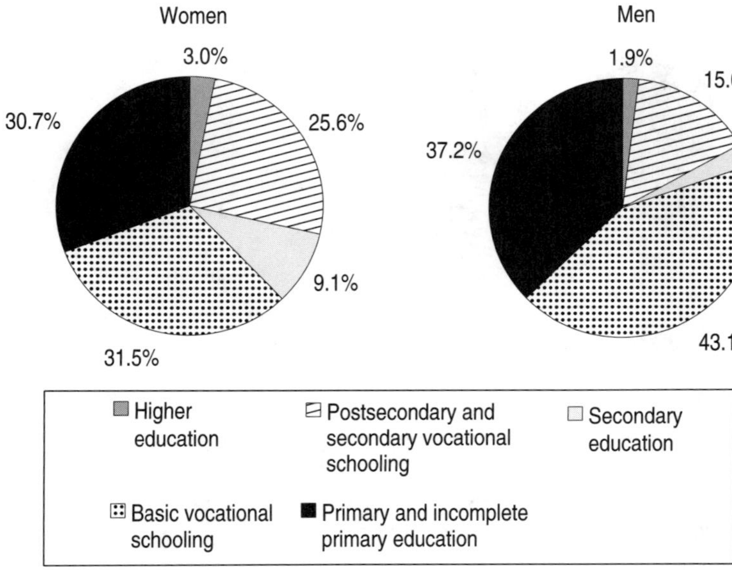

Source: Central Statistical Office.

FIGURE 6.15 UNEMPLOYMENT BY AGE, 2001
(percentage of total unemployment)

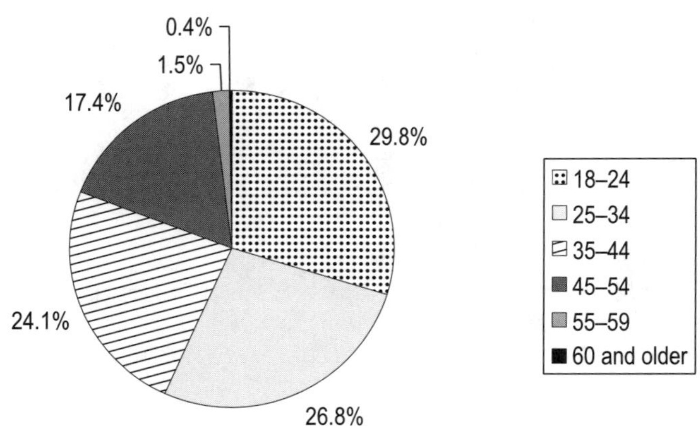

Source: Central Statistical Office.

FIGURE 6.16 UNEMPLOYMENT RATE BY AGE GROUP, 1992 AND 2000

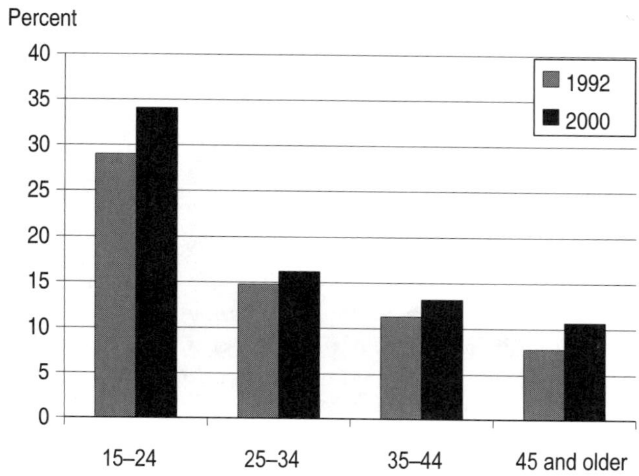

Source: Central Statistical Office.

FIGURE 6.17 UNEMPLOYMENT BY GENDER AND AGE, 2001

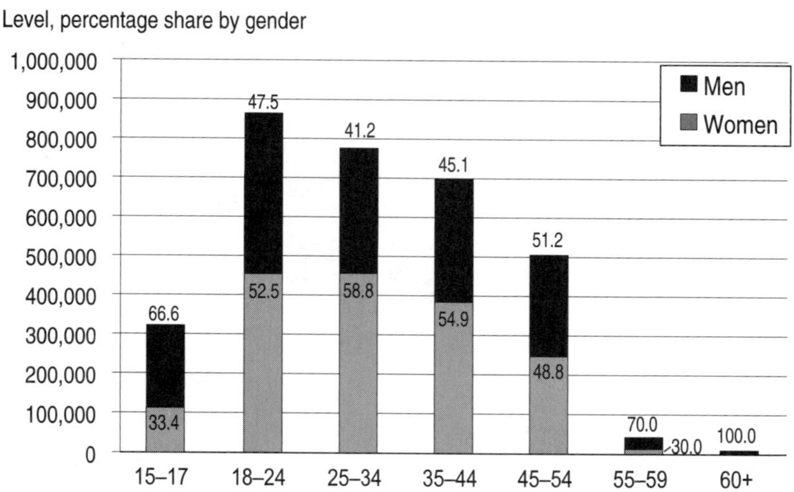

Source: Central Statistical Office.

For a variety of reasons, there have been changes over the past ten years in the proportion of unemployed entitled to unemployment allowance. In the early 1990s nearly 60 percent had such entitlement; currently it is some 20 percent. This decline results from tightened rules, but it also is indicative of the closeness of unemployment (particularly for high-risk groups) and the phenomenon of poverty. The lack of a job not only determines social status, but also influences the hazard of permanent transfer to the group of socially excluded. This applies to young people as well (given the high rate of unemployment among graduates).

Causes of Unemployment

One cannot characterize the causes of unemployment without pointing to the overlapping emergency of multiple causes and developments. The multiple-cause nature of Polish unemployment at the present time (it is no longer attributable simply to restructuring and economic slowdown, as it was in the early 1990s) presents the challenge of applying an array of remedial instruments.

Beyond question, there are several cyclical causes reflecting demographic and economic processes. The Russian crisis and its aftermath affected unemployment in many sectors. Slowing down the economic growth rate to the level of jobless growth, coupled with weak job creation in services and in small and medium enterprises (SMEs), pushes up unemployment. This particularly was the case when pursuit of a disinflation target was combined with stabilization of a high exchange rate of the Zloty (negative consequences for exporters), with money and credit becoming very dear. The observed demographic pressure also does nothing to help balance the supply and demand for labor. The actual supply is much too high, given the existing demand. On top of that come the elements important at the current juncture of economic transformations, namely, restructuring of multiple obsolete sectors and numerous enterprises (including firms where the protective umbrella of employment guarantees under privatization contracts no longer applies) having to face up to the challenge of competition.

Bleak development scenarios speak of unemployment climbing to 25 percent, should long-term economic growth remain at 2.5 percent GDP annually. The picture is bleak, especially since the second group of causes weakening the capacity of the economy to generate new jobs rapidly also acts to depress the market. This is linked with causes of a structural nature. Significant here are the following causes of unemployment.

Mismatch of Employee Qualifications

Analysis of the labor market indicates the importance of the "educational premium." Despite the high momentum in efforts to improve the quality and level of qualifications, the actual potential in terms of qualifications and competence is not very high. It should be remembered that 4.2 million young people have not benefited from educational reform, and the bridging forms of education offered them to help adapt their skills to the needs of the labor market were highly imperfect at best. The adult education network is underdeveloped, and the incentives for adults to join such educational efforts and attend retraining courses are also quite weak. (See figures 6.18 and 6.19 for the relationship between unemployment and education.)

Low Labor Mobility

The processes of occupational deactivation in the form of preretirement allowances and benefits have encompassed large groups of people, with the cost falling on the Labor Fund. The level of long-term unemployment, lack of possibilities for geographic mobility, lack of funds for programs training in active approaches and supporting mobility of many jobless on the verge of poverty due to lack of income—all of this defines a large population among the unemployed with a low mobility potential (correlated with low qualifications). (See figure 6.20 regarding the duration of the job search.)

FIGURE 6.18 LABOR FORCE BY LEVEL OF EDUCATION, 1992 AND 2000

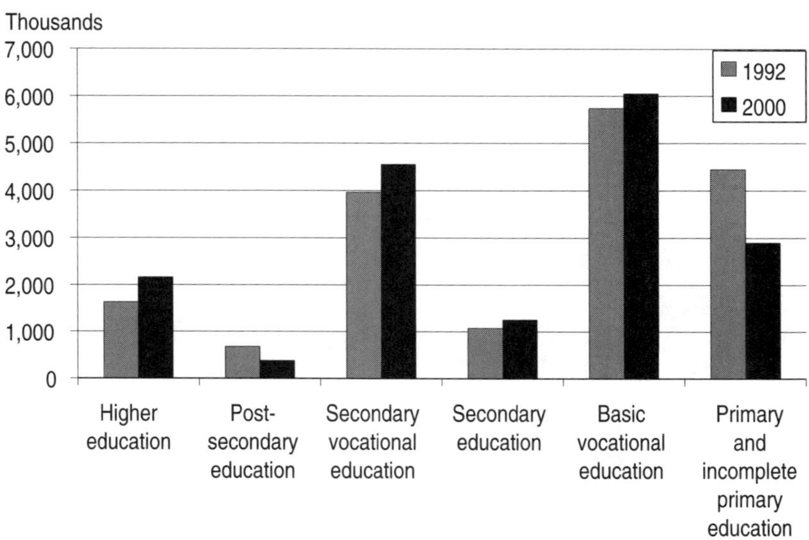

Source: Central Statistical Office.

FIGURE 6.19 UNEMPLOYMENT RATE BY LEVEL OF EDUCATION, 1992 AND 2000

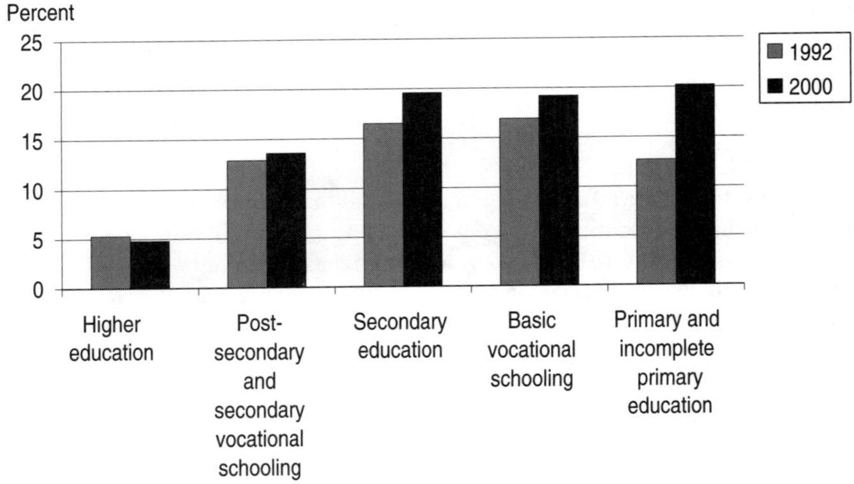

Source: Central Statistical Office.

FIGURE 6.20 UNEMPLOYMENT ACCORDING TO DURATION OF JOB SEARCH, 2001 (percent of total unemployment)

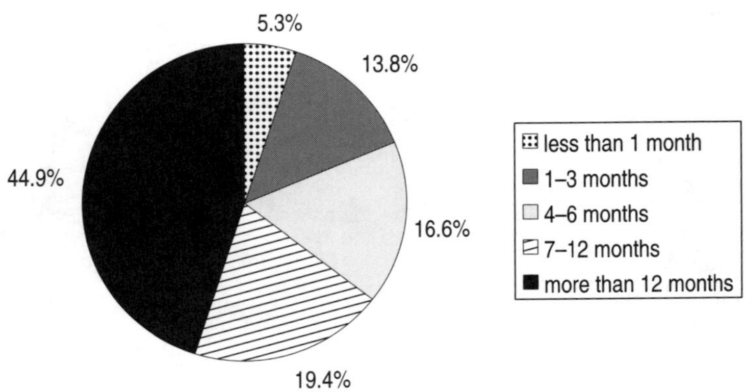

Source: Central Statistical Office.

Economic Modernization Requirements

Because of such requirements, there has been a move to accelerate restructuring of enterprises and entire sectors. In accordance with World Bank suggestions on job destruction and job creation, restructuring is still desirable although it eliminates jobs. At the same time care should be taken to create new jobs in services and in small and medium businesses.

Excessive Cost of Labor

Tax charges, high minimum wage (for many regions), or high nonwage charges on labor resulted in an evident slowdown in the rate of new job creation. Given the liabilities of the social security system, there is little chance that social security contribution rates could be reduced over the next few years, unless a decision were made to offer more employment subsidies. Still, consideration should be given to reducing taxes. Another significant element of the excessive burden on employers is the detailed legal and reporting requirement (bureaucracy). The requirements and procedures relating to company formation, operation, and employee provisions should be simplified and streamlined, particularly for small and medium businesses.

Excessive Rigidity of Labor Laws

Employers argue that, given the circumstances of the Polish labor market, there are too many obligations dictated by the Labor Code and other legislation, while the role of collective labor agreements has been diminished. With group dismissals (which often imply a difficult financial situation for the employer), there are high severance costs. This curtails the freedom to fire employees but also to hire them—that is, adjusting employment to changing market conditions. The rule requiring a permanent employment contract on third employment contract is too rigid. There are excessive overtime costs. Labor laws lack provisions allowing for atypical forms of employment so badly needed in, for instance, the service sector or when hiring women on a part-time basis. There is also no distinction made in selected employers' duties between large and small enterprises, something that is common in the European Union. Despite resistance from trade unions, talks on increasing the flexibility of labor law started in June 2000.

Regional Disparities

One of the most prominent causes of unemployment is the ever more set differentiation between regions. At the roots are the differences in economic potential, reflecting intrinsic underdevelopment of certain parts of the country. There is a need for the drafting of regional policy, incentives to investment in the weaker regions, and financial engineering that should allow tapping various sources for funding development-oriented initiatives in the area of infrastructure and improving educational opportunities for young people and adults. A huge role could be played here by both future and preaccession funds earmarked for infrastructure development. In sophisticated economies, new jobs are also created in the infrastructure of infrastructure (such as shops and service centers along motorways).

Managing the Labor Market

Decentralization of labor market management (submitting powiat-level labor offices to regional government controls), given the limited powers of these authorities as labor market instruments, has not yielded the expected positive results. Labor market policy in such a model becomes dispersed, poorly lending itself to cohesive programs. Instead of a cooperative approach by government and local authorities, one gets disputes over funding. A side effect, but one significant from the point of view of effective management of the labor market, was the high employment turnover (60 percent in one year) of employment service staff remunerated, for economy reasons, out of the budgets for intervention works. This has adverse consequences for the quality and scale of employment intermediation. Local government preferences for public works and organized occupational deactivation (fights to extend the scope of preretirement benefits) prevent application of more effective labor market policies.

Challenges and Actions

Acceptance that the reason for the so-called jump in unemployment (after 1998; second wave unemployment) has been a combination of several causes should lead to acceptance of an array of countermeasures focused on the prime objective of creating new jobs and adapting labor resources to job requirements. There is a need to continue eliminating unproductive jobs without a future in sunset sectors and firms requiring restructuring, to recognize the unavoidable nature of future rural restructuring and changes in agricultural employment, and to consider the demographic pressures at hand. With these objectives in mind, two types of solutions should be sought: solutions that would reduce unemployment and increase employment ratios, and solutions that would come to terms with a high unemployment rate for some time to come.

The key to success will be stable and sustainable economic development. But there is also a whole set of elements supporting improvement of the labor market situation. These should be perceived and applied as packages. They are linked to the European Union methodology, adopted by Poland, and map out targets of national employment strategy. The four pillars of such a strategy are improved labor skill levels, increased adaptability of enterprises and employees to new terms of economic competitiveness, development of entrepreneurship, and elimination of inequalities in the labor market that also reflect social inequalities. These strategies, through appropriate documents, have been adapted to the conditions prevailing in Poland.

They now are to be implemented through the adoption of a specific action program. In addition to the tasks carried out already, the program should be fundamentally extended to include the following program directions: work for young people, employment of women, labor market flexibility, improved labor qualifications, and employment services that take a more active stance. Each of these new tasks will be discussed in turn.

Actions to improve employment for young people must focus on better educational preparation of graduates, increasing their employment opportunities by differentiating minimum pay for persons just starting their employment careers. It also might be possible to further reduce the cost of their employment by additionally subsidizing their social security contributions from the Labor Fund.

Early elimination of legal provisions sanctioning unequal treatment of women in the labor market, coupled with programs to support occupational reintegration of women with little or no employment experience who are returning to the labor market after a break, should yield results. Important will be the right legal and economic terms to allow women to pursue at the same time their family functions and occupational aspirations.

The flexibility of the labor market can be increased in various ways: a new look at labor law and its economic functions, greater freedom in firing and hiring, more sensitivity in labor law to the different sense of operation in small firms, better terms for self-employment, and new forms of labor adapted to the new economy and new technology (distance working and call centers, contract jobs, the internet). All of this should be conducive to creation of new jobs.

Efforts to improve labor qualifications will yield results quickly. A more accessible and tax-attractive infrastructure for adult education is needed. Greater prominence should be given to occupational reintegration programs for employees with prolonged absence from active employment—with part of the funding from local governments and social welfare institutions. Transportation infrastructure will need to be improved to allow employment away from the person's place of residence. It is obvious that there should be support for school programs focused on future employment (computers, languages, communication skills).

The policy of employment services should be substantively more focused, standardized, and concentrated on employment intermediation. Given this, more attention should be paid to the quality of employment intermediation personnel. A supplementary role should be played by private job and temporary job agencies—for which the appropriate legal conditions should be created immediately.

In the present stage of Polish–European Union accession negotiations and with such a high level of unemployment, the issues of free movement of labor are becoming particularly critical. Figure 6.21 shows the scale of job migration (107,000 in 1990 and 330,000 in 2000). These observations do not warrant conclusions that long-term job migration is a solution yearned for by Polish employees. The fears of certain EU countries of a massive influx of labor are unfounded. This is particularly true since many of the jobs performed by Polish employees are in complementary markets, jobs that do not interest local employees. Equalizing

FIGURE 6.21 JOB MIGRATION, 1989–2000

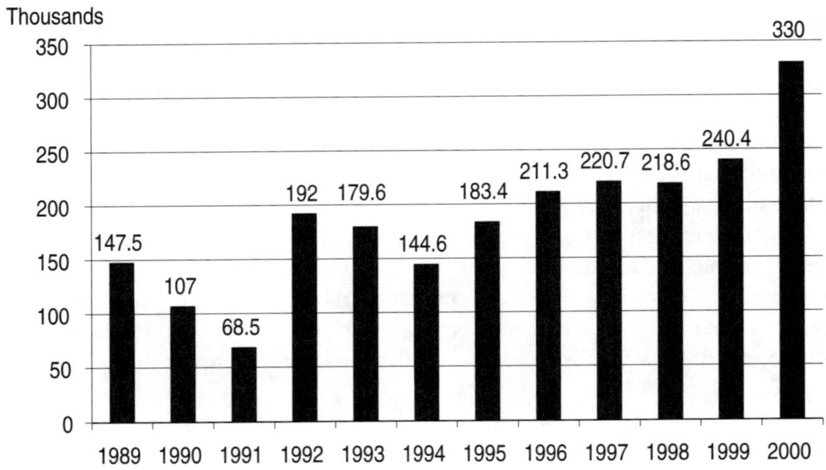

Source: Central Statistical Office.

living and earning standards, when it is relative, is not conducive to worker migration. Furthermore, those needing jobs the most are also the least mobile. One should not suppose that they will leap up overnight to take work in a completely alien environment.

Obviously, the estimates concerning illegal migration could give rise to fears, but any provisions concerning a temporary derogation from the free movement of labor will not address this particular problem. In assessing this question, one should keep in mind the problem of exporting unemployment to Poland (an estimated 300,000 jobs annually). This results from unrestricted trade flows or, in other words, the large scale of imports from the European Union. In addition, the impact that work by Polish nationals could have on EU countries with unbalanced demographic structures (such as the aging German population) on tax revenues collected from jobs held legally in these countries, will increase the level of social security there.

All of these questions must be addressed in the immediate future without bias, myths, or excessive emotions. Responding to labor market challenges, beginning dialogue with social partners on a "Pact to Create New Jobs," one cannot lose sight of the necessity for an alternative strategy that comes to terms with high unemployment prevailing for some time to come.

This would require action to greatly uplift the labor market, something that implies a high level of fluctuation in that market. There will be more redundancies, and more hiring, in part due to more flexible labor law. But there should also be radically less long-term unemployment, which requires good employment intermediation and programs to stimulate employee activity.

In such cases it will be necessary to have dual types of instruments addressing the unemployed. The strategy for action with the better educated and more mobile is obvious. Less obvious and much more costly is the package of social and economic policies to be applied to the high-risk groups. This will imply special programs for these groups that include economic incentives (cheaper jobs), legal incentives (greater flexibility of employment), and also psycho-social stimuli.

If, however, we want to avoid high and long-lasting unemployment and the permanent social exclusion that results, we must take up the challenges. In order to take them up, we should now, without any delay, redefine employment policy and labor market policy in Poland.

CHAPTER 7

Labor Market Trends and Issues in Lithuania

Rimantas Kairelis

The considerable changes in Lithuanian economy and society determined changes in employment and the labor market. The first stage of economic transformation, which ended in 1994, was characterized by decreased industrial production, reduction of domestic turnover in international trade, increased inflation, and falling standards of living. After 1994 the macroeconomic indicators began to take a positive direction until the end of 1998, when this positive trend was interrupted by an economic recession, influenced by Russia's financial crisis. The result was a decrease in gross domestic product in 1999 by 4.1 percent. The situation began to improve only in 2000, when GDP increased by 2.5 percent. This improvement was reflected in changes in economic activity and employment rates of the population.

Trends in Employment and Unemployment

Between 1990 and 2000 labor force participation in Lithuania decreased by only 3.5 percent. This was due to a small migration from the country and a successful pension reform in 1994, which eliminated the early pension retirement and prolonged retirement age. On the other hand, there was a significant decrease in the total number of employed by 14.4 percent (figure 7.1).

The most significant decrease in employment was in industry (figure 7.2). The main reason for it was a decrease in production and economic difficulties due to loss of markets, lack of capital, low quality and productivity, backward technology, and

FIGURE 7.1 ACTIVITY AND EMPLOYMENT RATES, 1990–2000

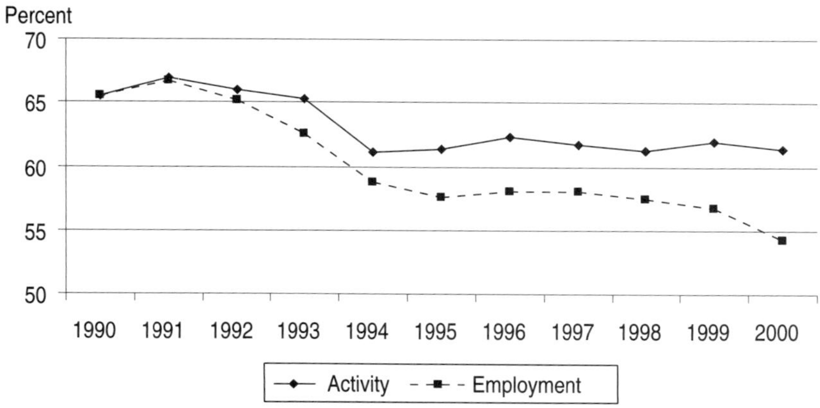

Source: Department of Statistics, Republic of Lithuania.

dependency on Eastern markets. A considerable increase in employment in agriculture until 1996 singles out Lithuania from other Eastern and Central European transition countries. The inflow of labor to agriculture was induced by restoration of private property for land and land restitution. Also it was a result of the population's response to the worsening economic and social conditions in Lithuania. People preferred hard and not very profitable work in agriculture to unemployment. At the same time the number of people working in agricultural cooperatives significantly decreased, and the number of individual farmers increased. A low level of mobility among the rural population resulted in the formation of an essentially closed, autonomous, and specific labor market. In the future the agricultural sector will face great difficulties because of the necessity to increase productivity and competitiveness in EU markets. Many workers will be forced out of agriculture into other sectors. Employment increased in services but mostly in the cities. In the countryside, because of the insufficient purchasing power of the population, service employment decreased.

After reforms in the economy began, the number of employed in public enterprises started to decrease considerably, while employment in private enterprises increased (figure 7.3). In 2000 the private sector employed about 68.4 percent of all employees. In the private sector the employment levels are 96.5 percent in agriculture, 94 percent in industry, and 95.5 percent in construction.

At the same time the average size of an enterprise decreased. Almost all large industrial and building enterprises have been privatized and split into smaller units.

FIGURE 7.2 EMPLOYMENT BY SECTOR, 1992–2000

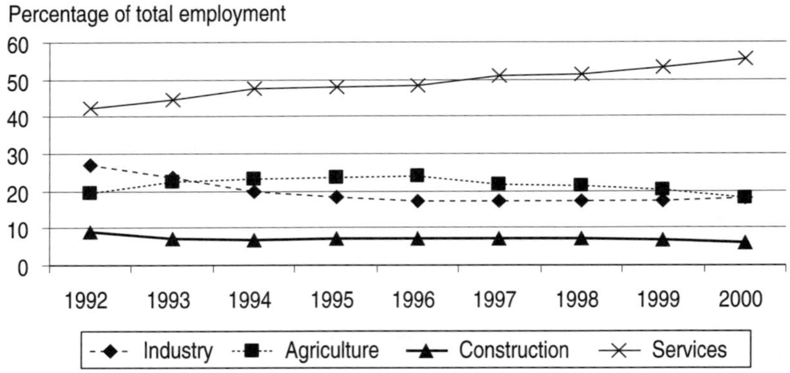

Source: Department of Statistics, Republic of Lithuania.

FIGURE 7.3 EMPLOYMENT IN PUBLIC AND PRIVATE SECTORS, 1990–2000

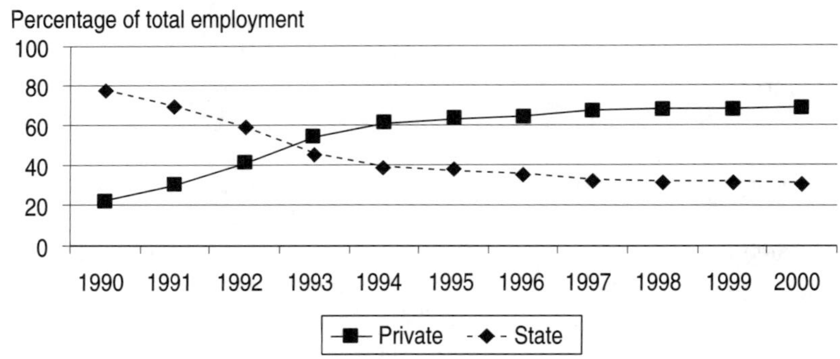

Source: Department of Statistics, Republic of Lithuania.

Small and medium business enterprises (up to 50 employees) developed very intensively. Among 128,000 registered enterprises in Lithuania, 80 percent were small and medium business enterprises. However, they employed only about 23 percent of the employed population.

Economic reforms and changes in enterprise ownership, together with the reductions in employees initiated by enterprises, meant that the first to be pushed out of the labor market were those workers with low qualifications and lower job productivity: women, older people working in industrial enterprises and construction organizations, and people with disabilities. On the other hand, changes in employment are stimulating workers to be more flexible and mobile and to seek retraining and education to upgrade their skills.

In Lithuania the participation of women and retired people in the labor market is quite high. Traditionally, high employment figures for women decreased during 1989 and 1999 from 53 percent to 49.2 percent of all employed. The old-age benefit is low (in 2001 the average old-age benefit represented 31 percent of the average monthly wage), and there is an early retirement age. About 25 percent of the population over the retirement age is still working.

It is difficult to evaluate how many people are employed unofficially. According to different sources, the shadow economy in 1990 accounted for more than 30 percent of GDP, and in 1998, 20 percent. Unofficial employment grew rapidly from 170,000 in 1992 to 370,000 in 1994 and then decreased to 220,000 in 2000. If we take into account unofficial employment, the employment level in Lithuania varied between 63 percent and 66 percent (in the transition period), according to an evaluation by Eurostat.

In sum, the main changes in employment were:

- From full employment to unemployment and to unofficial labor markets
- From the public sector to the private sector
- From a production sector to a services sector.

The first unemployed in Lithuania were registered on March 1, 1991, when labor exchanges began to function. Since that time registered unemployment has increased, reaching 13.2 percent in February 2001 (see figure 7.4 for the employment trend in the last decade). During the 1991–93 period, the unemployment rate grew slowly and did not exceed 5.5 percent, but it spread geographically and extended to new regions and social demographic population groups. From 1993 the official registered unemployment figure began to decrease due to intensive development in the private sector and to an expanding unofficial labor market. The year 1995 was marked by a continuing rise in unemployment related to economic restructuring. In 1996 the unemployment rate began to diminish, partially because of new legal provisions concerning more strict regulations on active and passive labor market measures. In 1997 the unemployment rate started to increase in response to new legal provisions on health insurance for the unemployed and social protection. Since 1998, increases in unemployment have been related to economic difficulties associated with the financial crisis in Russia. Some signs of economic recovery in the labor market are becoming clear. Registered unemployment started to decrease in April 2001.

FIGURE 7.4 UNEMPLOYMENT RATES, 1991–2000

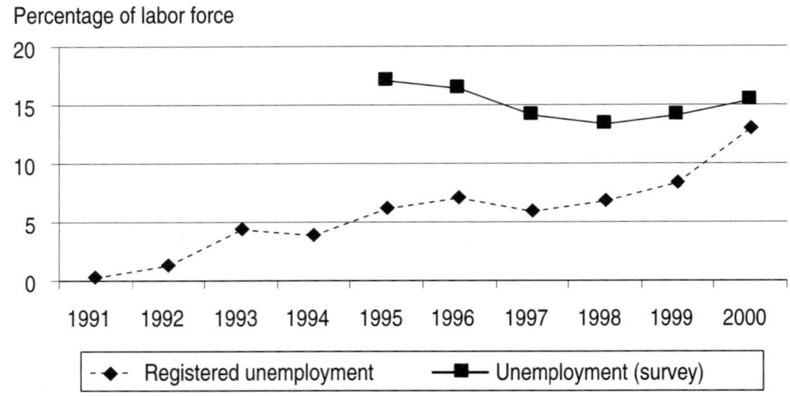

Source: Department of Statistics, Republic of Lithuania.

During this period, there were some clear tendencies in the structure of unemployment. The unemployment rate grew more rapidly in rural areas than in cities. Territorial differences now are fairly large. The proportion of unemployed men increased from 45 percent in 1994 to 54.1 percent in 2001. Increases in the number of young unemployed went from 4 percent in 1992 to 13 percent in 2001. The number of long-term unemployed increased to 30.6 percent. The number of those without professional skills grew from 25 percent in 1991 to 60 percent in 2001.

Employment Policy

The Lithuanian government responded to changes in the labor market by approving the national program for increased employment for 2001 to 2004. The strategic objectives of this program are to cope with the negative consequences of structural economic reforms and the external impact on employment and labor market. The program also plans to increase employment, reduce unemployment, restore balance in the labor market, and prepare for participation in the EU employment policy coordination process.

In implementing these objectives, the government will strive to curb the increase in unemployment in the first half of 2002 and to reduce registered unemployment to between 7 and 8 percent. During the period allotted for the implementation of the program, it is necessary to stimulate the development of business and investments, which would ensure the creation of 110,000 to 120,000 new jobs.

The employment and labor market policy will be based on the following strategic provisions. First, a high level of employment in the population is one of the main preconditions for the social and economic development of the country. Second, the problem of unemployment can be resolved by economic measures only. Therefore, the government will comprehensively encourage economic development, the creation of new jobs, and essential improvement in the business environment. Third, an array of policies (investment, fiscal, monetary, foreign trade, customs, regional development) will be used to increase employment. Fourth, good vocational education and training is needed to develop human resources and meet labor market demands. The goal is to develop the professional and creative potential of people and enable every individual to find his or her place in the labor market and to adapt to changes taking place therein. Fifth, in formulating and implementing strategic provisions of the social policy (for example, with regard to demographics, the family and youngsters, social insurance, social assistance, and the labor market), the government is seeking more cohesion between employment and social policy. Sixth, the government will encourage employment of individuals who have lost work, revive and improve professional skills, and restore and increase the ability of workers to establish themselves in the labor market. Finally, the capabilities of employers and employees to adapt to the changing environment will be promoted; bilateral and tripartite cooperation will be encouraged.

The main pillars of this program are as follows:

- Promoting job creation (enhancement of entrepreneurship)
- Improving support of employability
- Strengthening the capacity to adjust to changes
- Increasing equal opportunities in the labor market
- Enhancing employment policy integration.

Promoting Job Creation

The main actions to promote the creation of new jobs will include improvement of the overall system and of local employment initiatives. The problem is that new jobs are created too slowly. Since the system encouraging economic development and covering small, medium-size, and large businesses is implemented too sluggishly, there is no harmonious, self-regulating mechanism of job restoration. Due to imperfect regulation of assistance to business development, projects of local employment initiatives were not developed any further.

To make the system for the creation of new jobs operate more smoothly, it is expedient to:

- Plan specific actions on the national, regional (counties), and local levels (municipalities), and identify institutions related to business development, their competence and responsibility

- Follow the provision that business development will be determined not only by the scope of assistance provided by the state but also by the removal of obstacles that impede its development, ensuring an equal and favorable business environment for everybody in the market

- Create an economic and financial encouragement system, provide organizational measures for job creation, take up self-employment, and reduce differences between regions

- Increase the number of local employment and labor market policy measures that would create new jobs and reduce unemployment, encourage cooperation among local partners, and develop the local economy.

Improving Employability

The most important actions to improve the employability of workers will be activating the labor market policy, increasing the employability of young people and of the long-term unemployed, improving vocational training, and strengthening the cohesion between employment and social policy. The problem is that labor market policy is too poorly financed from national and municipality budgets. Difficulties in financing worsen the ratio between funds allocated to passive finance and active policy measures. The integration of young people in the labor market needs to be improved and their movement facilitated from school to work. Long-term unemployment becomes a severe problem of the labor market. The current system of vocational education and training is not wide enough and is unable to ensure general accessibility and sustainability of vocational education and training. A disproportion between the need for vocational training and the possibilities of satisfying this need has been observed. The current system of social assistance does not encourage an increase in employment. The possibility for unemployed persons to receive social assistance aid from several sources decreases their activity and does not encourage them to seek employment.

Taking into account the necessity to move to knowledge-based economics, to make wider use of information and communication technology, and to reduce social exclusion, the government has defined the major provisions of labor market policy in the following way:

- Labor market policy must be aimed at reviving and developing the skills of individuals who have lost jobs.

- Labor market policy must encourage the unemployed to seek employment and at the same time extend the possibilities that they can participate in active labor market policy measures.

- Labor market policy must make unemployment prevention more active, especially by encouraging employees to upgrade skills.

- Labor market policy must better ensure that spontaneous imbalance in the labor market will not result in material violation of the interests of the two major entities functioning in the labor market (the employers and the employees).

It is preferable to ensure the social security of individuals who have lost their jobs—socially vulnerable people in particular. Preventing youth unemployment needs to be strengthened by expanding and improving vocational information, guidance, and consulting. A greater number of young people, especially those under the age of 16, could study at secondary schools and receive a general education and other specific training. All young people need to acquire a basic education. Young people who have already obtained a vocational qualification must adapt to the workplace. The government should encourage their territorial mobility and develop labor market measures helping young people seeking their first employment to integrate into the labor market.

Other objectives of labor market policy are as follows:

- Improve the long-term unemployment prevention measures, and ensure conditions for the unemployed to voluntarily choose other social security options

- Rapidly reorganize the vocational education and training system consisting of basic and labor market vocational training, and strengthen the connections between training institutions

- Provide vocational education and training institutions with better technical equipment and teaching material, improve the curricula, develop the professional qualifications of teachers of different professions and tutors in practical training, separate functions of teaching and assessing to make better use of the possibilities provided by EU programs—or to develop labor resources

- Reform the current system of unemployment social assistance and reduce the social exclusion of the unemployed

- Change the criteria for applying for unemployment benefits and to incentivize job search.

Strengthening the Capacity to Adjust to Changes

The main actions increasing the ability to adjust to changes are development of flexible forms of work remuneration and organization, upgrading of employees' qualifications, and mitigation of the consequences brought by structural changes. The current legislation does not promote modern ways of work organization, nor does it promote the application of more flexible forms of employment and remuneration. Changes in labor costs are not always seen as having an impact on the competitiveness of undertakings and the employment rate. The participation of employee representatives in the process of solving the problems related to work organization and remuneration is not sufficient. The upgrading of employees' qualifications is not sufficiently developed. Thus a certain number of employees do not feel safe enough when faced with structural changes. Current legislation regulating restructuring, privatization, and mass dismissals fails to ensure timely solutions to social problems. Compensatory measures (applicable in cases when jobs are lost due to the introduction of new technologies and more efficient management and work organization) are not efficient.

In strengthening the capacity of Lithuanian workers to adjust to changes in the labor market, it would be expedient for the government to:

- Refine the legislation regulating labor relations so that it would provide for more flexible forms of work organization and contracts yet at the same time sufficiently protect social and employment-related rights of the employees

- Rreduce labor costs that have no proper justification

- Promote the conclusion of collective contracts and branch tariff agreements, better employee representation, provision of information and consultations to the employees

- make it possible for employees to upgrade their qualifications, provide incentives for employers and other social partners to take better care of the issue

- Develop preventive vocational education and training, especially in the undertakings that are planning to dismiss their employees

- Focus training on the upgrading of qualifications

- Develop a competitive system of employee requalification
- Organize vocational education and training of employees to upgrade their professional qualification
- Help persons who are to be dismissed find placement in new jobs as early as possible in the process, refine the early warning mechanism by involving all the stakeholders (employers, trade unions, and municipal and labor market institutions) in the preparation of procedures to mitigate the effects of dismissals and improve the employees' counseling
- Analyze the impact of mass dismissals on the labor market and employment of the population and draft social and economic development and employment programs at the local and regional levels, as well as target measures aimed at lessening the negative effect of dismissals.

If in the process of privatization and modernization the dismissal of employees is inevitable, the government should foresee means to help create new jobs, requalify employees, and plan other measures to provide employment, since privatization and restructuring are the means to provide employment. Business infrastructure is needed in rural areas. By promoting entrepreneurship among the population, the government will ensure more favorable conditions for the people to go into business.

Increasing Equal Opportunities in the Labor Market

The most important actions for equal opportunities in the labor market are the formation of a widely accessible labor market that ensures equal opportunities for men and women and supports the employment of the disabled.

The problem is that certain population groups are given priority. Obligatory employment quotas that employers must observe for those groups lead to negative social and economic consequences. Forced creation of new jobs and obligatory employment distort labor relations, impede business development, lead to an increase in social costs, and reduce the competitiveness of such undertakings. Despite progress in implementation of the principles of gender equality, the situation of women in the labor market is still worse than that of men. The state's support for employment of the disabled is not efficient enough. It is still the case that the disabled often are more inclined to look for social assistance and privileges than for a job.

Instead of obligatory employment quotas meant to help socially vulnerable individuals, it would be preferable to provide economic incentives. The development of preventive measures is better than focusing on activities to mitigate outcomes of elimination of the socially vulnerable groups from the labor market. The economic and social exclusion of these groups will be reduced by enhancing their social and economic security. Every person willing and capable of working must be given a chance to make his or her living by working. Ways must be found to encourage the socially vulnerable to become interested in employment. Their integration into the labor market will be made easier by linking it to the provision of social assistance.

To increase equal opportunities in the labor market, it also is necessary to:

- Refine legislation regulating the application of the principle of gender equality

- Strive for the situation where men and women can equally participate in all types of economic activities and are paid the same amount for the same type of work

- Promote the establishment of small and medium enterprises by women, their economic independence, and initiatives focused on the creation of new jobs

- Ensure opportunities for mothers and fathers to combine their professional and family duties (flexible organization of work, accessible childcare services of good quality, all types of social assistance to families)

- Create an employment support system that would be accessible to every disabled person willing and capable of working and that would enable them to compete in an open labor market or get employed in specialized undertakings, and strive for self-employment

- Enable the disabled to continuously upgrade their qualifications so they can adapt to dynamic social, economic, and technological changes and reduce the risk of getting pushed out of the labor market

- Increase the social and economic activity, independence, and self-confidence of the disabled as well as their responsibility for their own employment status.

Increasing Employment Policy Integration

The main actions ensuring the integration of employment policy are improvement of the employment and labor market management system, reorganization and strengthening of the labor market institutional system, formation of an open labor market, and development of a network of private employment agencies. Employment management structures of all levels lack their final shape. Major state governance and municipal institutions (with certain influence on employment rates and the labor market) insufficiently coordinate their activities. This impedes timely decisionmaking on different levels of state governance and results in the lack of needed and well-considered employment-related decisions. The current system of labor market institutions does not closely match the territorial administrative distribution and requirements brought about by public administration reforms. Therefore, it has limited possibilities to undertake uniform actions and ensure efficient implementation of the new provisions of the employment strategy. With unemployment soaring, the opportunity to find employment abroad becomes a very important measure of market regulation. There is a need to sign bilateral employment and social security agreements and promote the development of international employment mediation institutions. Lack of professionalism in the activities of private employment agencies evokes unnecessary tension and discontent with some of their functional elements. It is necessary to tighten the regulation of nonpublic employment agencies (companies) and increase their responsibility for the activities that breach the legislation in force or the rights of job seekers.

To better integrate employment policy, it is necessary to:

- Improve preparation of development strategies and programs for different sectors of the economy and coordinate their implementation as well as the formation of employment-promoting investment, tax, and financial policies

- Create at the national and regional level an employment and labor market information system and ensure that it functions

- Organize employment surveys, forecasts, and reviews nationwide and by region

- Prepare and implement employment and labor market policy programs and measures at the national and regional levels

- Coordinate interregional employment policy measures

- Define priorities concerning regional economic and social development guidelines and prepare and implement development programs

- Define regional employment and labor market policy and priorities

- Form regional employment support funds

- Promote local employment programs that comply with the regional employment strategy
- Prepare local infrastructure and economic development programs that best match the local situation and economic development traditions
- Identify the most serious employment-related problems and target programs to solve them
- Coordinate and in some cases consolidate economic entities in order to better solve general employment-related problems
- Promote local initiatives (business promotion funds, vocational education and training, institutions acting as employment mediators, and other non-public organizations helping to solve employment problems)
- Prepare local business development guidelines and a system of financial assistance and privileges for individuals beginning their own businesses
- Uphold employment guarantees provided for in the laws to the population in general and to specific groups
- Modernize territorial labor exchange offices, increase their responsibility for the situation in the labor market, and encourage more flexibility in the utilization of allocated resources to solve local labor market–related problems
- Iincrease the variety of services provided by territorial labor exchange offices to employers and introduce more efficient work methods and procedures to improve services to job seekers
- Improve the organization, execution, and quality of labor market vocational education and training
- Ensure the organizational environment necessary to make use of EU structural funds
- Get ready to cooperate with the national employment services of EU member states (that is, exchange information on employment opportunities via the EURES network and share best practices and implementation issues of common interest)

- Put more effort into expanding the labor market so that it can exceed the borders of national administration with the help of internationally recognized measures (highly qualified and comparatively cheap Lithuanian labor has to find its niche in the international division of labor)

- Conclude bilateral and multilateral agreements to enable a more active international movement of labor and eliminate obstacles impeding legal employment of Lithuanian citizens in foreign countries

- Use legal private employment agencies operating in Lithuania and abroad to place persons into jobs in foreign countries

- Create legal and institutional preconditions necessary for the future implementation of EU provisions regarding the free movement of workers

- Create the proper legal and organizational environment for the activities of private employment agencies

- Form a uniform employment mediation infrastructure by harmonizing the functions of labor exchange offices and private employment agencies

- Make use of the advantages of private employment agencies (for example, their ability to adapt quickly to the changing needs of the labor market.

First of all, employment services should be provided to the population by efficiently functioning and sufficiently financed public labor market institutions. In a market economy, employment mediation services (search for jobs and employees, vocational guidance and consulting, other employment-related services) should not be the state monopoly, with other economic entities having no right to provide them. Private employment agencies should supplement the activities of the labor exchange offices and contribute to the development of the labor market and implementation of the national employment policy. With the scope of privatization expanding, private employment agencies could assume some of the functions of labor exchange offices.

Modernization and Reform of Social Protection

Reform of social protection began in 1990 and ended in 1995 when the new pension system came into operation. At that time social protection conformed to the needs of the transitional period.

Since the initial reform years, the financial situation of social protection has worsened, and the deficit of the social insurance budget started growing. There are several reasons for this. There has been a rapid decrease in the ratio between the number of the insured and pensioners. The current level is 1.21 insured to one pensioner. There is still a high number of potential payers of social insurance contributions who work illegally or do not pay contributions in full. Despite the fact that the actual pension value is growing, it is still insufficient and the replacement rate is around 40 percent. Additional problems arise due to the predicted aging of the population. Social assistance benefits barely depend on the income level. The problem of social protection sustainability for the medium and long term becomes more obvious. It is also considered that social protection should play a more active role in promoting economic growth and employment. Those problems became particularly distinct during the economic recession and growing unemployment. Lithuania started modernizing social protection and preparing for the pension reform.

In the second and more extensive stage of social security reform, the government plans to gradually reduce its direct participation and its institutions in the social security system, thus creating the required preconditions to promote an accumulative principle for the financing of a nongovernmental system of social security. The government is taking concrete steps to shift from pay-as-you-go principles to accumulative pension insurance schemes. In 1999 the Parliament passed the Law on Pension Funds. It came into force on January 1, 2000. The law creates the legal framework for the system of personal additional voluntary pensions (additional voluntary social insurance), thus raising the income level in old age for the persons participating in this pension scheme. Pension funds will supplement the state pension system and will develop an additional pension insurance level.

In 2000 the concept of pension system reform was approved to reorganize and improve social security. The concept envisages the implementation of a three-stage pension system: pay-as-you-go pension schemes, compulsory accumulative pensions, and voluntary accumulative pensions.

Taking into consideration the experience of many foreign countries, the government will make an attempt to gradually introduce compulsory accumulative insurance in pension funds without any increase in the general pension tariff. This means that part of the current social insurance contributions should be directed to the individual accumulative accounts while every insured person could choose the pension fund. The compulsory accumulation will be applied only in relation to the old age pensions. Accumulative funds will be managed by the private pension funds that will be fully responsible for effective management. However, the state supervisory body (the planned State Commission on Securities) will regulate and strictly supervise the activities of pension funds. It will determine the conditions for compulsory participation as regards contributions and benefits. Eventually, persons who are insured in the compulsory pension funds will receive pensions from two sources: Sodra (State Enterprise for Social Insurance) and the private pension funds. The concept also provides for streamlining of the current social insurance system and guarantees its balance. Proposals will be made on how to change the system of state pensions paid from the national budget. These pensions should be gradually diminishing, and their allocation should be limited in order to eliminate unjustified privileges in the pension system.

The Lithuanian government approved the draft of the Law on Pension System Reform. Seimas (the Lithuanian Parliament) was expected to adopt this law in June 2001. The law aims at determining the major principles and trends for restructuring of the pension system.

In the draft of the Law on Pension System Reform, the Lithuanian government proposed that two groups of individuals would participate in the mandatory funded pension pillar. Participation in the mandatory funded pension pillar will be a must for all individuals younger than 40 years old and covered by an entire state social insurance pension. Individuals between 40 and 50 years of age and covered by an entire state social insurance pension will be entitled, on their own discretion, to participate in the mandatory funded pension pillar. Insured persons 50 years old and above will remain in the social insurance pension system only.

The proposed rate of the mandatory funded pension contribution is 5 percent of the participant's income, depending on the state social pension insurance contribution. The gross rate of the state social insurance contribution will not be subject to increase due to that reform. Pension system reform is planned to start in 2003.

The draft law on social assistance has been prepared in order to create a unified system of social assistance to the low-income population. The system is based on the principle of property and income assessment, and it is intended to be more employment friendly. The draft law on social assistance aims to allocate funds on a socially fairer principle. Social assistance will be targeted to the neediest families.

Provision of social assistance is foreseen for those low-income residents whose property and income do not exceed the established property and income levels. For this purpose, the residents applying for social assistance should declare their property and income. This makes it possible to establish the actual material condition of families and allocate assistance to the families in need.

The funds planned for the payment of social assistance amount to 164 million litas (Lt). At present, 88.6 million Lt are paid in the social benefit. A savings of 75 million Lt is foreseen by paying the family benefit only to mothers raising children under 1 year of age and raising this benefit to 1 million Lt. It is proposed that state-supported income be raised to 181 Lt, while the rate of the social benefit be lowered to 0.6. The guaranteed minimal income per person would then amount to 108.6 Lt.

Having raised state-supported income, the government expects the number of recipients of the social benefit to grow. In addition, quite a few restrictions concerning benefit recipients would be removed. All the employed and the unemployed with justifiable reasons, including persons searching for work through labor exchange offices, would be entitled to the benefit, taking into account the property in their possession and received income.

According to the data of the Department of Statistics on the household budget for 1999, about 20 percent of the population of Lithuania had income lower than 181 Lt. The assumption is made that, having introduced property and income declaration, about 10 percent of the country's population would be entitled to the social benefit.

If the norm of the social benefit is reduced, families will be more interested in having sources of income. The more a family earns, the higher is the family's income (including social assistance) and, consequently, the income per family member.

The residents would receive compensation not only for heating and cold and hot water expenses, but also for expenses for other major amenity services. If a family does not have any income at all, all expenses for all major amenity services would be compensated.

A family would have to pay a larger share. When the share of dwelling maintenance expenses covered by the family is increased to 60 percent, the family is encouraged to look for sources of income, since the more a family earns, the larger share of income remains for one member of a family after the payment for dwelling maintenance.

CHAPTER 8

Developments and Current Labor Market Issues in Romania

Ion Giurescu

The immediate interaction between the social and economic problems of Romania is the main reference point of the studies made on the evolution of the labor market, economic growth being a *sine qua non* condition in settling the majority of the current social issues, including the most sensitive issue—unemployment. The provisions that existed in 1990 in the social insurance field, child allowances and family allowances, measures of assisting disabled persons, have suffered modifications and have been improved by the introduction of new instruments of social protection.

The Romanian labor force market and social policies have characteristics in common with the policies of OECD countries; differences reside in the implementation conditions. Although Romania has smaller economic growth than any other country in the OECD, the Romanian labor market and its social policies contain most of the elements present in the corresponding institutions of OECD countries. As a result, political patterns implemented in these countries in the labor market field must be applied in our case with great precautions, taking into account the limited resources and the specific character of the social issues.

One of the major problems that must be addressed at this point is the extended economic impoverishment that affects a large social layer in Romania. If in 1990 the wage incomes were among the smallest in Europe, they have dropped since by 39.7 percent. Moreover, a great and differentiated percentage of the Romanian population is involved in small-scale agricultural activities, either as a main or secondary activity, and almost one-third of the total revenues are in kind. For this reason, only about one-half of the active population contributes to the social insurance system that collects one of the highest contribution rates in the world: about 60 percent from the wages (including the contributions of the employer and the employee).

Another difference between the labor market of Romania and that of OECD countries resides in the distribution of the revenue. While revenues are for the most part the same in Romania, the existing disparities seem unjustified from an economic point of view, since the relatively high wages exist in loss-making economic sectors. Like in other countries in transition, the private sector in Romania is in the process of development and contributes to wage disparities that are proportional to the qualifications of workers. In conclusion, overall poverty, insecure work places, and the continuous fluctuation of actual wages and prices have had a crucial role in the perception of economic instability for the great majority of socio-professional categories. An extended period of accelerated growth in the economy would be the best possible solution for the current problems confronting Romania.

In this context the objectives of reform in the labor force field must be oriented in two directions. The long-term objective will be to offer a social policy framework capable of generating solutions to the problems of a "modern" economy that is in the middle of development. The main aspects refer to the reduction of the dependence on in-kind revenues, ensuring a high-level mobility in the labor market and the necessity of preparing for the risks and problems inherent in a true market economy. At the same time, the decisionmakers must solve a great number of short-term problems that demand immediate intervention. Some problems are related to the consequences of economic restructuring; others relate to the great costs of social insurance, something that affects the economic development of the country and permits the unacceptable and dangerous spread of the "gray economy."

From the perspective of finding a solution to these negative aspects, we are in the process of implementing legislative and institutional reforms of our social policies, reforms that we consider to be ambitious but at the same time realistic and feasible. New public agencies were recently set up to administer the pensions, occupation and vocational training, and labor inspection. The additional reform packages now being prepared include a multipillar system of pensions, a new labor code, and a better framework for social assistance.

A brief analysis of the economic transition in Romania concludes that the process of restructuring must not only continue but be accelerated even if, in the short term, a higher rate of unemployment results. The registered rate of unemployment grew from 7.5 percent in 1997, to 9 percent in 1998, to approximately 12 percent in 1999. The 11.9 percent unemployment rate in January 2000 grew to 12.2 percent in February and then diminished to 9.9 percent in September as a result of increased labor demand due to seasonal activities (agriculture, tourism, construction). For the year 2001 the rate of unemployment is 10.8 percent.

The issues related to the transition, visibly greater in Romania compared with our neighbors from Central Europe, can be partially explained by flows inherited from the regime before 1989, but the slow rhythm in applying the reform policy after 1990 is the main cause of the current labor market. A number of socio-economic contexts are relevant to the Romanian territory; the data on employment, the pattern of job offers, and the structure of people's revenue confirm the connection between the broad sector of subsistence agriculture and the urban economy. Urgent restructuring of this connection is required. The unemployment rate in agriculture has grown as a result of massive layoffs in the industrial sector, since this was a seasonal occupation of the young labor force, and as an additional source of income for pensioners. The main issue that the labor market confronts is not unemployment but the prevalence of the underoccupation—employment in activities that produce very little or do not correspond to the economic necessities of the country. Our priority objective is the fast modernization of the economy according to the needs of the market.

The urban labor market is negatively influenced by the unmediated impact of the restructuring. Unfortunately, in Romania the loss-making companies represent an important part of the total rate of employment of the labor force. In contrast, the sectors that are developing—small and medium enterprises—represent a small share. Their main object of activity is retail and the low-scale production oriented toward consumers. In the medium term, we are preoccupied with relaunching these sectors that are in expansion—the main sources of places of work.

An apparent consequence of the insufficient creation of workplaces in the small and medium-size enterprise sector is the relatively low mobility of the labor force. Another problem is the very low geographical mobility in comparison with international standards. People who abandon the workplaces in industry involve themselves in small-scale activities (at the family level) in agriculture.

The relatively high duration of unemployment in Romania and the fact that the unemployment benefit is almost as high as the minimum wage do not motivate the unemployed to find a new job as soon as possible. This situation has prompted a reconsideration of social policy. Policymakers are rethinking the priorities to significantly increase the share of active measures (10 percent out of the National Employment Agency budget) in order to make the unemployed population more mobile. The extremely damaging practice of severance payments for workers dismissed from state-owned enterprises, payments not correlated with active measures of protection, has been abandoned. This practice generated a series of economic problems beginning in 1997 that cannot be combated in the short term. It also created a false impression among the population that the state plays a permanent supporting role. This is one of the myths that has to be shattered regardless of the degree of pain suffered by the ones aided by these measures and despite the price of image and popularity paid by the government.

Reform in the field of employment in Romania requires fast implementation of a program providing social protection for the personnel dismissed as a consequence of restructuring, privatization, or liquidation. Modernization of the employment services infrastructure and creation of an adequate institutional framework are particularly needed.

The National Employment Agency (NEA) has been functioning since 1999 as a public and national interest institution. Its main objectives are the implementation of strategies drafted by the Ministry of Labor and Social Solidarity, management of the unemployment insurance program, and institutionalization of social dialogue in this field. For this purpose the social partners are involved as members of the tripartite Governing Board. They implement policies in the field of employment, as well as in management of the fund for unemployment benefit payment. Another tripartite body, created in 1999, is the National Board for Vocational Training of Adults. It plays a consultative role in adopting politic decisions in the field of vocational training. These institutions have an active role in the regulation of problems related to the labor market and social protection and ensure the complete transposition of the acquis community.

In the legislative field, the regulations regarding wage setting, collective bargaining, and employment have a profoundly liberal character. The government's role is to impose a degree of procedural transparency and predictability. The liberal character of the Romanian legislation does not cover numerous practical deficiencies referring to the insufficient stimulative degree for employment, granting a principal role to the passive measures of protection of unemployed in the active measures disadvantage, insufficiently defining the attributions and responsibilities of different bodies and institutions acting on labor market and nonadequately correlated with the EU legislation and directives.

These deficiencies necessitated the drafting of a new law regulating implementation of strategies and policies designed to ensure a high level of employment, as well as to adapt the labor force to market demands. The new draft law:

- Increases the share of active measures for fighting unemployment to the detriment of passive ones.

- Provides a sole type of passive protection—the unemployment benefit—as an insurance benefit. The other allowances and aids are to be integrated in the social assistance benefits.

- Sets the unemployment benefit at 60 percent of the wage received at the time of dismissal, correlating it with the minimum wage and the guaranteed minimum income. The unemployment benefit shall be granted only after 12 consecutive months contributing to the Unemployment Fund; the amount shall be set in relation to a total period of contribution to this fund.

- Sets the categories of persons included in the compulsory system of insurance for unemployment risk (employees, public servants, cooperative workers).

An important stage in reforming employment policy and in EU integration is the National Action Plan for Employment (NAPE) —action necessary to prepare Romania for participating in the joint strategy in the field of employment promoted in the European Union and set by the Amsterdam Treaty. This plan shall be drafted by the Ministry of Labour and Social Solidarity and other institutions of the central public administration with responsibilities in this field. Other participants include social partners within a twinning project financed by the EU and run by the Federal Ministry of Labour and Social Affairs from Germany and the Ministry of Social Affairs and Employment from the Netherlands. NAPE shall be structured in accordance with the four pillars of the guidelines in the field of employment, shall take into account the existing situation in Romania and the short- and long-term effects of industrial restructuring, and shall define a package of priority measures in order to increase the employment rate.

For the success of any action in the field of employment, the involvement of social partners is necessary. In February 2001 a Social Agreement was signed that obtained the direct involvement of trade unions and employers' organizations in efforts to accelerate the implementation of European Union recommendations and directives applicable to our country in the field of labor legislation, and active measures for fighting unemployment, as well as management of the human resources and social policies demanded by the European Social Charter and European Code for Social Security. An integrated national multiannual program for training and upgrading human capital shall be drafted with the participation of the social partners in order to get a close correlation between the education system real needs of development as well as to introduce functional modalities of reconversion and multiqualification in the permanent education system.

The assumed main objectives set in the field of employment for 2001 are an increase in the employment rate and a reduction in the unemployment rate among some underprivileged categories (long-term unemployed, women, young people, handicapped persons).

Training, retraining, and guidance of the labor force in relation to the demands of the labor market are part of the active measures series. The following actions are envisaged: optimization of educational curricula, especially in the vocational education system, to reach an optimal balance between demand and supply in the labor market; vocational reconversion plans on the basis of prognoses concerning structural transformations of the national economy; and development of information, counseling, mediation and training services provided by NAPE.

The main active measures envisaged in the field of employment:

- Give small and medium-size enterprises credits with advantageous interest from the fund for unemployment benefit payment with a view to creating jobs for the unemployed

- Organize vocational training courses ensuring employment to 60 percent of the graduates in the first six months from the date of finishing the course

- Draft laws on stimulating the employment of graduates with the wage-tax exemption for the first two years of employment for university graduates, granting subventions (from the fund for unemployment benefit payment) in the amount of 70 percent of the negotiated net wage received by the graduated persons but which cannot exceed the average net wage from the employing institution

- Support special programs in order to create jobs for the community benefit

- Organize at the county level the General Labour Exchange as well as the Graduated Labour Exchange

- Draft (in cooperation with professional associations, the Commission for Occupational Standards, trade unions, and employers' organizations) the occupational standards, having in view the existing standards at the European level.

Another major concern is fighting against illegal employment, a problem that affects most of the countries in the transition process. The Labour Inspection, a specialized body of the central public administration, was created in 1999. It has the responsibility to verify the application in Romania of the legal provisions concerning industrial relations. It is being directly confronted with work without legal forms, a social phenomenon that during the last years became extremely damaging for the Romanian economy. The extent of this phenomenon is difficult to measure since the activities developed out of the legal limit are nonregistered and even hidden because some of them fall in the penal legislation incidence (illegal trade, trade of product with dubious provenience, etc.). To eliminate this scourge, public awareness measures have been taken through the media in order to make public the legal provisions concerning the work without legal forms. Meetings with entrepreneurs have been organized to provide consultancy in the field and permanent phone lines have been introduced providing information on these aspects. At the same time cooperation with police in carrying out unforeseen controls of different employers has been improved. In this case, too, the involvement of social partners is very important (their knowledge and popularization of the legal provisions in the field and their understanding of the rights and duties of employers and employees).

CHAPTER 9

The Main Challenges of the Slovenian Labor Market

Zdenka Kovac, Franci Kluzer, and Alenka Kaizer

The Slovenian labor market, like labor markets of other transition economies, faced severe and rapid changes in the 1990s. Out of almost 2 million people at the end of the 1980s, the active labor force was 948,400 persons. The great majority of employment was provided by big state-owned companies, just a small part (about 67,600 jobs) was provided by the privately owned craft sector, about 60,800 were farmers, and about 28,200 were unemployed. In the middle of the nineties the active population decreased to 864,000, from which 237,500 were employed in big companies and 286,800 in privately owned small and medium-size enterprises (SMEs). The number of farmers decreased to 55,000, and the number of unemployed reached one of the highest levels, with more than 120,000 unemployed.

At the beginning of 2000, the active population was 874,000, and the number of employees in big companies decreased further to 218,505. The number of employees in SMEs increased to 292,758, the number of unemployed decreased to 100,000, while the number of farmers stayed about the same.

If we assess carefully what led to the collapse in the nineties, we must identify at least two reasons. The first was the failure to answer the Yugoslavian economic crises of the 1980s. If at the beginning of the 1980s human resource development was considered a key factor of economic competitiveness, then we could say that up to that time, in this field, we had been fully in line with the market-driven economies. A broad network of public universities and in-company educational centers allowed free-of-charge learning for adults. But in the 1980s we began to lag behind rapidly. While market-driven economies, as a response to economic crises, have increased investments in human resource development (HRD) and research and development (R&D), the big publicly owned companies in Slovenia, in order to decrease costs, began to close internal R&D units, internal educational centers, and human resource management (HRM) functions. The government decreased financial support for adult learning. This resulted in a permanent decline in the competitiveness of our products in the global market. At the end of the 1980s, the Yugoslavian government began to promote entrepreneurship as a new economic force, but because of the political situation it was simply too late.

Second, political changes at the beginning of the nineties resulted in lost markets within the former Yugoslavia and the former Soviet Union. While Slovenian products were not competitive enough on global markets, still, because of the Slovenian industrial tradition and a fairly well-organized trading network within Eastern economies, Slovenian products were sold at relatively high prices in Eastern European markets. This fact probably led to wrong economic decisions in the 1980s, and over the first two years in the 1990s, these markets had been lost. Since big companies were not prepared to sell on the global market, the only possible answer was redundancy or, even more frequently, closure.

Evolving from a full employment situation for both genders, given the state jobs with reasonably high wages in big state-owned companies, a huge number of big companies closed almost overnight. The consequence was high unemployment and huge outflows from the active population to the pension system in the beginning of the 1990s. The unemployment rate in a few years grew from 2 percent to over 16 percent. The number of relatively young pensioners increased in just a few years by more than one-third.

The early nineties, in terms of economic and labor market development, could be described as a period of romantic expectations that the coming market-driven economy would resolve all economic problems and that everyone could become an entrepreneur, while we did not yet have a developed small-economy sector.

The government strongly supported self-employment, resulting in the establishment of about 23,000 new small businesses. Restructuring of many big companies led to spin-off units that also resulted in the establishment of SMEs. Some big companies with huge support from public funds (especially in the steel, paper, textile, and leather economy) remained in the market until the beginning of the new millennium. Also, the service sector, like banking, insurance, and transport, has not been totally privatized yet, which will bring new challenges for those employed in those sectors in the near future and will probably lead to new redundancy.

Recent Trends and Governmental Initiatives

Despite the fact that the Slovenian Development Strategy and the Employment Strategy for the new millennium have not been formally adopted by the Slovenian parliament, some positive trends in the labor market have been evident. After several years of decline and stagnation, in 1999 the first increase—of 1.8 percent—for the working-age population was registered. This change was due in part to temporary public work schemes, but mainly it was a result of very dynamic economic growth, which in 1999 exceeded 5.2 percent. Similar trends continued in 2000 with 4.8 percent economic growth and 1.3 percent employment growth. The main growth of employment was in the service and the construction sectors. Since the percentage of employed in industry and agriculture in Slovenia is still higher than in the European Union, it will probably face further declines in the future. The main provider of new jobs in recent years has been the SME sector, especially the so-called "gazelles," and probably the same could be expected for the years to come. Slovenia is a country with very low foreign investments. Therefore, new jobs could mostly be provided by the domestic industry.

Table 9.1 shows some basic indicators of the Slovenian labor market.

Labour Force Survey (LFS) figures show that the number of unemployed according to international standards for recent years has been circling around 70,000. The unemployment rate of between 7 and 8 percent in the third quarter of 2000 has fallen below 6.7 percent. Unemployment in Slovenia is therefore below the EU average and is on the average of OECD countries. The difference between the LFS unemployment rate and the registered unemployment rate has not been evident in Slovenia only, but the fact is that in Slovenia, the difference between these measures has been reasonably higher. The main reasons would be the following:

- A huge number of long-term unemployed, who through time became too passive and do not meet the criteria for active job searches

TABLE 9.1 BASIC INDICATORS OF SLOVENIAN LABOR MARKET

Indicator	*1996*	*1997*	*1998*	*1999*	*2000*
Unemployment rate[a]	7.3	7.4	7.9	7.6	7.0
Male	7.5	7.1	7.7	7.3	—
Female	7.0	6.3	8.1	7.9	—
Registered unemployment rate	13.9	14.4	14.5	13.6	12.2
Male	13.8	13.6	13.4	12.4	—
Female	14.0	15.3	15.7	15.0	—
Employment rate[b]	63.2	65.4	65.1	64.1	64.5
Male	66.5	69.8	69.5	68.5	66.7
Female	59.7	60.9	60.6	59.4	58.7
Employment growth[c]	–0.9	–0.5	0.0	1.0	1.0
Long-term unemployed	53.8	59.6	62.4	62.9	61.4
Average wage growth	—	2.4	1.6	3.3	1.6
Productivity growth	4.4	5.1	3.8	4.2	3.8

— Not available.
a. From the International Labour Organization (ILO).
b. From the Statistical Office of the Republic of Slovenia, Labour Force Survey.
c. For 1996–99, SURS; for 2000, Institute for Macroeconomic Analysis and Development (UMAR).

- An extensive gray economy and informal types of jobs, which are largely attributable to very rigid laws on labor relations and not enough stimulative fiscal policy

- Benefits within the social insurance and pension insurance system

- A fairly developed public employment services network compared with that in other transition countries.

The number of registered unemployed has been declining since 1998. In spring 2001 it fell to 100,000. The main reason is a new law on employment adopted in 1999. Unemployment benefits were shortened and lowered and new active employment measures to assist active job searches were introduced. The government also introduced the Employment Action Plan for 2000 and 2001. It was designed according to EU guidelines, and its main feature is that ministries responsible for economic development, labor, and education become commonly responsible for further development of new job opportunities and skills formation.

Under first pillar–employability, probably one of the most successful initiatives resulting from the Employment Action Plan was a common initiative of the Ministry of Labor, Family, and Social Affairs and the Ministry of Education called Program 5000. Under this program a second free-of-charge opportunity was offered in the past three years to more than 15,000 unemployed to attain a higher educational level according to the new needs of labor markets.

An increasing mismatch between new required skills and the existing skills of the registered unemployed has become the main obstacle to higher employment growth. The number of unemployed without basic vocational education has been circling around 45 percent. This problem is bigger due to the many long-term unemployed, which in the structure of unemployment exceeded 60 percent. An equally important factor is the huge number of disabled, which represents over 14 percent of the registered unemployment, and those of more than 40 years of age, a category that represents more than 50 percent.

Such a structure of unemployment leads to the situation where Slovenia, despite relatively numerous unemployed, must import labor mainly from former Yugoslav republics to cover some needs of the labor market. The number of employed foreigners varies from 35,000 to 40,000 and is largely based on temporary contracts. Mainly this is due to the needs of the construction industry but also to some types of trade and catering.

Lately, new information-technology job opportunities have emerged more quickly than skilled labor supply has been able to fill them, which increases the need for an imported labor force.

Youth unemployment has been slightly less in recent years because of two main reasons:

- The introduction of new measures (for example, Program 5000 and subsidized employment)
- High school graduates' tendency to continue their studies at a higher level.

Under second pillar–entrepreneurship, there were several common initiatives introduced to promote entrepreneurial culture and innovation in the country and to promote entrepreneurial skills among certain groups (young people, women, people from rural areas). The Ministry of Economy has worked with local communities to set up new infrastructure for SME development such as business zones, incubators, and technological and business-innovation centers.

Probably the most promising is the "Antibureaucracy Program." Its aim is to eliminate administrative barriers that prohibit development of new types of work, prohibit quicker development of domestic businesses, and inhibit foreign investments.

Structural imbalance in Slovenia has been evident at the regional level. Despite increased mobility (daily migration) toward capital, which is evident especially for high-skilled labor, the mobility of less skilled labor remains rather low. This is attributable to employers' unwillingness to cover relatively high transport costs and to the fact that attained wages have been too low to motivate people to take job opportunities that are out of the circle of 40 kilometers.

To face this problem, the government has created a more efficient, bottom-up approach by initiating local development partnerships. In the past few years about 26 local partnerships were established. This initiative was upgraded with the adoption of a regional development law, according to which 12 multiyear regional development programs would be designed and a regional development infrastructure set up. The ministries will designate special regional development support schemes and instruments according to the identified special needs of particular regions. One of the main focuses of these programs will be on employment challenges and human resource development.

Not enough has been done to promote the flexibility and adaptability of the work force and in the field of equal opportunities. These issues will be important challenges for the Slovenian government and social partners in forthcoming years. The low-skilled, long-term unemployed remain the most marginal group. The position of women in the labor market has worsened. Much more will have to be done to improve the position of the disabled. Despite positive trends in 2000, it is too soon to assess the new approach in employment policy adopted in 1999 with the new law on employment and the Employment Action Plan. For political reasons, employment policy measures in some fields have not been provided to the extent planned. An integrated approach is not yet fully in operation. The number of participants in some traditional employment schemes (public works and training) have been fewer than planned. The role of social partners in the design and implementation of employment policy has not been strong enough and is below expectations. Therefore, the main challenges of labor market policy in the forthcoming years remain mostly the same as they have been in the past.

The Accession Partnership pledges Slovenia to complete a joint employment policy overview each year to prepare the labor market for harmonization with EU policies. The first one was prepared for 1999. The National Plan for the Adoption of the Acquis also requires Slovenia to take the responsibility for preparing a long-term employment strategy.

Slovenia's Employment Policies: Future Objectives and Priorities

Slovenia, like other countries in Europe, already has begun facing the challenges of globalization, liberalization, adoption of "European" rules, and—in addition to the transition to a market economy—the transition from an industrial society to a knowledge-based society. All of this requires investment in the country's human resources. Slovenia also faces the problem of an aging population, which burdens the financing of the existing system of social security and necessitates the development and promotion of learning on a lifelong basis. This will require an increased flexibility and adaptability of the educational system.

In order to complete the transition process and to fulfill conditions for a successful EU accession, Slovenia must intensify the restructuring of its economy and reallocate resources in the next few years. The promotion of human resources will ease the restructuring of the economy and the institutional adaptation of EU rules. Within the internal EU market, labor market flexibility will become, along with a unified monetary policy, an even more important factor for securing the competitiveness and adaptability of the economy.

In order to efficiently promote labor market flexibility, the policy must take into account the fact that employability and flexibility are twins. A low-skilled labor force tends more toward security than a high-skilled labor force. Therefore, labor market flexibility requires increased investments in human resources.

In line with the European model, human resource development requires a comprehensive approach. It should become the core of Slovenia's employment strategy, and it has many different aspects:

- Human resource development and globalization of the economy imply the need for multilanguage training so workers can use information technology and participate in international exchanges of students and trainees.

- Human resource development and technological development imply more efficient investment in R&D and efforts to decrease the existing gap in the technological level of Slovenian products and production processes. The added value of Slovenian products has been one-third of the EU average.

- Human resource development and entrepreneurship development imply the need for innovativeness, creativity, and entrepreneurial skills among broaden broader target groups of the population and especially among the young, women, and people living in rural areas. Ensuring access to information, training, and advice will be crucial in this field.

- Human resource development and regional development imply the need for careful design of an education and training infrastructure that harmonizes the development objectives of particular regions in order to enhance the human capital of each region and reduce brain drain from less-developed regions.

- Human resource development and employability development imply the need for permanent skills development of the employed and unemployed in order to reduce unemployment and promote employment.

Above all, active cooperation among various ministries (such as economy, finance, labor and social affairs, education and science) is needed to implement the agreed employment policy objectives. The employment strategy up to 2006 proposed by the Slovenian government and in a phase of second reading in parliament is mostly meeting the above challenges. This will become an important part of the national development program until 2006. The central focus of the employment strategy is to strengthen the human capital of the country, the key to a competitive future for Slovenia. The strategy foresees the active involvement of social partners in the planning, implementation, and financing of employment policy, which is focused on the following four pillars:

- To increase the population's employability

- To promote entrepreneurship

- To increase adaptability of enterprises and employees

- To ensure equal employment opportunities.

Furthermore, the employment strategy takes into consideration all of the adopted development programs in related policy areas (education, regional development, entrepreneurship and SME development, competitiveness of industry development, agriculture and rural development). The proposals and suggested measures also reflect the findings and conclusions of the joint assessment paper (JAP) on the labor market in Slovenia, prepared in cooperation with the EU Commission.

Efficient implementation of the employment strategy will be ensured by the following actions: integration of the policies of economic and other line ministries with the employment policy; development of measures and guidelines for the active employment policy aimed at increasing the population's employability, especially under the conditions of an aging society; upgrading and improving the infrastructure of institutions implementing human resources and employment promotion programs at the national, regional, and local levels; and establishing a permanent monitoring system and undertaking progress reviews and evaluations.

The agreed strategic goals of labor market and employment policy for the next five years are:

- To increase the level of education and competence of the labor force through new opportunities for lifelong learning for adults

- To reduce the share of long-term unemployed (to around 40 percent) and the share of unskilled unemployed persons (to around 25 percent)

- To ensure the participation in active employment programs of all unemployed young people, who within 6 months of becoming unemployed have not found new employment, and for adults, who within 12 months of becoming unemployed have not found new employment

- To reduce regional disparities in the labor market through support of implementation of regional development programs

- To create more than 1 percent growth in employment in the period until 2006, which will help to reduce the unemployment rate (Labor Market Survey definition) to around 5 percent (or the registered unemployment rate to around 8 percent) by 2006

- To further develop social partnerships and strengthen the role of social partners in the design and implementation of employment policy on the national, regional, and local levels.

To reach these strategic objectives, the government is pursuing several key measures. For example, it is upgrading the legal framework regulating labor market relations. In addition to the law on employment, adopted in 1999, the law on labor relations remains one of the most important challenges for the government and social partners. The main dispute between social partners concerns the extent to which labor relations will be defined by law or by social bargaining. The final agreement cannot be foreseen despite five years of ongoing debate. The government expects that the law will ease the very rigid regulations, expensive for employers, governing the hiring and firing of workers. It has been prohibiting further growth of employment and has also been identified as one of the main obstacles to foreign investments. The law has been prepared for a second reading in parliament, where the final decision is expected. The law on employment of foreigners and the law on professional qualification through certification were adopted recently, but the implementation phase has brought many new challenges for administration. The law on mutual recognition of diplomas and professional qualifications will also promote the mobility of the labor force in order to prepare Slovenia to join the European Union. The law prohibiting illegal work has been adopted but needs to be implemented more efficiently. Despite the fact that the government in 1997 accepted the program identifying and sanctioning illegal work, the extent of the gray economy has not been declining.

A second key measure concerns the education of the labor force. The government intends to upgrade the educational attainment of the labor force and lower the skills gap in the labor market. The specific goals under this measure are to decrease the share of the low-skilled active population from 45 percent to no more than 25 percent by opening new opportunities for adult vocational education, diversifying and restructuring vocational schools' programs according to the new needs of the labor market, introducing dual vocational training for adults, offering personal skills development programs for marginalized groups, and opening new professional qualification opportunities through the certification system.

Third, the government is attempting to reduce by 5 percent the number of drop-outs from vocational, high, and posthigh schools by improving the quality of school programs and teachers; improving the quality of professional advisory services and assistance to young people with difficulties in learning; and offering dual vocational training.

Fourth, improvements are sought in the position of young people in the labor market. The main goal is to ease their transition from school to work so that no one will be unemployed for more than six months. The means to achieve this include new instruments to promote youth employment, new assistance in successful job searches, job-placed training, the provision of first-job opportunities in the framework of public works, and promotion of creativity and an entrepreneurial spirit among young people.

Fifth, the number of long-term unemployed must decline. The main goal is to decrease the share of long-term unemployed from 60 percent to less than 30 percent by:

- Strengthening the personal advice and group advice services through public and private networks of providers

- Increasing the share of public funding for active employment measures and lowering the share of passive employment benefits

- Devoting specialized providers of assistance to special target groups (for example, the aged unemployed and youth long-term unemployed) and promoting social development partnerships at the local level

- Legalizing the gray economy.

Sixth, the government is addressing the problem of unemployment through preventive measures. The main goal is strengthening social dialogue and social partnerships to improve the employability of employed and unemployed which will result in introducing preventive measures and join funding of costs of the measures through: introduction and development of labor and human resource development foundations on regional and sectarian level which will be managed by social partners.

Seventh, a culture of lifelong learning is needed if Slovenia's aging society is to cope with the rapidly changing technological and economic environment. A lifelong learning strategy includes the following: new support measures to assist adults in taking on learning challenges, a huge promotional campaign, a national certification center where professional qualifications can be attained, and new methods of long-distance learning.

Eighth, the government will attempt to foster an entrepreneurial culture by:

1. Promoting creativity, innovativeness, and entrepreneurial spirit through special training programs for different target groups such as youngsters, women, and people from rural areas

2. Eliminating administrative barriers for small business sector development and improving conditions for the creation of new jobs in enterprises

3. Improving space infrastructure for business development

4. Ensuring access to information and business-related services

5. Ensuring development of technological innovation centers as a common development infrastructure for SMEs

6. Promoting partnerships for ensuring sustainable development and the creation of new jobs within local employment initiatives

7. Monitoring constantly the impact of tax levies and incentives on employment

8. Increasing the flexibility and competitiveness of the economy.

Finally, measures to ensure equal access to the labor market will be adopted. The government will introduce alternative job opportunities and flexible working schedules; promote entrepreneurship and higher educational and professional attainment among women; promote new types of training adapted to the needs of the long-term unemployed; and promote new types of so-called social enterprises for the low-skilled and disabled.

Infrastructure for Strategy Implementation

The infrastructure for strategy implementation has two important components: institutions and funding.

Institutions

A special coordination and monitoring body constituted from representatives of government and social partners will play a crucial role in the follow-up process. A system of indicators for monitoring the employment strategy has already been set up together with the DG Employment representative. There has also been a list of indicators identified that should be developed in the future. The Ministry of Labour has prepared the "Phare project" to build up the labor market indicators system as a follow-up to the national employment strategy and the national employment action plan. According to the results of this analysis and the needs stated in the Employment Strategy, the system of indicators will be upgraded and made comparable to the system used in the EU (Eurostat, DG Employment/Social Affairs). EU compliant new indicators will have to be defined, suitable data collected, and related methodology developed. Different twinning programs (the Ministry of Labour, Family, and Social Affairs twinning with the United Kingdom and Employment Services of Slovenia twinning with Ireland) are working on these indicators as well. In establishing the monitoring system, the Ministry of Labour will work closely with the National Statistical Office, the Government Office for Macroeconomic Analysis and Development, the Employment Service of Slovenia, and the Monitoring and Evaluation Unit in the National Agency for Regional Development (NARD).

Several public institutions (Employment Services of Slovenia, the Small Business Development Center, the Slovenian Agency for Regional Development, the Center for Vocational Education, and the Center for Adult Education) will be involved in implementation of the strategy as well as nongovernmental, not-for-profit institutions at the regional and local levels. This network has been developed in recent decades but will need to be monitored in the future. The work of many of these institutions is specialized. For example, labor foundations assist the redundant workers, local development centers design local employment promotion projects and assist small businesses, and training institutions help the disabled and other hard-to-employ persons.

The core implementation institutions will continue to be the Ministry of Labour, Family, and Social Affairs and the Employment Services of Slovenia. The main challenge for both will be enhancement of performance efficiency. Associations of employers and employees are expected to take on a more important role in implementation of the strategy.

Funding

To ensure the realization of set goals, a system of transparent and EU comparable measures (grants, loans) will be introduced. Active social partnerships at the national level will result in additional fundraising human resource development, the key challenge of the Slovenian government and its social partners in order to achieve the long-term goals. The funding that could be provided directly from the budget will not be sufficient to satisfy the needs. Until Slovenia becomes a full member of the European Union and can benefit from structural funds to assist in the implementation of strategy, at least half of the necessary funding must be raised with the help of social partners and local communities. Arrangements with international institutions such as the Bank for Social Development and the European Development Bank are foreseen in order to ensure funding for necessary investments in implementation.

References

Employment Strategy, 2000-2006. Official journal of Parliament. Ljubljana.

European Commission. 2000a. *Proposal for Council Decision on Employment Guidelines for Member States' Employment Policies for the Year 2001*. Brussels.

———. 2000b. *Employment in Europe 2000.* Brussels.

———. 2000c. *European Economy: Economic Trends*. Brussels.

———. 2001. *European Economy (Supplement A): Economic Trends.* Brussels.

Institute for Macroeconomic Analysis and Development. 2000. *Analysis of Economic Trends*. Ljubljana.

———. 2000. *Employment Services of Slovenia: Monthly and Yearly Statistical Reports, 1991–2000.* Ljubljana.

Kovac, Zdenka. 2000. Intervention at Conference on European Employment and Social Policy and Enlargement. Prague. May 11–12.

Lonnroth, Karl-Johan. 2000. Intervention at Conference on European Employment and Social Policy and Enlargement. Prague. May 11–12.

Ministry of Labour, Family, and Social Affairs. *Employment Action Programme for 2000 and 2001*. Ljubljana.

The Slovenian Observatory of SME. 2000. *Small Medium Enterprises*. Ljubljana: Institute for Entrepreneurship and Management of SME.

CHAPTER 10

Discussant Notes

Michal Rutkowski

Three main facts dominate the picture presented in Part I. First, there has been a tremendous amount of restructuring in the countries of Central and Eastern Europe, both industrial restructuring and restructuring in the labor market.

Second, the labor market outcomes that we see are deeply troubling because of the high unemployment rate, the high share of long-term unemployed among the unemployed population, and the burden of unemployment falling on young women and the less educated. We saw huge regional differences in all the countries. A correlation clearly exists between unemployment and poverty. And there are great changes in terms of significant withdrawals from the labor market on top of increases in the unemployment rate and in long-term unemployment.

Third, both developments I have mentioned—quick restructuring and troubling labor market outcomes—have been in the presence of important rigidities in the labor markets in Central and Eastern Europe, high payroll taxes, relatively high and binding minimum wages, constraints to labor mobility, and generous social safety nets on a par with West European levels.

What we have seen suggests that restructuring per se does not really depend on the labor market. Other factors—macroeconomic policy, foreign direct investment, privatization—determine whether restructuring takes place or not. However, labor market performance influences who bears the burden of restructuring. So a particular pattern of losers in transition could be clearly linked to the labor market whereas the pace of restructuring cannot necessarily be linked.

Of course, to be able to delve more into that, one would have to run a counterfactual to see what would have happened in the absence of rigidities in the labor market, high payroll taxes, and high minimum wages. We do not have such a counterfactual, although we have some studies like the comparison of Estonia and Slovenia by Milan Vodopivec some time ago. Estonia and Slovenia in some sense are very different from each other with respect to labor market rigidities, with Estonia being the most deregulated and Slovenia being the most regulated. And I think this is a very important area of research.

What one can try to do is to move farther east and compare labor market developments in Central and Eastern Europe with developments in the Commonwealth of Independent States. This is an interesting comparison. In the Commonwealth of Independent States minimum wages are low and nonbinding, hiring and firing happens immediately, nobody bothers much about the labor code, and payroll taxes are significantly lower.

But if one looks at GDP dynamics or any indicator of restructuring, CIS countries are lagging far behind Central and Eastern Europe, despite having a more deregulated, if you like, labor market. Labor market outcomes or poverty outcomes are also different, with much more of a burden in the Commonwealth of Independent States borne by people who tend to be middle-aged, and there is much less bias toward the uneducated bearing the burden. The returns to education are not as high there as they are in Central and Eastern Europe.

If this hypothesis is true (that, in fact, restructuring does not depend on labor market performance, but labor market outcomes depend on labor market performance), what does this mean for the future? Does it mean that there is no reason to worry about what is happening with respect to labor market policies in the institutions? It seems to me that the answer is no for three reasons.

First, changes in some labor market policies could produce a significant improvement in welfare outcomes. For instance, the minimum wage (taking into account huge regional differences and the need to be flexible when applying different minimum wages in different regions) seems to be able to produce desirable outcomes pretty quickly in terms of employment of unskilled workers. So this is the first reason why there could be an improvement in welfare outcomes following a change in labor market policies.

Second, if Central and Eastern European countries would like to catch up with Western Europe, obviously the quick growth is not consistent with high payroll taxes and binding minimum wages. So the catch-up argument states that the challenge of growth targets for Central and Eastern European countries is simply too big, given their labor market performance. From that perspective, Central and Eastern European countries probably would like to have unemployment and productivity follow a U.S. style record rather than a West European type if one looks at the past 30 years.

Finally, trends clearly point to a shrinking effective labor force, both through withdrawals from the labor market and through long-term unemployment. This is very troubling. It is troubling from the point of view of social exclusion, but it is also troubling in the medium to long term from the macroeconomic perspective, given the growth prospects with a smaller number of people competing for jobs, with an unemployment-inflation balance moving farther away, and more difficulties in pursuing policies that keep inflation low and unemployment in check.

Despite quick restructuring, despite the clear success with respect to changes in the structure of industry and with respect to changes in the labor market, we need to worry about the labor market outcomes from the welfare standpoint. We also need to worry about growth prospects if institutions now in place are not reformed. The issue of payroll taxation is very important because of the issue of social security systems reforms in terms of bringing the payroll taxes down and restructuring the systems so that contributions to the social security system are not perceived as taxes. Policies with respect to minimum wages and flexibility in terms of hiring and firing will have to be reformed in order for Central and Eastern European countries to catch up and maintain growth rates corresponding with catch-up targets.

References

Vodopivec, M. 1999. "Worker Reallocation during Estonia's Transition to Market." World Bank, Washington, D.C. Processed.

CHAPTER 11

Discussant Notes

Eva Belabed

Because I represent the European Economic and Social Committee (Ecosoc), my contribution reflects the social partners' voice in the debate on labor market trends. In its continuous work on enlargement, Ecosoc has presented its views to European institutions on individual countries as well as on horizontal issues, such as the social dimension of enlargement. The social dimension was voted unanimously by all members of the committee, which means it has the support from all the groups in Ecosoc (employers, workers, and various other interests).

We also have organized regular conferences where we discuss important aspects of the enlargement process with representatives of social partners from the candidate countries, and we have established joint consultative committees with some of the candidate countries so their way to accession can be discussed in more depth. We thus follow a bottom-up approach in discussion with social partners and civil society of the candidate countries, integrating the results of these debates into our opinions on the enlargement process.

When dealing with the social aspects of enlargement, our message is very clear:

- Enlargement offers a historic chance for peace, security, and better living conditions for people all over Europe.

- The social effects of enlargement have to be taken into consideration to make sure the process is accepted by populations and to guarantee chances for improved living conditions for everybody.

In addition to the Copenhagen criteria, the social dimension forms a central element in the enlargement process, because transformation and the enlargement process have both economic and social effects. Georg Fischer has referred to the European Social Model and the debate on full employment that has been reopened in Lisbon in the context of making Europe the most competitive area in the world. Our intention is not to postpone accession or to prolong the process, but to make sure that the process is accompanied by suitable measures to take account of these effects.

The candidate countries have undergone a difficult process of transformation for more than ten years now. In this process they have achieved a lot of changes and reforms, but these reforms have not always brought immediate improvements for the population and—as Michal Rutkowski and others have noted—the burden is not equally shared by all groups in the population.

Structural changes have led to rising unemployment, as the figures presented by Hermine Vidovic show; unemployment gains momentum again. The reforms of the social systems together with budgetary constraints sometimes create difficult situations and therefore lead to growing scepticism in the population toward the process of transformation and EU accession. This results in political discontent and the electoral results we have seen recently.

When we look at the social dialogue in the candidate countries, we find very different pictures. In some countries social partners still encounter problems in getting involved in the accession process, and some governments still have problems with the role of social partners in accession. In addition, there are structural problems within social partners, which makes collective bargaining difficult. The European Union tries to help by emphasizing the development of social dialogue in the different accession programs (for example, the twinning program).

It is important to make enlargement socially sustainable, which means that in addition to the Copenhagen criteria, the social dimension has to play a central role. The enlargement process must:

- Include socially and environmentally sustainable strategies that are tailored to key problem areas (heavy industry and agriculture, for example)

- Develop new employment opportunities

- Accompany structural change with training, employment policy, and investments

- Improve conditions for small and medium enterprises
- Establish a social services system to help strengthen social cohesion and prevent exclusion and poverty
- Foster equal opportunities for all
- Promote and strengthen the social dialogue
- Develop dialogue with civil society and the population
- Develop cross-border cooperation (that is why the Commission is preparing a communication on this issue).

If we want populations in the Member States of the European Union and in the candidate countries to accept the process of transformation and enlargement, we have to give social aspects of transformation and enlargement their place in the process. Otherwise, we will run into problems.

PART II

Lessons from Previous Enlargements

CHAPTER 12

Employment Policies in Spain (1975–2000): Lessons for Central European Countries Acceding to the European Union

Juan Jimeno

This chapter discusses Spanish employment policies during the last quarter of the twentieth century and draws some lessons for the accession to the European Union of Central and Eastern European countries (CEECs) in this regard. At first sight, there are many differences between the scenario in which the Spanish accession to the EU took place in 1986 and that under which future CEECs accession will take place. For instance, the gaps in income per capita levels and labor productivity involved in the Spanish accession to the EU (figure 12.1) were smaller than in the case of the CEECs.[1] However, as in the Spanish case, EU eastern enlargements will deeply affect labor and goods markets in the CEECs and require substantial labor reallocation in these countries, from resource-intensive to labor-intensive activities, and from agriculture and manufacturing to services. Thus the analysis of the economic effects of alternative policy options coping with the labor adjustment process required by accession of CEECs to the EU can benefit from the analysis of the Spanish experience.

The chapter proceeds as follows. I begin with a brief sketch of the institutional framework and of the evolution of social and employment policies in Spain during the last quarter of the twentieth century. Then I describe macroeconomic performance and labor market trends in Spain during the 1975–2000 period. The next section comments on the role of labor market institutions and social policies during the process of economic reforms and integration into the EU. The chapter concludes with remarks on the lessons from the Spanish experience that may be relevant in future accession of CEECs to the EU.

FIGURE 12.1 GDP PER CAPITA AND GDP PER EMPLOYEE IN SPAIN, 1975–98 (PPS EU = 100)

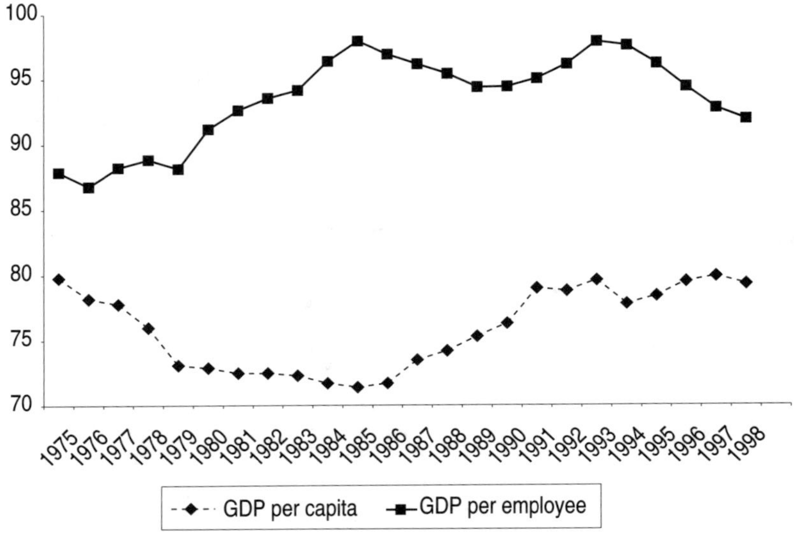

Source: Eurostat, *Statistical Appendix to European Economy*.

Social and Employment Policies in Spain

In the mid-seventies Spain was a relatively backward economy with underdeveloped social policies. Although some basic infrastructures for the public provision of social goods were put in place in the 1960s ands early 1970s, the objective of universal coverage of some social goods (such as health care and education) was not achieved until the late 1980s. Moreover, the social security system (pensions, unemployment benefits, and so on) was organized along corporatist rules, with many insurance schemes depending on workers' occupations, highly dispersed organization, and poor management (Guillén 1997).

The political reforms of the late 1970s and the economic reshuffling starting in 1975 generated social demands for the transition to a "modern Welfare State" that took place in the 1980s and 1990s. As seen in figure 12.2, public expenditures on social protection increased from about 15 percent of GDP in the late 1970s to surpass 20 percent of GDP in the mid-1990s, a level still below the EU average.

It is also illustrative to focus on the composition of social protection expenditures resulting from the increasing scope of social policies in Spain (table 12.1). Even in the current favorable cyclical situation, unemployment benefits amount to

FIGURE 12.2 GROSS SOCIAL PROTECTION EXPENDITURES IN SPAIN, 1980–95

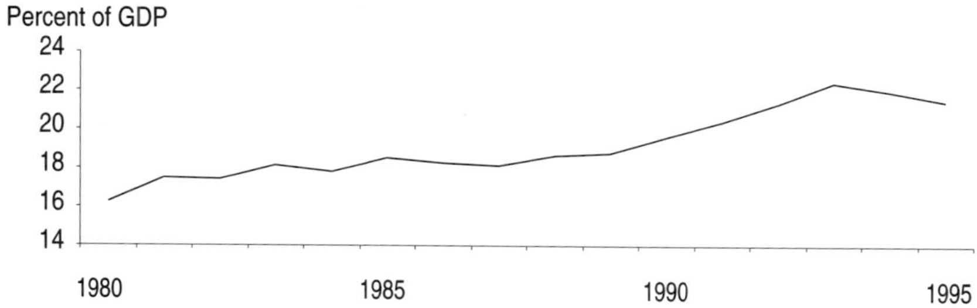

Source: OECD.

more than 2 percent of GDP, despite reforms in 1992 and 1993 that restricted eligibility criteria and lowered replacement rates. (Unemployment benefits amounted to 4.1 percent of GDP in 1991 and 5.2 percent of GDP in 1993.) Expenditure on old-age pensions is almost 9 percent of GDP, having increased by more than 1 percentage point since 1990. Early retirement schemes, very often connected to labor shedding in sectors with declining demand or going through a technological upgrading, were one of the main factors driving the evolution of pension expenditures. The other function with a significant increase of expenditure during the 1990s is sickness, which went from 5.7 percent of GDP in 1990 to 6.2 percent of GDP in 1998. Expenditures on housing, family, and social exclusion are far below the EU average.

TABLE 12.1 SPAIN'S EXPENDITURES ON SOCIAL PROTECTION (percentage of GDP)

Type	*1990*	*1995*	*1998*
Total expenditures	20.40	22.82	21.56
Social benefits	19.90	22.10	21.06
Sickness	5.70	6.40	6.16
Disability	1.50	1.63	1.61
Old age	7.60	8.80	8.85
Survivors	0.90	0.95	0.90
Family	0.30	0.38	0.43
Unemployment	3.60	3.67	2.87
Housing	0.10	0.14	0.07
Social exclusion	0.10	0.13	0.17

Source: Eurostat and European System of Integrated Social Protection Statistics (ESSPROS).

The main source of funding of social protection expenditures in Spain comes from social contributions. As seen in table 12.2, social security contributions remained more or less constant around 14 percent of GDP, until 1994, when they increased to 16 percent of GDP. Since then they have represented around 15 percent of GDP. In contrast to other EU countries, social security contributions are more unevenly split between employers and workers (75 percent for employers, 25 percent for workers). The rise in social protection expenditure that has taken place since 1990 (1.2 points of GDP) has been financed by a rise in social security contributions (of about 0.7 point of GDP) coming mostly from workers, and by higher government contributions (0.6 point of GDP). The fact that the latter are about three times higher than in 1980 reflects the process of extension toward universal coverage and the increasing weight of general taxation in the funding of social policies. The joint rise of social security contributions, labor income taxes, and indirect taxes led to a noticeable increase of the tax wedge, which some authors consider one of the main culprits of the rise of unemployment (Daveri and Tabellini 2000).

As for labor market regulation, the current institutional framework of the Spanish labor market dates back to 1980, with the approval of the so-called Workers' Statute (*Ley del Estatuto de los Trabajadores*). The main institutional features of the Spanish system of labor market relations are described below.[2]

The predominance of collective bargaining at the sectoral/provincial level as the means for establishing wages, working hours, and other employment conditions, is complemented by negotiations at other levels of bargaining (national, firm level). Collective bargaining agreements are enforced by law and applied to all

TABLE 12.2 SOCIAL PROTECTION RECEIPTS, 1980–98
(percentage of GDP)

Type	*1980*	*1985*	*1990*	*1994*	*1995*	*1996*	*1997*	*1998*
Actual employers' social contributions	9.1	8.4	9.1	9.9	9.0	9.3	9.4	9.3
Imputed employers' social contributions	2.5	2.2	2.1	2.5	2.3	2.3	2.2	2.1
Social contributions paid by the workers	2.8	2.9	2.9	3.6	3.3	3.5	3.5	3.4
Total social contributions	14.4	13.5	14.1	16.0	14.6	15.1	15.1	14.8
Reoriented social contributions	0.6	0.6	0.5	0.7	0.6	0.5	0.4	0.4
General government contributions	2.9	5.0	5.4	6.8	6.8	6.2	6.0	6.0
Other	0.2	0.3	0.5	0.5	0.6	0.7	0.7	0.7

Source: Spanish Ministry of Employment and Social Affairs 1998.

firms and workers within the sectoral/geographic scope of the agreement. There are elections within firms determining which trade unions are to bargain on behalf of workers. The coverage rate of collective agreements is relatively high (around 80 percent). Hence, collective bargaining agreements establish, de facto, a second layer of minimum wages above the national, statutory minimum wage, and it compresses the wage distribution at the bottom (Dolado, Felgueroso, and Jimeno 1997).

A high degree of employment protection is present against dismissals and against functional and geographical workers' mobility. Under the typical, full-time contract, firing costs are determined by workers' seniority and the reasons for dismissals. For individual "fair" ("unfair") dismissals (where "fair" or "unfair" is decided by the labor courts), severance payments are 20 (45) days of wages per year of seniority up to a maximum of 12 (42) months of wages. Collective dismissals need administrative approval, which is mostly conceded only when agreement has been reached between the employer and workers' representatives, and usually these agreements entail severance payments above those established for individual "unfair" dismissals.

A dualization of the labor market as a result of the liberalization of fixed-term employment contracts (FTCs) started in 1984. Instead of easing employment protection legislation (EPL) across the board, the Spanish government decided to introduce "flexibility at the margin." This allowed the use of temporary contracts for any kind of job, not only seasonal jobs or jobs of determined duration. As a result of this measure, the proportion of employees under FTCs increased very markedly to surpass 30 percent in the early 1990s.[3] More recently, there have been three labor market reforms (in 1994, in 1997, and in 2001) aimed at undoing the liberalization of FTCs in 1984 and at reducing the proportion of employees under FTCs.

In 1994 EPL was changed, widening the conditions for "fair" dismissals and restricting the conditions for the use of temporary contracts. In 1997 the employer confederation (Confederación EspaĖola de Organizaciones Empresariales) and the two major unions (Unión General de Trabajadores and Confederación Sindical de Comisiones Obreras) reached an agreement to reform the system of employment contracts and the structure of collective bargaining. The main novelty of the reform was the introduction of a new permanent employment contract with lower firing costs in case of unfair dismissals (33 days of wages per year of seniority with a maximum of 33 months of wages). This new contract could be used for most new hires, with the exception of males 30 to 45 years of age with unemployment spells below one year. It significantly reduced firing costs (the first time that Spanish unions conceded to this type of reduction).

The reduction was thought necessary to promote employment creation and, above all, to lower the incidence of temporary employment. The government supported this agreement by heavily subsidizing the signing of new permanent contracts and the conversion of temporary contracts into permanent ones. The subsidies were in the form of rebates to Social Security contributions in the range of 40 to 60 percent over a period of two years, depending on the individual characteristics of the employee. This new contract was supposed to be in effect until May 2001. In March 2001, after further negotiations between the trade unions and the employer confederations for additional labor market reforms, the government unilaterally both extended the eligibility of this new permanent contract to workers of other characteristics and allowed for the contract to be used further in the future.

A brief summary of the process of EPL reforms in Spain over the last two decades follows. Spain has one of the most rigid employment protection laws in the EU, and regulation of the collective bargaining system favors insiders' power. Therefore, flexibility "at the margin" was introduced in 1984 by easing the use of temporary contracts for nonseasonal reasons while keeping the protection of permanent contracts. As the proportion of temporary jobs surged, labor market reforms during the 1990s tried to get a more "balanced" situation between both types of contracts by restricting the use of temporary contracts and by reducing firing costs under permanent contracts. Recent labor market reforms have aimed at reducing the proportion of workers under temporary contracts, but this still remains above 30 percent. By contrast with the reforms of employment protection legislation, the regulation of the wage bargaining system introduced in 1980 remains more or less unchanged.[4]

Macroeconomic Performance and Labor Market Trends

As already seen in figure 12.1, during the second half of the 1970s and the first half of the 1980s, Spanish GDP per capita fell to less than 70 percent of the EU average. Since accession to the EU in 1986 and up to 1996, Spain improved its relative GDP per capita from about 70 percent to around 75 percent. Since 1996 Spain has had a growth rate above the EU average, and currently GDP per capita is above 80 percent of the EU average. Nevertheless, the evolution of GDP per capita conceals important differences in the evolution of labor productivity (GDP per employee) and of employment rates. Spain rapidly caught up in labor productivity in the 1975–86 period; since then it has remained at about 95 percent of the EU average. Obviously, the different patterns of convergence in GDP per capita and labor productivity arise from the evolution of employment rates (employment as a proportion of the working age population). In the EU-15 the average employment rate went from 65 percent in 1975 to about 60 percent in 1996 and back again almost to 65 percent by 2000. In Spain the decline of the employment rate was much more dramatic during the 1975–85 period (from about 57.6 percent in 1975 to less than 45 percent in 1985). The rate increased to 48.2 percent in 1996, recovering quickly in the second half of the 1990s to reach 57 percent.

EU Funds

In the EU, regional policies are high on the political agenda as a means to improve social cohesion among the member countries and to foster economic development in the laggard regions. Thus, in addition to private foreign direct investment, since 1986 some member countries have received transfers from the EU's budget that are devoted to improving the infrastructure base and human capital resources. As seen in table 12.3, EU Structural Funds in 1996 amounted to approximately 1 percent in Spain, an increase since the early 1990s. Figure 12.3 shows that, in relation to total investment, these funds have represented a significant and increasing share of capital accumulation.

TABLE 12.3 STRUCTURAL FUNDS AND COHESION FUNDS, 1986–96
(percentage of GDP)

Year	*Regional funds*	*European social fund*	*Other structural funds*	*Cohesion funds*
1986	0.13	0.07	—	—
1987	0.14	0.12	—	—
1988	0.19	0.14	—	—
1989	0.28	0.14	—	—
1990	0.36	0.16	—	—
1991	0.35	0.16	—	—
1992	0.45	0.18	—	—
1993	0.43	0.20	—	0.10
1994	0.33	0.16	—	0.10
1995	0.71	0.27	0.04	0.26
1996	0.46	0.39	0.06	0.24

— Not applicable.
Source: Doménech, Maudes, and Varela 2000.

FIGURE 12.3 TOTAL EU FUNDS AS A PERCENTAGE OF TOTAL INVESTMENT, 1985–96

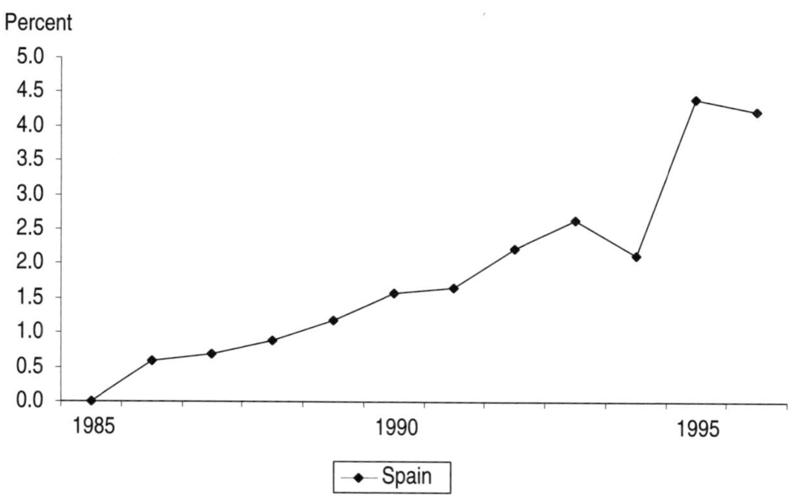

Source: Doménech, Maudes, and Varela 2000.

Unemployment and Inflation

Figures 12.4 and 12.5 plot the evolution of unemployment and inflation rates in Spain during the 1975–2000 period. The Spanish unemployment rates increased in the mid-1970s, immediately after the first oil shock and coinciding with political transition. They remained high until the mid-1980s. Since the mid-1980s, the Spanish unemployment rate has shown fluctuations similar to those in the EU average unemployment rate but at a much higher level and with a trend toward a reduction of this unemployment differential in the last three years 1998–2000.

As for inflation, after a huge increase following the oil shock in the early 1970s, Spain started a disinflation process in the late 1970s, although from a higher level and at a smaller pace than the core of the EU countries. In Spain the reduction of inflation from 10 percent to below 2 percent took 15 years and was associated with a rise of 13 percentage points in unemployment. Recently, the inflation differential with the EU has widened to around 2 points.

Sectoral Composition of Employment

Together with the rise of unemployment in the 1980s and 1990s, there have been significant changes in the sectoral composition of employment (table 12.4). Since

FIGURE 12.4 UNEMPLOYMENT RATE IN SPAIN, 1975–2000

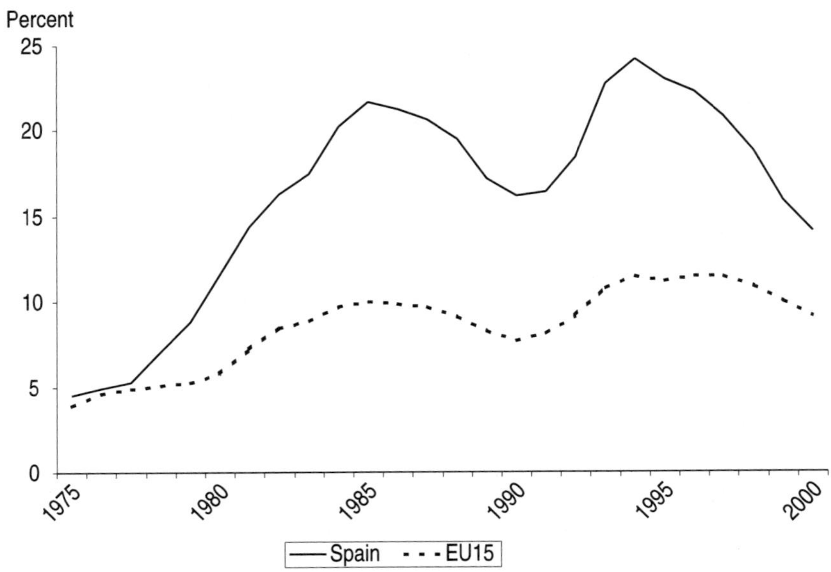

Source: Eurostat, *Statistical Appendix to European Economy.*

FIGURE 12.5 SPAIN'S INFLATION RATE, 1975–2000

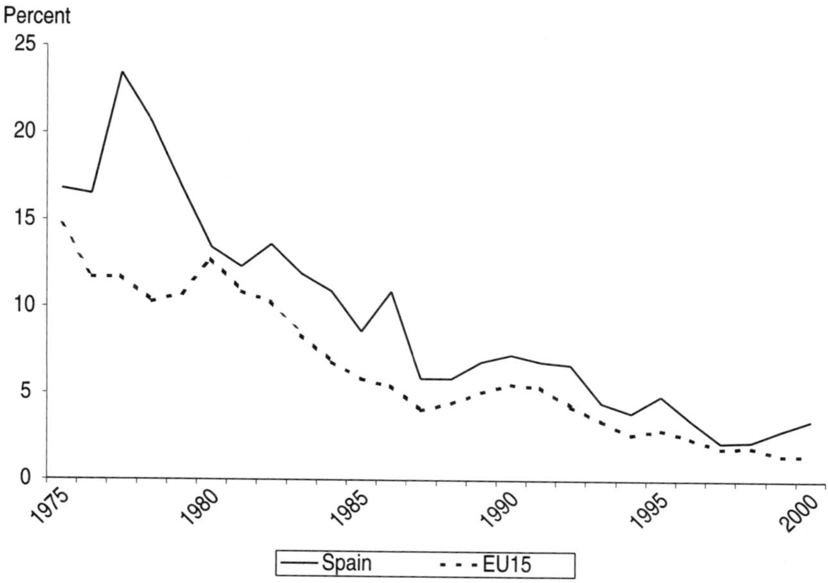

Note: GDP deflator at market prices.
Source: Eurostat, *Statistical Appendix to European Economy.*

TABLE 12.4 SECTORAL COMPOSITION OF EMPLOYMENT IN SPAIN, 1975–99

	1975	*1980*	*1985*	*1990*	*1995*	*1999*
Employment (thousands)	12,692	11,551	10,637	12,578	12,049	13,801
Self-employment (percent)	30.2	30.9	31.7	26.6	26.0	21.8
Agriculture (percent)	22.1	19.3	18.3	11.8	9.2	7.4
Manufacturing (percent)[a]	28.2	27.0	24.4	23.7	20.6	20.2
Construction (percent)	10.0	9.0	7.3	9.7	9.4	10.6
Services (percent)	39.7	44.7	49.7	54.8	60.6	61.9
Social services (percent)	14.5	17.9	21.2	23.3	26.6	27.2

a. Includes mining and quarrying and electricity, gas, and water.
Source: OECD 2000a.

1975 the weight of the agricultural sector in total employment has diminished by almost 15 percentage points while that of manufacturing has decreased from 28.2 percent to 20.2 percent. By contrast, the weight of employment in the service sector increased by more than 20 percentage points, mostly because of the expansion of social services (primarily in the public sector). Finally, employment in the building sector recovered to its 1975 relative level after a significant fall in this weight in total employment in the 1975–85 period. Hence, the sectoral composition of employment has converged to the average EU pattern, although some minor differences (lower employment weights for manufacturing and social services, slightly higher employment weights for agriculture and construction) are still noticeable.[5]

The Unequal Incidence of Employment and Unemployment

Another significant fact of the Spanish labor market performance over the last two decades is the unequal distribution of employment among different population groups. As seen in table 12.5, youth and female unemployment rates have been persistently higher than the unemployment rate of prime-age men. While the unemployment differential between men and women has increased, the relative youth unemployment rate has significantly decreased since the early 1980s.[6] Also noticeable is the rise of unemployment among workers close to the retirement age.[7]

As for the distribution of employment, the two most relevant developments are the rise of the employment rate of women ages 25 to 54 (by almost 20 pecentage points since 1983) and the decline in the employment rate of men ages 55 to 64 (by almost 15 percentage points during the same period). Besides the traditional explanations for the growing participation of women in the labor market,[8] there are two additional reasons for the increasing participation of Spanish women in the labor market. First, as in many traditionally Catholic countries, female labor market participation was very low in the 1960s and 1970s. Second, the educational upgrading of the female population (Dolado, Felgueroso, and Jimeno, 2000) and the decline in fertility (the total fertility rate has fallen from almost 3 in the late 1970s to around 1.1) have been spectacular since 1985. As for the fall of employment rates of men close to the retirement age, the main factor is the extension of early retirement schemes and its use as an instrument to adjust the labor force in firms with declining demand or subject to technological improvements.

Accession to the EU: How Spain Coped

The previous description of employment and social policies and macroeconomic developments in Spain over the last 25 years highlights the following facts:

- Preparation for accession and accession to the EU required quite significant changes in the Spanish economy that resulted in significant employ-

TABLE 12.5 EMPLOYMENT AND UNEMPLOYMENT RATES IN SPAIN (percent)

	1983			*1990*			*1999*		
Age Group	*All*	*Men*	*Women*	*All*	*Men*	*Women*	*All*	*Men*	*Women*
				Unemployment rates					
All ages	17.0	15.6	20.5	16.1	11.8	24.4	15.9	11.1	23.2
15–24	37.6	33.7	43.7	30.1	23.2	39.7	28.5	21.7	37.3
25–54	11.5	11.5	11.6	13.1	9.3	20.6	13.9	9.2	21.0
55–64	7.4	8.8	2.9	8.1	8.4	7.2	9.9	9.4	11.2
				Employment rates					
All	49.5	71.7	27.6	51.1	71.0	31.6	53.8	69.6	38.3
15–24	35.9	45.2	25.9	38.3	47.4	28.7	33.9	41.3	26.2
25–54	56.1	83.6	29.4	61.1	85.5	37.2	65.6	84.2	47.6
55–64	41.3	65.2	19.7	36.8	57.2	18.1	34.9	52.4	19.1

Source: OECD 2000b.

ment losses during the 1975–85 period and intense labor reallocation across sectors and occupations.

- Social expenditures increased to meet, to some extent, the higher demand for social protection. In particular, the coverage and duration of unemployment benefits and participation in early retirement schemes were extended to provide income support to displaced workers. This resulted in high long-term unemployment and a drastic decline in the employment rates of the population close to the legal retirement age.

- Wages and other employment conditions were determined by a multilayer, high coverage, noncoordinated wage determination system that led to a relatively high degree of real wage rigidity, at both the macroeconomic and microeconomic levels.

- Restrictive employment protection legislation did not prevent intense labor shedding and high job destruction rates in declining sectors. When employment protection legislation was finally reformed in 1984, it was done by the liberalization of fixed-term contracts resulting in a dualization of the labor market. The proportion of workers under fixed-term contracts increased to surpass 30 percent of all employees at the beginning of the 1990s. Although the introduction of flexibility at the margin contributed to employment creation in the second half of the 1980s (Bentolila and Saint-Paul 1992), it also had negative effects on the evolution of wages and productivity, and on wage inequality (Dolado, García-Serrano, and Jimeno 2001). In the 1990s, labor market reforms were primarily aimed at reducing the incidence of fixed-term employment contracts. There has been little success so far.

Overall, it seems that the Spanish institutions were not properly designed to accommodate the structural adjustments required by accession to the EU. In the mid-seventies Spain embarked on a path characterized by rapid modernization and technological upgrading and, therefore, high labor productivity growth. This structural change took place under a fairly rigid institutional framework and at times of negative supply and demand shocks. Not surprisingly, unemployment surged.[9] Moreover, some features of the institutional framework (increasingly long-lasting unemployment benefits, a high bargaining power of insiders, a wage determination together with segmentation of employment between permanent and temporary workers) also contributed to the persistence of unemployment (Dolado and Jimeno 1997) and to an unequal distribution of unemployment among population groups, increasing the relative unemployment rates of young and female workers (Jimeno and Rodriguez-Palenzuela 2001). The fact that unemployment mostly affected second-earners in the household, the role of the extended family as an additional provider of insurance (Bentolila and Ichina 2000), and the rise of expenditures in social protection explain why unemployment could remain at such high levels for so long.

In sum, as far as international integration is concerned, the Spanish experience can be judged as a qualified success. Fifteen years after accession to the EU, Spain is ninth in the ranking of EU countries by income per capita, since convergence in GDP per capita and labor productivity has proceeded slowly. As for the equity issue, although income inequality is high for EU standards and has increased during the last decade, the coverage of basic needs (such as education, health care, social assistance) is not very far from the standards of the "average European Welfare State." However, further economic development has been impeded by the workings of a labor market inefficiently regulated. As a result, the employment rate differential with the EU average has been on average around 15 percentage points during the last two decades. In the past five years this gap was closing very quickly, but it still remains to be seen if the improvement is due to the business cycle or if recent reforms have permanently reduced structural unemployment. The continuing process of labor market reforms is far from over. There are still unresolved problems: the segmentation of employment between insiders covered by a restrictive EPL and outsiders under temporary, atypical employment contracts; a multilayer wage determination system lacking coordination among many bargaining units; and the high incidence of long-term unemployment in some population groups (mainly unskilled young and female workers).

Final Observations: Any Lessons for CEECs?

Obviously, a single country's experience cannot provide a clear-cut recipe for CEECs undergoing structural reforms. The level of development and the international macroeconomic scenario are now very different from the situation prevailing when Spain took the route that the CEECs are now taking. Nevertheless, the economic literature on the relationship between labor market institutions and labor market performance singles out some "culprits" of the bad performance of the labor market.[10] Although the findings are not completely robust, there are some general lessons to bear in mind.[11]

Labor market institutions matter for labor market performance. Overly rigid labor legislation opposing structural changes rather than arranging them or coping with them is bound to fail. It will impede growth and will not preclude employment destruction.

Institutions matter, not only by themselves but also by their interactions among themselves and by their interactions with the demand and supply shocks hitting the economy. The effects may change as time goes by. For instance, the regulation of collective bargaining becomes almost irrelevant if firing costs are nonexistent. A too rigid institutional framework may convert temporary shocks to permanent shocks by generating hysteresis in unemployment dynamics.

Even apparently small differences in institutions matter. Countries with similar institutional features (Belgium and Holland, the United States and Canada, the United Kingdom and Ireland, Spain and Portugal) have shown dissimilar labor market performances.

There is not a unique set of labor market institutions that will create an efficient labor market delivering high employment rates. For instance, atypical work (part-time employment contracts) has contributed to lower unemployment in Holland but less so in Spain; active labor market polices are managed differently across countries with contrasting results.

In contrast to unemployment, there are institutions that unambiguously deliver lower wage dispersion. Flexible, less-regulated labor markets adjust to shocks by changes in relative wages. A centralized wage determination system, once the case in Scandinavian countries, reduces wage inequality (Bjorklund and Freeman 1997).

Economic agents react to institutions by shifts of their labor demand and labor supply and by changes in labor demand and labor supply elasticities. Decisions such as investment in human capital, participation in the labor market, and retirement are very much affected by the incentives implicit in social norms and labor market institutions.

Besides these general lessons, there are three broad conclusions that can be drawn from the Spanish accession to the EU in the mid-1980s.[12]

- First, as regards employment, flexible labor markets allow a better accommodation of the required labor reallocation by shifts to different specialization patterns, modernization, and technological upgrading. The Spanish case shows that restrictive employment protection legislation does not prevent intense labor shedding from reindustralization and changes in the sectoral composition of employment. It also shows that, when combined with a generous provision of long-lasting unemployment benefits, it contributes to augment hysteretic features of the labor market. Eventually, labor market reforms easing employment protection legislation is needed. In this case two-tier institutional reforms may result in a dual labor market where not only equity but also efficiency is negatively affected. As for equity, temporary employees (mainly young and female workers first entering the labor market) suffer the burden of the adjustment, while the insider power of workers under permanent contracts is strengthened. As for efficiency, human capital investment, training, and, subsequently, productivity growth are discouraged by the resulting employment segmentation. Finally, the use of early retirement schemes to ease the adjustment and to enhance the employment rates of the young is a nonstarter. The employment rates of the young do not increase as a result of the reduction of the adult labor supply. Rather, in a context of rising life expectancy and declining fertility, the financial viability of many unfunded pay-as-you-go social security schemes calls for delaying retirement, not the contrary.

- Second, as far as distribution is concerned, demands for social protection will increase and, unavoidably, social expenditures will also increase. The challenges are to accommodate those demands in a framework of stable macroeconomic policies and to design social protection schemes with the correct incentives, not to impede labor market participation and employment creation. For instance, in-work benefits seem superior to long-lasting unemployment benefits. Experience-rated unemployment benefits, as in the United States, may prevent excessive labor shedding instead of using them, as happened in Spain, as an incentive for firms to reshuffle their labor force. Active labor market policies should be targeted, well-designed, and properly evaluated, and they should not extend the duration of unemployment benefits.

- Finally, copying the West's institutions is also a nonstarter. The effects of institutions on labor market performance are, as indicated above, country and time specific, and they depend upon the shocks hitting the economy. For this reason harmonization of institutions with respect to the West could be counterproductive. For instance, the application of Western collective bargaining institutions can yield increasing, rather than decreasing, unemployment and wage differentials.

Notes

1. In 1985 Spanish GDP per capita relative to the EU average was around 72 percent. Excluding Slovenia and the Czech Republic, all candidates to join the EU from Central and Eastern Europe have income per capita gaps above 50 percent relative to the EU (Boeri and others 2001).

2. See Jimeno and Toharia (1994) for further details.

3. For a description of the regulation of FTCs and of the characteristics of temporary workers in Spain, see Cebrián and others (2001).

4. For a comprehensive survey on recent labor market reforms in Spain, see Segura (2001).

5. Marimón and Zillibotti (1998) argue that the rise of Spanish unemployment above that of other EU countries is due to the higher destruction of jobs in agriculture. Since job destruction in agriculture took place in Spain during a period of low job creation in the other sectors, while in other EU countries it took place earlier in the 1960s, unemployment increases more markedly in Spain than in other countries. Dolado and Jimeno (1997) argue against this view by pointing out the higher job creation in the public sector in Spain as a result of the development of the "Welfare State." They also note the case of Portugal as a counterexample of a country experiencing a similar downsizing of agriculture during the same period without a significant rise of unemployment.

6. The recent fall in youth unemployment may be related to the decreasing relative size of new young cohorts entering the labor market. For some evidence on a demographic factor in the evolution of youth unemployment rates, see, for instance, Korenman and Neumark (2000); Ahn, Izquierdo, and Jimeno (2000); and Jimeno and Rodriguez-Palenzuela (2001).

7. There are also significant and persistent unemployment differentials across regions (Jimeno and Bentolila 1998).

8. Dolado, Felgueroso, and Jimeno (2001) point out the following: on the demand side, greater firms' willingness to hire women due to various factors such as the rise of service sectors and the decline of manual/production sectors, the development of new technologies that allow firms to substitute male for female workers, antidiscrimination policy measures, and the huge increase of higher education among women; on the supply side, lower fertility rates, the availability of new household technologies, and the emergence of flexible-time work.

9. On this the comparison with Portugal is very illustrative (Jimeno and others 2000). Portugal adopted a labor-intensive, broad-based growth strategy, with more flexible labor

institutions that delivered lower labor productivity and wage growth but a higher employment rate.

10. Just to cite three of the most recent ones, see Nickell and Layard (1999), Blanchard and Wolfers (2000), and Bertola, Blau, and Kahn (2001).

11. These lessons draw from Dolado, Felgueroso and Jimeno (2001).

12. Similar conclusions are in Boeri and others (2001).

References

Ahn, N., M. Izquierdo, and J. F. Jimeno. 2000. "TamaĖo de la población y desempleo juvenil: un análisis con datos agregados, regionales y microeconómicos." Documentos de Economía 7. Foundation Caixa Galicia, CIEF.

Bentolila, S., and A. Ichina. 2000. "Unemployment and Consumption: Are Job Losses Less Painful near the Mediterranean?" Working Paper 0010. Center for Monetary and Financial Studies (CEMFI), Madrid.

Bentolila, S., and G. Saint-Paul. 1992. "The Macroeconomic Impact of Flexible Labor Contracts: An Application to Spain." *European Economic Review* 36: 1013–97.

Bertola, G., F. Blau, and L. Kahn. 2001 "Comparative Analysis of Labor Market Outcomes: Lessons for the U.S. from International Long-Run Evidence." *The Roaring Nineties: Can Full Employment Be Sustained?* A. Krieger and R. Solow, eds. New York: Russell Sage and Century Foundations.

Bjorklund, A., and R. Freeman. 1997. "Generating Equality and Eliminating Poverty: The Swedish Way." In R. Freeman, R. Topel, and B. Swedenborg, eds., *The Welfare State in Transition.* Chicago: University of Chicago Press.

Blanchard, O., and J. Wolfers. 2000. "Shocks and Institutions and the Rise of European Unemployment: The Aggregate Evidence." *Economic Journal* 110(1): 1–33.

Boeri, T., and others. 2001. "The Impact of Eastern Enlargement on Employment and Labor Markets in the EU Member States." Draft. European Integration Consortium.

Cebrián, I., and others. 2001. "Atypical Work in Italy and Spain: The Quest for Flexibility at the Margin in Two Supposedly Rigid Labor Markets." In S.

Houseman and M. Osawa, eds., *Nonstandard Work Arrangements in Japan, Europe and the United States.* W.E. Upjohn Institute for Employment Research.

Daveri, F., and G. Tabellini. 2000. "Unemployment, Growth and Taxation in Industrial Countries." *Economic Policy* 30: 47–48.

Dolado, J. J., F. Felgueroso, and J. F. Jimeno. 1997. "The Effects of Minimum Bargained Wages on Earnings: Evidence from Spain." *European Economic Review* 41: 713–21.

———. 2000. "Explaining Youths' Labor Market Problems in Spain: Crowding-Out, Institutions, or Technology Shifts?" Processed.

———. 2001. "Mercado de trabajo y políticas de empleo en el inicio del siglo XXI." *Moneda y Crédito* 212: 11–59.

Dolado, J. J., and J. F. Jimeno. 1997. "The Causes of Spanish Unemployment: A Structural VAR Approach." *European Economic Review* 41: 1281–1307.

Dolado, J. J., C. García-Serrano, and J. F. Jimeno. 2001. "Drawing Lessons from the Boom of Temporary Jobs in Spain." Draft. Universidad Carlos III, Universidad de Alcalá y FEDEA.

Doménech, R., A. Maudes, and J. Varela. 2000. "Fiscal Flows in Europe: The Redistributive Effects of the EU Budget." *Review of World Economics* 136(4): 631–56.

Eurostat. *Statistical Appendix to European Economy.*

Guillén, A. M. 1997. "Welfare State Development in Spain: A Historical and Explanatory Approach." In *Comparing Social Welfare Systems in Southern Europe*, vol. 3. Florence Conference. Paris: MIRE.

Jimeno, J. F., and S. Bentolila. 1998. "Regional Unemployment Persistence (Spain 1976–1994)." *Labor Economics* 5: 25–51.

Jimeno, J. F., and D. Rodriguez-Palenzuela. 2001. "Youth Unemployment in the OECD: Demographic Changes, Labor Market Institutions, and Macroeconomic Shocks." Draft. FEDEA y European Central Bank.

Jimeno, J. F., and L. Toharia.1994. *Unemployment and Labor Market Flexibility: Spain.* Geneva: International Labor Office.

Jimeno. J. F., and others. 2000. "Integration and Inequality: Lessons from the Accessions of Portugal and Spain to the EU." In *Background Papers: Making Transition Work for Everyone.* Washington, D.C.: The World Bank.

Korenman, S., and D. Neumark. 2000. "Cohort Crowding and Youth Labor Markets: A Cross-National Analysis." In D. G. Blanchflower and R. B. Freeman, eds., *Youth Employment and Joblessness in Advanced Countries.* Cambridge, Mass.: National Bureau of Economic Research.

Marimón, R., and F. Zillibotti. 1998. "'Actual' versus 'Virtual' in Europe: Is Spain Different?" *European Economic Review* 42(1): 123–54.

Nickell, S., and R. Layard. 1999. "Labor Market Institutions and Economic Performance." In O. C. Ashenfelter and D. Card, eds., *Handbook of Labor Economics*, vol. 3C. Amsterdam: North-Holland.

OECD (Organisation for Economic Cooperation and Development). 2000a. *Labour Force Statistics.*

———. 2000b. *Employment Outlook.*

Segura, J. 2001. "La Reforma del Mercado de Trabajo EspaĖol: Un Panorama." *Revista de Economía Aplicada* IX(25): 157–90.

Spanish Ministry of Employment and Social Affairs. 1998. *Anuario de Estadísticas Laborales*. Madrid.

CHAPTER 13

How Is Germany's Labor Market Coping with Unification?

Viktor Steiner

German unification was accompanied by a dramatic decline in employment and an unprecedented increase in unemployment in East Germany. Registered unemployment in East Germany increased from virtually zero to about 20 percent. In addition, there is a large share of "hidden" unemployment related to early retirement and active labor market programs. These adverse labor market developments are closely related in East Germany to wage policy, which right from the beginning of the unification process has been aimed at reaching parity with West German wages. Active and passive labor market policies have been excessively used to support the transition process. The financial burden of unemployment compensation, early retirement pensions, and active labor market programs, to a large extent financed by social security contributions and other transfers from West Germany, by increasing labor costs has also had negative effects on economic growth there. This, in turn, has repercussions on economic growth in East Germany, which has recently fallen even below the modest West German growth rate. Average labor productivity in East Germany is stagnating at a level of about 60 percent of that in West Germany, while average effective wages in East Germany have reached about 80 percent of the West German level and in some sectors have already reached parity. In comparison to other former communist countries, East Germany has experienced a much stronger increase in unemployment and real wages as a result of a policy aimed at fast equalization of living standards in East and West Germany. This policy has been supported by generous income support schemes for the unemployed and large-scale "active" labor market policies, which could only be financed by huge transfers from West Germany. Such a policy was clearly not feasible for other transition countries.

Given this general background, the chapter describes the development and structure of unemployment and wages in East Germany relative to West German developments, discusses active and passive labor market programs intended to cope with the high level of unemployment in East Germany, and evaluates the success of these programs on the basis of available empirical evidence. The main conclusions I draw from the experience of German unification are that (1) wage convergence outpaced relative productivity growth between East and West Germany resulting in mass unemployment, (2) downward wage rigidity is related to the level of income support for the unemployed relative to employment in the low-wage sector of the East German economy, and (3) active labor market policies may have contributed to downward wage rigidity and have been mostly ineffective in reducing unemployment.

Labor Market Developments

To set the scene for the following discussion of the main causes of the labor market problems in East Germany and their potential solutions, I briefly describe in this section relevant labor market developments including employment and labor force participation, the structure of unemployment, and wage and productivity developments.[1]

Employment and Labor Force Participation

Employment in East Germany fell dramatically from almost 9 million employed people to fewer than 6 million at the end of the nineties. The lion's share of this decline occurred in the first two years after currency union in July 1990. The employment decline has been continuing at a modest rate since the mid-nineties despite positive GDP growth rates in East Germany. By the end of the nineties, economic growth in East Germany no longer exceeded West German growth rates and average labor productivity stagnated at about 60 percent of the West German level.[2] The employment decline in East Germany was very much concentrated in the manufacturing sector, which, by the late nineties, was only half the size of this sector in West Germany. Private services and especially the construction sector expanded strongly in the nineties, but this could not compensate for the employment decline in manufacturing. In fact, the oversized construction sector, which in relative terms is about three times as large as in West Germany, as well as the still overstaffed public sector will have to shrink in the future, inducing further employment reductions.

To some extent, changes in labor force participation mirror the employment decline in East Germany. In 1991 the average participation rate in East Germany was 81.6 percent, exceeding the West German rate by about 10 percentage points.

This difference was mainly related to the much higher female participation rate of about 77 percent in East Germany, compared to only about 58 percent in West Germany. By the end of the nineties, the participation rate of East German men had declined by more than 5 percentage points, reaching the West German level of about 80 percent. For men this marked decline in participation rates is mainly related to special early retirement schemes that provided rather generous pension benefits until 1992 for people age 55 years or older. The labor force participation rate of East German women also declined by about 5 percentage points in this period. This is partly related to the increased costs of child care facilities in East Germany.

At the end of the nineties, the participation rate of East German women still exceeded the West German rate by more than 10 percentage points. This difference is all the more remarkable as the share of part-time work among West German women is much higher than in East Germany. Furthermore, the average working hours of full-time workers in East Germany are, both for men and women, still considerably higher than in West Germany. Accounting for these factors, the level of employment in East Germany is still higher than the measured employment figures indicate and may, in fact, be not much different from the West German level (Schneider and others 2000).[3]

Unemployment

The decline in employment and labor force participation was accompanied by a dramatic increase in registered unemployment in East Germany that reached about 20 percent by the end of the nineties. Starting from a level of virtually zero in the former German Democratic Republic (GDR), registered unemployment strongly increased immediately after currency union and has been increasing more or less steadily since then. Although unemployment in West Germany also increased markedly following the severe economic recession in 1993–94, this increase was much less pronounced and, since cyclical unemployment began to decline in the late nineties, apparently of a different nature. Furthermore, the high level of registered unemployment of about 20 percent only gives an overly optimistic picture of the unemployment problem in East Germany. Adding "hidden" unemployment, which consists of participants in "active" labor market programs (ALMP) and people on early retirement schemes, to the registered unemployed yields a corrected unemployment rate of almost 30 percent in 1998 (Sachverständigenrat 2000).

As to the structure of unemployment, the most important development in East Germany concerns the strong increase in long-term unemployment, both for men and women. East German and West German figures are similar: currently about 30 percent of all people in the unemployment stock have been unemployed for at least one year. Older workers, women, and disabled persons are overrepresented among the long-term unemployed. Overall, the structure of unemployment differs little between East and West Germany.

Wages and Labor Productivity

The development of wages plays a decisive role in the East German transitions process.[4] In 1991 average wages in East Germany amounted to 46.7 percent of the West German wage level, while relative labor productivity was only 31 percent. Thus unit labor costs in East Germany exceeded the West German level by about 50 percent at the beginning of the period (table 13.1). Between 1991 and 1998 the relative wage increased to about 74 percent, compared to an increase in relative labor productivity of about 60 percent. By the end of the period, unit labor costs in East Germany still exceeded the West German level by about 25 percent. These figures indicate that convergence of the East German economy has come to a halt, although relative productivity and wage levels in the two regions are still far from being in balance.[5]

Small surprise then that employment has declined markedly and unemployment has soared in East Germany. But why do wages not adjust to the lower level of labor productivity in East Germany? The usual explanation is that collective bargaining agreements prevent downward wage flexibility. However, this cannot be the full story because, as described in Franz and Steiner (2000), union coverage in East Germany is relatively low and collective bargaining agreements are often not binding even in the covered sector due to the prevalence of "emergency" clauses (*Öffnungsklauseln*). Therefore, other factors must prevent wages to balance supply and demand in the East German labor market. One important factor that may sustain wages at relatively high levels despite sky-rocketing unemployment in East Germany is the level of income support for unemployed people.

Income Support for the Unemployed

One recurrent theme in the public policy debate on unemployment in Germany concerns the size of the differential between the level of the social minimum of non-employed households and potential net income from gainful employment (Sinn

TABLE 13.1 EAST-WEST GERMAN COMPARISON OF BASIC LABOR MARKET INDICATORS, 1991 AND 1998

Indicator	*1991*	*1998*
Gross nominal wages[a]	46.7	73.9
Labor productivity[b]	31.0	59.4
Unit labor costs[c]	150.6	124.1

Note: Ratios of East German to West German figures multiplied by 100.
a. Gross labor income per employee.
b. Nominal GDP per employee.
c. Domestic gross labor income per employee divided by labor productivity.
Source: Compiled from Franz and Steiner (2000), table 2.

2000a). The main income support scheme related to unemployment in Germany is unemployment compensation. If a person is not eligible for unemployment compensation, or if the amount of unemployment compensation is below the social minimum, he or she may apply for social assistance. Income support may be conditional on other household income and wealth (means-tested), or it may be granted without a means test. There are basically no differences in regulations for unemployment compensation and social assistance between East and West Germany, although there remain some differences in the average level of income support. To a large extent, these differences are related to still existing wage differentials and differences in living costs in the two regions.

Unemployment Compensation

There are two forms of unemployment compensation: unemployment benefits (UB) and unemployment assistance (UA).[6] The level of UB is related to previous earnings, and eligibility depends on a minimum insured employment period. It is not means-tested, and the entitlement period depends on the duration of previous employment and on age. The income-replacement ratio (the ratio of the UB amount to net earnings in the previous job) is 67 percent for persons with at least one child and 60 percent for persons without children. UA is means-tested and is initially granted for a maximum period of 12 months but may be renewed as long as the means test is passed. The UA income-replacement ratio is 57 percent for persons with at least one child and 53 percent for persons without children. Depending on the level of previous earnings and household size, the level of unemployment compensation may be below the social minimum. In this case, one can apply for social assistance (see below). The regulations in East Germany are the same as in West Germany.

Between 1991 and 1998, the number of recipients of unemployment compensation and total expenditures per recipient increased markedly in both regions (table 13.2). This reflects both the increase in the level and changes in the structure of unemployment. Almost 20 percent of the East German labor force received unemployment compensation in 1998. In East Germany, in particular, the explosion in the number of UA recipients reflects the dramatic increase in long-term unemployment. Between 1991 and 1998, total expenditures on unemployment compensation in East Germany increased from 11.3 billion to 28.2 billion Deutschemark (DM).

Recipients of unemployment compensation are allowed to work as an employee or be self-employed for a small number of hours and earn additional income. For example, until 1998 recipients of UA could work up to 18 hours a week and keep 50 percent of earnings exceeding a small basic allowance of 30 DM per week until the sum of earnings and the remaining amount of UA reached 80 percent of the level of the net income in the previous job. For earnings exceeding this threshold, the remaining amount of UA was withdrawn at a rate of 100

TABLE 13.2 RECIPIENTS AND EXPENDITURES: UNEMPLOYMENT COMPENSATION IN EAST AND WEST GERMANY, 1991 AND 1998

Recipients and expenditures	*Country*	*Unemployment benefits*		*Unemployment assistance*	
		1991	*1998*	*1991*	*1998*
Recipients (in thousands)	West Germany	721	1,238	391	955
	East Germany	673	749	24	549
Recipients (percent of labor force)	West Germany	2.69	4.46	1.46	3.44
	East Germany	7.63	10.61	0.28	7.78
Total expenditures (in billions DM)[a]	West Germany	18.63	34.65	8.04	20.40
	East Germany	10.91	18.18	0.38	10.04
Expenditures per recipient (in 1,000 DM per month)[b]	West Germany	2,155	2,332	1,713	1,780
	East Germany	1,351	2,023	1,298	1,524

a. All amounts are deflated by the consumer price index (1998=100) and refer to the budget of the Federal Labor Office only.
b. In addition to the monthly amount of unemployment compensation, contributions to the public pension and health insurance funds.
Source: Compiled from Hagen and Steiner (2000), tables 7 and 8.

percent. Similar regulations also exist for UB recipients (Steiner 1997a, 1997b). However, these regulations seem to have had little effect on work incentives. For example, in 1998 only 0.9 percent (1.5 percent) of all recipients of UA in West (East) Germany chose that option.

The extent to which unemployment compensation contributes to unemployment has been analyzed in a number of microeconometric studies. For West Germany, Steiner (1997b) finds that the entitlement to UB or to UA increases long-term unemployment substantially, whereas marginal reductions in the income replacement ratio have only small effects on an individual's job-finding rate. Similar results were obtained for East Germany by Steiner and Kraus (1995), whereas Schneider and others (2000) report that even marginal reductions of the income replacement ratio at the beginning of an unemployment spell reduce its duration substantially.

Social Assistance

Social assistance is available to every legal resident in Germany whose income from other sources is below a socially determined "cultural" subsistence level (the so-called social minimum).[7] There are two types of social assistance payments: general assistance to cover subsistence expenditures (*Hilfe zum Lebensunterhalt* or HLU) and assistance under special circumstances (*Hilfe in besonderen Lebenslagen*). Since the latter type of social assistance is of little relevance for the question of work disincentives induced by social assistance, the following discussion will be restricted to HLU.

The social minimum consists of a basic subsistence level, which I will call "basic HLU-rate," housing costs (including heating) and irregular payments and benefits in kind the household can apply for under special circumstances. In 1999 the average basic HLU-rate for the head of the household was 546 DM in West Germany and 527 DM in East Germany (including East Berlin). Within the two regions these basic rates differ little (by less than 5 percent). Other adults living in the same household receive 80 percent of the household head's rate; for children the rate ranges between 45 and 90 percent, depending on their age.

Table 13.2 compares the monthly social minimum to the respective net income in employment for various types of households in the two regions. According to the Federal Social Assistance Act, the social minimum for a couple household with three children should, on average, be below the net income of a corresponding household with one member employed full time in the lower range of the earnings distribution. Earnings are calculated for a full-time worker receiving at least the wage defined by collective bargaining agreements. This so-called wage-differential rule (*Lohnabstandsgebot*) should provide incentives for HLU recipients to take up work. The respective wage differential by household type is shown in table 13.3.

For a couple with two children, the wage differential is about 20 percent in West Germany and 15 percent in East Germany. This regional difference is related, to a large extent, to still markedly higher wages in West Germany. For larger households and for single parents, the wage differential gets even smaller. Effective wages in East Germany are frequently below contract wages. Therefore, the numbers in table 13.3 are likely to overstate the true wage differential. In fact, for couples with two children and one spouse working full time in the East German low-wage sector (for

TABLE 13.3 AVERAGE SOCIAL MINIMUM AND DISPOSABLE INCOME BY HOUSEHOLD TYPE IN WEST AND EAST GERMANY, 1999

	West Germany			*East Germany*		
Household type	*HLU*[a]	*Net income*[b]	*%D*[c]	*HLU*[a]	*Net income*[b]	*%D*[c]
Couple with						
two children	2,931	3,658	19.9	2,683	3,183	15.7
three children	3,462	4,056	14.6	3,154	3,558	11.4
Single mother or father with						
one child less than 7 years of age	1,941	2,646	26.7	1,745	2,279	23.4
two children between 7 and 13 years of age	2,556	2,925	12.6	2,323	2,673	13.1

a. The amount of the social minimum in DM.

b. Disposable household income for a household with one full-time employed unskilled worker, net of taxes and social security contributions and including child allowances and housing subsidies.

c. $\%\Delta = (1 - \text{HLU/net income}) \times 100$.

Source: Bundesministerium für Arbeit und Sozialordnung 1999.

example, hotels and restaurants, retail trade), the wage differential may even become negative (Schneider and others 2000, 127).

Between 1991 and 1997 the number of HLU recipients increased from about 2 million to almost 2.9 million. As a share of the German population, the HLU caseload increased from 2.5 percent of the population at the beginning of the eighties to 3.5 percent by the end of the nineties. In 1997 expenditures on HLU reached about 20 billion DM, or approximately 0.55 percent of GDP. In East Germany the average number of HLU recipients increased from about 220,000 to 410,000 people in the period 1991 to 1998. This doubling of the HLU caseload reflects the increasing importance of long-term unemployment.

Several recent proposals to improve work incentives for recipients of social assistance are motivated by the observation that the number of employed people among recipients of social assistance is very small. For example, calculations by Buslei and Steiner (2000) have shown that of those 1.3 million people in the age group of 18 to 60 years of age who received social assistance at the end of 1995, only about 100,000 were employed, while 450,000 were registered as unemployed.

Active Labor Market Policy

The income support schemes described in the previous two sections are also known as "passive labor market policy" in contrast to "active labor market policy" (ALMP). While providing income support, ALMP mainly aims at integrating the unemployed into the regular labor market. The following discussion focuses on public works and training programs, by far the most important measures of ALMP in East Germany. Compared to other transition countries like Poland, the Czech Republic, and Hungary (see Lehmann 2001 for a comparative analysis), the programs are run on a much larger scale in East Germany.[8]

Public Works Programs

In terms of both the number of participants and expenditures, public works programs (PWP) constitute the most important active labor market policies in East Germany. According to the Employment Promotion Act, PWP should be aimed at improving the employment prospects of particular groups in the labor market, especially long-term unemployed people. Public works programs are intended to support activities not provided by the private market and are, therefore, restricted to nonprofit organizations in principle. In East Germany the subsidy amounts to 100 percent of the refundable wage, which is typically the relevant contract wage (including social security contributions) contained in collective bargaining agreements. As a rule, the wage subsidy is paid for a period of 12 months but can be prolonged up to 24 months. Until 1995 even more generous regulations were in existence in East Germany (Kraus, Puhani, and Steiner 2000). In 1998 the average number of PWP participants in East Germany was about 150,000 people, or 2 percent of the labor force, compared to only about 60,000 people in West Germany.

A special type of PWP are the so-called Structural Measures Adjustment (*Strukturanpassungsmaßnahmen*). These come either as Structural Measures Adjustment in the Nonprofit Sector (SMA-NP) or Structural Measures Adjustment for the Private Sector (SMA-PS). SMA-NP were introduced in East Germany in 1993 and in West Germany in 1994. In East Germany, they are typically run on a large scale by so-called Societies for Employment Promotion and Structural Development (ABS-*Gesellschaften*) with a focus on infrastructure and environmental development.

For SMA-NP, the amount of the wage subsidy is determined by the average level of unemployment compensation, including social security contributions, and must not exceed 80 percent of earnings in comparable jobs. As for PWP, this requirement is usually met by adjusting the working time accordingly. The wage subsidy is typically paid for a maximum period of 36 months; it may, however, be prolonged to 48 months if the employing institution agrees to employ the participant after the termination of the program. SAM-PS were introduced in 1997 and are available to employers in the private sector in East Germany. The amount of the wage subsidy is similar to an SMA-NP program. In 1998 the average number of participants in SAM-PS programs was 162,000 people.

Publicly Financed Training Programs

The second large-scale ALMP are publicly financed training programs (PFTP). Their aim is to improve the future employability of participants with too little or outdated human capital. Whether these programs are successful in this respect is discussed in the next section. In East Germany, in particular, the aim of publicly financed training programs often was to provide income support for unemployed people whose entitlement to unemployment benefits had been exhausted. Until 1998 participation in PFTP automatically renewed the entitlement to unemployment benefits. During participation in the program, the level of income support is the same as the amount of an individual's previous unemployment benefits.

The number of participants in PFTP in East Germany peaked in 1992 with an average stock of about 500,000 people. This number declined substantially to about 150,000 people in 1998, compared to about 200,000 in West Germany. In that year average expenditures per participant were about DM 3,200, and total expenditures amounted to almost DM 5.5 billion in East Germany and about DM 7 billion in West Germany. The naive "bookkeeping" effect of deducting full-time participants in PFTP from the number of unemployed people in 1998 reduced the East German unemployment rate by about 2 percentage points.

The Effectiveness of Active Labor Market Policies in East Germany

According to the German Employment Act, the main aim of active labor market policies is to reintegrate unemployed people—especially the long-term unemployed, the disabled, women, and youth—in private sector employment and to increase their future employability. However, empirical evaluation studies suggest that, more often than not, such policies fail to reach this goal in practice. Since most of these studies refer to East Germany, the following discussion is restricted to the East German experience with active labor market policies, and to public works programs and publicly financed training programs in particular.[9]

Microeconomic evaluation studies of these programs are typically concerned with whether participating in a PWP or PFTP improves the average participant's employment prospects compared to the (hypothetical) situation had he or she not participated in the program. Most of these studies find *negative* effects of PWP on individual re-employment probabilities in regular jobs. In other words, the employment prospects of unemployed people would have been better had they not participated in such programs. To some extent, this result can be explained by the nature of public works programs. By definition, they are not intended to qualify participants for a job in the regular labor market. Furthermore, participants tend to search less intensively for a job in the regular labor market while on a PWP than do those registered as unemployed at the labor office. This is known as the "locking-in" effect in the literature. Finally, people may stay unemployed after the termination of a PWP because participation in such a program renews eligibility for unemployment benefits, which in turn provides an opportunity to participate in another PWP, and so on (the "carousel effect").

Most microeconomic evaluation studies of PFTP find either no significant or even *negative* employment effects for East Germany. One exception is the study by Kraus, Puhani, and Steiner (1999). They report significant positive effects of PFTP on participants' future employment stability, especially for women. However, because of data limitations, all these studies estimate only average short-run employment effects and do not distinguish by type of PFTP. Therefore, it is possible that positive employment effects of well-designed PFTP are masked by ineffective ones. Moreover, most of these studies identify only the short-run effects of PFTP. The presence of negative short-run effects may be related to the "locking-in" effect referred to earlier. The "carousel effect" also may have been of some relevance for PFTP in the past. However, since 1998, participation in PFTP has not led to a renewal of eligibility for unemployment benefits, in contrast to participation in a public works program.

By their nature, microeconomic evaluation studies have to assume that participation in active labor market policies does not affect labor market outcomes for nonparticipants. Thus these studies neglect direct and indirect program effects, such as substitution and displacement effects. For large programs, like PWP in East Germany, this may yield overly optimistic results concerning the overall program effects and even lead to biased estimates of the employment effects for program participants. Aggregate impact studies of the labor market effects of large-scale programs are therefore a necessary complement to microeconomic evaluation studies.

However, there have only been a few such studies for East Germany to date. A recent study by Hagen and Steiner (2000) based on panel data on regional labor market districts finds that PWP raises the regional unemployment rate significantly because of its increasing effect on the regional unemployment inflow. Perhaps more surprising is the result that publicly financed training programs also increase the unemployment rate, where this effect is also related to the increase in the unemployment inflow associated with a higher previous level of participation in PFTP. These results can partly be explained by the locking-in effect. They also confirm the suspicion mentioned earlier that large-scale PWP may be associated with substantial substitution and displacement effects. Overall, the study by Hagen and Steiner (2000) suggests that the effectiveness of active labor market policies in East Germany is even worse than already indicated by the results from microeconomic evaluation studies.

Conclusion

At the beginning of German unification, politicians and economists alike thought that the transition to a market economy and convergence to West German living standards would be much less painful than it eventually turned out to be. While average real wages in East Germany converged quickly toward the West German level within a few years, employment declined markedly, and unemployment soared to a much higher level than observed in other transition countries. By the late nineties the convergence process seemed to have come to a halt. Economic growth in East Germany was even below the modest West German growth rate, and East German labor productivity was still only about 60 percent of the West German level, with the ratio of average wages converging to 80 percent. Given the implied cost disadvantage and the high level of labor force participation, there is little reason to believe that unemployment in East Germany will markedly decline in the near future.

Union wage policy has played an important role in this development, but it cannot fully explain the downward rigidity of wages because union coverage in East Germany is relatively low. One important factor that may explain wage rigidity despite mass unemployment is the high level of income support for the unemployed relative to average wages in East Germany. I have presented evidence that seems to support this view. Another factor is the widespread availability of active labor market programs, especially public works and publicly funded training programs that often provide more generous income support than regular employment in the low-wage sector. Furthermore, evaluation studies of these programs indicate that they are not effective in increasing participants' employment prospects and may even, through substitution and displacement effects, increase overall unemployment. Although there is little empirical evidence on their effects on the level of wages in Germany, economic reasoning suggests that these programs are likely to contribute importantly to downward wage rigidity and thus to the persistently high level of unemployment in East Germany. Reducing unemployment permanently would therefore call for a reduction of large-scale active labor market programs, in particular public works programs, and fundamental reforms of income support schemes for the unemployed.

Notes

1. If not stated otherwise, the following facts are taken from Franz and Steiner (2000) and Hagen and Steiner (2000). An analysis of labor market developments after unification set in a broader economic context is given by Sinn and Sinn (1992).

2. Sinn (2000b) considers this as the most alarming weakness of the East German situation and discusses possible reasons for it.

3. However, the share of people in "active" labor market programs in East Germany is much larger than in West Germany (see later discussion).

4. This section draws on Franz and Steiner (2000).

5. Sinn (2000a, section 4) discusses various reasons for this development and concludes that there is no convincing single explanation.

6. This section draws on Steiner (1997a, 1997b).

7. If not stated otherwise, this section draws on Bundesministerium für Arbeit und Sozialordnung (1999).

8. There also exist various wage subsidy programs that aim at increasing employment of low-productivity workers by paying wage subsidies to firms employing such workers. These programs are targeted at special groups whose employment prospects in the labor market are poor for various reasons, such as old age, low skills, and disability. Furthermore, benefit withdrawal rates of less than 100 percent in unemployment compensation and social assistance programs can be viewed as part of ALMP. For a general survey of wage subsidies in Germany, see Buslei and Steiner (2000).

9. This section draws on Hagen and Steiner (2000) as well as Kraus, Puhani, and Steiner (1999, 2000).

References

Bundesministerium für Arbeit und Sozialordnung. 1999. *Grundinformationen und Daten zur Sozialhilfe*. Bonn.

Buslei, H., and V. Steiner. 2000. *Beschäftigungseffekte von Lohnsubventionen im Niedriglohn-bereich.* ZEW Wirtschaftsanalysen 42. Nomos-Verlag: Baden-Baden.

Franz, W., and V. Steiner. 2000. "Wages in the East German Transition Process: Facts and Explanations." *German Economic Review* 1(2): 241–70.

Hagen, T., and V. Steiner. 2000. *Von der Finanzierung von Arbeitslosigkeit zur Förderung von Arbeit: Analysen und Empfehlungen zur Steigerung der Effizienz und Effektivität der Arbeitsmarktpolitik in Deutschland.* ZEW Wirtschaftsanalysen 51. Nomos-Verlag: Baden-Baden.

Kraus, F., P. A. Puhani, and V. Steiner. 1999. "Employment Effects of Publicly Financed Training Programs: The East German Experience." *Jahrbücher für Nationalökonomie und Statistik* 219(1 and 2): 216–48.

———. 2000. "Do Public Works Programs Work in Eastern Germany?" In S. Polachek, ed., *Research in Labor Economics* 19: 275–314.

Lehmann, H. 2001. "Active Labor Market Policies in Central Europe: First Lessons." In R. T. Riphahn, D. J. Snower, and K. F. Zimmermann, eds., *Employment Policy in Transition: The Lessons of German Integraton for the Labor Market.* Berlin: Springer.

Sachverständigenrat zur Begutachtung der Gesamtwirtschaftlichen Entwicklung. 2000. *Jahresgutachten 1999/2000.* Stuttgart.

Schneider, H., and others. 2000. "Die Effizienz der Arbeitsmarktpolitik in den neuen Bundesländern: Eine Bilanz der Vergangenheit und Ansätze für künftige Reformen." *Sonderhefte* (March 2000). Halle, Germany: Institut für Wirtschaftsforschung Halle.

Sinn, G., and H.-W. Sinn. 1992. *Jumpstart: The Economic Unification of Germany.* Cambridge, Mass.: MIT Press.

Sinn, H.-W. 2000a. "Sozialstaat im Wandel." In R. Hauser, ed., *Die Zukunft des Sozialstaats, Schriften des Vereins für Socialpolitik* 271. Berlin: Duncker & Humblot.

———. 2000b. "Germany's Economic Unification: An Assessment after Ten Years." *CESifo WP* 247. Munich.

Steiner, V. 1997a. "Extended Benefit: Entitlement Periods and the Duration of Unemployment in West Germany." ZEW Discussion Paper 97–14. Center for European Economic Research (ZEW), Mannheim.

———.1997b. "Kann die Effizienz der deutschen Arbeitslosenversicherung erhöht werden?" *Beihefte zur Konjunkturpolitik (Applied Economics Quarterly)* 46: 137–68.

Steiner, V., and F. Kraus. 1995. "Structural Differences in Long-Term Unemployment between West and East Germany after Unification." *Beihefte zur Konjunkturpolitik (Applied Economics Quarterly)* 43: 111–34.

PART III

Spatial Disparities and Labor Mobility

CHAPTER 14

Poland: Regional Dimensions of Unemployment

Jan Rutkowski and Marcin Przybyla

The Polish economy has enjoyed nine consecutive years of expansion. However, despite relatively high growth rates, unemployment in Poland has been higher than in many other transition economies in Central and Eastern Europe. After a period of decline in the mid-1990s, unemployment levels began to rise and reached over 18 percent in 2001 (according to the Labor Force Survey), largely as a result of accelerated industrial restructuring. The situation, however, varies significantly across regions. There are regions where employment is growing and unemployment is low, while in others employment is falling and unemployment remains high.

The purpose of this chapter is, first, to document the latest trends in labor market developments with a focus on regional disparities; second, to identify factors behind the low internal migration flows, despite very large differences in unemployment rates across regions; and finally, to identify structural and institutional factors, such as minimum wage regulation, influencing creation of job opportunities at the regional level.

Regional Disparities

The transformation of the Polish economy that began in the early 1990s led to a sharp decline in employment in those regions (voivodships) where there was little output diversification. The most severely affected were northern regions dominated previously by large state-owned farms, and single-industry regions and towns, such as Lodz with the initial concentration of the textile and clothing industry, Starachowice with the automobile assembly industry, and Walbrzych with coal mining. As a result, the economic geography of Poland is now characterized by striking differences in availability of job opportunities (figure 14.1) and unemployment rate differentials (table 14.1).

The regional disparities in unemployment rates that emerged in the early 1990s have proven to be remarkably persistent. Regions where unemployment was high in 1993 still have high unemployment rates in 2001, despite several years of sustained economic growth. In the period 1993–98, the dispersion of unemployment rates between voivodships (measured as a ratio of maximum to minimum unemployment rate) increased almost twofold, even though an overall unemployment rate for the whole country decreased to its lowest levels (table 14.1). The ratio dropped in 1999, but this is due to the administrative reform, effective January 1, 1999, that changed the boundaries of existing voivodships and reduced the overall number of voivodships from 49 to 16. The larger regional units imply smaller disparities in unemployment rates among them.

Given existing large and persistent unemployment rate disparities accompanied by increasing wage differentials across regions, one could expect internal migration flows to increase.[1] The next section presents the evidence that it did not happen and gives the explanations for the low levels of internal migration.

FIGURE 14.1 HIRING RATE BY VOIVODSHIPS, 1999
(Poland = 100)

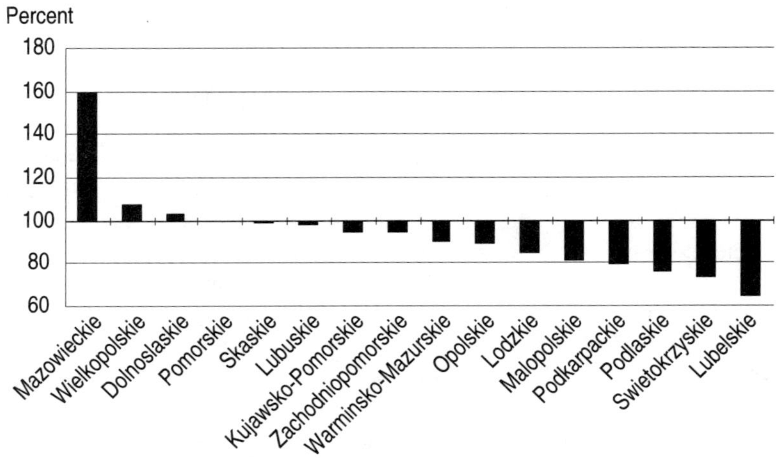

Source: Central Statistical Office 2000.

TABLE 14.1 REGIONAL UNEMPLOYMENT RATE DIFFERENTIALS, 1993–2001 (percent)

	1993	*1994*	*1995*	*1996*	*1997*	*1998*	*1999*[a]	*2000*	*2001*[b]
Poland	16.4	16.0	14.9	13.2	10.3	10.4	13.1	15.0	15.8
Maximum	30.3	29.8	28.4	25.7	21.2	20.5	21.4	24.5	25.6
Minimum	7.6	6.5	5.4	4.1	2.7	2.6	8.7	11.1	11.9
Maximum/minimum	4.0	4.6	5.3	6.3	7.9	7.9	2.5	2.2	2.2

a. The administrative reform, effective January 1, 1999, changed the boundaries and number of the voivodships.
b. April.
Source: Data from the Central Statistical Office, *Statistical Bulletin*, various issues.

Internal Migration

The internal migration flows remain at a very low level, despite large regional differences in unemployment rates. In 1998 the official statistics reported a total net inflow to urban areas of 8,600 persons, a negligible number (even assuming that migration is substantially underestimated) compared with over 1.8 million registered unemployed at that time. Cross-sectional analysis shows that migration is highly correlated with the unemployment rate and hiring rate at the voivodship level (with correlation coefficients –0.6 and 0.7 respectively).[2] Inward migration flows are higher in the regions with a low unemployment rate and high hiring rate (figure 14.2A and B).

One can identify three major sets of factors that explain this low level of internal migration: operation of the housing market, the skills mismatch, and incentives to stay in the rural areas. The key factor that inhibits migration within Poland is the poorly functioning housing market. People cannot move to desirable locations due to very high housing prices in the major cities that discourage migration.

A second important factor hindering migration is that the skills required by employers in more developed regions of Poland usually differ significantly from the skills possessed by potential migrants, who tend to come from less-developed regions. Most of the new jobs have been created in the service sector, and many of those jobs require better educated workers, while a vast majority of migrants (80 percent) have only a basic vocational education or less (World Bank 2001).

Finally, there exist a number of incentives not to leave rural areas. Many people from rural areas consider their farmland as a safety net, and this reduces their willingness to migrate. Additionally, the low prices of farmland reduce the incentive to sell it, which makes it more difficult for small farmers to move from rural areas. Finally, the significant difference in contributions between the Farmers' Social Security Fund (KRUS) and the regular Social Security Fund (ZUS), given that both systems offer similar benefits, is equivalent to a tax on the movement of workers out of farm employment (World Bank 2001).

FIGURE 14.2A MIGRATION FLOWS BY VOIVODSHIPS, 1998

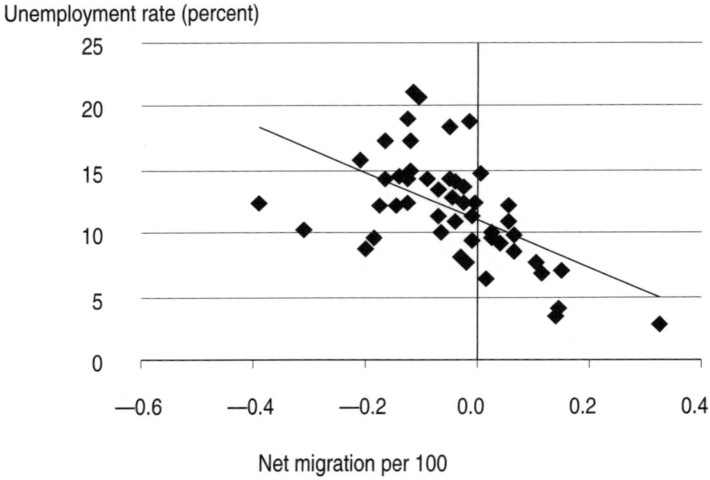

Source: Central Statistical Office 1999.

FIGURE 14.2B MIGRATION FLOWS BY VOIVODSHIPS, 1998

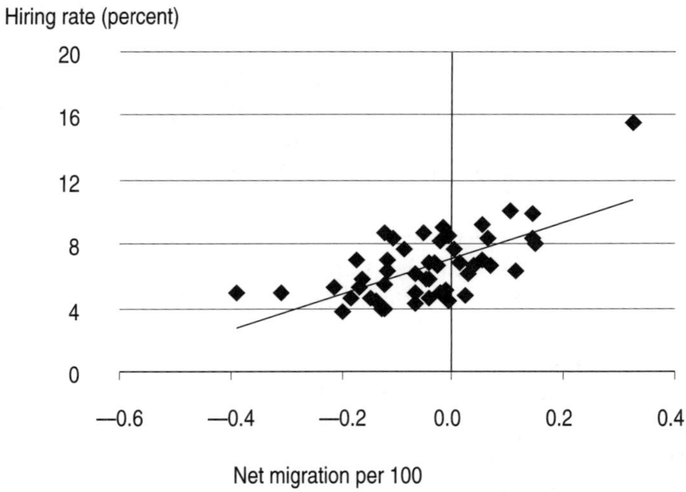

Source: Central Statistical Office 1999.

Structural Factors Affecting Job Creation

In this section we deal with the role of structural factors in determining the availability of job opportunities at the regional level. We try to explain why some regional labor markets are more buoyant than others. Our focus is on the role of exogenous initial conditions and structural factors rather than on the endogenous growth variables.

We identified five broad components of economic structure that can be relevant for job creation: (1) industrial structure, (2) capital and productivity, (3) human capital, (4) labor market structure, and (5) physical infrastructure. For these components we considered the following indicators:

Industrial structure

- Services (as a share of total employment)
- Industry and construction (as a share of total employment)
- Private sector outside agriculture (as a share of total employment)[3]
- Small- and medium-size firms (as a share of total employment)[4]

Capital and productivity

- Capital-to-labor ratio
- Labor productivity (output per worker)

Human capital

- Population with less than secondary education (as a share of total population)
- Population of working age (as a share of total population)

Labor market structure

- Wage level
- Labor cost per unit of output (wage/productivity)
- The decile ratio (top decile/bottom decile wage)
- Bottom decile/median wage

Physical Infrastructure

- Urban population (as a share of total population)
- Road density
- Railways density
- Telephone lines (per 100 persons)

In table 14.2 we present correlation coefficients between the hiring rate and the proposed indicators in order to see if they are indeed good predictors of the availability of job opportunities.

All correlation coefficients have an expected sign and are statistically significant, which means that the chosen indicators are relevant correlates of the hiring rate. Put differently, all specified structural factors significantly affect the availability of job opportunities at the regional level. Some of the most interesting relationships are presented in figures 14.3A–E.

The analysis of the correlation matrix indicates that four factors are key in determining the hiring rate. First is the industrial structure. In particular, regions with a developed service sector hire many more workers than do regions where services play a less important part (figure 14.3A).

The second factor is human capital. The hiring rate is higher the larger the proportion of the population with secondary or higher education (figure 14.3B).

Infrastructure, especially the communication infrastructure, is the third factor. The greater the density of telephone lines—a proxy for communication opportunities and access to information—the higher the hiring rate (figure 14.3C).

Finally, there is the wage level and structure. The hiring rate is significantly higher in regions where productivity is high relative to wages, that is, in regions with relatively low labor costs (figure 14.3D). Also the hiring rate tends to be higher in regions with a less compressed wage structure, that is, where wages are more flexible (figure 14.3E).

Naturally, the variables relating to different aspects of the economic structure are not independent. Instead they are a part of a larger syndrome—let us call it the

TABLE 14.2. CORRELATION COEFFICIENTS BETWEEN THE HIRING RATE AND SELECTED INDICATORS OF ECONOMIC STRUCTURE
(percent)

Indicator	*Hiring rate*
Hiring rate	1.000
Share of services in employment	0.870
Share of industry in employment	0.454
Capital-to-labor ratio	0.540
Productivity	0.662
Population with less than secondary education	–0.850
Working-age population	0.713
Wage level	0.597
Labor costs	–0.639
Decile ratio	0.535
Bottom decile/median wage	–0.441
Urban population	0.790
Road density	0.254
Rail density	0.476
Telephone lines density	0.824

Note: For 49 voivodships, 1997.
Source: Central Statistical Office 1997.

job creation potential—and they are related to each other. For example, the density of telephone lines is strongly correlated with urbanization, and urbanization in turn is strongly correlated with the share of the service sector. This gives rise to the issue of assessing an independent impact of the variables, which can be addressed in a standard way by means of multivariate regression analysis.

The results of the regression analysis of the determinants of the hiring rate are presented in the appendix (table 14.A1). The regression analysis reveals that, after adjusting for the effect of other variables, indicators of the infrastructure (telephone density, road density, rail density, urbanization) do not have a significant effect on the hiring rate. The impact of these variables is almost fully captured by other variables, and they are in a sense redundant. Thus, we have searched for a parsimonious version of the regression equation by means of stepwise estimation.[5] The result—an equation that includes only significant variables that contribute to the model's explanatory power—is presented in appendix table 14.A2.

Regression analysis confirms that the industrial employment structure, educational attainment of the labor force, labor costs, and wage flexibility play a crucial role in laying down a basis for job creation. Knowing these five factors, one is able

FIGURE 14.3A HIRING RATE AND THE SERVICE SECTOR

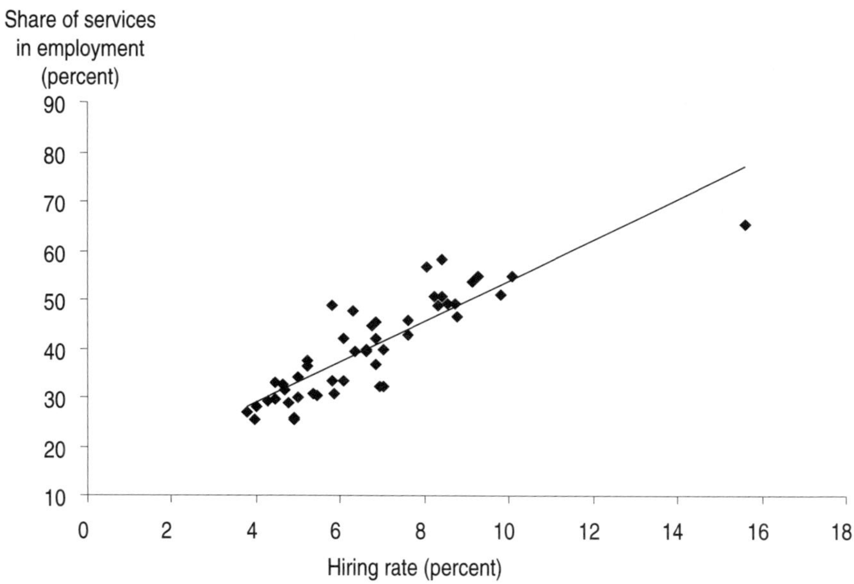

Source: Central Statistical Office 1997.

FIGURE 14.3B HIRING RATE AND EDUCATION

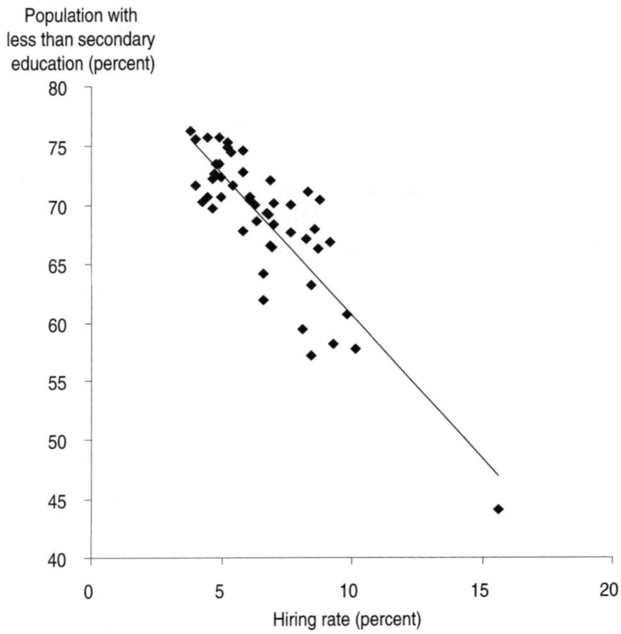

Source: Central Statistical Office 1997.

FIGURE 14.3C HIRING RATE AND THE COMMUNICATION INFRASTRUCTURE

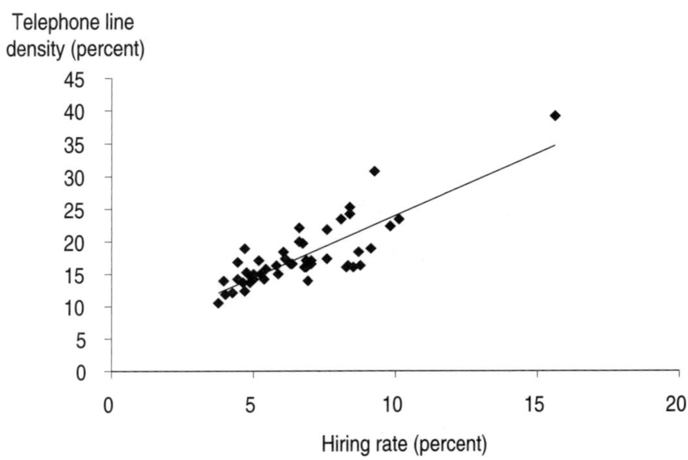

Source: Central Statistical Office 1997.

FIGURE 14.3D HIRING RATE AND LABOR COST

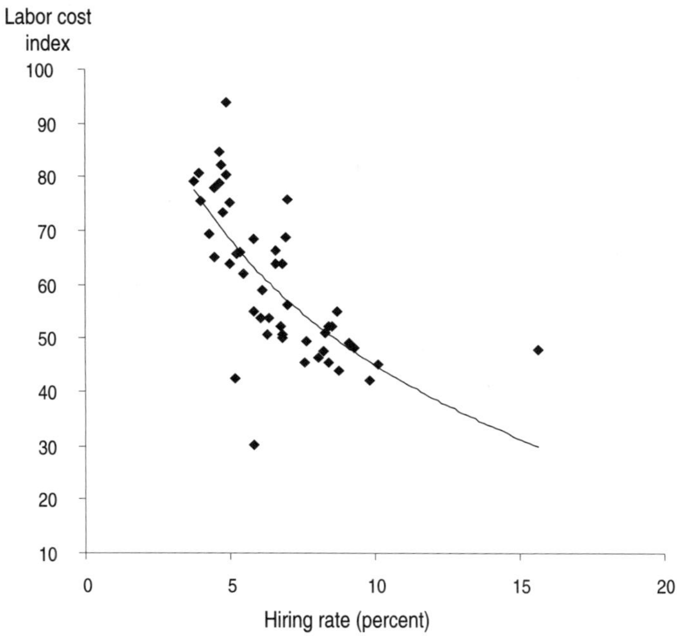

Source: Central Statistical Office 1997.

FIGURE 14.3E HIRING RATE AND WAGE STRUCTURE

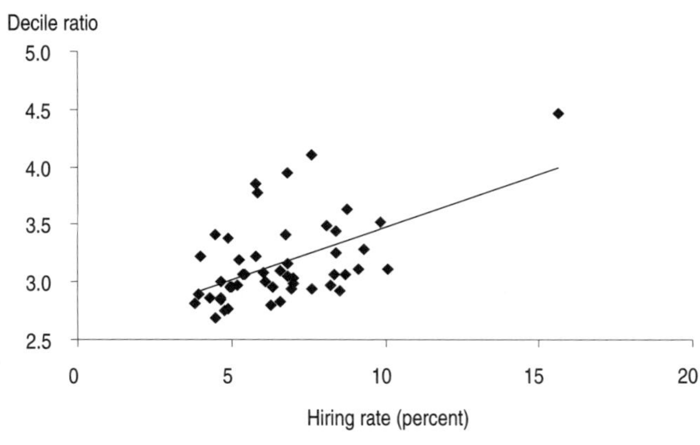

Source: Central Statistical Office 1997.

to explain about 85 percent of the variance in the hiring rate. In other words, just a few major elements of the economic structure account for most of the regional variation in the availability of job opportunities.

The effects of structural variables are not only statistically significant, but they are also quite strong. The strongest are the effect of education and employment structure. A one standard deviation increase in the share of population with secondary or higher education will lead to a 0.45 standard deviation increase in the log hiring rate (all else held equal). A similar effect on the hiring rate would occur with the one standard deviation increase in the share of services in employment.

The hiring rate is also sensitive to changes in wages and labor costs. If the level of wages in a region were to rise by 1 percent, then we might expect the hiring rate to fall by 0.9 percent (productivity and other variables held constant). Put differently, an increase in the wage level, if not matched by a proportional increase in productivity, is likely to result in lower hiring.

In addition, the hiring rate is influenced by wage dispersion. A more compressed wage distribution, especially at the bottom, results in lower hiring. Specifically, a 10 percent increase in the ratio of the bottom decile wage to the median (P_{10} ratio) results in a 12.7 percent decrease in the predicted hiring rate.[6] (A 10 percent increase in the P_{10} ratio would occur if wages of the bottom decile earners rose by 10 percent, while the median wage remained constant.) This result implies that raising the minimum wage is likely to negatively affect the hiring of less-skilled workers. We examine the issue of minimum wage regulations and their impact on the regional labor markets in the next section.

Minimum Wage Regulations

The minimum wage in Poland is set around 40 percent of the average (mean) wage. This figure indicates that an average worker earns substantially more than the minimum wage, which—according to popular perception—implies that the minimum wage is very low, with no negative effect on employment. However, this aggregate figure seems to obscure the real effect or the "bite" of the minimum wage. This effect is given by the answer to the following question: "How far is the minimum wage from the wage that low-productivity workers can bargain for in the labor market?" If the minimum wage is close to the actual wages of low-productivity workers, then the minimum wage is likely to limit the demand for this category of workers.

In order to measure the bite of the minimum wage, one needs to define the local labor market for a specific category of workers. We do so by using *median* regional wages for various categories of workers who represent low-productivity workers.[7] We define the bite of the minimum wage for a given category of workers as the ratio of the national minimum wage to the region-specific and category-specific median wage. The results are shown in appendix table 14.A3.

The regional variation in the bite of the minimum wage is quite substantial. In the Warszawskie (capital) region, the minimum wage accounts for only 36 percent of the region's median wage. At the other extreme, in the Ciechanowskie and Bialskopodlaskie regions, the minimum wage accounts for as much as 58 percent of the regional median. This means that, in the depressed regions of Poland, the national minimum wage is relatively close to the "going" regional wage, much closer than in the buoyant regions. Accordingly, in the depressed labor markets, the national minimum wage is likely to distort the wage adjustment mechanism and thus contribute to unemployment.

Naturally, the bite of the minimum wage is particularly marked in the case of weak worker groups. For a median worker the bite is 48 percent, but it is 65 percent for young workers, 72 percent for workers in elementary occupations, and as much as 82 percent for bottom-quintile workers. These figures suggest that the minimum wage truncates the wage distribution for less-productive workers and thus is likely to bar them from employment.

The effect comes out even stronger when one looks at the bite of the minimum wage for low-productivity workers across regions. In the most depressed regions of Poland—such as Slupskie, Wloclawskie, or Ciechanowskie—the national minimum wage accounts for well over 90 percent of the median wage for bottom quintile workers. In particular, in the Slupskie region the bottom quintile workers earn on average only 3 percent more than the national minimum wage! This makes one wonder how many low-productivity workers in, say, the Slupskie region, who are out of jobs, would have been employed if there were no minimum wage. These figures provide a strong indication that the seemingly low minimum wage may cost a nonnegligible number of jobs in the depressed regions of Poland.

Does the national minimum wage contribute to unemployment in the depressed, low-productivity regions? Does it inhibit chances to find a job? Below we present some evidence that points to positive answers to these questions. As before, we measure the effect of the minimum wage using the ratio of the minimum wage to the region's bottom decile wage, and refer to this ratio as the bite of the minimum wage.

Correlation analysis indicates that there is a distinct association between the bite of the minimum wage and regional labor market conditions. Unemployment is higher in regions where the minimum wage is high relative to wages of low-productivity workers (figure 14.4A), and the association between these two variables is quite strong (correlation coefficient $r = 0.61$). Similarly, the hiring rate tends to be low in regions where the minimum wage is high relative to the first decile wage (figure 14.4B).[8] This suggests that the nationwide minimum wage may limit job opportunities and contribute to unemployment in those regions of Poland where the bite of the minimum wage is particularly strong.

However, bivariate correlation alone provides insufficient evidence for causality. Hence, we performed regression analysis to test for the independent (net)

FIGURE 14.4A THE BITE OF THE MINIMUM WAGE AND THE UNEMPLOYMENT RATE, 1998

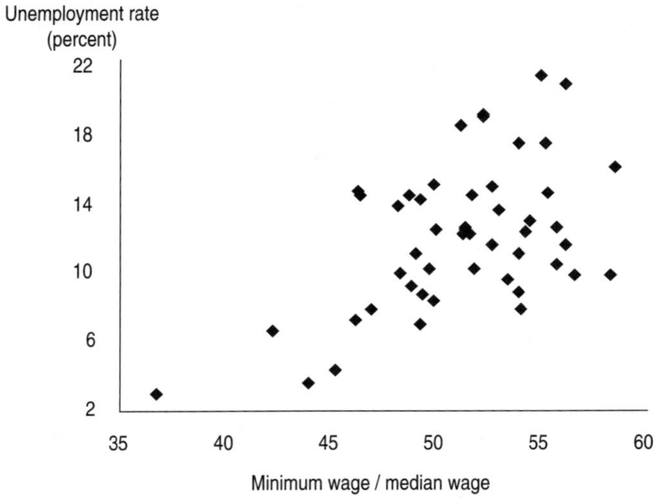

Note: For bottom quintile workers in 49 regions.
Source: Central Statistical Office 1998 and 1999.

FIGURE 14.4B THE BITE OF THE MINIMUM WAGE AND THE HIRING RATE, 1998

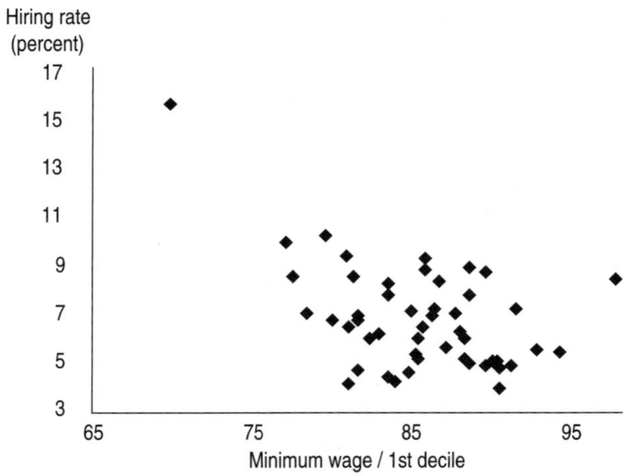

Note: For bottom quintile workers in 49 regions.
Source: Central Statistical Office 1998 and 1999.

impact of the minimum wage on regional unemployment. To control for the regions' economic status, we used variables related to the regions' GDP per capita, investment, level of human capital, employment structure, and infrastructure. The results are presented in appendix table 14.A4.

Regression analysis corroborates the hypothesis that when the national minimum wage is high relative to the region's bottom decile wage, it is likely to prevent low-productivity workers from employment. The detrimental impact of the high minimum wage is considerable. All else held equal, a 1 percentage point increase in the ratio of the minimum wage to the first decile wage would be associated with an increase in the region's unemployment by a 0.34 percentage point. This 1 percentage point increase would occur in an average region if the minimum wage were raised by about 1.2 percent. Put differently, a 1 point decrease in the unemployment rate in an average region would require a 3.6 percent decline in the nationwide minimum wage (other things held constant). However, an important caveat should be made: this prediction is based on a pattern observed in cross-sectional data, which does not necessarily hold in a dynamic setting. The estimate is presented solely for illustrative purposes and should be treated with necessary caution. The same remark refers to the estimates of the impact of the minimum wage presented below: they are meant to show the expected magnitude of the minimum wage effect, not a precise prediction.

Looking at the impact of the minimum wage from a different angle, we find that a 10 percent increase in the nationwide minimum wage would be expected to lead to about a 2.8 point increase in the unemployment rate in regions where the bite of the minimum wage is around the mean value (82 percent). In low-productivity regions, this impact would be still larger. For example, in regions such as Bialskopodlaskie, Nowosadeckie, Siedleckie, or Zamojskie (where the minimum wage accounts for 90 percent of the first decile wage), a 10 percent increase in the minimum wage would bring about a 3.1 percentage point increase in unemployment, other things held constant. This is a considerable effect, associated with a substantial social cost.

Conclusion

The broadly conceived economic structure is a key factor influencing the availability of job opportunities. Hiring is higher in regions that are urbanized, with a high level of human capital and with a modern (service-oriented) employment structure. Hiring is also higher in regions characterized by low labor costs, that is, by high productivity relative to wages. Furthermore, hiring is higher in regions with more flexible labor markets (for example, with a more flexible wage structure). Finally, hiring is higher in regions with well-developed modern infrastructure, especially related to communication.

Remarkably, only a few structural variables can explain some 80 percent of the regional variation in the hiring rate. This implies that the independent contribution of variables related to economic growth is quite limited. This is probably owing to the fact that they are strongly influenced by and thus correlated with structural variables. Hence, one does not necessarily need "growth variables" in order to satisfactorily explain regional differences in hiring. Information on economic structure is sufficient to predict the hiring rate and other key variables characterizing labor market conditions.

The policy implications of the analysis are straightforward. The results of the regional analysis support and reinforce fundamental principles of the economics of growth. In order to create jobs, regions and the whole country should:

- Promote industrial restructuring and the development of the service industry
- Invest in human capital
- Invest in physical capital and promote the development of the modern infrastructure (for example, communication)
- Foster competitive labor markets and the flexible wage structure.

These measures are likely to lead to greater labor market dynamics, better labor market prospects, including better chances to find a job, higher outflows from unemployment, and shorter job search duration. The relatively high minimum wage limits employment chances of low-productivity workers, especially in less-developed regions of Poland. In such regions the nationwide minimum wage accounts for some 90 percent of wages awarded to low-paid workers. This truncates the earnings distribution and thus is likely to contribute to unemployment. This prediction is borne out by the evidence. An increase in the national minimum wage would most likely lead to an increase in unemployment among low-skilled workers in depressed regions of Poland. Thus one can presume that a lower national minimum wage, or a minimum wage differentiated by regions so as to factor in the degree of labor market slack, would help to reduce unemployment.

Appendix

TABLE 14.A1 REGRESSION OF THE HIRING RATE ON VARIABLES RELATED TO ECONOMIC STRUCTURE

Source	SS	df	MS			
Model	3.56079828	7	0.508685469	Number of obs	=	49
Residual	0.58463814	41	0.014259467	F(7, 41)	=	35.67
				Prob > F	=	0.0000
				R-squared	=	0.8590
				Adj R-squared	=	0.8349
Total	4.14543642	48	0.086363259	Root MSE	=	0.11941

lhrate	Coef.	Std. Err.	t	P>|t|	[95% Conf. Interval]	
Service[a]	0.0134357	0.0046534	2.887	0.006	0.0040379	0.0228334
Pooredu[b]	–0.0181868	0.0086198	–2.110	0.041	–0.0355948	–0.0007788
lktol[c]	–0.0446322	0.1652802	–0.270	0.788	–0.3784224	0.2891579
Productivity	0.2393695	0.1298605	1.843	0.073	–0.022889	0.501628
Wages	–0.8553322	0.4140516	–2.066	0.045	–1.691526	–0.0191379
Decile ratio	–1.258512	0.5957177	–2.113	0.041	–2.461588	–0.0554358
ltelef[d]	0.1100145	0.155808	0.706	0.484	–0.2046462	0.4246752
Constant	6.350816	3.746115	1.695	0.098	–1.214616	13.91625

a. Share of services in employment.
b. Population with less than secondary education.
c. Capital-to-labor ratio.
d. Telephone line density.

TABLE 14.A2 REGRESSION OF THE HIRING RATE ON VARIABLES RELATED TO ECONOMIC STRUCTURE: A PARSIMONIOUS VERSION

Source	SS	df	MS			
Model	3.553529	5	0.7107058	Number of obs	=	49
Residual	0.591907422	43	0.013765289	F(5, 43)	=	51.63
				Prob > F	=	0.0000
				R-squared	=	0.8572
				Adj R-squared	=	0.8406
Total	4.14543642	48	0.086363259	Root MSE	=	0.11733

lhrate	Coef.	Std. Err.	t	P>|t|	Beta
Service[a]	0.0131943	0.0039268	3.360	0.002	0.4561787
Pooredu[b]	–0.0220275	0.0058564	–3.761	0.001	–0.4546573
Productivity	0.2474971	0.1213938	2.039	0.048	0.2502439
Wages	–0.9231423	0.3401929	–2.714	0.010	–0.3250676
Decile ratio	–1.267448	0.5837353	–2.171	0.035	–0.1783697
Constant	7.747325	2.354791	3.290	0.002	.

a. Share of services in employment.
b. Population with less than secondary education.

TABLE 14.A3 MINIMUM WAGE AS A PERCENTAGE OF THE MEDIAN WAGES BY VOIVODSHIP, 1998

Voivodship	*All workers*	*Low-productivity workers*[a]	*Young workers*[b]	*Elementary occupations*[c]	*Primary education*
Poland	47.6	81.6	65.0	72.0	57.3
Warszawskie	36.3	69.2	48.7	60.4	48.6
Bialskopodlaskie	57.9	90.6	76.4	79.0	69.9
Bialostockie	48.9	79.4	69.5	74.6	56.2
Bielskie	48.8	80.5	62.4	71.7	57.4
Bydgoskie	47.8	81.0	62.7	72.6	56.2
Chelmskie	52.2	84.3	72.0	69.4	66.3
Ciechanowskie	58.1	92.2	75.4	76.4	69.8
Czestochowskie	49.5	85.7	63.4	71.6	58.3
Elblaskie	51.8	88.0	69.2	79.1	68.0
Gdanskie	45.7	83.0	66.8	71.3	54.7
Gorzowskie	51.0	89.1	71.5	74.8	63.8
Jeleniogorskie	51.3	81.7	65.4	69.4	60.4
Kaliskie	55.7	87.5	73.5	74.4	66.8
Katowickie	41.8	77.9	60.0	71.4	47.1
Kieleckie	50.9	85.8	71.7	77.7	57.3
Koninskie	45.8	81.0	67.5	72.5	56.0
Koszalinskie	51.8	85.3	67.4	73.2	61.2
Krakowskie	44.8	77.0	59.5	68.3	50.7
Krosnienskie	52.5	83.0	73.6	74.4	57.9
Legnickie	46.0	83.0	68.6	76.9	58.4
Leszczynskie	53.0	84.7	71.3	70.6	62.3
Lubelskie	48.4	81.0	66.3	70.3	55.9
Lomzynskie	55.3	89.8	78.6	73.5	68.0
Lodzkie	48.6	80.3	68.7	67.2	57.2
Nowosadeckie	53.5	89.9	76.3	76.1	66.2
Olsztynskie	50.7	85.2	65.2	73.3	63.5
Opolskie	49.3	82.3	69.8	72.2	54.8
Ostroleckie	49.5	83.4	71.3	75.1	55.6
Pilskie	54.0	87.1	66.8	78.0	65.7
Piotrkowskie	48.8	84.9	71.0	73.9	55.4
Plockie	48.3	87.7	72.0	74.3	61.1
Poznanskie	43.5	76.5	59.4	69.5	55.1
Przemyskie	53.8	89.1	78.8	71.0	65.5
Radomskie	54.9	86.6	78.9	75.0	66.1
Rzeszowskie	51.2	84.4	69.9	72.9	56.9
Siedleckie	53.5	90.0	83.0	76.1	64.3
Sieradzkie	56.2	88.1	75.5	73.1	68.8
Skierniewickie	53.6	87.8	68.7	77.3	72.4
Slupskie	55.7	97.2	81.9	82.0	68.5
Suwalskie	54.6	91.0	77.5	76.4	65.9
Szczecinskie	47.9	80.8	64.7	70.1	59.8
Tarnobrzeskie	49.6	80.5	73.2	78.3	54.9
Tarnowskie	51.4	84.8	72.0	74.4	57.3
Torunskie	52.2	88.0	66.7	68.9	61.6
Walbrzyskie	53.5	85.1	68.8	75.3	62.7
Wloclawskie	54.8	93.8	78.5	79.4	72.5

Voivodship	*All workers*	*Low-productivity workers*[a]	*Young workers*[b]	*Elementary occupations*[c]	*Primary education*
Wroclawskie	46.5	79.0	62.8	72.8	56.8
Zamojskie	55.3	89.5	78.6	75.6	65.2
Zielonogorskie	51.0	86.1	65.8	81.7	64.6
Percentage of all workers	100.0	20.0	8.6	10.0	14.5

Note: The minimum wage is 40 percent of the average (mean) wage; the median is calculated separately for each category of workers. Earnings by occupation in October 1998.
a. Bottom quintile workers in a given region. The median wage for the bottom quintile workers is the first decile wage.
b. Workers age 24 or less.
c. Elementary occupations include sales and service elementary occupations, agricultural laborers, and laborers in mining, construction, manufacturing, and transport.

TABLE 14.A4 REGRESSION OF THE REGIONAL UNEMPLOYMENT RATE ON THE BITE OF THE MINIMUM WAGE AND VARIABLES INDICATING REGIONS' ECONOMIC STATUS

Variable	*Regression (1)*	*Equation (2)*
Bite[a]	0.266*	0.344†
GDP[b]	–1.017	—
Invest[c]	–1.396	—
Pooredu[d]	0.424‡	0.439†
Service[e]	0.254†	0.225†
Telefon[f]	–0.028	—
Constant	–29.717	–56.253
R2	0.500	0.488
Adj R2	0.429	0.454
N	49	49

— Not applicable.
* Significant at the 10 percent significance level.
† Significant at the 1 percent significance level in a two-tailed test.
‡ Significant at the 5 percent significance level in a two-tailed test.
Note: The parsimonious specification (column 2) was produced by means of stepwise regression (backward selection method).
a. The national minimum wage as a percentage of the region's bottom decile wage.
b. Log GDP per capita.
c. Log investment per capita.
d. Population with less than secondary education (as percent of total population).
e. Services as a percent of employment.
f. Telephone lines per 100 population.

Notes

1. Deichmann and Henderson (2000) found that the relative wage variance across regions increased in manufacturing from 0.62 in 1994 to 0.76 in 1998, and in services from 0.54 to 0.75 respectively.

2. Rutkowski (2000) shows that the hiring rate is the best indicator of the availability of job opportunities.

3. The data are not available at the voivodship level.

4. The data are not available at the voivodship level.

5. We performed both a forward and a backward selection search and obtained identical results.

6. Alternatively, a 10 percent increase in the decile ratio would lead to an 8.5 percent increase in the predicted hiring rate.

7. Specifically, we look at the following proxies for low-productivity workers: bottom-quintile workers, young workers, workers in elementary occupations, and finally workers with only primary education.

8. The hiring rate is defined as the number of hires relative to the population of working age (18 to 64), and it reflects the probability of being hired.

References

Central Statistical Office. Various issues. *Statistical Bulletin.* Warsaw.

———. 1997. *1997 Enterprise Survey*. Warsaw.

———. 1998. *The Survey of Earnings by Occupation.* Warsaw.

———. 1999. *Statistical Yearbook of Voivodships.* Warsaw.

———. 2000. *Statistical Yearbook of Voivodships.* Warsaw.

Deichmann and Henderson. 2000. "Urban and Regional Dynamics in Poland." Policy Research Working Paper 2457. World Bank, Washington, D.C.

Rutkowski. 2000. “Structural Determinants of Job Creation.” Draft. World Bank, Washington, D.C.

———. 2001. “Low-paid Employment in Poland.” Draft. World Bank, Washington, D.C.

World Bank. 2001. *Poland—Labor Market Study: The Challenge of Job Creation*. Washington, D.C.

CHAPTER 15

Regional Disparities in Unemployment in Central and Eastern Europe: The Case of Hungary

Károly Fazekas

Full employment, social equality, and balanced regional development were major policy goals during the planned economy era in Central and Eastern European countries (CEECs) for more than four decades. It was in this field of "socialist achievements" that the most dramatic changes occurred over the last 10 years of transition. Where full employment, high activity, scarcity of labor, low wage levels, and limited income dispersion used to be the norm, the situation now is just the opposite in many respects. The transition in these countries has been accompanied by a considerable increase in open unemployment, a high level of inactivity, and growing income disparities. One of the most shocking outcomes of the transition was the emergence of large regional disparities in terms of labor market activity and wage and income indicators.[1]

Regional labor market imbalances had been expected already at the start of the transition, given the high spatial concentration of industries most sensitive to the collapse of the COMECON market and also because of the fast decrease of agricultural employment in rural regions. What causes the real worry is that there are no signs of reversal of this negative trend. In the case of Hungary, indicators of regional labor market differences have been showing a steady upward trend.

In the first part of this chapter we describe regional disparities in the Hungarian labor market. The second part deals with the most important explanatory factors of regional labor market differences. The third section discusses an adjustment mechanism re-equilibrating regional inequalities. This will be followed by conclusions and a few policy relevant messages.

Regional Labor Market Disparities in Hungary

After the collapse of the old regime, large-scale job destruction and fast increasing unemployment rates were accompanied by considerable spatial differences. Dispersion of regional unemployment rates has been increasingly correlated with the regional wage dispersion. However, regional unemployment rate differentials in Hungary are not particularly high when compared with other countries (OECD 2000). We should note that regional labor market indicators cannot be readily compared across countries, since they are considerably affected by the size of regions and the degree to which administrative regions correspond to the actual size of the local labor markets (Boeri, Burda, and Köllő 1998) International studies are usually confined to macro-level comparisons. In the case of Hungary, this method gives a distorted picture since regional differences are much more pronounced at the lower levels of regional classification. Table 15.1 shows that the Hungarian labor market is highly fragmented. Many regional differences are within the meso and macro regions. To get relevant information on regional labor market imbalances, one should focus on the appropriate regional level.

Regions, Subregions, and Local Labor Markets

In Hungary there are four levels of regional nomenclature: the macro level with 7 large regions, the meso level with 20 regions (19 counties plus Budapest, which has a county status), the micro level with 150 microregions, and the settlement level with 3,135 communities (23 districts of the capital, 221 cities, and 2,913 villages—see maps in the appendix).

International comparisons of regional unemployment rate differences are usually based on national labor force surveys. Unfortunately, the sample size of the Hungarian Labor Force Survey is not suitable for a statistically meaningful analysis of labor market status at the micro level (CSO 2000). Thus, to analyze labor markets at this level, we used unemployment data from the register of the Hungarian Labor Market Center (HLMC). Registered unemployment rates at micro and meso

TABLE 15.1 DISPERSION OF REGISTERED UNEMPLOYMENT RATES BY TYPE OF REGION, MARCH 2001
(percent)

Type of region	*Range*	*Minimum*	*Maximum*	*Standard deviation*
Micro regions	22.81	2.36	25.17	4.22
Meso regions (counties)	13.54	2.36	15.91	2.91
Macro regions	9.99	3.13	13.12	2.95

Source: Institute of Economics, Hungarian Academy of Science (IE-HAS), regional database.

levels are calculated by the HLMC from the number of the registered unemployed and from the estimated number of the employed population in the regions. There is no complete, regular statistics for the employed population at the settlement level, except for the years of the census.[2] Thus in the case of the settlements, the ratio of the registered unemployed to the working-age population could be used as an indicator of local unemployment.

The most important patterns of regional labor market differences at the four regional levels can be summarized as follows:

Macro-Level Dispersion of Labor Activity

Table 15.2 shows unemployment rates and employment ratios of macro regions. The central region (Budapest and its agglomeration) is in the best position. There is a clear East-West division of the country's regions. Eastern regions have the worst labor market conditions, while the western regions are much better off (map 15.1). Data show increasing top-to-bottom differences in registered unemployment rates between 1992 and 2000.

Table 15.3 shows selected labor market indicators of the 19 counties plus Budapest. Budapest, the capital, had the lowest unemployment rates throughout the transition. Borsod and Szabolcs counties along the East-Slovakian and Ukrainian border were in the worst position; Győr and Vas counties close to the Austrian border were in the most favorable position (maps 15.2 and 15.A2).[3]

MAP 15.1 UNEMPLOYMENT RATES IN MACRO REGIONS, MARCH 2001

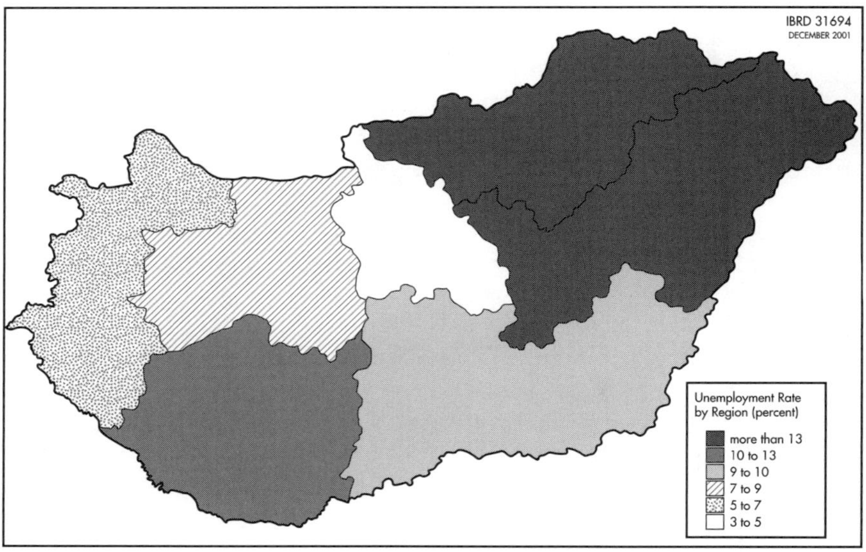

TABLE 15.2 LABOR MARKET ACTIVITY OF WORKING-AGE POPULATION BY MACRO REGIONS, 1992–2000
(percent)

Macro regions	*1992*	*1993*	*1994*	*1995*	*1996*	*1997*	*1998*	*1999*	*2000*
Employment ratio									
Central Hungary	68.7	64.6	63.3	63.1	62.7	62.5	63.4	65.7	68.1
Central Transdanubia	63.9	61.4	61.0	59.5	58.8	59.7	62.3	65.1	66.9
Western Transdanubia	69.5	67.9	67.3	65.7	66.3	66.5	68.2	69.6	70.6
Southern Transdanubia	64.7	59.8	59.1	54.8	56.7	56.3	57.5	58.9	62.5
Northern Hungary	58.6	55.7	54.0	52.5	51.7	51.5	52.3	54.2	59.6
Northern Great Plain	58.6	54.0	53.2	51.7	51.0	50.4	51.4	53.8	58.2
Southern Great Plain	64.4	60.0	59.6	59.6	59.1	59.8	60.1	61.4	63.4
Country	64.5	60.8	59.9	58.7	58.4	58.4	59.6	61.6	64.5
Top-to-bottom ratio	128.2	125.7	126.5	127.1	130.0	129.1	132.7	129.4	121.3
Unemployment rate									
Central Hungary	7.4	9.8	8.7	7.3	8.1	6.9	5.6	5.2	5.3
Central Transdanubia	11.4	12.4	10.6	10.8	10.3	8.0	6.7	6.0	4.9
Western Transdanubia	7.2	8.9	7.7	6.8	7.1	6.0	6.0	4.4	4.3
Southern Transdanubia	9.5	12.7	11.8	11.9	9.3	9.9	9.4	8.3	7.8
Northern Hungary	13.9	15.9	15.0	15.8	15.3	13.9	12.2	11.5	10.2
Northern Great Plain	12.3	14.6	13.6	13.6	13.0	11.9	11.0	10.1	9.3
Southern Great Plain	10.1	12.2	10.5	9.2	8.3	7.3	7.1	5.7	5.2
Country	9.8	11.9	10.7	10.2	9.9	8.7	7.8	7.0	6.4
Top-to-bottom ratio	193.0	178.6	194.8	232.3	215.5	231.7	217.9	261.4	237.2

Sources: CSO 2000 and LFS 2001.

Micro- and Settlement-Level Dispersion of Unemployment

Map 15.3 shows the average unemployment rates of micro regions as of December 2000. Most of the high unemployment regions are situated at the eastern, north-eastern part of Hungary along the East-Slovakian and Ukrainian border, but there are hard hit regions even within the most developed western Transdanubian regions and counties.

Table 15.4 shows the unemployed as a percentage of the working-age population at settlement levels. There is a strong correlation between these ratios and the type and the size of the settlement. The highest ratios can be found in villages (14.8 percent) and in settlements with fewer than 500 habitants (17.2 percent). Map 15.4 reveals an extremely fragmented picture of unemployment in settlements. Even in the most developed western part of the country, one can find settlements with higher than 50 percent unemployed/working-age population ratios.

There is no "travel to work" (TTW) nomenclature of Hungarian settlements similar to that in the United Kingdom, but according to studies on job searches, commuting, and migration, micro regions are close to the size and geographical distributions of local labor markets.[4] To investigate regional differences in local

TABLE 15.3 COUNTY-LEVEL PARTICIPATION RATIOS AND UNEMPLOYMENT RATES, 2000

	Participation ratios		*Unemployment rates*	
Budapest and counties	*Percent*	*Standard error*	*Percent*	*Standard error*
Budapest	57.6	1.2	5.3	0.7
Baranya	49.8	2.3	7.2	1.3
Bács-Kiskun	53.6	1.9	5.7	1.1
Békés	47.7	2.8	5.8	1.4
Borsod-Abaúj-Zemplén	46.5	1.6	11.8	1.5
Csongrád	53.2	2.9	3.9	1.7
Fejér	55.9	2.1	5.2	1.2
Jász-Nagykun-Szolnok	51.4	2.5	9.4	1.9
Győr-Moson-Sopron	57.9	2.2	4.2	0.9
Hajdú-Bihar	49.4	2.5	7.2	1.5
Heves	51.5	2.6	7.6	2.1
Komárom-Esztergom	54.8	2.3	5.4	1.3
Nógrád	50.8	2.7	9.1	1.8
Pest	56.0	1.3	5.2	0.9
Somogy	51.6	2.5	8.3	2.7
Szabolcs-Szatmár-Bereg	44.7	2.2	11.3	1.7
Tolna	52.7	2.5	8.3	1.8
Vas	61.2	2.4	4.7	1.1
Veszprém	55.8	1.7	4.1	1.1
Zala	57.3	2.3	3.9	1.3
Country	53.4	0.5	6.4	0.3

Sources: CSO 2000 and LFS 2001.

MAP 15.2 UNEMPLOYMENT RATES IN COUNTIES, 2001

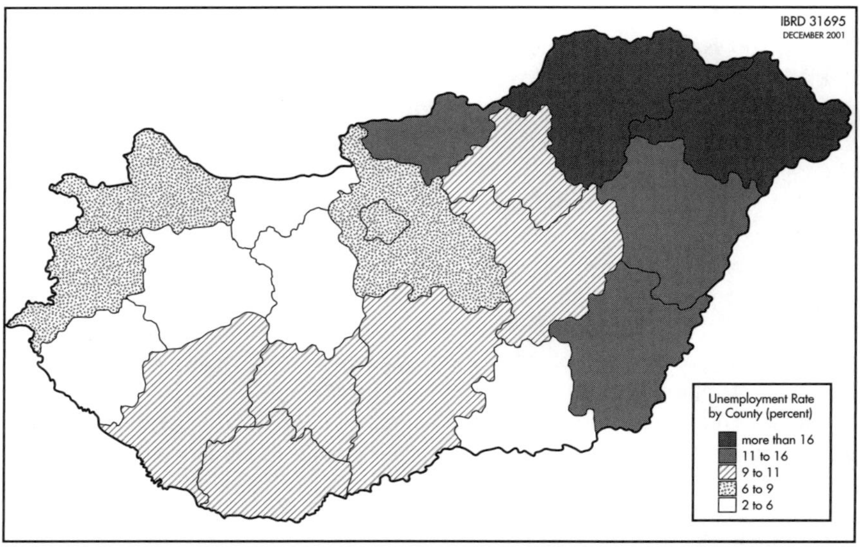

MAP 15.3 UNEMPLOYMENT RATES IN MICRO REGIONS, 2001

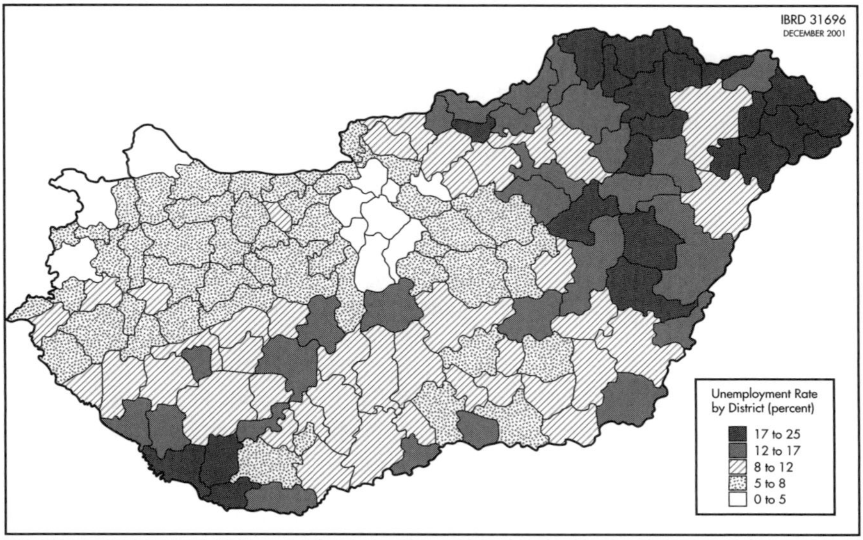

TABLE 15.4 REGISTERED UNEMPLOYED AS A PERCENTAGE OF THE WORKING-AGE POPULATION BY TYPE AND SIZE OF SETTLEMENTS, 1999

Type and size of settlement	*Mean*	*Number of observations*	*Standard deviation*	*Minimum*	*Maximum*	*Range*
Settlement type						
Capital	2.5	1	—	2.5	2.5	0.0
County level city	7.7	22	4.52	1.8	20.9	19.1
City	11.2	199	6.77	1.1	33.9	32.8
Village	14.8	2,909	11.30	0.0	79.8	79.8
Population size						
Fewer than 500	17.2	1,032	13.17	0.0	77.5	77.5
501–2,000	14.4	1,337	10.47	1.0	79.8	78.8
2,001–5,000	11.8	483	7.97	0.9	51.0	50.1
5,001–50,000	10.7	253	7.05	0.9	38.7	37.8
More than 50,000	6.7	21	3.50	1.8	16.6	14.8
Total	14.55	3,126	11.09	0.0	79.8	79.8

— Not applicable.
Source: IE-HAS regional database.

labor markets in Hungary, the best solution is to choose the micro level of the regions.

Unemployment Rate Differences in Micro Regions

Figure 15.1 shows the evolution of the average unemployment rate of the top and the bottom decile and that of the median microregions. Time paths follow a simple pattern. Unemployment rates increased until March 1993 and then decreased. In March 1993 the average ratio of the top decile was 23.8 percent, and the average rate of the bottom decile was 7.1 percent. In March 2001 the respective figures were 19.2 percent and 3.1 percent. The top-to-bottom ratios were doubled during this time from 3.1 percent to 6.2 percent.

Because of the small size of the country, the differences in unemployment rates on the micro-regional level can be evaluated as relatively high. Besides the wide range of dispersion, the long-term tendency of the figures is alarming. Regional differences have continuously increased, and disadvantages have accumulated over the years of transition. Figure 15.2 gives more detailed information on the time path of the relative differences. Expressing mean unemployment rates of the different deciles in percentages of the median (50th centile) at each period of time gives us a picture of the time path of unemployment rate differentials. This measure of relative differential is, by definition, independent from the actual levels of unemploy-

MAP 15.4 UNEMPLOYMENT AS A PERCENTAGE OF THE WORKING-AGE POPULATION AT THE SETTLEMENT LEVEL, 1999

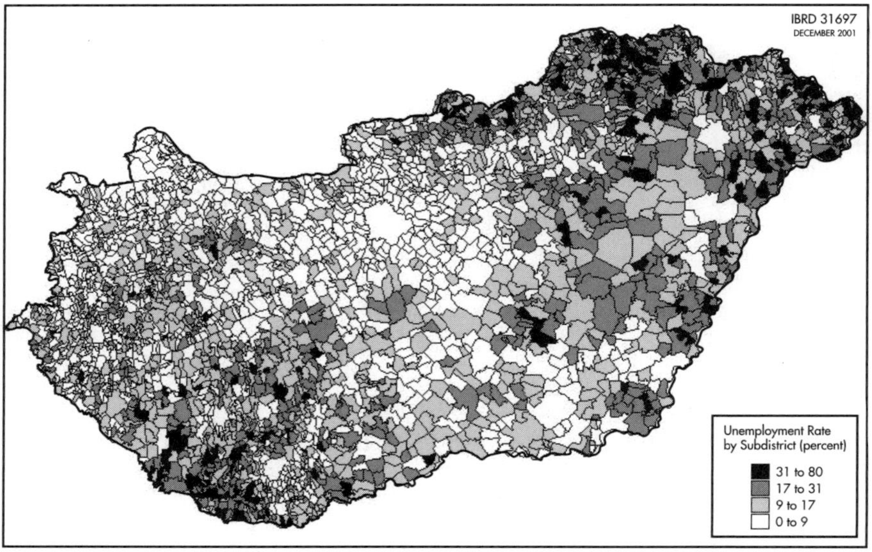

FIGURE 15.1 EVOLUTION OF AVERAGE UNEMPLOYMENT RATE OF TOP AND BOTTOM DECILES AND THE MEDIAN MICRO REGIONS, 1991–2001

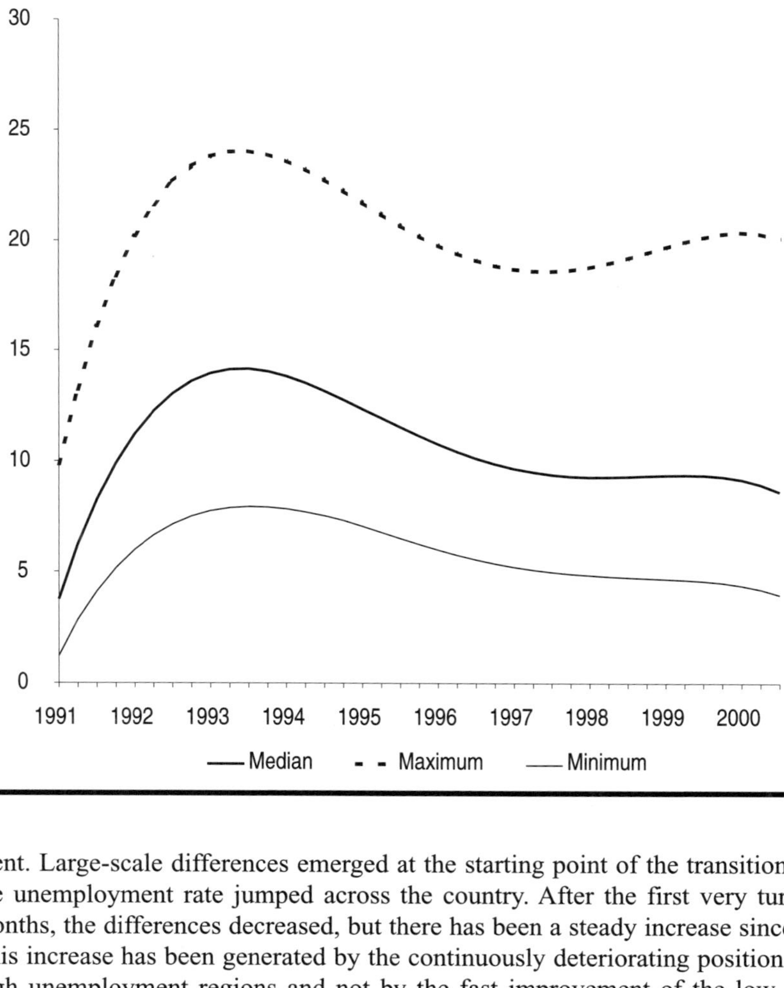

ment. Large-scale differences emerged at the starting point of the transition when the unemployment rate jumped across the country. After the first very turbulent months, the differences decreased, but there has been a steady increase since then. This increase has been generated by the continuously deteriorating position of the high unemployment regions and not by the fast improvement of the low unemployment regions.

Unemployment Rate Stability in Micro Regions

Increasing unemployment rate disparities are accompanied by high stability in the position of regions. The ranking of micro regions by their unemployment rates has not changed over the years of transition. Those that were the winners of the first transitional period turned out to be the winners of the post-transitional period. This ten-

FIGURE 15.2 TIME PATH OF RELATIVE UNEMPLOYMENT RATE DIFFERENTIALS, 1991–2001

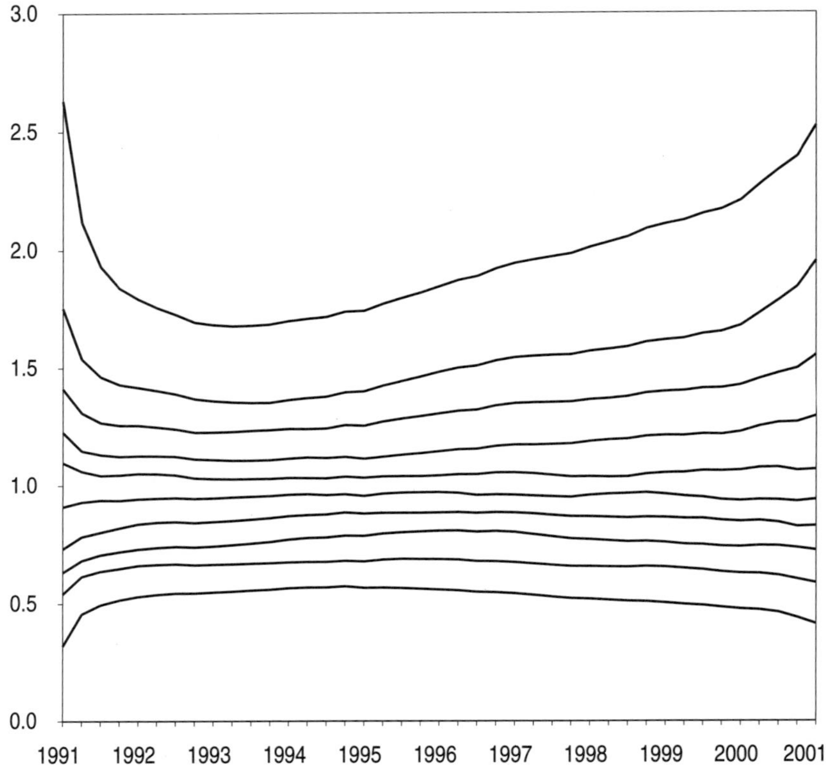

dency confirms the observation that there are stable long-term explanatory factors behind regional disparities in the labor market. This stability is shown in table 15.5. Most of the cases are found in the neighborhood of the main diagonal. Only five micro regions (3.3 percent) changed position by more than one quartile.

Accumulation of Regional Disadvantages in Hard-Hit Micro Regions

The unemployment rate is an important indicator, though by no means the only one, of employment tensions. In the worst-off regions one could observe a higher ratio of the hard-to-place (poorly educated, long-term) unemployed (Fazekas 2000b). Higher unemployment is accompanied by a higher outflow from the labor

TABLE 15.5 INTERQUARTILE UNEMPLOYMENT RATE TRANSITIONS, MARCH 1993–MARCH 2001

	Unemployment rate transition from March 1993 to March 2001				
Quartile	*Lowest quartile*	*Second quartile*	*Third quartile*	*Highest quartile*	*Number of micro regions*
Lowest quartile	25	11	1	0	37
Second quartile	10	18	10	0	38
Third quartile	2	7	20	9	38
Highest quartile	0	2	7	28	37
Number of micro regions	37	38	38	37	150

Source: IE-HAS regional database.

market. Figure 15.3 illustrates that high inactivity was concentrated in regions with higher than average unemployment rates.

The Main Causes of Regional Labor Market Disparities

Pre- and Post-transitional Causes

The emerging regional differences in transitional labor markets are often explained by the high degree of spatial concentration of industries that suffer most by transitional crises (Jackman and Rutkowski 1994). This explanation is partly challenged by the results of regional analyses in Hungary. No doubt, one of the reasons for today's regional disparities is the lack of diversification of pretransitional economic activities. Trade orientation toward the COMECON countries, and the availability of natural resources in certain regions, led to large-scale industrialization in some northeastern regions of Hungary. Nevertheless, the collapse of old industrial centers explains just a minor part of the labor market differences. These differences are much more related to the spatial distribution of the emerging new local economies during transition. While the intensity of job destruction in the first phase of transition shows an equal regional distribution, the intensity of job creation follows a quite uneven pattern (Nemes-Nagy 2001).

First Hungarian analyses of transitional local labor markets have shown that emerging unemployment rate differentials can be attributed mainly to differences in the *entrepreneurial* and *industrial* capacity of regions at the starting point of transition. Hungarian data indicate that the dominance of state-run large-scale industry on its own was negatively related to the level of unemployment emerging in a given local economy. The dominance of big state industry has led to higher unemployment only in those regions where this dominance was coupled with low entrepreneurial capacity. By entrepreneurial capacity we mean the extent to which infrastructure and the social conditions of local economic development "were

FIGURE 15.3 INACTIVITY RATE AND UNEMPLOYMENT RATES IN MICRO REGIONS, MARCH 2001

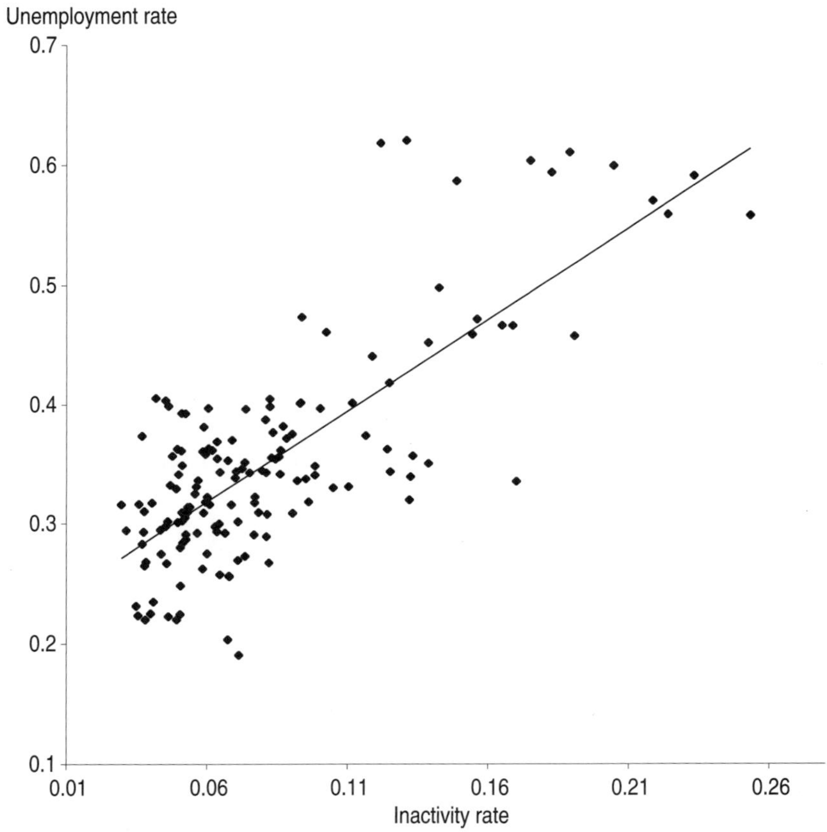

ready" at the starting point of transition (Fazekas 1996; Faluvégi and Komjáthy 1995).

Recent analyses of post-transitional characteristics of unemployment differences have shown that the explanatory power of the industrial capacity of regions has diminished, while that of the distance of regions from Budapest and the western border has increased. Post-transitional unemployment is typically high in remote agricultural regions with poor infrastructure, low educational levels, poorly developed services and trade, and large Gypsy communities.[5] The core-periphery division has become stronger in the last few years. The central agglomeration, and regions along the main East-West transport routes toward Graz and Vienna, recovered faster and benefited from the massive inflow of foreign direct investment. The worst-hit regions are typically rural, located near the east Slovakian, Romanian, and Ukrainian borders.

There are important labor market differences between urban and rural settlements even within the micro regions. Villages and smaller towns lag behind larger cities in terms of physical infrastructure and human capital endowments. Many villages are isolated from urban labor markets because of the lack of public transport, and they have a high unemployment rate for this reason (Ábrahám and Kertesi 1998; Fazekas 2000b; Kertesi and Köllő 2000).

Spatial Characteristics of Job Creation: The Effect of FDI Inflows on Local Labor Markets

The location preferences of investors have also changed since the pre-1990 era. The Hungarian data on firm creation, small business start-ups, physical capital formation, and foreign direct investment (FDI) suggest increasing rather than decreasing regional differentials in the density of firms and capital endowments. Existing labor cost differentials have not motivated the investors to move to the depressed, high unemployment regions.

According to the predominant view, foreign capital can decisively promote economic restructuring of local economies, providing capital, modern technologies, and work organization practices. Foreign capital is also a means for integration into the global economy. Several studies confirmed that FDI was key to the economic success of Hungary (Nemes-Nagy 2000, 2001; Fazekas 2000a). Most analyses agree that regions with a higher ratio of foreign firm employment perform much more successfully in the labor market (Fóti 1995; Hunya 1997; Hamar 1999).

Empirical results of a recent study on the impact of FDI inflows on local labor markets (Fazekas 2000a) showed that micro regions with higher educational levels and a closer location to the western trade portals attracted more foreign capital than did the others. Urban centers with a high concentration of skilled workers and proximity to the western border offer the most favorable conditions for foreign enterprise employment development. Border position had a positive impact if other variables, including distance, are held constant.[6] Budapest and its agglomeration are in the most attractive position. It has to offer a wide selection of "goods" producing external economies such as a direct link with the political and financial decisionmakers, spillover effects due to high firm density (twice as high as the national average), and cooperation with universities (Fazekas and Ozsvald 1998; Kertesi and Köllő 1999).

Generally, the impact of educational levels has been increasing, but the data suggest some FDI growth in some of Hungary's less developed (and least educated) regions in recent years. The analysis of FDI in urban versus rural areas partially explains recent developments. Foreign direct investment in urban areas is positively affected by schooling levels and negatively affected by distance to the trade portals.

Distance seems to matter even more in the case of rural areas. Perhaps surprisingly, rural regions with lower educational levels attracted more FDI than did their more educated counterparts, other things being equal. This dichotomy seems to be similar to that described in the international FDI literature. Skill-intensive technologies look for an educated work force and region-specific external economies of more developed areas. Low-skill technologies may reach the less-developed regions, but their expansion is constrained by transport cost considerations. In the particular case of Hungarian regions, FDI in some low-skill industries like food, clothing, and mining has reached the remote, poorly educated eastern part of the country, but the urban centers of these regions are handicapped in the race for skill-intensive FDI.

The impact of FDI inflow on the change of unemployment rates appears to be weak. Low unemployment regions attracted more investment recently, but no significant correlation was found between the change of FDI employment and the change of unemployment. This may be explained by the relatively high share of takeovers as opposed to "green-field" investment during transition, the relatively low labor intensity of foreign investments (compared to domestic enterprises), as well as the practice of hiring from the ranks of employed workers rather than from the pool of unemployed persons.

Adjustment Mechanism to Mitigate Regional Unemployment Differences

Demand-Side Adjustment: The Effect of the Regional Wage Curve on Spatial Distribution of Job Creation

The initial pretransition level of earning dispersion was rather low by international standards. Then the increase in wage dispersion moved the post-communist countries into the group of medium and high inequality countries. In Hungary, Kertesi and Köllő (1999, 2000) estimated the link between regional relative wages and registered unemployment, and they analyzed factors affecting regional relative wage costs, such as changes in regional productivity levels and differences in the search intensity of the unemployed. Regional wage adjustment was analyzed with repeated cross-section regressions using large data sets comprising both individual and firm-level data. The Hungarian findings suggest that by 1996 the elasticity of individual earnings with respect to local registered unemployment reached a value of minus 10 percent, a typical estimate for mature market economies.[7] The unemployment elasticity of wages increased faster in smaller firms, but after the liberalization of wage settings in 1993, the differentials by firm size gradually disappeared.

Analyzing the impact of location on the cost of labor holding, registered unemployment, and other wage determinants, Kertesi and Köllő (1999 and 2000) found that in the second phase of transition, labor cost fell in Budapest and in the central agglomeration relative to the peripheries. The same applies to large cities relative to small towns. This phenomenon is largely due to the fact that relative productivity levels changed in favor of the more developed centrally located urban districts.

The role wage adjustment could play in re-equilibrating regional differences is an open question. Despite the fact that in Hungary wages have responded to the pressure of unemployment, wage costs are considerably lower in depressed regions. Labor and capital move very slowly toward higher earnings and lower labor costs. According to estimations by Fazekas (2000a), the low wage costs that are typical of remote underdeveloped rural regions with high unemployment rates had no significant impact on the spatial distribution of foreign investment enterprises' employment. The fact that there is no significant negative effect resulting from relative wage cost differences indicates the weakness of the demand-side adjustment mechanism diminishing regional labor market differences.

Supply-Side Adjustment: Migration and Commuting

Using aggregate in and out migration data by settlements, Kertesi (2000b) has shown that the magnitude of migration is (contrary to common belief) far from negligible in Hungary and that migration behavior also reacts to economic incentives. Regions with a high level of unemployment suffer migration losses, whereas those with low levels of unemployment make migration gains. The magnitude of this effect, however, is quite modest. Using the results of some settlement-level computations and putting them into the framework of a simple simulation model, Kertesi has shown that even a migration of considerable size would not lead to a sufficient narrowing of the regional unemployment rate differentials.

The other potentially equalizing mechanism could be the daily commute of the rural population to surrounding towns. The impact of transport costs on the openness of local labor markets was estimated using aggregate unemployment data and estimated rural-urban travel costs by settlements. Results have shown that the equalization of regional unemployment rate differentials is strongly limited by the high costs of commuting and the resulting segregation of the local labor markets. High commuting costs result in large local unemployment rates, since the disadvantages of rural labor markets are less eased by the existence of nearby towns (Köllő 1997; Kertesi 2000b).

Kertesi examined how the geographical position of villages—the costs of availability of better urban labor markets—affect the probability of work for those people who could not find jobs or did not have job offers rewarding enough in their own places of residence. He found strong effects, particularly for the male labor force, and the impact of schooling was especially strong. The more educated a person is, the higher his or her chances are of finding employment that requires daily commuting, since the person can afford to pay the high transportation costs.

Education raises the chances of employment by commuting enormously: travel cost differentials induced by job finding are very large for unskilled workers, whereas similar travel costs have only trivial consequences for the job finding chances of people with higher education. According to Kertesi's estimations, regional and transport disadvantages may create a 35 to 50 percent differential in job finding probabilities for people with low education.

Conclusion

In most Central and Eastern European countries, regional labor market inequalities are high by the standards of the European Union. As a result of substantial changes in the economic structure of local labor markets, industrial job destruction or job creation does not seem to play a major role in the intensity of regional employment tensions. The long-lasting, stable differences in unemployment rates can be traced back to other factors related to historical and cultural traditions, economic development, and hard-to-change endowments rather than to the job destruction that occurred during the first years of transition.

Regional labor market differences described in the previous sections hold a number of lessons for policymakers.[8]

Policies Related to Human Capital

Educational expansion in Hungary took place without opening new public schools or increasing their capacity in backward regions. Among the 3,200 communities of the country, only 200 have any kind of institution for secondary education. The network of dormitories is extremely underdeveloped; accommodation prices both in dormitories and in sublets are prohibitively high. This, together with the high cost of books, transportation, and school programs, creates severe obstacles to school continuation, especially in the case of children coming from rural low-income families (Kertesi and Köllő 2000). The most effective means of raising the educational level of the young generation is extending the age of compulsory schooling through mandatory general education until the age of 18. The extension of compulsory education requires policy action to promote backward communities in several fields. It is necessary to increase the capacity of schools and to open new schools, particularly in regions where there is an acute shortage of secondary schools. The travel and accommodation of students from communities without schools should be assisted.

Policies Encouraging Inter-regional Migration and Commuting

Provided there is a priority for supporting migration, the most important policy action is the expansion of the rental housing sector, together with the development of mortgage financing. Short-distance geographical mobility is heavily dependent on the availability of public transport. In Hungary gasoline prices are high compared to public transport fares. Public transport policies should therefore play an important role in maintaining the availability of urban centers for village dwellers. The subsidization of fuel prices should be excluded from options because of the enormous dead-weight loss implicit in such a policy. The subsidization of public transport companies raises similar concerns but should be considered in Hungary. Given the external economic effect of public transport, there seems to be a strong case for mixed finance. (For example, projects aimed at maintaining or starting particular coach services, with the financial contribution of affected local governments and firms, should be considered for state support.)

The Need for a Coherent Framework for Regional Development Policy

The postaccession period will require a new set-up of regional development and employment development policy. The new system should be based on increased local and regional autonomy. One of the most serious problems in the practice of regional development in Hungary is that it does not provide clear guidelines for decisionmakers at the national, regional, and local levels. If the reduction of regional inequalities of nonemployment is high on the priority list of regional development and the differences in nonemployment are mostly determined by the degree of urbanization, distance from economic centers, and the ethnic composition of the regions, central and local actors responsible for regional development should be encouraged to prefer (1) development of the transport system, (2) investment in decisive fields of urbanization to prevent the country from regional segregation, and (3) special programs for the Gypsy minority to increase their employment chances in local labor markets. Similarly, if the level of education is the crucial factor determining entrepreneurial capacity and the attractiveness of regions for FDI inflows, policymakers should concentrate on the longer term development of education in backward regions.

Last but not least, the European support programs should take into account that high unemployment/high dependency ratios, the deficiencies in educational systems, and the increase and persistence of regional crises all imply risks in the integration process. Hungarian studies call for making a high priority the development of secondary education and the development of a public transport network. Assistance in these areas could help Hungary and the other CEECs move from low employment equilibrium and high regional differences to higher rates of activity and more balanced regional labor markets.

Appendixes

MAP 15.A1 MACRO REGIONS IN HUNGARY

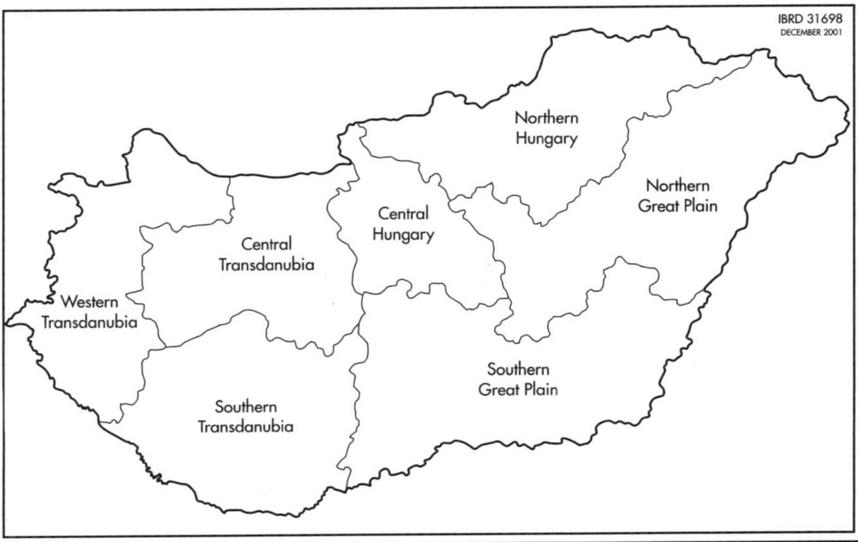

MAP 15.A2 MESO REGIONS (COUNTIES) IN HUNGARY

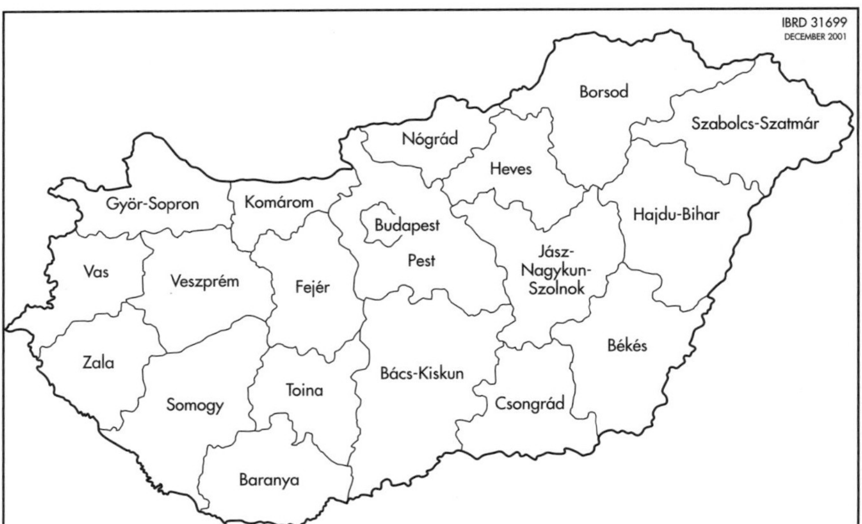

Notes

1. This has been pointed out by Burda (1993), OECD (1995, 2000), Scarpetta (1995), Boeri and Scarpetta (1996), and Boeri, Burda, and Köllő (1998).

2. Although the last census was carried out in March 2001, data are still only available from the 1990 Census.

3. For a detailed county-level analysis of regional unemployment rate differences, see Günther (1998).

4. The average size of micro regions is 620.2 square kilometers, the average local population is 77,279 persons, and the average density of population is 108.5 persons per square kilometer (Faluvégi 2000).

5. Ábrahám and Kertesi (1998) and Kertesi (2000a) give a detailed analysis of the changing employment pattern of Hungarian Gypsy communities during transition.

6. International comparisons show the same pattern in other Central and Eastern European countries (Hunya 1997; Pavlinek and Smith 1998).

7. The Hungarian elasticities are slightly higher than those estimated for Poland and the Czech Republic and markedly higher than those for Romania (Köllő and Vincze 1999).

8. Recommendations in this chapter were selected from a comprehensive set of policy recommendations formulated within the framework of recent research programs carried out by János Köllő, Gábor Kertesi, Dominic Redor, Maria Vince, and Károly Fazekas. *Wage Inequality in East-Central Europe* and *Regional Inequalities in Hungary: Some Aspects of Diagnosis and Cure.*

References

Ábrahám, Á., and G. Kertesi. 1998. "Regional Unemployment Rate Differentials in Hungary, 1990–1995: The Changing Role of Human Capital." In L. Halpern and Ch. Wyplosz, eds., *Hungary: Towards a Market Economy.* Cambridge: Cambridge University Press.

Boeri, T., and S. Scarpetta. 1996. "Regional Mismatch and the Transition to a Market Economy." *Labour Economics* 3: 233–54.

Boeri, T., M. Burda, and J. Köllő. 1998. *Mediating the Transition: Labour Markets in Central and Eastern Europe.* London: CEPR.

Burda, M. 1993. "Unemployment, Labour Markets and Structural Change in Eastern Europe." *Economic Policy* 7: 101–28.

CSO (Central Statistical Office). 2000. *Labour Force Survey, 1992–1999.* Budapest.

Dorenbos, R. 1999. *Labour Market Adjustment in Hungary and Poland.* Labyrinth Publications.

Faluvégi, A. 2000. "A magyar kistérségek fejlettségi különbségei~" ("Differences in the Level of Development between Hungaria Micro-Regions"). In *Területi Statisztika* 4: 19–46.

Faluvégi, A., and Komjáthy, eds. 1995. *Kistérségi vonzáskörzetek: A regionális térszerkezet jellemzői az átmenet éveiben.* (*Micro-regions: Spatial Characteristics of Transition.*) Budapest: Central Statistical Office.

Fazekas, K. 1996. "Types of Micro-regions, Dispersion of Unemployment, and Local Employment Development in Hungary." *Eastern European Economics* 34 (3): 3–48.

———. 2000a. "Impact of Foreign Direct Investment Inflows on Regional Labour Markets in Hungary." SOCO Project Paper 77c. Vienna: Institute for Human Sciences.

———. 2000b. "Regional Labour Market Differentials during Transition in Hungary." In G. Petracos, G. Maier, and G. Gorzelak, eds., *Integration and Transition in Europe: The Economic Geography of Interaction.* London: Routledge.

Fazekas, K., and J. Köllő. 1999. "A külföldi érdekeltségű vállalatok munkaerőkeresletének jellemzői Magyarországon 1995-ben." ("Labor Demand of Foreign Investment Enterprises in Hungary in 1995.") In Fazekas and others, eds., *Relokáció: A munkahelyek áttelepülése Nyugat-Európából Magyarországra.* (*Reallocation of Jobs from Western Europe to Hungary.*) Budapest: MHISM.

Fazekas, K., and E. Ozsvald. 1998. "Transition and Regional Policies: The Case of Hungary." In M. Keune, ed., *Regional Development and Employment Policy: Lessons from Central and Eastern Europe.* Budapest/Geneva: International Labour Office.

Fóti, K. 1995. "Some Impacts of Foreign Direct Investment on Employment and Labor in Hungary." Budapest: Institute for World Economics, Hungarian Academy of Sciences. Processed.

Günther, J. 1998. *Regional Unemployment Differentials and Spatial Labour Mobility in Hungary*. Budapest: Diplomarbeit (Social Science Department, Osnabrück University).

Hamar, J. 1999. "A külföldi működőtőke beáramlás Magyarországon belüli területi jellemzői." ("Regional Characteristics of Foreign Direct Investment in Hungary.") *Külgazdaság* 43 (March): 47–69.

Hunya, G. 1997. "Foreign Direct Investment and Its Effects in the Czech Republic, Hungary, and Poland." Research Report 168. Vienna: Vienna Institute for International Economic Studies.

Jackman, R., and M. Rutkowski. 1994. "Labour Markets: Wages and Employment." In N. Barr, ed., *Labour and Social Policy in Central and Eastern Europe*. Oxford: Oxford University Press.

Kertesi, G. 2000a. "A cigány foglalkoztatás leépülése és szerkezeti átalakulása 1984 és 1994 között." ("Deterioration and Structural Change of Gypsy Employment in Hungary.") *Közgazdasági Szemle* 5.

———. 2000b. "Migration and Commuting: Two Potential Forces Reducing Regional Inequalities in Economic Opportunities?" SOCO Project Paper 77a. Vienna: Institute for Human Sciences.

Kertesi, G., and J. Köllő. 1999. "Unemployment, Wage Push and the Labour Cost Competitiveness of Regions." Budapest Working Paper on the Labour Market 1999/5. Budapest: Institute of Economics.

———. 2000. "Wage Inequality in East–Central Europe." Budapest Working Paper on the Labour Market 7. Budapest: Institute of Economics.

———. 2001. "Economic Transformation and the Revaluation of Human Capital: Hungary, 1986–1999." Budapest Working Paper on the Labor Market 2001/4. Budapest: Institute of Economics.

Keune, M., and J. Nemes-Nagy. 2001. *Local Development, Institutions and Conflicts in Post-socialist Hungary*. Budapest: International Labour Office.

Köllő, J. 1997. "A napi ingázás feltételi és a helyi munkanélküliség Magyarországon." ("Daily Commuting and Local Unemployment in Hungary.") *Esély* 2.

———. 2000. "Patterns of Non-employment in Hungary's Least Developed Regions." SOCO Project Paper 77a. Vienna: Institute for Human Sciences.

Köllő, J., and K. Fazekas. 1998. "Regional Wage Curves in the Quasi-Experimental Setting of Transition: The Case of Hungary, 1986–95." IFO Discussion Paper 47. München: IFO Institut für Wirtschaftsforschung.

Köllő, J., and M. Vincze. 1999. "Self-employment, Unemployment and Wages: Regional Evidence from Hungary and Romania." Budapest Working Paper on the Labour Market 7. Budapest: Institute of Economics.

Nemes-Nagy, J. 2000. "The New Regional Structure in Hungary." In G. Petracos, G. Maier, and G. Gorzselak, eds., *Integration and Transition in Europe: The Economic Geography of Interaction.* London: Routledge.

———. 2001. "Regional Processes at the End of the Millennium: An Overwhelming Transformation with Individual Courses of Development." In M. Keune and J. Nemes-Nagy, eds., *Local Development, Institutions and Conflicts in Post-socialist Hungary.* Budapest: International Labour Office.

OECD (Organisation for Economic Co-operation and Development). 1995. *The Regional Dimension of Unemployment in Transition Countries: A Challenge for Labour Market and Social Policies.* Paris.

———. 1996. *Lessons from Labour Market Policies in the Transition Countries.* Paris.

———. 2000. *Employment Outlook.* Paris.

Pavlinek, P., and A. Smith. 1998. "Internationalisation and Embeddedness in East-Central European Transition: The Contrasting Geographies of Inward Investment in the Czech and Slovak Republics." *Regional Studies* 32 (7): 619–38.

Scarpetta, S. 1995. "Spatial Variations in Unemployment in Central and Eastern Europe: Underlying Reasons and Labour Market Policy Options." In *The Regional Dimension of Unemployment in Transition Countries: A Challenge for Labour Market and Social Policies.* Paris: OECD.

CHAPTER 16

Lessons from East Germany on Labor Mobility

Jennifer Hunt

In the next several years people in Central and Eastern European countries will be able to move freely into the labor markets of the current European Union, as EU membership is extended toward the East. Both old and new members are interested in knowing which people will move and why, how long they will stay outside their own country, and how many people will move. Economically these questions are important because of their implications for income gains for movers, and the impact on wages of workers in the source and receiving countries.

The reunification of East and West Germany is an obvious place to look for answers to these questions. Since Hungary began allowing citizens of the German Democratic Republic to cross into Austria in August 1989, East Germans have had access to the West German labor market. This access became less costly with the fall of the Berlin wall in November 1989.[1] Figure 16.1 shows the flows between East and West from 1957 to 1999.[2] The outflows in 1989 and 1990 each represent 2.5 percent of the East German population. Emigration from the East fell quickly after 1990, with net emigration becoming almost zero, but it has recently risen once more. This outflow of people to the West has contributed to a large reduction in the East German population, with a large decline in the birth rate being the other main contributor. Table 16.1 decomposes the population decline of 8.7 percent into excess deaths and net emigration to the West, with net immigration from abroad offsetting the population decline slightly.

FIGURE 16.1 GERMAN EAST-WEST MIGRATION, 1957–99
(thousands of people)

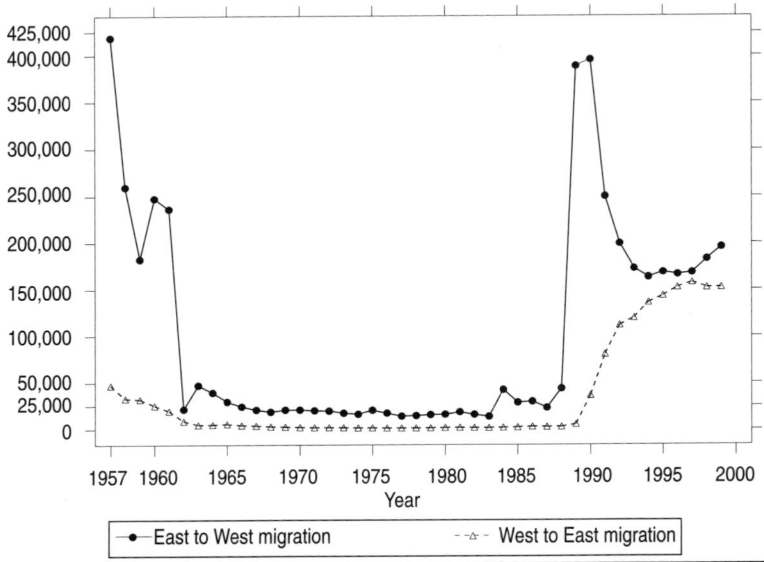

TABLE 16.1 DECOMPOSITION OF POPULATION DECLINE IN EAST GERMANY, 1989–99
(number of persons)

Indicator	*Number of persons*	*Absolute change*	*Change as percent of population on December 31, 1988*
Population on December 31, 1988	16,675,000	–1,458,000	–8.7
Registered population on December 31, 1999	15,217,000		
Deaths, 1989–1999	–1,998,000	–779,000	–4.7
Births, 1989–99	1,220,000		
Moved to West, 1989–99	–2,448,000	–1,204,000	–7.2
Moved from West, 1989–99	1,244,000		
Moved abroad, 1989, 1991–99	—	422,000	2.5
Moved from abroad, 1989, 1991–99	—		
Calculated population on December 31, 1999	15,114,000	n.a.	n.a.
Discrepancy	103,000	n.a.	n.a.

n.a. Not applicable.
— Not available.
Note: Statistics on migration to and from abroad are not available for 1990.
Source: Statistisches Bundesamt 2000.

In this chapter I analyze data from the German Socio-Economic Panel and refer to existing research on migration to attempt to shed light on the main questions of interest.

Data

The data are drawn from the 1990–99 interview years of the German Socio-Economic Panel. West Germans had been interviewed and followed through time since 1984, and the first wave of eastern interviews was conducted in June 1990, just before monetary union. The survey therefore does not shed light on migration that took place before this time. People are followed if they move between East and West, and the survey also asks people if they work in the opposite region of the country (East or West). I refer to these individuals as commuters.[3] Unless otherwise specified, the wages of workers are deflated by the price index for their region (East or West), adjusted to make purchasing power comparable across regions (Krause 1994).

What Sort of People Moved?

The existence of the enclave of West Berlin and the long border between the two Germanies meant that commuting was a very feasible substitute for emigration for many easterners. Some easterners report having changed their workplace from East to West without having changed employers. I refer to these as "transferred" commuters or emigrants. The relative importance of commuters and transferred commuters is shown in table 16.2. Over the whole period 62 percent of people who moved either their home or their workplace to the West were commuters. Thirty-one percent of commuters were transferred, 19 percent of emigrants were transferred, and the share of transferred commuters rose over time. Commuters work in the West for a less extended period than emigrants live in the West, however, and account for only 31 percent of mover time in the West.

TABLE 16.2 TYPES OF MOVERS TO THE WEST
(percent)

	Year left the East		
Type of mover	*1990–92*	*1993–99*	*1990–99*
Commuters	49	39	43
Commuters (transferred)	11	25	19
Emigrants	33	28	30
Emigrants (transferred)	6	8	7
Total	100	100	100

Note: Sample weights are used. Individuals are age 18 or older. Sample size is 385.
Source: German Socio-Economic Panel 1990–99.

Hunt (2000) conducts detailed analyses of which easterners emigrate and commute. Two common types of movers are young people going to study in the West, and tertiary education graduates who move immediately after graduation. Movers are particularly likely to report having been laid off in the previous year. Table 16.3 shows that movers of all kinds are significantly younger than stayers, and that 30 percent of commuters had recently been laid off. Transferred commuters and migrants by definition continued working with the same employer and could not have been laid off. Table 16.3 also shows that people living in a country (Kreis) right on the border with the West commute rather than emigrate. The behavior of Berliners, who both commute and migrate more than nonborder residents, is an exception. The commuters include people who return home only on weekends (about one-third of the commuters), so commuting fairly large distances is feasible.

Why Did They Move?

Up until the parliamentary elections in East Germany in March 1990, the main motivation for emigration was political, with family reunification the secondary motivation.[4] At that point it became clear that unification with the West would come rapidly, and economic reasons became dominant. Work with data on migration flows between all regions of Germany by Hunt (2000) underlines the importance of the wage gap as a determinant of emigration from East Germany. As is well known, the tendency of individuals to move between two places is closely related to the distance between them, and Hunt also finds this. The individual-level data discussed above show that unemployment and layoffs are also an important impetus for migration (or commuting).

TABLE 16.3 CHARACTERISTICS OF STAYERS AND MOVERS, 1990–99

Category	*Average age (years)*	*Laid off between interviews spanning move (percent)*	*Living in county on former border with West, 1990 (percent)*
Stayers	46.6	6	18.4
Commuters	32.0	30	46.0
Commuters (transferred)	36.0	0	51.0
Emigrants	33.0	15	19.0
Emigrants (transferred)	33.0	0	21.0

Note: Sample weights are used. Individuals are age 18 or older.
Source: German Socio-Economic Panel 1990-1999.

How Long Did They Stay?

As already mentioned, commuters have shorter spells in the West than emigrants do. Table 16.4 tabulates the ratio of westward departures to eastward returns. The number of commuters who stop working in the West is 64 percent of the number of commuters who start working in the West. If commuters who become emigrants are included, the proportion of commuters who cease commuting is 73 percent. The number of easterners moving back East from the West is 29 percent of the number emigrating to the West. This number is sensitive to the use of the sample weights and is lower if the raw percentage is used. There is thus substantial return migration, but most emigrants have remained in the West.

Flows from New EU Members

Many people who look at figure 16.1 and table 16.1, and who note that the wage gap between old and new EU members is larger than the inter-German wage gap was, fear that a large proportion of the populations of the accession countries will move to the EU. They further note that social safety nets in the new member countries are less generous than in East Germany, and that the populations of the countries involved are large.

However, there are many important differences with the East German case that suggest emigration and commuting could be less significant for the new EU members. The political reason for emigration, which spurred perhaps half of the cumulative outflows from East Germany, is now absent in the accession countries. Furthermore, the economically motivated emigration from East Germany from March 1990 onwards occurred at the time of the mass layoffs in the East. The accession countries are gaining mobility well after the shock of price liberalization

TABLE 16.4 RETURN PROPENSITIES OF COMMUTERS AND EMIGRANTS (percent)

Category	*Ratio of returns to departures*
Commuters	64
Commuters (alternate definition)[a]	73
Emigrants	29

Note: Sample weights are used. Individuals are age 18 or older.
a. The alternate definition of returning from commuting describes all ends to commuting, including ends due to emigration to the West.
Source: German Socio-Economic Panel 1990–99.

and other events that led to dramatic output falls. It is also unclear to what extent the opening of the borders will constitute a significant relaxation of mobility constraints, given that considerable migration has already taken place.

Language and culture are less similar than in the German case, and family ties between the source and destination region play less of a role. Family ties are important not only as a direct cause of migration, but also as an indirect one, through the facilitation of information about jobs and housing. In addition, for much of the population in the accession countries the distances involved are much greater, and the closest thing to the unique Berlin is the proximity of Bratislava and Vienna. Finally, fewer workers are likely to be transferred by their companies.

Economic Impact for Migrants

The study of the economic impact of migration is often very difficult. The one certainty is that immigrants themselves benefit a lot. Table 16.5 shows the real wage growth (ratio of wages in adjacent years) for stayers and all mover types for East Germans. Commuters, who benefited from the low consumption prices in the East, doubled their monthly wages by moving to the West. This compares to average yearly wage growth of 14 percent for stayers. Transferred commuters gained much less, 31 percent on average, apparently because they were earning western wages to start with (table 16.6). Emigrants gained 83 percent on average. As a check, the real wage growth for those who stop commuting or who return to live in the East is also reported. Return commuters have an insignificant 2 percent wage growth (again compared to 16 percent for stayers), while return migrants experience a wage cut of about a third.

In 1999 male movers (migrants and commuters) earned a statistically insignificant 5 percent lower nominal wage than did western men (controlling for their characteristics), while female movers earned the same as their western counterparts.

Impact on the Destination

Theoretically, the impact of immigration on the receiving labor market is ambiguous. It is important to realize that if the immigrants are similar to the natives, there is no reason to expect immigration to have any impact once capital stocks and housing stocks have had a chance to adjust. A hypothetical experiment where every person in a country acquires a twin suggests only short-run effects. On the other hand, immigration of less-skilled workers could reduce the wages of less-skilled natives. It is important to remember that in this case high-skilled workers or firm owners would benefit, and that in all cases allowing people to work where they are most productive is good for overall efficiency.

TABLE 16.5 REAL WAGE GROWTH BY MOVER TYPE IN THE YEAR OF THE MOVE (ratio of wages in adjacent years)

Category	*Year left the East (except for stayers)* 1990–92	1993–99	1990–99
Stayers	1.23	1.09	1.14
	(0.009)	(0.005)	(0.005)
Commuters	2.44	1.41	2.11
	(0.06)	(0.07)	(0.04)
Commuters (transferred)	1.52	1.24	1.31
	(0.11)	(0.05)	(0.05)
Emigrants	1.85	1.81	1.83
	(0.11)	(0.10)	(0.08)
Emigrants (transferred)	1.08	1.47	1.32
	(0.14)	(0.10)	(0.08)
Returning commuters	0.88	1.07	1.02
	(0.09)	(0.05)	(0.04)
Returning migrants	—	0.68	0.68
	—	(0.12)	(0.13)

— Not available.
Note: Standard errors are in parentheses. Sample weights are used. Individuals are 18 or older. Wage change is computed only for individuals with positive wages in both years considered.
Source: German Socio-Economic Panel 1990–99.

TABLE 16.6 MONTHLY REAL WAGE BY MOVER TYPE IN THE YEAR BEFORE THE MOVE (1991 DM)

Category	*Year left the East (except for stayers)* 1990–92	1993–99	1990–99
Stayers	1,966	2,940	2,578
	(11)	(14)	(10)
Commuters	1,932	2,549	2,145
	(84)	(187)	(101)
Commuters (transferred)	2,436	3,333	3,094
	(160)	(156)	(124)
Emigrants	1,834	2,299	2,054
	(115)	(197)	(125)
Emigrants (transferred)	3,544	3,257	3,371
	(212)	(278)	(200)
Returning commuters	3,640	3,230	3,341
(who continue working)	(132)	(130)	(103)
Returning commuters (who	4,202	2,648	2,850
stop working)	(283)	(178)	(153)
Returning migrants	3,548	3,019	3,068
	(441)	(228)	(201)

Note: Standard errors are in parentheses. Sample weights are used. Individuals are 18 or older.
Source: German Socio-Economic Panel 1990–99.

The empirical literature is somewhat inconclusive, with zero impact and large impacts being ruled out, but the exact size of the medium impact is uncertain.[5] The opportunity to study the huge immigration to West Germany of the ethnic Germans (or Aussiedler) cannot be seized due to data difficulties. However, the wage structure of West Germany was remarkably stable over the 1990s, and there have been no marked changes in unemployment over the long term.[6] I have attempted to use the German Socio-Economic Panel to look for particular wage or unemployment changes along the border with the East, but the sample size is such that only large changes can be ruled out.

Impact on the Source Country

This is an interesting topic which space does not allow me to pursue. Since inequality is now higher in the accession countries than in West (and East) Germany, it is likely to be the less-skilled who have the most to gain from moving, unlike in the East German case.[7] The young will be those most likely to leave, and remittances will play a role.

Implications for Migration from EU Accession Countries

The young and the unskilled will be the typical movers, and commuting will be important along the Bavarian and Austrian borders, and along the Italian border with Slovenia. Little commuting to East Germany is likely to occur based on foreign migration trends in the past. The probability of emigration could be lower than in the East German case. The emigrants and commuters will have very large wage gains, and allowing labor mobility is thus the surest way of helping citizens of the accession countries. There is no convincing evidence that immigration and commuting will have serious negative consequences for the receiving countries.

Policy Recommendations

Receiving economies must adapt their capital stock and housing stock to the arrival of immigrants. This argues for a quota system that gradually increases the number of citizens of accession countries who are allowed to live in the EU. The quotas should be extended until they are no longer binding, with this occurring at the latest in about 2007 (assuming that the accession countries only join in 2004).[8] All citizens from accession countries should be permitted to enter a lottery randomly allocating the right to live and work anywhere in the EU. A procedure could be used that is similar to the American Green Card lottery. To allow for this gradual process, the quotas should be introduced now. This will have the additional benefit of signaling to accession countries that the EU is serious about granting membership. Delaying labor mobility for seven years and then introducing it all at once serves no obvious purpose.

Notes

1. Grundmann (1998) gives more detail on the events of 1989 and 1990.

2. Data are from the Statistisches Bundesamt.

3. Wagner, Burkhauser, and Behringer (1993) describe the data.

4. See references to surveys of emigrants in Grundmann (1998).

5. Friedberg and Hunt (1995) survey the theoretical and empirical literature.

6. Prasad (1999) documents the lack of change in the wage structure for males.

7. See Brainerd (2000) for wage inequality numbers. The German numbers are from my own calculations.

8. See Boeri and Brücker (2001) for a similar suggestion.

References

Boeri, Tito, and Herbert Brücker. 2001. "Eastern Enlargement and EU-Labour Markets: Perceptions, Challenges and Opportunities." *World Economy*. Forthcoming.

Brainerd, Elizabeth. 2000. "Women in Transition: Changes in Gender Wage Differentials in Eastern Europe and the Former Soviet Union." *Industrial and Labor Relations Review* 54 (1): 138–62.

Friedberg, Rachel, and Jennifer Hunt. 1995. "The Impact of Immigrants on Host Country Wages, Employment and Growth." *Journal of Economic Perspectives* (Spring): 23–44.

Grundmann, Siegfried. 1998. *Bevölkerungsentwicklung in Ostdeutschland: Demographische Strukturen und räumliche Wandlungsprozesse*. Leske und Budrich: Opladen.

Hunt, Jennifer. 2000. "Why Do People Still Live in East Germany?" Yale University working paper.

Krause, Peter. 1994. "Armut im Wohlstand: Betroffenheit und Folgen." Discussion paper 88. Berlin: Deutsches Institut für Wirtschaftsforschung.

Prasad, Eswar. 1999. "The Unbearable Stability of the German Wage Structure: Evidence and Interpretation." Working paper. Washington, D.C.: International Monetary Fund.

Statistisches Bundesamt. 2000. *Statistical Yearbook of the German Democratic Republic.* Berlin.

Wagner, Gert, Richard Burkhauser, and Friederike Behringer. 1993. "The English Language Public Use File of the German Socio-Economic Panel Study." *Journal of Human Resources* 28 (2): 429–33.

CHAPTER 17

Departure from the Periphery: Reflections on Regional Labor Markets without Borders in Austria

Christof Schremmer

This analysis on the regional impact of labor markets without borders in Austria focuses on the development of Austria's regional economic situation along the border and provides some reflections on the labor market impacts there. Figure 17.1 shows the specific spatial situation in Austria. The perspective for the future is represented by the dark line, the Schengen border, and how it shall move to the East after accession. The question is: how, in the near future, will Austria's close location to its neighboring countries affect the regional labor markets?

The particular situation is, of course, a result of developments in the twentieth century. The Schengen border symbolizes the periphery of developed Western Europe. So Austria and the peripheral regions within Austria—in a historical context—became the hinterland of the European Union.

Sixty percent of Austria's population lives in those peripheral areas along the Schengen border, and about two-thirds of the country's jobs are located in this area, which includes the major cities of Vienna, Graz, and Linz.

Within 60 kilometers of the Schengen border (a daily commuting distance), you have wage differentials of between 1 to 6 and 1 to 7, and they have improved slowly in the past 10 years (table 17.1). The gap may be closing in Poland, but not in the neighboring countries so far. The reason for this is not purchasing power; it is the difference between exchange rates and purchasing power in the accession countries. Purchasing power differentials are a lot closer. This is not a problem. But the differential in actual nominal wages in the regions is the relevant issue. Closing the gap between exchange rates in accession countries and the European Union will necessitate a substantial climb in the value of the currencies by a factor of two or three. This will be a big problem.

Figure 17.2 shows the differential in gross domestic product between Austria and the eastern neighboring countries in purchasing power. Here you can see the gradient of GDP per capita reaching from the West, from Bavaria and western Germany and upper Italy to Austria, and continuing across the EU borders to the East. (There is also a traditional West-East differential within Austria, but it is diminishing.)

The pattern of regional economic development in Austria in the 1990s showed the eastern border regions catching up, contributing to the reduction of the West-East differential within Austria (figures 17.3 and 17.4). GDP and job creation in the eastern regions are better than in the western parts of Austria.

With a protecting border in the 1990s, the eastern border regions, which traditionally lagged behind, began to catch up. For decades the eastern part of Austria was an economically sealed-off hinterland. The catching-up process, however, has not been nearly as successful in the capital, Vienna, and this is the basis for heated discussions about the impact of open borders on the labor market of the capital.

Comparing the unemployment rates in the neighboring regions (figure 17.5), one can see that Vienna, in the center, has surprisingly the highest unemployment rate in the region. By comparison, Austria's peripheral, traditionally poor regions have developed very well in labor market terms. In these peripheral regions, the

FIGURE 17.1 PERIPHERY TRANSITION ENLARGEMENT

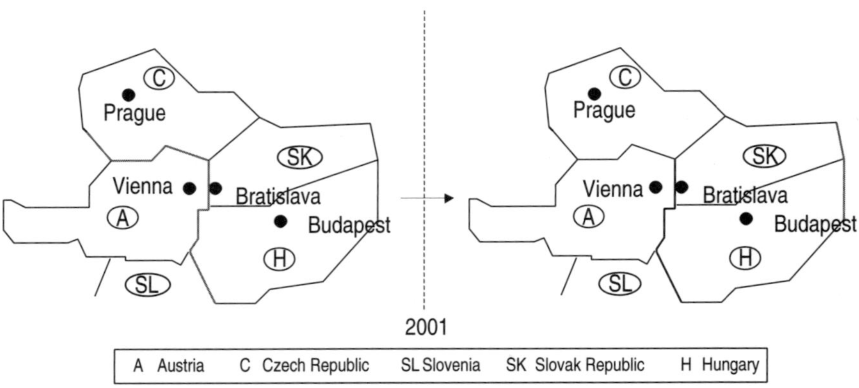

Source: Österreichisches Institut für Raumplanning (ÖIR).

TABLE 17.1 CEEC AVERAGE MONTHLY GROSS WAGE

Country	*1990*	*1999*	*Difference in percentage points*
Czech Republic	9	16	+7
Hungary	11	14	+3
Poland	6	19	+13
Slovak Republic	9	11	+2
Slovenia	46	41	–5
Bulgaria	25	5	–20
Romania	8	6	–2
Austria	100	100	0

Source: ÖIR.

FIGURE 17.2 GROSS DOMESTIC PRODUCT IN AUSTRIA AND ITS EASTERN NEIGHBORS, 1996

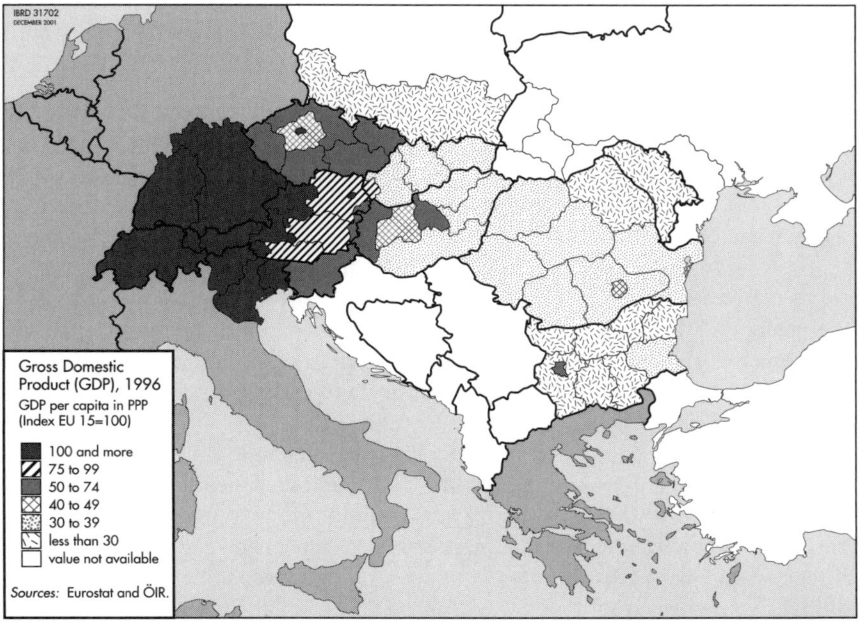

FIGURE 17.3 DEVELOPMENT OF GDP PER CAPITA IN AUSTRIA'S REGIONS, 1989–98

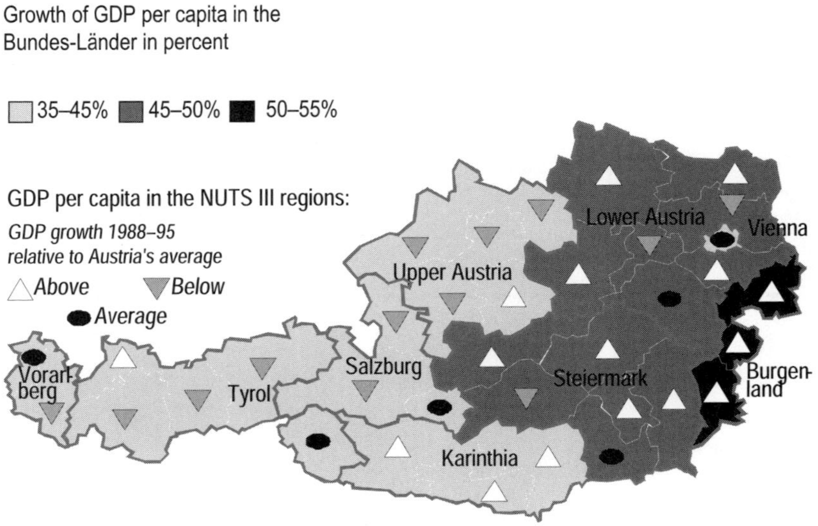

Source: ÖIR.

ones with the highest proportion of foreign workers have the lowest unemployment rates. So there has been no pushing out of Austrian workers by foreign workers so far. The foreign workers mostly have come from former Yugoslav countries and Turkey. Only a small portion of the foreign workers in Austria has come from the neighboring countries.

There have been positive developments in the cities, but in Vienna not as positive as expected. Development in the 1990s in the border regions was better than anticipated, and this was attributed to small-scale development of small and medium enterprises (SMEs) in the border regions. Substantial structural changes have occurred as well: losses in the textile industry and clothing industry and gains in other, more advanced manufacturing industries.

The positive development of SMEs shows a closing of the productivity gap compared to small enterprises in central regions, and there seems to be an increase in the activity radius of SMEs, partly across the border and partly within Austria. Firms located in border regions do market their products and services more in central regions and also across borders. This seems to be a very important development that gives some reason to hope for the future. Even small firms have started to act

FIGURE 17.4 DEVELOPMENT OF EMPLOYMENT AND GROSS WAGES IN AUSTRIA'S EASTERN BORDER REGIONS, 1989–99

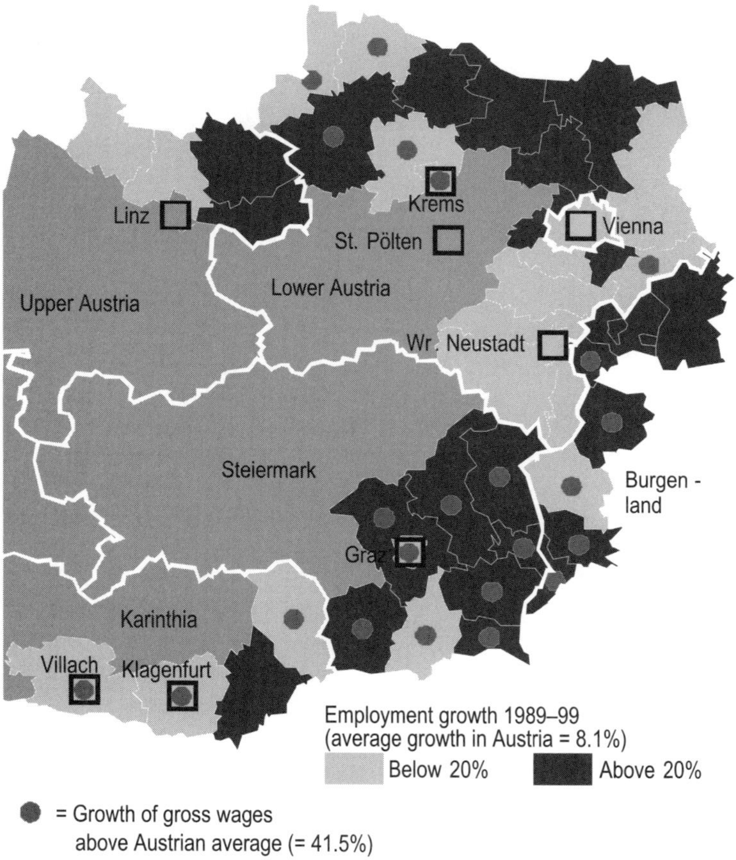

Source: HVSV and ÖIR.

transnationally. This took a long time, but there is some tendency toward innovation and upgrading of firms in Austria's border regions.

At least two-thirds of the Austrian population potentially is affected by the commuting option. Consider the commuting distances shown in figure 17.6. With a car and open borders, commuters from neighboring centers can reach all of the major cities of Austria in 90 minutes. The regional labor market open for daily commuting is prompting fears and heated political debate in Austria. In my opin-

FIGURE 17.5 UNEMPLOYMENT RATES IN NUTS III REGIONS, 1998–99
(percent)

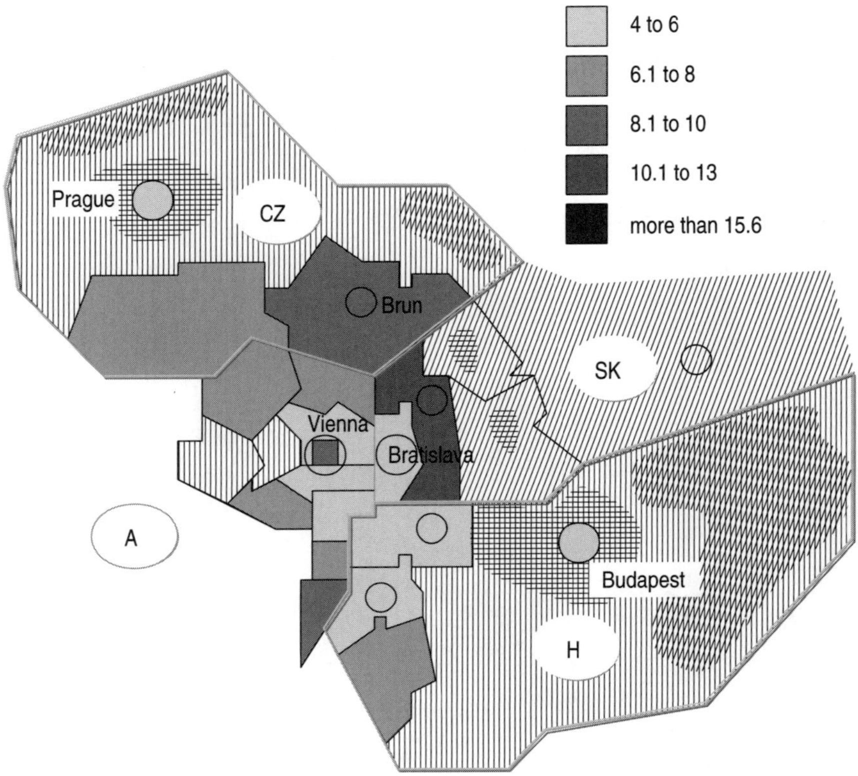

Source: ÖIR.

ion the issue of commuting will be of greater significance for Austria than migration.

In the long run migration is not expected to become a major problem. In terms of commuting, however, the accession of the Slovak Republic, with the close vicinity of the two centers—Vienna and Bratislava—will make a major difference for the eastern Austria labor market and the Vienna labor market in particular.

Timing will also make a difference. It is a question of how fast the accession and the opening up of labor markets will take place. Therefore, transitional regulations will make a difference. The slower the accession, the less positive the economic impacts will be, but there may be less political friction. This seems to be the tradeoff heavily discussed in Austria.

FIGURE 17.6 ACCESSIBILITY OF AUSTRIAN BORDER REGIONS FROM CITIES IN NEIGHBORING COUNTRIES, WITHIN 90 MINUTES BY CAR

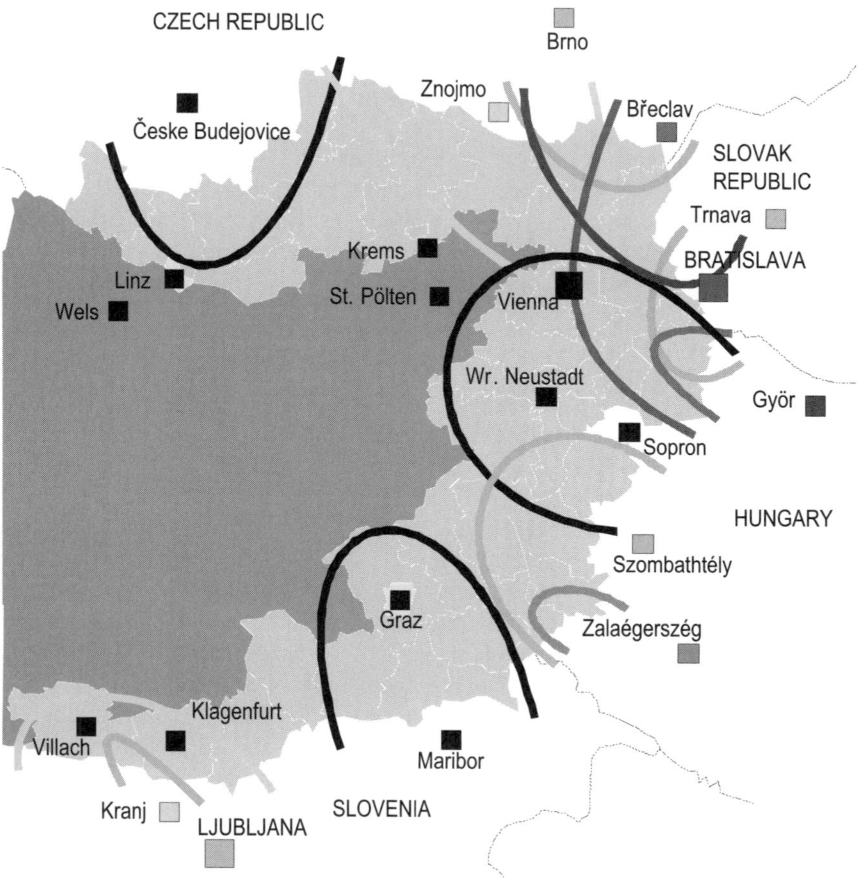

Source: ÖIR.

The regional impacts on the cities are expected to be positive, particularly in the short to mid term, with declining impacts in the long run. As Jennifer Hunt pointed out in her chapter, the influx of human capital and a certain amount of competition can contribute to inner-city and central region growth.

In the hinterland in the classic border regions, we expect some positive growth effects, but there will be a more mixed pattern there, at least for the near future.

There will be high competition in production, particularly in services, in the construction sector and also in household services and other social services. This will be relevant to the labor market in those sectors and to small firms. There will be more direct competition from firms producing at much lower labor costs, and of course with free commuting there is a high degree of flexibility. There is, however, a long list of uncertainties. Which labor markets will be affected, and who is going to commute?

The effect on the new member states will also be important, as noted in Hunt's chapter. Commuters will gain experience and hard currency money to transfer to their families back home, improving the quality of living and housing there. Some of the former commuters and migrants may eventually come back and invest in their own businesses after a couple of years. That is, of course, an effect that will be very important to the new member countries. This effect is probably underestimated in the discussion in the EU.

What are the policy options for the future? We need a governing regime for handling labor market impacts, and this governance should be dealt with in a joint way between Austria and its neighboring states. The proposed transitional arrangements, with respect to labor market flows and open movement of labor, will provide some time, and at least in political terms, time is needed to handle those adaptation processes. For instance, all INTERREG-programs (joint development programs between Austria and its neighboring states) contain preparatory measures for labor market adaptation. The neighboring states will work together on the observation of labor markets before and after accession and will take preparatory steps to develop labor markets on both sides of the border. And for the implementation of these measures, transitional arrangements will be helpful.

The proposed measures must be differentiated regionally. It is a different situation between Vienna and Bratislava than between Graz and Ljubljana or between Klagenfurt and Kranj. A lot more labor market tension is to be expected in the Vienna region, I think, than in other regions of Austria, and so more preparatory action will be needed there.

Considering these bilateral measures, I suggest a slow, step-by-step opening up of the labor markets along the Austrian border over the next five to seven years. The results should be monitored and documented closely as well as analyzed by scientists and politicians from both sides. It will be essential to reach a common understanding of what is happening in the regions close to the borders. Representatives of the neighboring countries need to assess the same facts and developmental problems. It will not be easy. Interpretations differ considerably, leading to more debate. However, there is enough reason to hope for a well-prepared and well-timed procedure for accession and for economically integrated regional development across (former) borders in the future.

CHAPTER 18

The European Integration: A Policy toward Stability, Growth, and Employment

Peter Tempel

This conference, jointly organized by the Bertelsmann Foundation, the European Forum, the Institute for Public Affairs in Bratislava, and the Bruno Kreisky Forum, addresses the important issue of labor, employment, and social policies in the enlargement process.

The Göteborg European Council recently declared, and I quote: "Provided that progress towards meeting the accession criteria continues at an unabated pace, the road map should make it possible to complete negotiations by the end of 2002 for those countries that are ready. The objective is that they should participate in the European Parliament elections of 2004 as members."

Never before has the commitment of the European Union to welcome new members been stated more clearly and more precisely than in Göteborg. The process has become irreversible. The Union is willing to meet the challenge that enlargement is posing.

The enlargement process is unprecedented in terms of its scope and diversity, as well as in its political and strategic significance. To be more precise:

- Compared with the "southern enlargement" (Spain, Portugal) in the eighties, the acquis communitaire has developed enormously: since then the internal market has been created, the Economic and Monetary Union has been established, justice and home affairs (including the Schengen Treaty) have become part of a community policy, and security and defense policy has become closely coordinated in the Union, including crisis management tasks and the intended creation of a rapid reaction force.

- If all 13 countries that are currently part of the enlargement process join the Union, then its population and geographical area would grow by 30 percent. But initially, only 8 percent would be added to the Union's Gross Domestic Product. In other words, those 100 million people produce together as much as the 16 million people in a country such as the Netherlands.

- But this is also the good news. The economic reforms in candidate countries are paying off. Their economic growth exceeds that in the Union. This opens up opportunities for exporters and investors. Already the region as a whole is our second most important trading partner after the United States. Foreign direct investment contributes to their future and to our shareholder value. Economically we are therefore talking about a win-win situation.

These are some of the considerations we should bear in mind when discussing the enlargement process and the negotiations in particular. These negotiations take place on the basis of a number of important principles—in particular, the principle that each candidate should be able to progress according to its merit, as well as the principle that the countries where negotiations started later should have a real possibility to catch up with the first group.

To give you an overview of the complexity of this task, let me tell you that each individual candidate must transpose into its own law something like 70,000 pages of Community law. For the purposes of negotiation, we have divided these 70,000 pages into 30 chapters that form the subject of individual negotiations. With 12 countries, we are therefore talking about 360 chapters to be negotiated.

Where do we stand in this process? With the first group of six countries and after three years of negotiations, we have provisionally closed more than half of these chapters. For some candidate countries, we are even at two-thirds. With the second group, which started a little more than a year ago, we are about 45 percent down the road.

In fact, if one looks closely at the European Council's conclusions in Helsinki, Nice, and Göteborg, a very clear window of opportunity becomes discernible. This window of opportunity does not need to be made more precise. What is lacking however, is how we get there.

For this reason the European Commission proposed, in November 2000, very concrete commitments by the Union regarding the content of the accession negotiations. Sometimes candidate countries have accused the Union of not being clear on the terms of negotiations on certain sensitive issues. Therefore, the Commission proposed what it called a "road map" covering the period until the end of the Spanish presidency in the first half of 2002. In this road map it proposed for each subsequent presidency a number of negotiating chapters for which the EU should lay down its definitive position.

For instance, under the Swedish presidency the EU has laid down its positions on such sensitive chapters as free movement of workers, free movement of capital, and the environment. Concretely, this means that the Commission proposes to the Council certain negotiation positions regarding requests for transitional arrangements. These requests most often come from the side of the candidates. For the first group of six countries, there are 500 such requests, of which 350 are in the agricultural field. Sometimes, however, it may also be in the interest of the Union to ask for such arrangements.

Free movement of workers is an example. There have been numerous studies about the potential for migration into the Union from the candidate countries. Some 850,000 nationals from Central and Eastern European countries now live in the Union. According to some estimates, accession of all candidates could lead to immigration in the first year of more than 300,000 workers, including their families. In subsequent years this number would gradually decrease, but nevertheless it would imply a substantial increase compared to the current number of Eastern European nationals.

Macroeconomically, these figures may seem small or even insignificant. But what if, as the studies predict, 70 percent of the inflow ended up in Germany and Austria? And what if, of these 70 percent, most migrants ended up in the border regions? Admittedly, this is only one of the possible scenarios. But it is a scenario that leads to questions, if not outright opposition to the idea of enlargement, among sometimes important parts of the population of the countries concerned. We can then do two things. We can ignore these fears and act as if nothing is going to happen. This entails the risk of rejection of the enlargement process as a whole and may even endanger the accession ratification procedures. Or we can try to find a solution that responds to these fears, be they justified or not.

I think that the solution we have found offers an elegant way out. We have proposed a flexible transitional period of a maximum of seven years, with reviews after two and five years. This approach has already been accepted by Hungary, Cyprus, Latvia, the Slovak Republic, and Malta.

How does it work in practice? Under the transitional arrangement for the free movement of workers, citizens from the candidate countries can get work permits in the EU for some years after accession. This applies not only to "blue collar" workers but also to anybody who wants to sign an employment contract with an employer in one of the present Member States. This is the normal system that applies internationally, and the idea is to move gradually toward the EU system, where people can freely get a job anywhere they want.

After two years the Commission will report on the situation, and the Member States will have to announce what system they wish to use from then on. Those countries that choose to liberalize their labor markets would maintain only a "safeguard." This means that in cases of unexpected disturbance in the labor market or in some region or profession they could ask to reintroduce work permits temporarily. Such safeguards have usually been available in the past but never used.

Three years later the remaining Member States will again be invited to open their labor markets, provided that there is no serious disturbance in the labor market. In any case, two years after this no Member State will be allowed to require work permits.

As regards the requests from the candidates, let me come back to the two other examples that I mentioned: free movement of capital and the environment. For free movement of capital the most important requests for transitional periods concern the acquisition of secondary residences and of agricultural land. For secondary residences, I am very glad to say that we have found a solution in the negotiations with several candidates that could serve as a model for other countries.

The acquisition of agricultural land is not so much an economic problem as a political problem. There are the fears of the candidates for a sell-out of their land for purely speculative reasons. Indeed, this is not excluded if one compares the living standards in the candidates with those in the Union. On average, income per capita in the candidates is only 35 percent of that in the Union. On the other hand, the demands, which sometimes go as far as 18 years, may be exaggerated. Since this does not concern a real disturbance of the internal market as long as acquisition of land for investment purposes is possible, we are offering limited transitional periods. Also this approach has been accepted by some candidates.

Finally, the environment. Here the candidates face an unequal fight. In order to comply with Community legislation, they would need to invest some 120 billion Euro. We cannot demand that this happen overnight. On the other hand, there should be a clear commitment and investment schedule in order to comply with our high environmental standards in the medium term. I am happy to say that this approach has had a fruitful start. We have already been able to close provisionally the environment chapter with several candidates under the Swedish presidency.

These are some examples of how we intend to tackle the difficult obstacles on the road before us. Nevertheless, we have difficult negotiations ahead. We are now touching on issues that directly influence certain economic sectors or have immediate social consequences. I refer, for instance, to the energy sector, where the candidates need to follow our pace in opening the market; transport, where huge differences remain in technical, environmental, and social standards; fisheries, where a good balance needs to be found between environmental and economic considerations regarding the protection of certain fishing areas; and taxation, where the immediate adoption of the minimum excise or VAT levels of the Union can imply considerable price increases for basic necessities. Furthermore, we will start substantial discussions on technical aspects of agricultural policy.

I conclude with these observations concerning the enlargement process:

- The Göteborg summit lent a more precise definition to the time window outlined in the Nice conclusions. In so doing, the Union has opened up the realistic prospect of completing the negotiations with the most advanced of the candidate countries by the end of 2002 and set the aim of enabling them to take part in the 2004 European elections as members.

- The time factor introduced into the negotiations by means of the Commission's road map has proved realistic. The Swedish presidency's excellent agenda management and resolute conduct of the negotiations made a decisive contribution to this result. The prospects for bringing the accession negotiations to a successful conclusion are better than ever.

- The negotiations will continue to be conducted strictly on the basis of the established negotiating principles: progress in the negotiations in accordance with the individual merits of the candidate countries; differentiation in the negotiation process; and the possibility that countries where negotiations began at the start of 2000 can catch up.

- The timetable for the further conduct of the negotiations will be decided by reference to these negotiating principles and the time window defined in Nice and Göteborg. Ten candidate countries have pledged themselves to use this time window. We do not want to discourage any candidate country from resolutely continuing to pursue this objective. As things stand at present, none of the candidate countries has a guarantee of accession within this time window, but neither is accession to be excluded for any of them. The time window is open for all 10 countries.

- The enlargement process will be successful only if it is given adequate political support. This requires an adequate measure of flexibility in the negotiations in order to take account of the justified concerns and demands in the candidate countries. Due consideration must be given to the social costs that people in the candidate countries must bear. Neither can we make excessive demands on the accession countries concerning the financial burdens they have to bear in adopting EU standards. The budgetary requirements of implementing the acquis are enormous: on the basis of credible investment plans, we have sometimes granted very long transition periods. This flexibility by the Union is absolutely needed if we want to ensure public support for enlargement and minimize the disruption in the economic and social situation in the candidates due to the takeover of the acquis.

- Further efforts must be made in the Member States to project Europe's chances as a political and economic power in a globalized world. Europe will be able to play a decisive part in the shaping of politics only if there is a lasting guarantee of stability, security, and peace. We also have to make it even clearer that the candidate countries are aspiring to this common European future and are prepared to assume enormous burdens of adjustment, both now and in the future, in order to achieve this objective.

For the present Member States, enlargement will open up many types of advantages. We are setting up a large common market with high growth rates not only for the candidate countries but also for the present Member States. The candidate countries will adopt the European environment standards and thereby contribute to the lasting protection of the environment on the European scale. They are also adopting our rules on how to combat organized crime and other illegal activities.

The concerns of the population of the Member States must be taken seriously. But we can offer them solutions. The agreement reached on the matter of freedom of movement for persons and cross-border services—within the EU-15 and with a range of candidate countries—shows this very clearly. The solution found offers adequate protection for those Member States that need it for a certain period and at the same time opens up the possibility of immediate liberalization for those that want it. Some Member States have already announced their intention to permit unrestricted free movement of persons from the point of accession.

Justified concerns must not be dismissed as national egotism. On the contrary, in the negotiations we must seek proper solutions. A limited period of transition arrangements is preferable to the risk that at the end of the process the necessary political support for the outcome will be lacking. The Commission will continue to arrive at proper solutions.

These deliberations make it compellingly clear: there can be no going back. The momentum of the enlargement process must be kept up. The Göteborg European Council strongly underlined the irreversibility of the accession process.

CHAPTER 19

Immigration Aspects of European Enlargement

Rita Suessmuth

For decades most of the Western European countries have ignored the realities of migration.[1] One of the front-runners was Germany with its political and normative guiding principle of the past that "Germany is not an immigration country." As a rule of history, however, you cannot escape from realities forever. The time comes when you must face them. Meanwhile, each country has defined or is still defining its own framework to deal with this issue. For the first time in its history, Germany installed a so-called "Independent Commission on Migration." Its work is based on the assumption that there is a vital need for migrants and for a broad set of instruments to manage migration and integration.[2]

In addition to the search for a consensus at the national level, parallel negotiations at the European level are needed that take into account the upcoming enlargement of the European Union (EU). The deficit in the current debate is the lack of knowledge about developments at the national level within the EU countries and about the proposals on the table at the European Commission in Brussels. Both discussions—the national and the European—run parallel without any real linkage. An overall plan setting clear objectives is necessary for the structuring of migration and integration—to do justice to humanitarian responsibilities, to contribute to the safeguarding of economic prosperity, and to improve the collective living situation of migrants and their host societies and encourage integration.

Facing the Contradictions

The European Union prepares for the accession of new Member States. Despite only a minimum consensus reached in Nice, the enlargement process has entered its crucial phase. The EU, as well as the accession states, now faces certain questions related to EU enlargement in more concrete and immediate terms, and fears and syndromes of overload become obvious. The debates on European migration and asylum policy are reflecting these syndromes more clearly than in every other policy field. If one were to assess the status quo of European migration policy, one would see many contradictions. There are more contradictions than clear positions.

Political leaders in the EU are not getting tired of announcing that they are fully in favor of enlargement. But under which conditions? The agreement on transition periods for the introduction of the free movement of labor is being decided right now and demonstrates that the interests and fears of the EU-15 are the major yardstick of enlargement. Moreover, rising unemployment rates and reservations about opening borders for labor migrants from third (that is, non-EU) countries raise other dilemmas.

The argument in favor of transition periods includes the following elements. First, transition periods are to help control the unhampered influx of migrants expected from Central and Eastern Europe after the enlargement. This influx of labor is said to be boosted by the gap in prosperity between the old and the new members, causing displacement effects in the domestic labor market, especially for low-wage jobs. This, in turn, results in a reduction in wages and will overload the social security systems in the countries of destination. Second, the accession is expected to provoke illegal immigration of labor. The new member countries would benefit from transition periods, since they were a means of preventing the majority of highly qualified workers from immigrating to Western European countries. The impact of the brain drain from East to West would at least be cushioned. Such presumed linkages—for example, between the increase in illegal migration and the enlargement of the European Union—must, however, be analyzed in a rational way.

Articulating the Facts

The adoption of the *acquis communautaire*, the European Union's common property, by the accession states is to lead to a maximum convergence of economic, political, and social structures among the old and new Member States. For the time being, however, this will not remove the considerable gap in prosperity, even after the accession of the first Central and Eastern European countries. The disparities are the result of the absence of an integrated market and social policy at the European level caused by failed national policies.

Like any enlargement, the EU enlargement will create incentives for parts of the new EU population to offer their manpower in another EU country. Countries—like Germany and Austria—that border the new Member States will be affected more strongly than others by the influx of labor from Central and Eastern Europe. This labor potential, however, does not automatically mean an additional or even unbearable burden on the respective national labor markets or social security systems. On the contrary, in the medium and long term, the countries initially most affected by the influx of labor will be exactly the ones where the most favorable impacts on the economy as a whole will occur. Therefore, workers from Central and Eastern Europe will not trigger a displacement process for local workers. As a rule, they will take complementary jobs. In other words, they will be employed in branches where there is a lack of local labor. An automatic increase in illegal immigration as a result of enlargement is not to be feared either. Anyway, it is a problem the European Union has to tackle—with or without enlargement. The problem requires solutions in the short term at the national level and in the medium term also at the European level.

It is indisputable that there actually have been displacing effects for local labor in low-wage industries such as the construction industry during the last few years. However, these reductions in wage levels and displacing effects should not be overestimated. On the one hand, control over the labor market in low-wage industries is a problem that has to be approached at the national level; on the other hand, workers from Central and Eastern Europe will themselves choose those branches offering skilled or less-skilled jobs. On average, the formal education levels of immigrants from Central and Eastern Europe are significantly higher than those of immigrants from other parts of the world. Nevertheless, this does not necessarily mean that the attractiveness of Western European countries especially for highly skilled workers is so great as to induce them to leave their native countries immediately after the accession. In general, this professional group distinguishes itself by a high level of mobility. These people often return to their native countries after a certain period of time abroad and contribute to their economic development by setting up businesses, for example.

Globalization is opening economic opportunities, but it is also placing new demands on the competitiveness of the national economies and on the competitiveness of the EU. In the modern industrial nations, prosperity is based on a high state of technology and knowledge. Knowledge continues to gain importance and is increasingly acquired internationally. In addition, Western European countries (for instance, the United States and Canada) compete with other countries in the world for the best brains. In most cases higher wages and lower barriers to language, as well as the clear perspective of integration, make them decide in favor of countries other than those in Europe. This trend has to be faced in connection with the demographic developments all over Europe. The figures are speaking for themselves. The declining birth rate and the aging of the population will have unwanted effects on economic developments, the employment market, the national budget, the per capita debt, and the ability to innovate if these demographic trends are not counteracted by preventive policies. In Germany, for instance, the drain on the social security system brought about by the aging of the population will double within the next 50 years. When we take the current demographic developments in Central and Eastern Europe into account, we come straight to the conclusion that the countries of the EU and the accession countries are in the same boat. For instance, the birth rate of Italy, 1.2 percent, is similar to that of Hungary. Western European politicians fear uncontrolled migration flows from EU enlargement. Their assumption is based on EU figures. The figures from Central and Eastern Europe, however, lead to a completely different assumption. Therefore, what is missing is a common methodology in finding these demographic figures to establish a common database that allows for reliable "enlarged analyses."

Structuring Migration

Future demand for labor cannot be forecast with certainty, particularly in relation to individual occupational groups. However, the general demand for highly qualified labor and for employees in the service sector will intensify, and the need for graduates of colleges and universities will increase. Therefore, considerable efforts are necessary to use the existing national labor force better than before. Unemployed persons must have the opportunity to improve their education skills. The necessary measures must be part of a structured migration policy that is not only determined numerically but also defined in terms of qualifications.

A flexible migration system is needed that can help adjust supply and demand in the employment market. It is particularly important to gain highly qualified migrants to the EU whose innovative abilities and technological knowledge could make a decisive contribution to securing a better economic future. The "competition for the best brains" must be intensified. The leading personnel from the business world as well as from science and research should be offered considerably simplified entry rules and optimal conditions of residency. The EU must become more attractive for qualified migrants, and at the same time it must define mechanisms to deal with migrants with temporary residency. The German Independent Commission on Migration has proposed a point system. This system takes the abilities of migrants to integrate into the society and the employment market into consideration.

It must be guaranteed that, as far as possible, all sides win through the international mobility of labor. A decisive element for this is to allow and encourage this mobility in both directions and to create incentives for a return to the countries of origin. But any future European legislation on migration oriented to the employment market must take the principle of subsidiarity into account. In this context, the differing conditions of national employment markets should be taken into consideration.

Besides this "self-interested" kind of migration, there must always be an unselfish humanitarian approach to those who need help. However, it must combat undesirable developments and, where possible and feasible, not forgo limitation and management. Thus, the obligation to take a humanitarian approach is the feature of a migration policy that challenges the host society but does not burden it. The candidate countries have become not only transferring countries but also receiving countries from asylum seekers. These movements confront them more than the EU countries. The challenges presented by asylum seekers and refugees require a common and coherent European asylum system. Thus the quick attainment of the objectives for refugees and asylum policies set in the Amsterdam Treaty is indispensable. Moreover, there is the necessity to establish minimum standards for asylum procedures.

Strengthening Integration

The integration of people migrating to the EU presents a special challenge; it is a complex and long-term undertaking. There is a close connection between migration and integration: if it is agreed that there will be migration to the EU, successful integration of those who are already living in the European countries must be sought. Integration is a societal process that includes all people living in the country. As a political task, integration efforts should allow migrants coming to the EU to participate on equal terms in the economic, cultural, and political life of the host country. Integration entails responsibilities for both sides: the host society must provide migrants with permanent residency prospects and access on equal terms to the employment market and the education system; migrants are required to learn the language of their host country and are obliged to respect and follow its constitution and laws. Various surveys have confirmed that language capabilities are the port of entrance for successful integration. Access to the education system and the employment market are also of major importance. Migrants to the EU are affected by educational deficiencies. In the worst case, foreign youths drop out of school completely, lessening their chances for a successful entrance into professional life. Many young migrants lack information about education programs and service training.

To eliminate the existing deficits, numerous coordinated measures are necessary. For instance, migrant youths and their parents should be clearly informed about the significance of scholastic and vocational education for finding a job in the host country. For economic reasons and reasons related to integration policy, migrants having realistic prospects of permanent residency should be granted immediate unlimited access to the employment market of their host country.

Family solidarity must be encouraged. The legally secured option of reuniting immediate family members should be a matter of priority in the EU. For the age of entry of dependent children, the following applies generally: a positive course of integration is generally facilitated if the entry takes place as early as possible. However, a separation of parents and their minor children must be rejected for reasons based on family policy.

Selling the Added Value

In the past decades migration and asylum policy was defined as a more or less artificial playground for scientific experts, especially in Germany. The picture has changed completely. Today's migration and asylum policy is at the center of political decisionmaking at the national and European levels.

Given that

- the countries of the EU will remain a destination for migrants from all over the world
- the geographical landscape for migration will expand with EU enlargement
- national differences in dealing with migration within this landscape will increase
- the EU as well as the accession countries will depend on migrants for demographic reasons,

the Europeans should develop a common coherent framework for migration and asylum policy. Political decisionmakers and society as a whole need to understand that the effective management of migration is of vital interest for each country. The issue must be seen beyond national perspectives within a European framework. That is why we need to do a better job selling the added value of migrants for our societies to our citizens. For this reason, we need a new communication strategy that is based on a new, more sensitive vocabulary. Instead of speaking of illegal migration, uncontrolled migration flows, migration pressure, social dumping, and "Fortress Europe," we should use terms with positive connotations that stress the social and economic added value of migrants for our societies. In general, we must initiate a broader discussion about our perceptions of migration. A societal climate of acceptance is an important prerequisite for the success of social integration processes.

In addition to these efforts, we must institutionalize the exchange of expertise and the flow of information about current developments in migration and asylum policy between the national governments and the decisionmakers in Brussels. Only a clear analysis of the legislation and political debates in each country will enable us to identify the possibilities for a consensus at the European level. It will take decades to change the understanding of migration in our Western societies, but it is an effort we must make sooner than later. The way in which the Europeans resolve migration policy will influence the competitiveness of the enlarged EU in a globalized world.

Notes

1. This chapter includes recommendations of the *Report of the Independent Commission on Migration to Germany*, published on July 4, 2001, in Berlin.

2. The term "migration" must be defined in a much broader sense than in the past. Today migration includes all kinds of migrants—those who are in their host country on a temporary protection basis and those who are able to stay for an undefined period of time and have a clear long-term perspective for integration in their new country.

CHAPTER 20

Discussant Notes

Werner Sengenberger

Ms. Suessmuth in her paper presented the key findings and recommendations of the German Commission on Immigration that she has been chairing. The Commission's report can clearly bring more realism and rationality to the German policy on migration. It recognizes that contrary to the rhetoric in part of the political spectrum, de facto immigration has been happening for quite some time, and it rightly emphasizes that immigration may be beneficial to the German labor market and the level of welfare. Starting from the observation of serious shortages of skilled labor in Germany, notably in relation to information technology and biotechnology, the Commission recommends—in line with the immigration policy of many developed countries—a redirection of German immigration policy on qualified labor in order to alleviate the skill gap.

From the perspective of the International Labour Organization (ILO), the general issue to be addressed is how a global framework for international worker migration can be designed that accommodates the interests of both the receiving countries and the sending countries. First, such a framework will have to take into account that labor migration can be an instrument for reducing imbalances in the supply and demand of labor resources across countries. Outmigration of labor from developing countries not only may reduce the volume of surplus labor, but also is often part of government policy to raise capital inflow from the remittances of the country's expatriate workers. At the same time, if developing countries lose skilled labor, this may harm their development prospects, and it may further exacerbate the development gap between the high-income countries and the poor countries, if the former receive labor with skills paid for by the latter. Therefore, to the extent to which such skill transfers are deemed useful by both the sending and the receiving countries, a mechanism of financial compensation for human capital formation may be considered.

Second, any immigration policy must seek adequate solutions to the problem of unskilled immigrants, many of whom are illegal entrants or refugees and asylum seekers working illegally. These workers are often without protection. They are likely to become victims of discrimination and to be treated as second-class citizens. This holds even if they become permanent citizens, and it applies also to their offspring.

Third, as a recent report of the International Organization of Migration has revealed, there has been a rising level of trafficking of women, including girls, from developing and transition countries into the affluent countries of Europe and North America for the purpose of prostitution. A good deal of this type of migration is forced, and it violates basic worker rights under ILO's Declaration of Fundamental Principles and Rights at Work, among them ILO Convention 182 concerning the worst forms of child labor.

The papers by Rutkowski, Przybyla, and Fazekas analyze the persistent, and even increasing, regional disparities in Poland and Hungary. I concur with many of the comments made by Michael Landesmann. I take issue with the conclusion in the paper on Poland that identified the minimum wage as a major cause of the regional differential in unemployment. For several reasons, it would be problematic to conclude that minimum wages produce unemployment.

- The decisive cost criterion for the decisions on location is not labor costs as such but unit labor costs, that is, the ratio of labor costs to productivity levels; productivity tends to be low where wages are low because the latter cannot attract skilled and motivated workers.

- An important factor for investment decisions is the social and physical infrastructure.

- Statistical association is not to be equated with causation; even if it could be established that there is a link between minimum wages and levels of growth, employment, or unemployment, it does not follow that lowering the minimum wage is the only or best prescription for alleviating regional disparities.

There are countries in Europe, such as Denmark, with comparatively high minimum wages, or relatively small gaps between the minimum wage and the average wage, that have attained high levels of employment, low unemployment, and comparatively high regional equality. At the same time there are countries with low levels of minimum wage, such as the Czech Republic, that have seen high and widening regional employment disparities. Labor market regulation does not necessarily create labor market rigidities. Rather, it can contribute to raising functional-type flexibility. There need not be a tradeoff between flexibility and security arrangements.

Minimum wages pose a problem for employment only if we follow the tenets of orthodox economics—the view that wages and wage distribution are the exclusive or main clearing mechanism in the labor market. In this view, large wage differentials undisturbed by a minimum floor are indeed required for efficient resource allocation. Minimum wages—and other interventions that set minimum standards or compress differentials—create imperfections and distort labor market adjustment. Consequently, the policy prescription is to remove such distortions to restore equilibrium.

The paper on Hungary by Károly Fazekas indicates, however, that the self-regulating market may not work in the expected way. Regional unemployment disparities in Hungary increased despite increased wage dispersion. Freeing the labor market from regulations has not diminished the regional disparities in Hungary. On the contrary, the unregulated inflow of foreign direct investment has accentuated the employment and income gaps that existed at the beginning of the transition period. Most of the inward investment flew to the most-developed, high-cost regions of Budapest and northwest Hungary. The reason was their better infrastructure in terms of education, housing, and transport. A serious problem generated by large wage differentials is the working poor, since those with low wages tend to be unable to cover living expenses.

I tend to agree with the analysis and conclusions of Fazekas's paper. It sees the main cause of the Hungarian regional disparities in a lack of aggregate demand for labor and the uneven endowment of the regions in terms of physical and social infrastructure. The remedy will be a proactive approach to balance this infrastructure, notably to invest in education, vocational training, housing, and health in the depressed regions as part of public policy. Private investment flows alone will not redress the existing unevenness because private enterprises will not just look to labor costs, but will seek skilled labor, entrepreneurial capacity, good transport, and communication facilities. Active public policies toward labor and other regional resources are thus an alternative to the use of large wage differentials, and the concomitant low wages, for gaining flexibility for adjustment. The advantage is that high relative poverty can be avoided.

Wages are important not merely for allocating labor, but for securing minimum income and consumption power, and also for productivity and innovation. According to the orthodox position, a wage floor creates disincentives for employment. But a wage floor may lead to efforts by firms to reach productivity levels commensurate to pay the minimum wage. They may do this through better management, process and product innovation, skills training, and better work organization. Thus minimum wages may spur investment into human capital and the efficient use of labor. Conversely, the absence of minimum standards may elicit complacency and lack of competitiveness.

It would be misleading to equate the active, interventionist approach to the labor market with rigidities, or lack of freedom for employers. While it is true that an active approach may block some options for adjustment, it tends to open up other channels for flexibility, such as the one associated with the use of an educated and skilled labor force. It gives firms "freedom for" particular actions, whereas the free market approach emphasizes the "freedom from" employer constraints through regulation.

CHAPTER 21

Discussant Notes

Michael Landesmann

Let me start with two comments on Professor Suessmuth's presentation. Research on migration by Western European countries and African countries comes out with very similar estimates because the methodologies used are very similar. They use gravity models that examine the impact of region, geographic proximity, and wage gaps, and unemployment or labor market differentials in the different regions. It depends, of course, on what group of countries or regions are being compared. But research on Poland in this topic, or at least things I know from the Czech and Hungarian research, shows that the estimates are very similar to Western European and African estimates.

Among the researchers at least, there is not much disagreement. There is a lot of convergence in methodology and also in terms of the overall numbers. Whether these results come through at the political end of the debate is probably more questionable.

Second, economic researchers in Europe must take much more seriously the analysis of the dynamic impact of migration. The types of studies that were made in preparation of EU enlargement by the research community analyzed the static impact—mostly, of course, the distributional impact—of migration on labor markets. There is probably, at the moment, insufficient attention given to the dynamic impact. Particularly in relation to comparisons of the United States and Europe, this dynamic or growth impact is essential.

Now I will discuss the Rutkowski-Przybyla and Fazekas papers. They cover a lot of topics, and I will pick out a few things that I found particularly interesting or innovative, and I will err more on the critical side than on the positive side when I debate some of the results. Both papers emphasize the persistence and widening of regional inequalities. Quite straightforwardly, they both stress the importance of education and the dissemination or dispersion of educational capacities across the regions, which is probably the single most important variable.

The issues that give rise to more critical debate are the issue of wages and the minimum wage. I begin with some points in Mr. Fazekas's paper. When we look at regional unemployment, we should not take a partial view of the issue. We should not focus only on the labor market. Regional unemployment, of course, is closely linked to the dynamics of regions, so it is linked to growth, to the development of income generation, and to structural change in the regions. I am a bit skeptical about papers that look at the issue of regional labor markets by analyzing the labor market by itself. I like Mr. Fazekas's paper because it does not do that.

It is clear that distance matters, distance from the western regions. In the applicant countries an enormous gap is opening between capital cities and the rest of the economy. More comparative research of Western Europe and the applicant countries is needed on whether this dispersion is wider compared to the normal structure of income and labor market gaps between the capital city and the rest of the country. In this context it would be interesting to know whether the gap between the capital city and other urban centers is also widening, except the ones that are on the western border. Is development of urban agglomerations below the capital city developing in line with what you could observe in other economies? The issue that is most clearly emerging in Hungary, compared to the other applicant countries, is the enormous impact of foreign direct investment. In his paper, Fazekas mentions that the evidence for employment generation from FDI is rather low, although again it is a direct measure of FDI impact on labor markets rather than the overall impact on value-added generation and income generation.

Labor costs combine two variables, productivity and wage rates. And the two papers emphasize either one or the other. In the Fazekas paper, it is pointed out that in regions where labor costs fall relatively, there is a positive employment effect or a positive effect on the labor market situation. As noted, this is due to productivity differentials. These regions are undergoing very high productivity growth.

In the Rutkowski-Przybyla paper, the same variable labor costs are used to emphasize the importance of wage differentiation rather than productivity differentiation. So one can interpret these variables in both ways, and I think it is worthwhile to decompose the effects, in fact, in both papers. The Rutkowski-Przybyla paper says that the magnitude of migration from high-unemployment regions is far from negligible. And the paper shows an interesting interaction effect between the level of schooling and the effect of transport costs.

Now let me come to the more controversial issue of wage flexibility and the minimum-wage effect. The Rutkowski-Przybyla paper is a starting point, but it does not provide a robust basis for showing that wage flexibility has a positive impact on employment developments or reductions of unemployment or the issue of the minimum-wage effect. In fact, to acknowledge that, the paper says it may have an *effect* not that it has a *proven effect*. Let me take an example. The simple table on correlations, you give about importance of various factors, some variable correlations. With the hiring rates, you use as an indicator for wage flexibility the gap between the bottom-decile wage and the medium wage. How is this to be interpreted? We know that in the areas that are doing rather well, there is a lot of differentiation on the upper end of the wage scale or the income scale, and of course the medium wage would be lifted. So one would expect that this wage differentiation effect in the higher income regions could drive this variable. It is, again, not sufficient to emphasize here the wage flexibility at the bottom end. And, of course, the issue of causality and the problems with causality run throughout the paper and are not resolved in the current formulations.

The analysis of the "biting factor," namely, the relationship between the minimum wage and the wages paid to different groups of workers, can be interpreted in a number of ways. It could be interpreted as wage flexibility, that represents, obviously, the wage structure in an economy. Now, in the regression presented in the Rutkowski-Przybyla paper, a significant effect of this variable of the biting factor on the hiring rates was found. But again we do not know what is cause and what is effect. The analysis is restricted to a one-point-in-time regression analysis across regions, so we cannot follow in which way these wage differentiations are caused by differences in unemployment rates or hiring rates or whether they are in any way causally linked. The causation has to be looked at in the other way.

So I would be rather cautious with the policy statements toward the end on the basis of the research done so far that wage flexibility and a reduction of the minimum wage would be helpful for the poorer regions.

CHAPTER 22

Discussant Notes

Arvo Kuddo

In their papers Juan F. Jimeno, Viktor Steiner, and Jennifer Hunt focus on two main questions. First, what are the patterns of labor market mobility (especially geographical mobility) in transition countries after inclusion to the European Union based on the experience of East Germany? Second, how have labor market institutions and the work force (in particular, in the 1980s and 1990s in Spain and in the 1990s in the eastern part of Germany) adjusted to the new political and economic environment?

Labor migration is a major source of contention within the European Union and between the EU and the CEE-10. In the European Union the free movement of workers and their families, students, and pensioners between the Member States is guaranteed. Equal treatment should be pursued to take up available employment, as well as equal treatment in remuneration, in dismissals, in registration as unemployed, in taxation, and in social protection. The European Commission has proposed a transition period of up to seven years for free movement of labor from accession countries to the 15 current members of the EU.

In fact, emigration of labor from Central and Eastern Europe to the EU has already been significant. In the 1990s, approximately 830,000 people from CEE accession countries resided in the EU, of whom 300,000 were legally employed. However, albeit significant in absolute numbers, this amount of labor represents only 0.2 percent of the total EU labor force and 6 percent of non-EU workers (Oxford Analytica Brief 2001).

By the estimates of the Ministry of Social Affairs of Estonia, in the 1990s around 15,000 people (out of a total population of 1.37 million based on the census of 2000) left to go to Western Europe, mostly for family reasons, and around 5,000 of them are working (including 2,000 in Finland). In 1990–2000 the total registered net migration was about 86,000 people, which means that most migrants actually left to go to CIS states (SOE 2000).[1]

Current projections of migration flows, in particular from the Baltic region, tend to be heavily exaggerated. For example, Finnish trade unions estimate that around 400,000 labor migrants might move from Estonia to Finland, although the working population of Estonia equals around 600,000. In Lithuania recent polls suggest that around 300,000 people out of 3.49 million might leave the country after the accession (*Postimees* 2001).

The wage gap as well as differences in the level of social guarantees between the CEE-10 and EU-15 is indeed enormous. In addition, unemployment and mass layoffs are an important impetus for migration. Unemployment rates in most accession countries are at present much higher than the average for the EU. In early 2001 in the Slovak Republic, Poland, and Estonia the unemployment rate equaled 19, 16, and 14 percent, respectively, but the rate was much less in the Czech Republic, and Hungary—8 and 6 percent, respectively. Regional disparities in unemployment rates in all accession countries are much higher. Especially among youth, the unemployment rate is stubbornly high. This would amplify the pressure on labor migration from Central and Eastern Europe.

On the other hand, importing labor from outside the EU is also necessary because of the demographic structure of its population. The United Nations estimates that the EU will require an annual net migration of 1.4 million people per year between now and 2050 to maintain a stable working population. The aging of the population would specifically facilitate recruitment of highly skilled social care and health care workers. Importing labor from outside the EU is an alternative to a labor shortage. Moreover, labor mobility within the EU is very low compared to the U.S. level, and liberalization of labor markets may facilitate geographical mobility and contribute to efficient utilization of the work force.

Hunt's paper, with data based on the German Socio-Economic Panel, provides valuable information on the dynamics and structure of migration flows between East and West Germany. Young people are moving to the West to study, and tertiary education graduates are moving immediately after graduation. Laid-off workers represent another major group of migrants. In migration flows in East Germany, commuters prevail. During the survey period, 63 percent of people who moved either their home or workplace to the West were commuters.

Despite the obvious attraction for labor to relocate from the Central and Eastern European applicant countries, there exist serious impediments for massive migration flows. Qualification requirements still stand. Cultural and language barriers have a significant importance. Although workers from Central and Eastern

Europe compete for jobs that are typically less attractive, and their wage demands are lower, the availability of vacant jobs limits migration flows even if the structural mismatch in the local labor markets is involved. Capital stocks and housing stocks need to be adapted to accommodate potential labor migrants. The number of people actually ready to leave their country once it joins the EU will not be as high as the numbers expressed in public polls.

Numerous surveys in the CEE region confirm that geographical mobility as well as occupational mobility resulting from inappropriate qualifications of the population is very low, especially in high unemployment regions. Among labor migrants, commuting within the same county prevails. Therefore, emigration from distant regions of the CEE will probably be much more limited than in the case of East Germany.

Some surveys in accession countries confirm that there are high expectations for the EU as a vehicle of development. However, among the priorities people think can be solved within the framework of the EU, new employment opportunities are not valued as highly as many other aspects. Most Estonians expect that accession to the EU will improve economic development, national security, foreign trade possibilities, and the environmental situation. Only 36 percent of respondents agreed that the EU will lead to better possibilities to find a job; 20 percent feared that EU membership will make it harder to find employment (Ruutsoo and Kirch 1999).

While the impact of labor displacement on EU labor markets has attracted wide attention, less debate has been focused on the impact of accession on the labor markets of the applicant countries themselves. Due to a rapid decline in birth rates in the 1990s, the continuous aging of the population, and the potential migration flows of the most active and qualified part of the work force to current EU-15 countries, the prospect of a mounting labor shortage and an escalating dependency ratio in CEE-10 countries will become apparent at the end of this decade. This emphasizes the need for labor reforms in accession countries.

Despite high unemployment rates, the structural mismatch in the labor markets of accession countries is significant, and further large-scale labor migration will have a significant negative impact on some segments of the economy. In the EU the labor markets of the accession countries have to compete with the rest of the Union. The Spanish experience in this regard is very instructive, as Juan Jimeno points out in his paper. The Spanish institutions were not properly designed to accommodate the structural adjustments required by accession to the EU.

The prospect of EU membership has already become one of the most powerful incentives for undertaking difficult reforms, including institution-building. However, in several areas progress has still been slow. Thus labor market institutions need to be adjusted for the work force to stay flexible and competitive in EU labor markets.

In particular, labor legislation in most accession countries (like in Spain before the 1984 reforms) tends to be too rigid and restrictive, especially with respect to the freedom of employers to dismiss workers (see chapter by Riboud, Silva-Jauregui, and Sánchez-Páramo in this volume). As an example, in many EU countries (Belgium, Denmark, Finland, Germany, Sweden), the notification period is relatively short, and severance pay is not even legislatively mandated (OECD 1999). In several accession countries it can still take six or more months to dismiss workers on personal grounds or because of economic redundancy, and it can take even longer in the case of collective dismissals. Also in CEE-10 countries, collective bargaining needs to be enhanced to strengthen industrial relations and facilitate labor market flexibility.

Although the EU regulations do not regulate minimum standards on employment services in detail, accession countries need to adjust their employment services. In particular, according to EU Directives, the unemployment benefit is paid by the country in which the job seeker was employed last. Low social guarantees in case of unemployment (or strong protection in the current EU-15) may discourage workers from the Eastern bloc countries.

Social security schemes in accession countries need to be brought into compliance with EU standards. This will increase associated costs, as happened in Spain in the 1980s and 1990s. The challenge is that the tax burden on labor in the CEE-10 is already much higher than the average in the EU.

With the exception of Poland and Hungary, accession countries spend modest amounts of budgetary resources on active and passive labor market policies. (Estonia spent as little as 0.2 percent of GDP.) In recent years outlays for unemployment benefit payments increased, which squeezed spending on active labor market programs.

The educational and professional structure and qualifications of the work force in many sectors of the CEE-10 economies do not reflect the needs of the national economy. To tackle the skills gap, education and training systems need to be modernized, and their links to the workplace strengthened. A significant portion of the youth population is leaving the education system without any professional education. Vocational schools specifically are to be restructured for compliance with European standards. Curriculum and equipment in schools should be updated with the support of EU funds. Adult training, retraining, and lifelong education are also a key to improving the quality of labor.

In the last 10 years labor reallocation across sectors has been intense, and in most applicant countries the structure of the work force has already adjusted to EU levels. The private sector and the services sector dominate in all accession countries. Nevertheless, productivity in the economy lags behind Western levels. Thus the key to labor market policies is that workers should be equipped to take up new employment opportunities locally, at higher productivity levels and higher wages.

An important aspect of the accession process is that the CEE-10 will become border regions for the CIS states. This may lead to the opening of the borders for migration from CIS countries. Currently migration to Estonia is limited by immigration quotas as well as by requirements to obtain special permits for employment and temporary residence in Estonia. Quotas equal 0.05 percent of the resident population, or around 650 people annually, but quotas exclude Estonian nationals, EU countries, and some other Western countries (for example, the United States, Norway, Iceland, Canada). However, despite high unemployment rates, there is already a shortage of labor in several professions, a shortage that may become even more acute after accession. Thus the pressure from the business community and outside to loosen migration policies may become a reality.

Since wage gaps are much more significant, and social safety nets are less developed, the relative gap between Eastern and Western Europe will probably persist much longer than in the case of Spain and the rest of the EU.

In sum, the work force in accession countries has a significant advantage in terms of labor costs compared to the EU countries. Proximity to new markets, especially in the CIS, and other factors will make investments in the economies of CEE-10 countries attractive enough. Opening up the EU markets will also significantly affect the growth of exports. The enlargement will spur East European countries' real GDP growth and elevate their per capita income levels.

Note

1. In the 1990s migration flows were heavily underreported.

References

OECD (Organisation for Economic Co-operation and Development). 1999. *OECD Employment Outlook.* Paris.

Oxford Analytica Ltd. 2001. "Eastern Europe/EU: Labour Displacement." *Oxford Analytica Brief* (April 2).

Ruutsoo, Rein, and Aksel Kirch. 1999. "Estonia at Europe's Threshold." *The Baltic Review* 14. Tallinn.

SOE (Statistical Office of Estonia). 2000. *Statistical Yearbook of Estonia.* Tallinn.

Virki, Tarmo, and Erkki Behovski. 2001. "Soome valitsus on tööjôu vabale liikumisele vastu." *Postimees*. April 28.

PART IV

European Social Model or Eurosclerosis?

CHAPTER 23

Does Eurosclerosis Matter? Institutional Reform and Labor Market Performance in Central and Eastern European Countries

Michelle Riboud, Carolina Sánchez-Páramo, and Carlos Silva-Jauregui

Whether or not labor market rigidities are an important contributor to persistently high levels of unemployment remains at the center of an important debate in Europe. European labor markets are often viewed as rigid and inflexible, unlike those in North America where legislation is less protective of employment and fosters greater mobility. The fairly high unemployment rates that persist in numerous parts of Europe are often attributed to these rigidities.

The debate has renewed relevance with the potential entry of new countries to the European Union (EU). Since those countries are compelled to have laws and policies consistent with the *acquis communautaire*, an interesting question is whether they have introduced in their labor markets the same rigidities that exist in other European countries. An even more fundamental question is whether those rigidities, if they exist, are slowing down the adjustment of labor markets in these economies, wasting potential for productivity growth and leading to a persistently high level of unemployment. In other words, are Central and Eastern European countries (CEECs) likely to contract a European disease, commonly called "eurosclerosis" on their way toward accession into the EU? Does this disease really matter?

The chapter will thus attempt to answer the following questions:

- To what extent have the CEECs—which aspire to enter the EU—adopted labor market institutions (job security provisions, support programs for the unemployed, and other related policies) that make the functioning of their labor markets relatively inflexible and rigid?

- How do their policies and legislation compare with those in the member countries of the EU and the Organisation for Economic Co-operation and Development (OECD)?

- To what extent have these institutions shaped labor market adjustment dynamics in these economies during the transition? How does the impact of institutions on labor market outcomes compare to that of macroeconomic and structural reforms? Have labor market institutions and policies had an impact on the effectiveness of economic reform programs? In other words, to what extent do they "matter"?

In our search for answers, we examine labor market institutions during the 1990s for a group of EU accession countries (the Czech Republic, Estonia, Hungary, Poland, the Slovak Republic, and Slovenia), following the methodology used by the OECD (1997, 1999). This allows us to compare our results for the CEECs with those presented by the OECD for its member countries, including EU countries. We then discuss the role played by these institutions in the context of the ongoing macroeconomic and structural reforms. In doing so, we relate to the economic literature that views labor market adjustment not uniquely as a function of labor market institutions, but rather as the result of the interaction between such institutions and other factors outside the labor market (Blanchard and Wolfers 1999).

We show that:

- CEECs, although adopting the set of policies and institutions common to European countries, do not constitute a monolithic group. There is diversity among them, and as a result some countries have a more flexible labor market than others. However, when compared to EU and OECD members, most of these countries tend to be in the middle of the "labor market flexibility" scale.

- CEECs have experienced tremendous changes in their labor markets in terms of labor reallocation across economic sectors, changes in patterns of labor force participation and employment-to-population ratios, and emergence of unemployment. These changes would not have taken place without wide-ranging economic reform programs. Changes in fiscal and monetary policy, price and trade liberalization, privatization, and introduction of financial regulations have had a huge impact on labor market dynamics.

- Even if the impact of labor market institutions has remained modest and hard to uncover, one should not conclude that they are insignificant. A number of signs (low employment creation, a rising proportion of long-term unemployed, specific patterns of labor force participation, and the size of the informal economy) reflect the impact of labor market institutions. One can also relate differences between countries to the diversity of policies and institutions.

The chapter begins with a description of selected labor market institutions in these countries and a comparison with labor market institutions in EU and OECD countries. The next section documents the main labor market developments. We then discuss macro and structural reforms implemented during the 1990s and their effect on the labor market compared to the effect of institutional changes. A conclusion follows.

The Flexibility of Labor Markets in Central and Eastern European Countries

Measuring the degree of flexibility or rigidity of labor markets is not an easy task due to the lack of a *unique* quantifiable indicator that can serve as a barometer. As pointed out by Freeman (1999), "there is no generally accepted taxonomy for classifying economies into different institutional groupings, not even a scale to measure the distance between particular institutional settings. Are Japanese institutions closer to those of the United States or Germany? Are United Kingdom institutions more American or European? We have no measures of institutions to answer these questions definitely."

It is nevertheless possible to take into consideration a set of indicators and classify countries on the basis of existing knowledge of the policy relevance of these indicators. This is the approach followed by Lazear (1990), Nickell (1997), Blanchard and Wolfers (1999), and the OECD in its *Jobs Study* and *Employment Outlook* (1994, 1999). We have adopted a similar approach in this chapter and discuss different sets of indicators of labor market policies and institutions. This set includes (1) an employment protection legislation index; (2) various measures of the coverage, cost, and effectiveness of passive and active labor market policies; and (3) indicators of union strength and the tax burden on labor (for example, payroll taxes).[1]

Using these indicators, we find that:

- CEECs do not constitute a monolithic group. Despite their common recent history and similar steps to join the EU, they have adopted somewhat different labor policies. In terms of employment protection, Hungary seems to have adopted the most flexible legislation and Slovenia the least flexible.

- Despite some disparity, these countries—when compared to EU and OECD members—tend to be in the middle of the "labor market flexibility" scale (with the exception of Slovenia). Their labor markets are definitely less flexible than those in the United States or the United Kingdom, but certainly not as rigid as those in Southern Europe.

- Although CEECs have adopted—again with some degree of variation—the set of policies (passive and active) common to all EU and OECD countries, they are devoting modest amounts of budgetary resources to the unemployed and, in this respect, are closer to the United States, the United Kingdom, and Southern Europe than to Central and Northern Europe.

Finally, these countries have moved away from a centralized wage bargaining system and toward a more liberalized system of wage negotiation. However, institutions and social norms inherited from the previous regime still play an important role in the bargaining process. Also the tax burden on labor in these countries is the highest in Europe. We comment on the differences and the commonalities with respect to each type of indicator.

Employment Protection Legislation

Employment protection legislation refers to regulations that restrict the employers' freedom to dismiss workers. While their objective is to "protect" the welfare of employees by reducing their exposure to unfair actions and to the risk of fluctuating incomes, these regulations may increase the costs of employing workers. The consequence can be a reduced flow of vacancies and thus lower employment levels.

We construct two different Employment Protection Legislation indices (EPL, versions 1 and 2) for the six CEECs using the OECD methodology. Version 1 considers exclusively legislation on permanent and temporary employment, while Version 2 expands the scope of the index to account for legislation on collective dismissals. Both indices aim at measuring the degree of strictness of the legislation. The use of the OECD methodology in both cases allows us to make comparisons not only among CEECs but also with EU members and other OECD countries.

Although we construct both indices below, we will only discuss the expanded version (Version 2).[2] This version of the EPL is a weighted average of 22 indicators, some readily available in quantitative form (for example, notice period or severance payment), some constructed from qualitative information (for example, difficulty of dismissal).[3] The indicators for the Czech Republic, Poland, and Hungary are based on OECD data, and the indicators for the remaining, non-OECD countries are based on the review of their most recent labor legislation. The EPL index takes values 1 to 6, and the higher the value the stricter is the employment protection legislation.

Clearly, countries in Central and Eastern Europe do not constitute a monolithic group. When we compare the value of the EPL index for all six countries, we find substantial disparities (table 23.1). Hungary has the most flexible labor legislation, with an EPL index value of 1.7, closely followed by Poland (2.0) and the Czech Republic (2.1). The Slovak Republic and Estonia occupy the middle ground, with an index of 2.4 and 2.6, respectively. Finally, Slovenia has the most restrictive labor regulations, with an EPL index value of 3.5.[4]

These disparities can, in turn, be explained by differences in regular employment legislation, temporary employment legislation, and collective dismissals legislation, with differences in temporary employment legislation being the largest. (The standard deviation of this indicator represents 50 percent of its mean value, compared to 15 percent for the other two indicators.)

Regular employment legislation establishes the rules for hiring and firing procedures for permanent workers, notification requirements, and severance payments. This legislation is most flexible in Hungary and Poland, with index values of 2.1 and 2.2, respectively. In Hungary a written statement to an employee is sufficient for the dismissal to take place, while in other countries the notice of dismissal must be shared with a third party, usually an employee representative body. In addition, in Hungary and Poland "unsatisfactory performance" and "job redundancy" are sufficient reasons for dismissal, whereas in the Czech Republic, Estonia, the Slovak Republic, and Slovenia employers are required to take into account social considerations, to look for retraining, or even to ensure the worker's transfer to another suitable position. Finally, in both Hungary and Poland the notice period is short and the severance payment small.[5]

Temporary employment legislation regulates the use of fixed-term contracts, their renewal and maximum duration, as well as the functioning of temporary work agencies. The Czech and Hungarian bills stipulate the least amount of restrictions (index values of 0.5 and 0.6, respectively), while the Estonian, Polish, and Slovak bills are stricter, with index values that are two to three times higher. Slovenia is an outlier in the group with the most restrictive legislation of all and an index value of 2.4.

These differences respond mainly to the fact that in the Czech Republic and Hungary temporary contracts can be used with almost no restrictions or limits to their number or duration, while in other countries they can be used only for specific reasons and for a limited period. In contrast, differences in the regulation of temporary work agencies are nil, with the exception of Slovenia where their use is limited to two months.[6]

Collective dismissals legislation defines the term "collective," as opposed to "individual," and stipulates notification requirements and payments associated with such dismissals. As was the case with regular and temporary employment, Hungary and Slovenia have the least and most restrictive legislation, with index values of 3.4 and 4.8, respectively, while the remaining countries fall in the middle. Although the definition of "collective dismissal" and most notification requirements are very sim-

TABLE 23.1 EMPLOYMENT PROTECTION LEGISLATION IN EU ACCESSION COUNTRIES, LATE 1990s

Country	*Regular employment legislation*	*Temporary employment legislation*	*Collective dismissals legislation*	*EPL Strictness Version 2*[a]	
				Index	*Rank*[b]
Czech Republic	2.8	0.5	4.3	2.1	3
Estonia	3.1	1.4	4.1	2.6	5
Hungary	2.1	0.6	3.4	1.7	1
Poland	2.2	1.0	3.9	2.0	2
Slovak Republic	2.6	1.4	4.4	2.4	4
Slovenia	3.4	2.4	4.8	3.5	6
Slovenia[c]	(2.9)	(0.6)	(4.9)	(2.3)	(4)
CEEC average	2.7	1.2	4.1	2.4	—
EU average[d]	2.4	2.1	3.2	2.4	—
OECD average[e]	2.0	1.7	2.9	2.0	—

— Not applicable.
a. Weighted average of indicators for regular contracts, temporary contracts, and collective dismissals.
b. All rankings increase with the strictness of employment protection.
c. Based on proposed labor code.
d. Does not include Greece and Luxembourg.
e. For the average for all OECD countries, see table 23.A1.
Sources: OECD 1999 and World Bank estimates for Estonia and Slovenia.

ilar in all these countries, there are some differences regarding the additional delays and costs imposed on employers in the case of collective dismissals versus individual dismissals.[7] For example, in Poland an additional month delay is required for the notification to take place, while in the Czech Republic the delay amounts to almost four months. Similarly, in Hungary and the Czech Republic there are no additional costs associated with collective dismissals, whereas in the other four countries the employer has to disburse additional severance pay or provide additional compensation, such as retraining or re-employment.

Differences in employment protection legislation not only exist among CEECs, but also, and to an even greater extent, among the members of the European Union and other OECD members. As already shown by the OECD studies (1994, 1999) as well as by Nickell (1997), the EPL index ranges from 0.7 to 3.7 among OECD countries (figure 23.1 and table 23.A1).[8] This large diversity is fully reflected within the EU, which includes countries such as the United Kingdom, Ireland, and Denmark that do not have strict legislation and, at the other side of the spectrum, countries in Southern Europe (Italy, Spain, and Portugal) that have by far the most protective legislation (with an EPL index equal to or larger than 3.1). Germany, France, and some Scandinavian countries occupy the middle of the range.

What constitutes no surprise is the comparison with the United States. That comparison does support the frequent assertion that European labor markets are much less flexible than the U.S. labor market. The U.S. index is the lowest of all. However, it is closely followed by the Anglo-Saxon countries that are part of the European Union, the United Kingdom and Ireland.

The comparison between the two sets of countries shows that CEECs tend to be in the middle of a "labor market flexibility" scale. Slovenia is the exception and falls at the end of the range (until the new legislation under preparation is approved). Labor markets in Central and Eastern Europe are definitely less flexible than in the United States, the United Kingdom, or Canada, but certainly not as rigid as in some countries of Southern Europe. Out of a total of 26 countries classified by order of increasing EPL index: (1) Hungary, Poland, and the Czech Republic hold positions 9, 10, and 11, respectively; (2) the Slovak Republic and Estonia hold rank 16 and 18, respectively; and (3) Slovenia is number 25. If Slovenia adopts its new labor code, it would climb up the ladder to rank 16 (table 23.A2).

These cross-country differences in the overall ranking, although not large, are enough to suggest that, when adopting new labor legislation during the transition period, the CEECs may have been influenced more by geographical or cultural proximity than by the desire to imitate a single European model. For instance, Estonia is close to Norway or Sweden in terms of the EPL index, while Slovenia seems closer to Italy or Germany.

FIGURE 23.1 EMPLOYMENT PROTECTION LEGISLATION INDEX IN SELECTED OECD AND EU ACCESSION COUNTRIES

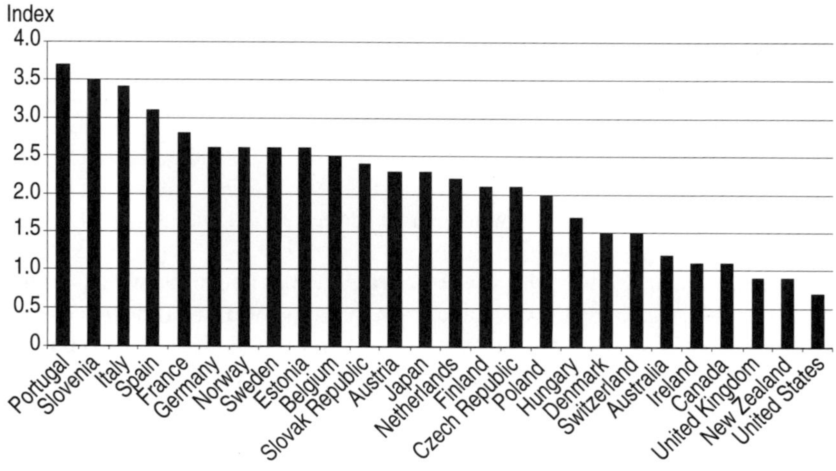

Note: Data are provided in table 23.A1.

Passive and Active Labor Market Policies

We analyze here the different policies adopted by the CEECs to support the unemployed. We distinguish between passive policies (for example, an unemployment insurance system) and active policies (for example, job assistance, training, public works, and wage subsidies). While passive labor market policies may create incentives to remain unemployed for a longer period of time, active policies aim at facilitating the re-entry into the labor market. The final impact on unemployment will depend on the features of the various programs, notably their relative generosity and importance in budgetary terms.

We again find that diversity prevails. Although CEECs have adopted a package of measures similar to those of other European countries, they differ significantly in terms of benefits, coverage, and duration of their programs, as well as in terms of their relative preference for passive or active policies.

PASSIVE LABOR MARKET POLICIES: UNEMPLOYMENT INSURANCE (UI)

The generosity (or lack thereof) of a particular unemployment insurance system depends on the quantity and duration of the benefits, and the system's eligibility rules. Hence, we concentrate on these features.

A simple way to compare *benefit quantity* across the CEECs is to look at benefit replacement ratios—the initial level of benefits divided by some average measure of previous earned income. Replacement ratios in the CEECs range from 40 to 64 percent, except in the case of Estonia where this number is 10 percent (table 23.2).[9] An alternative way to perform this comparison is to express benefits as a fraction of the minimum and average wages in each country. Then unemployment benefits represent between 60 and 100 percent of the minimum wage and between 10 and 45 percent of the average wage (table 23.3). Although they are within the EU and OECD ballpark (35 to 75 percent), these numbers reveal important differences across countries.

Benefit duration also varies from country to country. For instance, maximum duration in the Czech Republic and Estonia is 6 months, compared to 12 months in Hungary and the Slovak Republic, or even 24 months in Poland and Slovenia (table 23.2). These figures are similar to those in the EU and OECD countries (for example, 6 months in the United States, 12 months in the United Kingdom, 24 months in Spain, no limit in Belgium).

Instead of directly comparing *eligibility rules* across countries, which would be rather cumbersome, we use the coverage rate as a proxy indicator—the percentage of unemployed receiving unemployment insurance benefits (table 23.3). Coverage rates in the Czech Republic and Estonia are around 40 to 50 percent, having remained fairly stable over the last decade. This has also been the case in Hungary, although coverage is much higher there (70 to 75 percent). In contrast, the remaining three countries saw coverage rates fall continuously throughout the 1990s, from 80 to 20 percent in Poland and the Slovak Republic, and from 40 to 30 percent in Slovenia.

TABLE 23.2 FEATURES OF THE UNEMPLOYMENT INSURANCE SYSTEM IN EU ACCESSION COUNTRIES, LATE 1990s

Country	*Year of data*	*Benefit replacement ratio (percent)*	*Benefit duration (months)*
Czech Republic	1998	50	6
Estonia	1998	10[a]	3–6
Hungary	1997	64	12[b]
Poland	1996	40[c]	12–24[d]
Slovak Republic	1996	60	6–12[e]
Slovenia	1998	63	3–24[e]
CEE average	—	48 (55)[f]	—
EU average[g]	—	60	—
OECD average[h]	—	58	—

— Not applicable.

Note: Description of categories: (1) benefit replacement ratio—initial benefit level divided by previous earned income, (2) benefit duration—maximum duration, in months, depending on various criteria (age, family status, employment record/ contributive history).

a. Benefits are set at 60 percent of minimum wage. This amounts to approximately 10 percent of the average wage.
b. Requires four years of employment.
c. Forty percent of the average wage for the year prior to unemployment.
d. Increases with previous employment tenure.
e. A function of the worker's contributive history.
f. Figure in parentheses does not include Estonia.
g. Does not include Greece and Luxembourg.
h. Average for all OECD countries in table 23.A3.

Sources: OECD 1995, 1999; IMF 1999; IMF Article IV—Consultation with the Slovak Republic; World Bank estimates for Estonia and the Slovak Republic; World Bank 1998a, 1999.

Not surprisingly, such differences in benefit quantity and duration, and in coverage rates, translate into differences in *unemployment insurance spending*. The CEECs spend less than 1 percent of GDP on unemployment insurance, with the exception of Poland where this figure is 1.7 percent (table 23.4). Nevertheless, even at this low level, there is significant variation across countries, with Slovenia spending 0.9 percent and Estonia spending less than 0.1 percent.

These aggregate spending figures, however, can be misleading since they are partly a function of the number of unemployed.[10] To correct this caveat, we consider the ratio of GDP spending to the unemployment rate (both in percentage terms) as an alternative measure of expenditure. We then find that these countries have been spending a relatively small amount of resources to support the unemployed (between 0.01 and 0.12 percent of GDP per percentage point of unemployment).

These numbers are generally lower than those of EU and OECD members, which devote more than 1 percent of GDP (0.25 percent of GDP per percentage point of unemployment) to unemployment insurance (table 23.A4). In this regard, unemployment insurance policies in CEECs are closer to those of the United States, the United Kingdom, and Southern Europe than to those of countries in Central and Northern Europe (box 23.1).

TABLE 23.3 UNEMPLOYMENT INSURANCE SYSTEM IN EU ACCESSION COUNTRIES, 1991–98

Country	*1991*	*1992*	*1993*	*1994*	*1995*	*1996*	*1997*	*1998*
Czech Republic								
Coverage rate	—	46.5	50.5	47.1	44.2	50.1	51.4	49.2
% minimum wage	—	63.8	75.2	83.3	93.5	92.2	102.7	88.1
% average wage	—	30.2	28.4	26.6	25.2	23.8	24.0	20.0
Estonia								
Coverage rate	—	—	56.4	46.3	39.9	45.4	53.6	55.1
% minimum wage	—	—	60.0	60.0	40.0	35.3	28.4	27.3
% average wage	—	—	16.9	10.4	7.6	8.0	6.7	7.2
Hungary								
Coverage rate[a]	76.8	78.1	74.1	76.7	79.0	73.5	71.3	73.6
% minimum wage	75.0	75.0	75.0	75.0	75.0	—	—	—
% average wage	28.1	26.9	24.6	23.4	23.3	—	—	—
Poland								
Coverage rate	79.0	52.3	48.3	50.1	58.9	51.9	30.5	22.9
% minimum wage	100–305	100–310	95.3	98.0	81.0	110.0	—	—
% average wage	up to 100	up to 100	36.0	36.0	36.0	45.0	—	—
Slovak Republic								
Coverage rate	82.0	34.0	34.0	23.0	23.0	28.0	27.0	28.0
% minimum wage	—	—	—	61.7	72.2	70.6	106.9	109.3
% average wage	—	—	—	24.0	24.6	23.4	31.3	32.8
Slovenia								
Coverage rate	40.0	45.0	43.1	42.1	30.3	30.3	32.6	32.6
% minimum wage[b]	100–300	100–300	100–300	100–300	100–300	100–300	100–300	187.2
% average wage[b]	—	32.7	44.1	47.1	43.3	43.4	43.1	43.9

— Not available.

a. Includes unemployment benefits and income support once unemployment benefits are exhausted.

b. Data from the annual reports of the Slovene National Employment Office, the Bank of Slovenia Monthly Bulletin, and Slovenia: Labor Market Issues (World Bank 1998b).

Sources: Employment and Labor Market country reports prepared by the European Training Foundation 1999, EBRD 1999, Central Bank of Estonia, and OECD 1999.

ACTIVE LABOR MARKET POLICIES

Active labor market policies cover a vast array of programs, including job search assistance and counseling, training for the unemployed and youth, employment subsidies, direct job creation, and special measures for disadvantaged groups. Given the extensiveness and varied nature of all of these different programs, we feel that a detailed cross-country comparison of their features and roles is beyond the scope of this chapter. We therefore limit our analysis to spending in active labor market policies.

The EU accession countries spend between 0.08 and 0.83 percent of their GDP in active labor market policies (table 23.4). Even though these are not large amounts, they reveal important differences across countries. For example, Slovenia spends a share of its GDP that is 10 times higher than that spent by Estonia. When we adjust this measure to account for differences in unemployment rates, these countries spend between 0.01 and 0.11 percent of GDP per percentage point of unemployment.

TABLE 23.4 SPENDING ON PASSIVE AND ACTIVE LABOR MARKET POLICIES IN EU ACCESSION COUNTRIES

Country (year of data)	*Unemployment rate*	*Passive policies*		*Active policies*	
		% GDP	*Spending per unemployed*[a]	*% GDP*	*Spending per unemployed*[a]
Czech Republic (1999)	8.8	0.31	0.04	0.19	0.02
Estonia (1998)	9.9	0.08	0.01	0.08	0.01
Hungary (1997)	8.7	0.56	0.06	0.40	0.04
Poland (1996)	14.3	1.71	0.12	0.49	0.03
Slovak Republic (1996)	11.1	0.54	0.05	0.56	0.05
Slovenia (1998)	7.9	0.89	0.11	0.83	0.11
CEEC average	—	0.68	0.06	0.42	0.04
EU average[b]	—	1.73	0.26	1.16	0.16
OECD average[c]	—	1.43	0.23	0.92	0.14

— Not applicable.
a. Ratio of GDP spending on unemployment insurance to unemployment rate (both in percentage terms).
b. Does not include Luxembourg.
c. Average for all OECD countries in table 23.A4.
Sources: OECD 1997, 1999; Country Economic Memorandum (CEM) Slovak Republic; Estonia Labor Force Survey (ELFS) 1998.

BOX 23.1 SUPPORT TO THE UNEMPLOYED IN SELECTED OECD AND EU ACCESSION COUNTRIES

The ratio of GDP spending to the unemployment rate can be interpreted as the amount out of each dollar produced by a labor force member that is spent on the unemployed. For instance, if the Czech Republic spends on unemployment insurance 0.04 percent of GDP per percentage point of unemployment, we can also say that out of each dollar produced by a labor force member, 4 cents are given to the unemployed in the form of UI.

On average the CEECs spend 6 cents on passive labor policies out of every dollar produced by a labor force member, and an additional 4 cents on active labor market policies. In contrast, EU (OECD) countries spend 26 (23) cents on passive polices and 16 (14) cents on active policies out of every dollar. This is more than a sevenfold difference (table B1.1).

However, substantial differences exist among OECD members. The Netherlands, Denmark, and Austria are among the countries that spend the most per unemployed worker, with 85 (55), 60 (34), and 32 (14) cents spent on passive (active) policies, respectively. When compared to this group, the CEECs seem to be spending even smaller amounts in support of the unemployed.

(Box continues on the following page.)

BOX 23.1 *(continued)*

TABLE B1.1 SPENDING ON PASSIVE AND ACTIVE LABOR MARKET POLICIES

	Passive policies		*Active policies*	
Country	*% GDP*	*Unemployed*[a]	*Spending per % GDP*	*Spending per unemployed*[a]
EU average[b]	1.73	0.26	1.16	0.16
OECD average[c]	1.43	0.23	0.92	0.14
OECD—high spending				
Netherlands	2.81	0.85	1.80	0.55
Denmark	3.12	0.60	1.77	0.34
Austria	1.22	0.32	0.52	0.14
OECD—low spending				
United States	0.25	0.06	0.18	0.04
Japan	0.52	0.13	0.09	0.02
United Kingdom	0.82	0.12	0.37	0.05
Spain	1.41	0.09	0.81	0.05
CEEC average	0.68	0.06	0.18	0.04
Czech Republic	0.31	0.04	0.19	0.02
Estonia	0.08	0.01	0.08	0.01
Hungary	0.56	0.06	0.40	0.04
Poland	1.71	0.12	0.49	0.03
Slovak Republic	0.54	0.05	0.56	0.05
Slovenia	0.89	0.11	0.83	0.11

Note: Data from different years (see table 23.4).
a. Ratio of GDP spending on UI to unemployment rate (both in percentage terms).
b. No data for Luxembourg.
c. Average for all OECD countries in table 23.A4.
Source: OECD 1997, 1999; CEM Slovak Republic, ELFS 1998.

In contrast, countries like the United States, Japan, and Spain spend much smaller amounts on both passive and active policies. All three devote between 6 and 13 cents out of every dollar to UI, and between 2 and 5 cents to active policies. These numbers are significantly closer to those of the CEECs. Hence, even though on average the CEECs spend less on the unemployed than OECD and EU members do, their policies are fairly similar to those of some OECD/EU countries. Data for a larger selection of OECD countries can be found in table 23.A4.

Compared to the EU and the OECD, spending in active labor market policies in these six countries is fairly low on average, but substantial variation exists among the former. For example, the United States and Japan spend less than 0.2 percent of GDP on active policies, while the Netherlands spends 0.8 percent (table 23.A4). This suggests that, in general, the CEECs have followed closely the practices of the first group, devoting a modest amount of resources to these programs (box 23.1).

RELATIVE WEIGHT OF ACTIVE AND PASSIVE LABOR MARKET POLICIES

When choosing between active and passive policies, the CEECs have a mixed experience. Estonia, the Slovak Republic, and Slovenia spend almost the same on both types of programs, measured as the share of GDP per percentage point of unemployment, while the other three countries favor passive policies over active ones.

In doing this, they are closer to the average OECD member. In fact, most countries in the EU and the OECD devote more resources to their passive labor market policies than to their active ones, the exceptions being Italy, Norway, and Sweden.

Strength of Unions and the Tax Burden on Labor

We discuss here two of the main factors that influence wage formation and determine labor costs, namely, the role of unions in the collective bargaining process and the tax burden on labor. We choose to concentrate on these two measures for the sake of comparability between our results for the CEECs and Nickell's results for the OECD countries.

In most European countries, with the exception of the United Kingdom, trade unions play a significant role in wage determination and, even when the number of unionized workers is fairly low, agreements reached under collective bargaining can extend to nonunion members, thus covering a large fraction of the labor force. Furthermore, the impact that collective bargaining can have on wages is likely to depend on the degree of coordination that exists between different unions and employer associations, as well as on the extent to which the government is involved in the negotiation process.

Similarly, payroll and other taxes can increase the cost of labor, even in the absence of upward pressure on wages. Although, in theory, part of the tax burden can be passed on to workers through lower wages, it is not unreasonable to expect that high taxes on labor may have a negative effect on hiring and firing decisions.

We find that, compared to countries in the EU and the OECD, the CEECs fall in the middle of the range in terms of union strength and coordination regarding collective bargaining. In contrast, they have very high payroll and other taxes, well above those in Spain, Italy, or the Netherlands, which set the upper limit in the EU.

WAGE BARGAINING: THE ROLE OF UNIONS AND EMPLOYER ASSOCIATIONS

The CEECs offer a fairly homogeneous picture regarding wage bargaining and the role of unions and employer associations.[11] During the last decade, these countries have all started to move away from a centralized wage bargaining system toward a more liberalized regime of wage negotiation, and these changes have been especially relevant for newly created firms. As a result, although union density and coverage are still high, there are important differences between the public and the private sectors, with unions holding a much weaker position in the latter.

We present data on union membership and *de facto* union coverage, as well as on the degree of coordination among unions and employer associations. Membership is measured as the percentage of all salaried workers who belong to a union, while coverage is captured through a coverage index that takes a value of 1 when collective agreements cover less than 25 percent of all salaried workers, 2 if this number is between 26 and 69 percent, and 3 when coverage is above 70 percent. Finally, the degree of union and employer coordination is measured through an index that ranks from 1 (low) to 3 (high).

Union density ranges from a low of 34 percent of all salaried workers in Poland to a reasonably high 62 percent in the Slovak Republic. *Union coverage*, however, is large (above 70 percent) in most countries, with the exception of the Czech Republic and Estonia (table 23.5).

However, this does not translate into high union bargaining power due to low coordination among unions (table 23.5). In fact, although basic guidelines are sometimes established through tripartite negotiations with the government, most wage bargaining takes place at the industry or the firm level, and, in practice, in the private sector wages are set by employers.

TABLE 23.5 THE ROLE OF UNIONS AND PAYROLL TAXES IN EU ACCESSION COUNTRIES

Country	*1*[a] *Union density (%)*[b]	*2 Union coverage index*[c]	*3 Coordination*		*4 Payroll tax rate (%)*	*5 Total tax rate (%)*
			Union	*Employer*		
Czech Republic	42.8	2	1	1	47.5	73.4
Estonia	36.1	2	2	1	33.0	63.3
Hungary	60.0	3	1	2	44.0	81.5
Poland	33.8	3	2	1	48.2	80.0
Slovak Republic	61.7	3	2	2	50.0	81.0
Slovenia	60.0	3	3	3	38.0	69.1
CEEC average	49.1	—	—	—	43.4	74.7
EU average[d]	44.4	—	—	—	23.5	53.0
OECD average[e]	39.6	—	—	—	19.5	45.4

— Not available.

a. All data for 1995, except for Denmark, Ireland, Italy, Spain, and Sweden (1993), and estimated data for Slovenia.

b. Percentage of salaried workers that belong to a union.

c. 1: less than 25 percent of salaried workers are covered by collective agreements; 2: between 26 and 69 percent are covered; 3: 70 percent or more are covered.

d. No data for Greece and Luxembourg.

e. Average for all OECD countries in table 23.A5.

Sources: The Bank of Estonia, Business Eastern Europe, Deloitte Touche Tohmatsu International 1998, EIU 1998, ILO 1997, OECD 1997, the Polish Agency for Foreign Investment, and the World Bank.

In contrast, EU and OECD members present a more varied picture. Both union density and union coverage differ substantially across countries, with the United States and Sweden representing the two extremes (table 23.A5). In addition, coordination levels have changed substantially over recent years, with no identifiable unique trend. For example, unions and employer associations in Scandinavian countries and Central Europe tend to coordinate their wage bargaining activities, while very little coordination exists in the United Kingdom or in the United States (OECD 1997, Nickell 1997). This places the CEECs somewhere in the middle of the range, together with countries like Belgium or the Netherlands.

PAYROLL TAXES

Payroll taxes in Eastern European countries are high, even by Western European standards. Rates range from 33 percent in Estonia to 50 percent in the Slovak Republic. Only France, Italy, Spain, and Sweden have rates above 30 percent, and in no case higher than 40 percent (table 23.5 and figure 23.2).

During the transition period the fiscal pressure to maintain high payroll taxes, or even to increase them, was extremely strong. Unemployment was on the rise, and this forced governments to continuously increase spending on unemployment insurance systems and active labor market policies. An aging population and declining employment rates also put additional strain on the public pension system, through falling revenues and increased outlays. Finally, a decrease in other types of tax proceeds because of the economic contraction obliged the governments to look for alternative sources of revenues to cover public expenditures, in particular for health and social assistance.

Despite these problems, some countries, such as Hungary, have recently started to lower their payroll taxes, albeit at a very slow and gradual pace, and there is reason to believe that others will follow as the economic situation improves, bringing unemployment down. Moreover, the tax burden on labor exceeds the amount of the payroll tax. Consumption and income taxes also affect labor income and are part of the tax wedge between labor costs and take-home pay. When both consumption and income taxes are considered, the total tax burden on labor varies greatly between countries, and Eastern Europe continues to exhibit the highest total tax rates (table 23.5 and figure 23.2).[12]

Thus, according to the evidence presented in this section, we can say that, by the end of the 1990s, the EU accession countries had adopted labor market institutions that indeed resembled those in EU countries. However, in doing so they followed neither the most nor the least flexible "role models" but opted instead for a fairly moderate set of institutions. This placed them in the middle range of the flexibility scale. It is only with respect to payroll taxes that CEECs stand at the extreme end of the range.

Output and Labor Market Dynamics in the Transition

Before trying to assess the role played by labor market institutions in shaping the labor markets of CEECs, we consider the economic and social context in which

FIGURE 23.2 TAX BURDEN ON LABOR IN SELECTED OECD AND EU ACCESSION COUNTRIES

A. Payroll tax rate

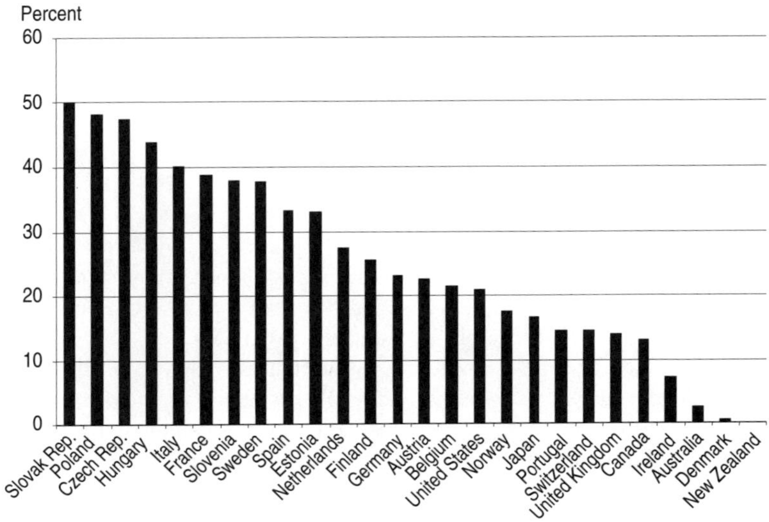

Note: Data are provided in table 23.A5.

B. Total tax rate

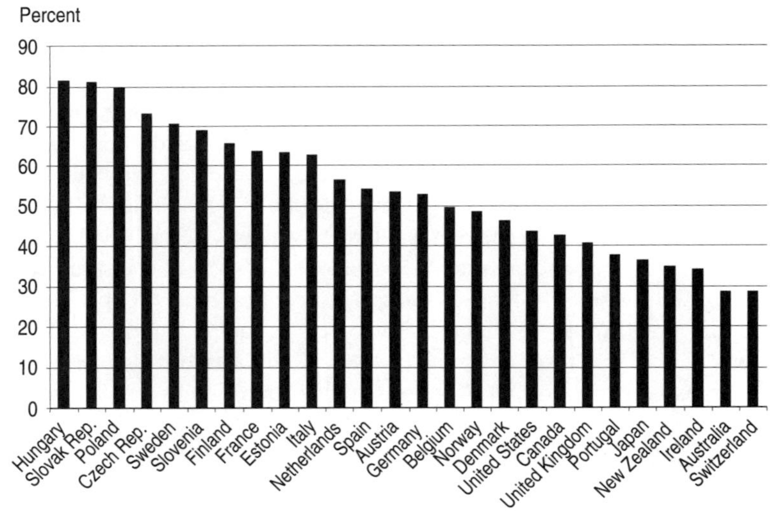

Note: Data are provided in table 23.A5.

these institutions were introduced or modified. The past decade was a time of dramatic transformation in Central and Eastern Europe. The fall of the Soviet bloc and the transition from command to market economy produced remarkable changes in the social, political, and economic infrastructures of CEECs. From an economic point of view, these changes were most important in real output (as measured by GDP) and factor markets, particularly in labor allocations, since the rules of economic interactions between members of the ex-Soviet bloc, and between them and the rest of the world, changed dramatically with the introduction of market-based practices. While in the command-economy system the risks of open unemployment and dislocation due to economic fluctuations were virtually nil, efficiency in the allocation of resources was poor. The rewards that market systems assign to different degrees of human capital or to specific skills were practically undifferentiated, and labor and capital productivity was low. Wages in the command production system were centrally determined and highly compressed. Labor mobility was for all practical purposes nonexistent. In a nutshell, job security was the prize, but this came at the expense of efficiency and distorted market incentives that eventually generated fatigue in the socialist production model.

Output

As the old socialist economic model was breaking apart, real output collapsed in every country of the Soviet bloc, albeit with different intensities (figure 23.3). In response, the new leaders of the Central and Eastern European economies formulated reform strategies focusing on macroeconomic stabilization and structural

FIGURE 23.3 GDP IN EU ACCESSION COUNTRIES, 1990–2000

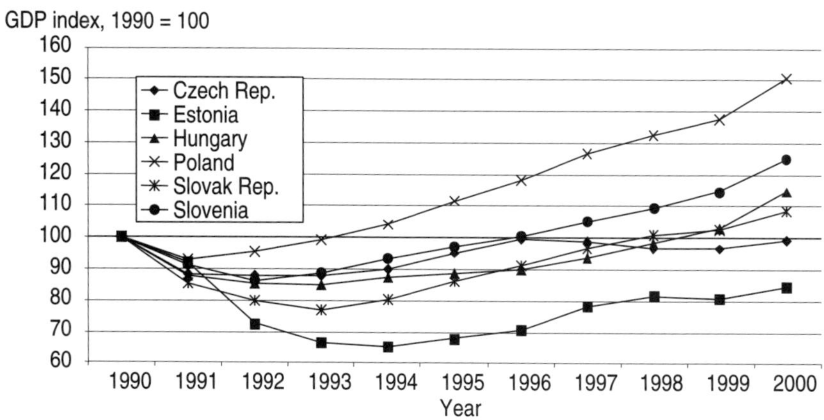

Note: Data are provided in table 23.A6.

reforms at the micro level. Modern market structures were gradually introduced. Labor markets adjusted to the new economic environment by reducing employment and labor force participation, especially of women, which was unusually high in Central and Eastern Europe, and by increasing open unemployment to rates unseen in this part of the world.

In addition to changes in the level of GDP, the restructuring process involved a significant shift in economic activity across sectors. By 1998 the contribution of agriculture to total GDP had fallen in all countries to at least half its 1989 level (table 23.6). A decline also occurred in the industrial sector over the decade, with its share of GDP falling between 7 percentage points for Slovenia (from 45.6 to 38.6 percent) and 27 percentage points for the Slovak Republic (from 58.5 to 31.6 percent). As a result of these changes, the service sector share of GDP grew significantly.

Even more drastic than these sectoral shifts was the transformation from public-sector-dominated to private-sector-dominated economies. The share of GDP produced by the private sector went from a low 5 percent in the former Czechoslovakia in 1990 to as much as 80 percent in the Czech Republic and Hungary in 2000. Only in Slovenia was this transformation less intense, and the private sector, while dominant, is smaller than elsewhere.

Employment, Unemployment, Labor Force Participation, and Wages

The transition had significant repercussions on labor market outcomes in terms of both levels and composition. The level of employment responded to the initial output decline (figure 23.4). As a result, aggregate employment fell substantially at the beginning of the 1990s and continued to decline in most countries, although at a slower pace, throughout the decade. Output started to grow in the mid-nineties and in some cases surpassed the pretransition levels (Poland, Slovenia), but employment levels have not recovered.

TABLE 23.6 OUTPUT PER SECTOR IN EU ACCESSION COUNTRIES (percentage of GDP)

	Agriculture		*Industry*		*Services*		*Private sector*	
Country	*1989*	*1998*	*1989*	*1998*	*1989*	*1998*	*1990*	*2000*
Czech Republic	8.5	4.2	57.7	39.2	33.8	56.6	5.0	80.0
Estonia	21.0	6.3	40.6	26.7	38.4	67.0	10.0	75.0
Hungary	15.6	5.5	46.7	28.2	40.7	66.3	20.0	80.0
Poland[a]	12.9	4.9	52.4	32.0	34.7	62.4	25.0	70.0
Slovak Republic	9.4	4.4	58.5	31.6	32.2	64.0	5.0	75.0
Slovenia	5.5	4.0	46.6	38.6	48.9	57.4	10.0[b]	55.0

a. Data for 1997 instead of 1998.
b. Data for 1991 instead of 1990.
Source: EBRD 2000.

FIGURE 23.4 GDP AND AGGREGATE EMPLOYMENT LEVELS IN EU ACCESSION COUNTRIES, 1990–2000

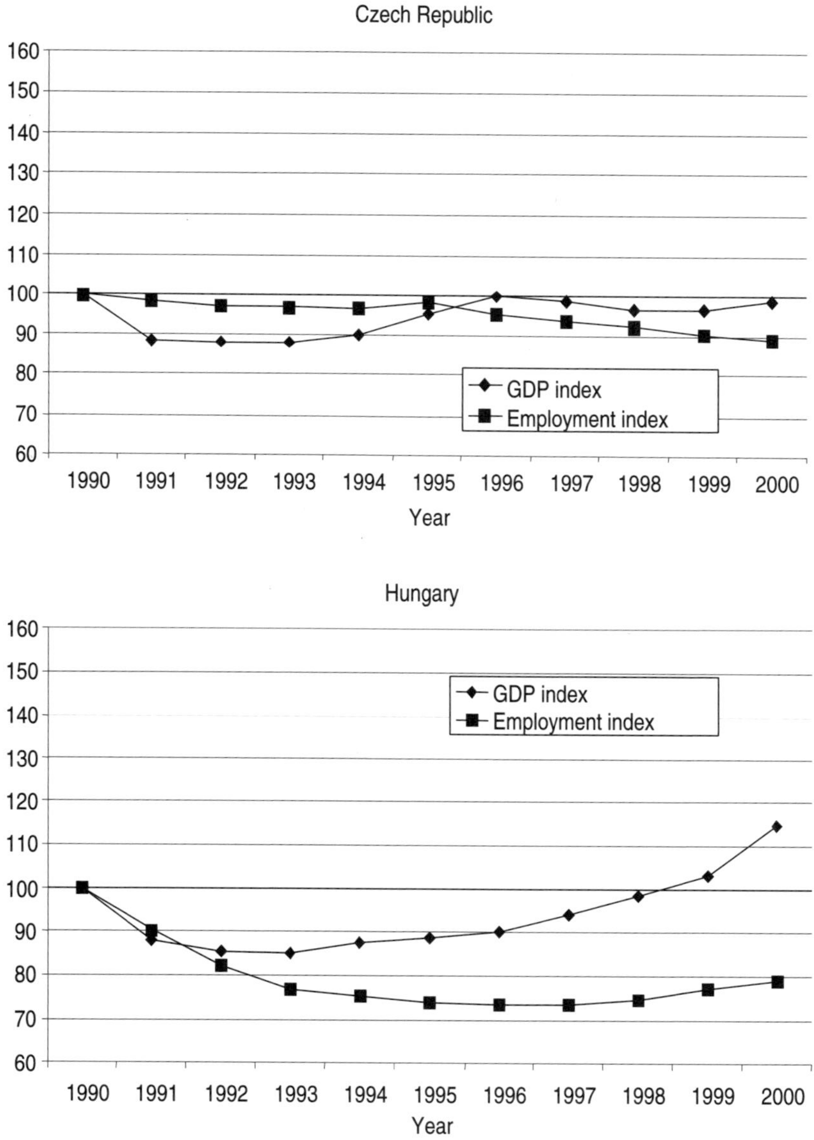

(Figure continues on the following page.)

FIGURE 23.4 (*continued*)

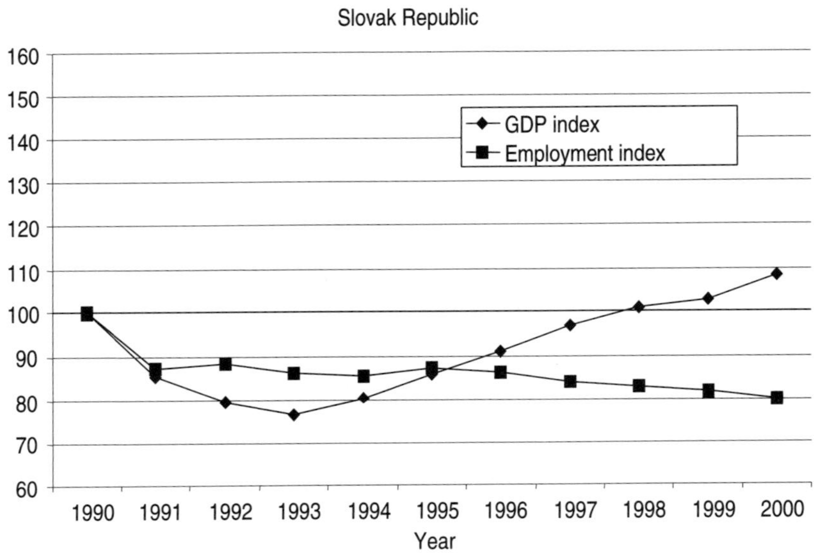

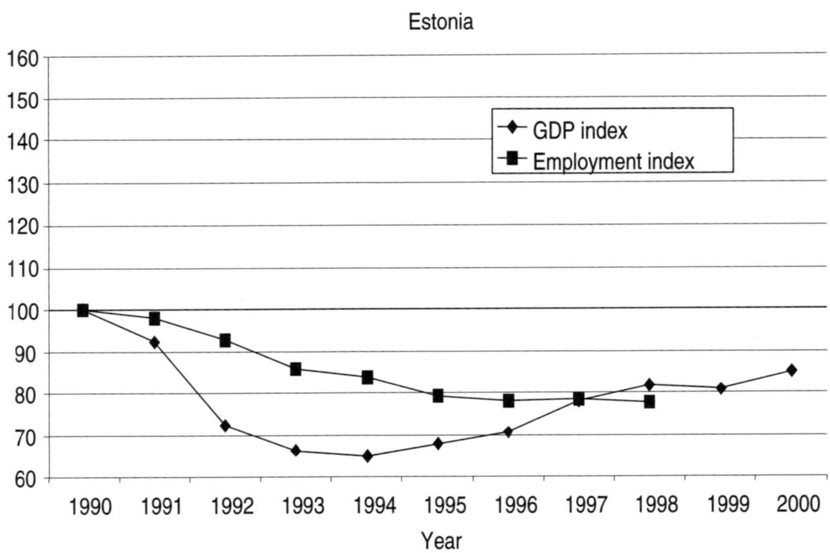

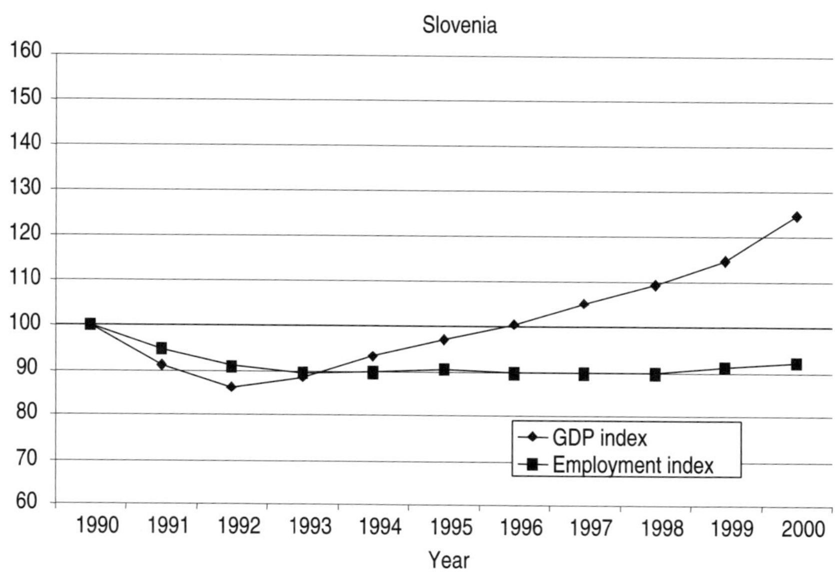

Note: Data are provided in tables 23.A6 and 23.A7.

The flip side of such employment performance was, not surprisingly, a substantial increase in unemployment. With the exception of the Czech Republic, all countries saw their unemployment rates move rapidly to double-digit figures during the early 1990s (figure 23.5). Although some of them have been able to bring those numbers down in recent years, high unemployment is still one of the most important concerns of policymakers in the region.

However, unemployment is not the only margin of adjustment when employment creation is weak. In the light of dim employment prospects, jobless workers can decide to exit the labor force instead of looking for a job. During the transition labor force participation rates fell substantially in these countries (table 23.7). This fall was so large in some cases that it brought overall participation rates back to their 1960–64 levels, after continuous increases in the 1970s and 1980s.

Changes in the labor market, however, were not limited to the ups and downs of employment, unemployment, or labor force participation. The substitution of centralized commands by market forces as the mode of labor allocation also altered the composition of these pools of workers, as certain characteristics of workers become more valuable than others in the labor market. There was significant labor relocation away from agriculture and industry and toward services as a consequence of sectoral shifts in economic activity. This relocation was accompanied by a shift in labor demand toward a different skill mix and higher education levels. This affected the "employability" of different types of workers.

FIGURE 23.5 UNEMPLOYMENT RATE IN EU ACCESSION COUNTRIES, 1993–99

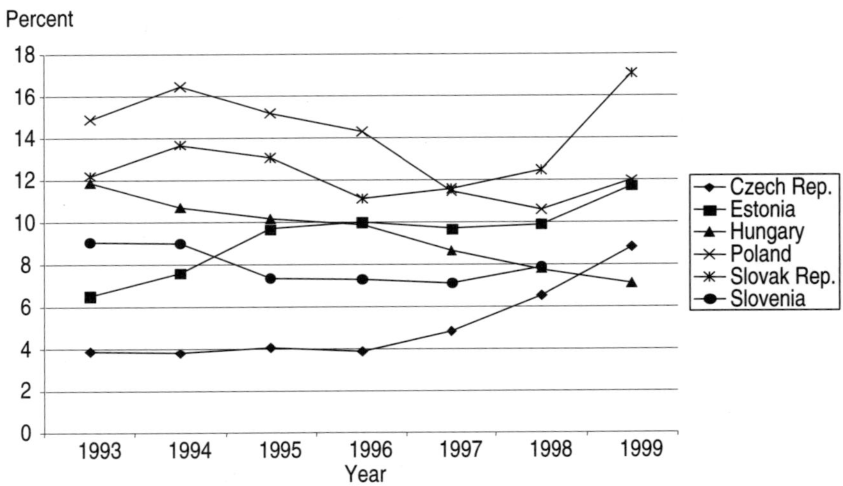

Note: Data are provided in table 23.A9.

More and more the unemployed became either young or old workers, or workers with low education or skills, giving rise to patterns that closely resembled those of the unemployed in the EU (box 23.2).

Finally, real wages fell in most countries as a consequence of rising inflation levels. However, the decline was less than necessary. Real wages needed to decline to facilitate the reallocation of labor, but in some countries, like Hungary and Poland, real wages (when measured with a production price index) did not fall rapidly or far enough to facilitate the reallocation of workers. In some countries, like Slovenia, real wages actually grew rather than declined (table 23.8).[13] This reduced job turnover and prevented a more rapid absorption of the growing unemployment.

What Explains These Labor Market Dynamics?

Labor market dynamics can be seen as the outcome of interactions between labor market institutions and other economic forces. In the case of CEECs, the fall of the former Soviet Union and the transition from a command to a market economy were

TABLE 23.7 LABOR FORCE PARTICIPATION RATES IN EU ACCESSION COUNTRIES (percent)

Country	*Workers*[a]	*1960–64*	*1970–74*	*1980–84*	*1990–94*	*1995–99*
Czech Republic[b]	All	68.5	73.8	76.1	73.4	72.2
	Female	49.1	61.6	68.6	69.3	64.0
Estonia	All	75.7	81.4	82.0	79.4	78.7
	Female	67.3	77.6	78.9	75.9	74.9
Hungary	All	68.4	72.6	73.3	68.6	69.0
	Female	46.9	57.2	62.1	59.3	60.3
Poland	All	75.4	76.5	75.9	73.4	71.8
	Female	62.1	67.4	67.7	65.1	65.6
Slovak Republic[c]	All	66.4	68.9	76.4	70.8	69.0
	Female	47.3	56.1	69.3	65.1	62.8
Slovenia	All	65.9	65.1	74.4	70.7	70.2
	Female	44.2	46.2	67.2	64.8	64.8

a. Ages 15 to 64.
b. Data for 1990 to 1999 from OECD. Data for 1960 to 1984, estimated by the authors.
c. Data for 1990 to 1999 from Lubyova (1999).
Source: Rama and Artecona, unpublished.

BOX 23.2 SIMILARITIES IN THE DEMOGRAPHICS OF THE UNEMPLOYED IN THE SLOVAK REPUBLIC AND SPAIN

The evolution of unemployment in the CEECs has been such that the characteristics of the unemployed resemble substantially those of unemployed workers in most EU countries. To illustrate this point we study the characteristics of the unemployed from 1994 to 2000 in the Slovak Republic and compare them to the characteristics of the unemployed in Spain, also a high unemployment country, in 1997.

Unemployment rates in the Slovak Republic vary widely with education and age. Consistently unemployment rates have been negatively correlated with education, so that workers with a college education have performed much better than those with primary or even secondary studies (table B2.1). In addition, differences across education groups have widened over time. While in 1994 the unemployment rate for workers with an apprenticeship degree was 15 percent, compared to 4 percent for those with a college degree, in 2000 these rates were 20 and 5 percent, respectively. That is, while in 1994 the unemployment risk of a worker with an apprentice degree was three times that of a worker with a college degree, in 2000 the unemployment risk of the former was five times that of the latter.

TABLE B2.1 UNEMPLOYMENT RATES IN THE SLOVAK REPUBLIC BY EDUCATION LEVELS

Education	*1994*	*1995*	*1996*	*1997*	*1998*	*1999*	*2000*
Less than basic	44.2	39.5	64.3	66.7	88.5	—	—
Basic	27.4	26.9	23.7	27.6	25.8	33.6	39.0
Apprenticeship low	14.4	13.1	10.8	11.0	12.7	17.4	20.6
Vocational low	13.6	12.7	10.0	11.3	10.8	18.95	19.9
Apprenticeship complete	15.3	9.5	8.1	10.6	9.6	15.6	19.6
Vocational complete	9.8	7.1	7.4	8.2	8.7	13.10	14.0
Grammar	13.1	14.3	11.8	14.6	13.8	17.12	17.7
University (+)	3.8	2.9	3.4	3.2	4.2	5.5	4.8

— Not available.
Source: Slovak Labor Force Survey.

Unemployment has also been much higher among young workers (15 to 24 years of age) than among prime-age ones (table B2.2). However, unlike in the previous case, relative differences across the two groups have been fairly stable over time, with unemployment rates increasing by about 40 percent for both groups between 1994 and 2000. As a result, the unemployment risk of a young worker has remained at a level that is about twice that of prime-age workers.

In contrast, unemployment has been systematically lower among older workers than among prime-age ones—a response to differences in participation rates between both groups rather than to a relative preference for older workers among employers. What is more important is that such a difference has become smaller over time, as the risk of unemployment among older workers has increased by 65 percent compared to 40 percent for prime-age ones.

TABLE B2.2 UNEMPLOYMENT RATES IN THE SLOVAK REPUBLIC BY AGE GROUPS

Age group	*1994*	*1995*	*1996*	*1997*	*1998*	*1999*	*2000*
15–24	26.5	22.4	19.4	23.5	26.6	33.7	35.9
25–49	11.5	10.4	9.2	9.8	9.5	13.8	15.8
50–64	8.2	7.1	5.7	6.6	6.8	10.2	13.4

Source: Slovak Labor Force Survey.

Finally, when we compare the characteristics of the Slovak and the Spanish unemployed, we find them to be fairly similar: unemployment rates are high among the least educated and the young (table B2.3).

TABLE B2.3 UNEMPLOYMENT RATES IN SPAIN BY EDUCATION AND AGE GROUPS, 1998

Education group	*Percent unemployed*	*Age group*	*Percent unemployed*
Less than upper secondary	17.0 (12.6)	15–24	34.1
Upper secondary	15.3 (10.0)	25–49	16.5
College or more	13.1 (8.5)	50–64	10.3

Note: Data for male unemployment in parentheses.
Source: Spanish Labor Force Survey.

the sources of tremendous economic shocks that necessarily interacted with the labor market.

Thus, whatever impact institutions may have had in the determination of labor market dynamics, they were clearly not the only factors affecting labor market outcomes in Central and Eastern Europe during the transition years, particularly during the early transition. Factors outside the labor market had an enormous impact and may have been the driving force behind the significant shifts observed in the labor market at the beginning of the transition. Big changes in employment, unemployment, and labor force participation could not have happened without stabilization

TABLE 23.8 REAL WAGES IN EU ACCESSION COUNTRIES: GROWTH RATE AND LEVEL

Country	Indicator		1990	1991	1992	1993	1994	1995	1996	1997	1998	1999
Czech Republic	Real growth		—	–26.3	10.2	3.7	7.7	8.7	8.8	1.9	–1.3	4.5
	Index (1990 = 100)		100.0	73.7	81.2	84.2	90.7	98.6	107.3	109.3	107.9	112.7
	After initial decline	Index (1991 = 100)	—	100.0	110.2	114.3	123.1	133.8	145.6	148.3	146.4	153.0
Hungary[a]	Real growth		–0.2	–3.7	1.7	–0.5	5.1	–8.9	–2.6	3.4	3.5	—
	Index (1990 = 100)		100.0	96.3	97.9	97.4	102.4	93.3	90.9	94.0	97.3	—
	After initial decline	Index (1991 = 100)	103.8	100.0	101.7	101.2	106.4	96.9	94.4	97.6	101.0	—
Estonia	Real growth		—	15.0	–59.4	2.3	10.1	6.2	2.1	7.6	6.7	3.7
	Index (1990 = 100)		100.0	115.0	46.7	47.8	52.6	55.8	57.0	61.4	65.5	67.9
	After initial decline	Index (1992 = 100)	—	—	100.0	102.3	112.7	119.6	122.1	131.5	140.3	145.4
Poland[b]	Real growth		–24.4	–0.3	–2.7	–2.9	0.5	3.0	5.7	6.8	—	—
	Index (1990 = 100)		100.0	99.7	97.0	94.2	94.7	97.5	103.1	110.1	—	—
	Decline prior to 1990		—	—	—	—	—	—	—	—	—	—
Slovak Republic[c]	Real growth		–5.6	–26.3	8.9	–3.8	3.0	4.3	7.1	6.5	2.8	—
	Index (1990 = 100)		100.0	73.7	80.3	77.2	79.5	82.9	88.8	94.6	97.3	—
	After initial decline	Index (1991 = 100)	—	100.0	108.9	104.8	107.9	112.5	120.5	128.4	132.0	—
Slovenia[d]	Real growth		—	12.0	0.7	11.7	4.7	5.1	5.1	2.4	1.6	—
	Index (1990 = 100)		100.0	112.0	112.8	126.0	131.9	138.6	145.7	149.2	151.6	—
	No initial decline		—	—	—	—	—	—	—	—	—	—

— Not available.

a. Hungarian Statistical Office.

b. Polish Statistical Office.

c. Slovak Statistical Office.

d. Data for 1993 to 1999 from Slovene Statistical Office (rate of growth of gross real wages).

Source: European Training Foundation 1999, and Central Bank of Estonia.

policies and structural reform measures. The relevant question is whether the newly introduced labor market institutions facilitated (or hindered) these changes and to what extent they affected the structure and composition of supply and demand.

This section analyzes labor market performance during the transition from the perspective of the impact of other reform policies that affected labor market outcomes. We pay particular attention to the role of macroeconomic stabilization and structural reform policies, and their impact on labor market outcomes. We then turn our attention to a discussion of the role of labor market institutions.

Macroeconomic Stabilization Policies

Initial conditions were an important factor in shaping the dynamics of the transition process rather than its outcome, since Central and Eastern European economies were quite heterogeneous. The degree of centralization and state control, imbalances in macroeconomic fundamentals (both domestic and external), the level of public indebtedness, and the degree of interaction with the West varied tremendously among CEECs before the transition. This heterogeneity, in conjunction with developments in the political elite structure, influenced the policy agenda of reform in a number of areas, including the speed of reforms, how much foreign direct investment (FDI) was embraced as a restructuring tool, the mechanism of privatization of state assets, the rigidity in the imposition of hard budget constraints, the degree of fiscal adjustment, and the design of the monetary policies and the exchange rate regime. Through many of these channels, the dynamics of the labor markets were affected as the Central and Eastern European economies redefined their economic interactions.

The need to cope with macroeconomic stabilization in the early stages of the transition forced the authorities to implement reform strategies that affected labor and other factor markets. Inflation was an important source of concern, particularly in Estonia, where annual inflation rates peaked at 1,069 percent in 1992, but also in Poland and Slovenia (table 23.9). Tight monetary policy was essential to establish control over inflation. Some countries also opted to use the exchange rate as a nominal anchor in an attempt to cope with inflationary pressures. This, with a loose fiscal stance, limited credit to the private sector in many countries, slowing down the absorption of the unemployed.

The need to ensure fiscal sustainability forced the authorities to impose fiscal discipline and strong fiscal adjustment measures. As a result, fiscal policy changed its supportive role. This in turn reduced the availability of prevailing support mechanisms to the economy, both in the form of price supports and direct or indirect subsidies de facto imposing hard budget constraints to public enterprises and forcing their restructuring (table 23.10).

Overall, macroeconomic stabilization policies helped to impose hard budget constraints on the Central and Eastern European economies and encouraged enterprise restructuring, which forced the reallocation of labor and other factors of production from inefficient sectors and activities to efficient ones. This produced

TABLE 23.9 INFLATION RATES IN EU ACCESSION COUNTRIES (percent)

Country	*1990*	*1991*	*1992*	*1993*	*1994*	*1995*	*1996*	*1997*	*1998*	*1999*	*2000*
Czech Republic	10	57	11	21	10	9	9	9	11	2	4
Estonia	23	211	1,069	90	48	29	23	11	8	3	8
Hungary	29	35	23	23	19	28	24	18	14	10	10
Poland	586	70	43	35	32	28	20	15	12	7	12
Slovak Republic	10	61	10	23	14	10	6	6	7	11	9
Slovenia	550	118	207	33	21	14	10	8	8	6	8

Note: Year-to-year change in annual Consumer Price Index, in percentage.
Sources: Statistical Information Management and Analysis (SIMA)—WDI database and Unified Survey FY01 database, national authorities, IMF, and the Bank country team estimates.

TABLE 23.10 SUBSIDIES TO THE ENTERPRISE SECTOR IN EU ACCESSION COUNTRIES (percentage of GDP)

Country	*1989*	*1993*	*1994*	*1995*	*1996*	*1997*
Czech Republic	25.0	4.4	3.1	2.7	2.2	2.4
Estonia	—	—	0.9	0.5	0.4	0.3
Hungary	12.1	4.1	4.5	3.8	3.9	3.3
Poland	12.9	3.0	3.3	2.9	2.5	2.4
Slovak Republic	25.0	4.8	3.2	2.8	2.4	2.2
Slovenia	—	—	1.6	1.6	1.2	1.3

— Not available.
Source: World Bank 2000.

enormous shifts in labor demand (and supply) from industrial and agricultural activities to services, and from the public to the private sector. In conjunction with price liberalization policies, the imposition of hard budget constraints triggered the breakdown of state enterprises and helped to encourage the development of a new private sector. At the same time it fostered enterprise sector restructuring, changing the face of the Central and Eastern European labor markets. As a result, unemployment appeared as a real and open phenomenon in Central and Eastern Europe, one that will require the attention of the authorities for years to come. Labor force participation rates also changed significantly, particularly with the withdrawal of females from the labor force and the use of early retirement schemes in some countries to cope with the growing unemployment. These changes reshaped labor markets in CEECs to resemble European labor markets.

Structural Reforms

Structural reforms played an even more important role in the shaping of the dynamics of labor markets during the transition. Market institutions were introduced in Central and Eastern Europe via structural reform policies that liberalized trade and domestic prices, eliminated many state monopolies (particularly important was the monopoly in the banking systems), privatized state enterprises, promoted (or abstained from hindering) the development of a dynamic private sector, facilitated competition and efficiency, and redefined property rights and the legal and regulatory systems. These reforms reshaped the new Central and Eastern European economies and had a dramatic impact on labor and other factor markets, encouraging reallocation and restructuring in the real sector.

With the liberalization of prices, the removal of restrictions to private sector development, and the reduction in direct and indirect subsidies, hard budget constraints were imposed on state firms, many of which could not cope with the new market conditions and the competition of the growing private sector. The state sector declined, shedding labor, while the private sector grew. However, resources released from the public sector were not fully absorbed by the private sector. In part this was the result of a mismatch in skills, since the new production platforms demanded higher educated workers and workers with different skills. The lack of absorption capacity was also the result of other factors including a weak financial sector still not able to intermediate resources effectively, thus limiting the availability of credit to the new private sector.

Banking crises compounded the credit problem, affecting the capacity of firms to grow and generate more employment opportunities. As a result of all of these measures, employment declined, and unemployment grew rapidly in the newborn market economies. As mentioned earlier, employment levels have not recovered despite the return of strong output growth that increased productivity throughout the 1990s (figure 23.6).

While these factors were common in most transition economies, the dynamics of labor markets varied from country to country as a rainbow of policy options was implemented. Some countries, like Poland, used early retirement schemes to cope with the growing open unemployment; others, like Slovenia, used the privatization process to slow down or even delay the adjustment of labor, maintaining the structure of employment as much as possible and reducing the speed of reform. The use of a mix of different policies explains the different labor adjustment dynamics.

Privatization played a critical role in shaping labor markets dynamics, accelerating or retarding the adjustment in the real sector and turnover in labor markets. Different modalities of privatization of state assets were introduced, from restitution and insider buyouts (sometimes at a discount) to management control and strategic investor involvement. Mass privatization schemes and direct sales to outsiders (both domestic or foreign) completed the picture (table 23.11). These different privatization techniques implied differences in the imposition of hard budget constraints to the firms and thus different adjustment paths.

FIGURE 23.6 AGGREGATE EMPLOYMENT IN EU ACCESSION COUNTRIES, 1990–2000

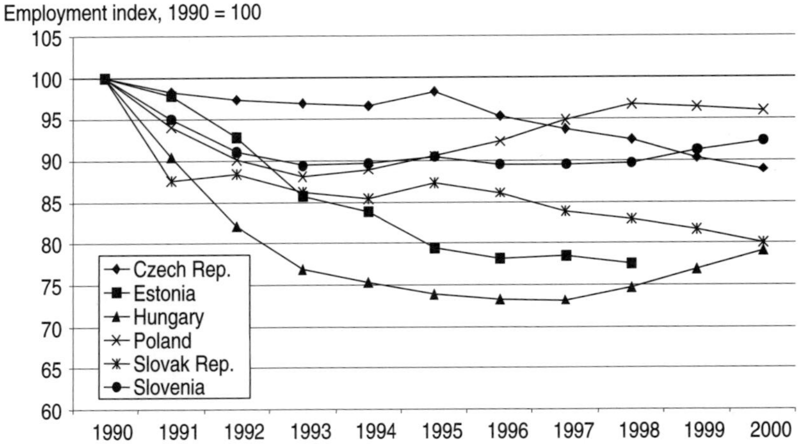

Note: Data are provided in table 23.A8.

TABLE 23.11 PRIVATIZATION MODALITIES FOR MEDIUM AND LARGE ENTERPRISES IN EU ACCESSION COUNTRIES

	Insider buyouts		*Mass privatization program*		*Sales to outsiders*		
Country	*Employees*[a]	*Managers*[b]	*Equal access for the whole population*	*Concessions to insiders*	*Large foreign share*[c]	*Little foreign share*[d]	*Other*[e]
Czech Republic	n.a.	n.a.	Primary	n.a.	n.a.	Secondary	Tertiary
Estonia	n.a.	Secondary	n.a.	n.a.	Primary	n.a.	Tertiary
Hungary	Secondary	n.a.	n.a.	n.a.	Primary	n.a.	Tertiary
Poland	Primary	n.a.	Secondary	n.a.	n.a.	n.a.	n.a.
Slovak Republic	n.a.	Primary	Secondary	n.a.	n.a.	n.a.	n.a.
Slovenia	Secondary	n.a.	n.a.	Primary	n.a.	n.a.	Tertiary

n.a. Not applicable.
a. Employees' share exceeds 75 percent of total assets privatized.
b. Management share exceeds 25 percent of total assets privatized.
c. Foreign share is more than 25 percent of total assets sold.
d. Foreign share is less than 25 percent of total assets sold.
e. Includes restitution and assets sales through insolvency proceedings.
Source: World Bank 2000.

Employment, unemployment, and labor force participation levels were affected by the privatization options used in combination with other structural reform policies and the degree of flexibility of labor markets. For example, in Slovenia job turnover was slow since most firms were privatized to insiders (managers, workers, and pensioners), and this maintained the status quo. Estonia and Hungary focused more on attracting foreign strategic investors, accelerating the adjustment process and boosting job turnover.

The initial reform focus was on privatization and restructuring of state enterprises rather than on facilitating the development of new firms. With time, small and medium-size enterprises (SMEs) started to emerge in the manufacturing sector, in spite of the limitations imposed by the weak credit markets. With hindsight, more support may have been needed for SMEs, which have become not only one of the key engines of growth, but also one of the few areas where new job opportunities have been created in the manufacturing sector. Privatized firms engaged much more in job destruction than in job creation, relying on increases in productivity to survive.

Other economic policies (or the lack thereof) also affected the dynamics of key labor market variables. For instance, the housing stock was determined by the needs of the previous production model, thus limiting the capacity for labor mobility and reallocation during the transition. This bottleneck was reinforced by a poorly developed (sometimes nonexistent) mortgage market. As a result, regional disparities in labor market outcomes emerged.

Labor Market Institutions

Clearly, labor market dynamics in CEECs were significantly affected by the structural reform agenda. The sharp decline in total employment and relative increase in private sector employment, the shift in economic activity and reallocation of labor between sectors, the changes in the skills mix, and the reduction in real wages that was observed over one decade would not have happened without wide-ranging structural reforms.

What, then, has been the impact of labor market institutions? Should we consider it as modest and relatively unimportant? Although data limitations do not permit us to perform a thorough econometric analysis, we use evidence drawn from previous research to make a number of observations that invite a more cautious conclusion.[14] In particular, we believe that labor market institutions may have contributed to shaping the adjustment of key labor market variables, affecting the rhythm of reform, even though their impact may have been "masked" by the dramatic impact of other reforms.

First, employment levels have not recovered. Although output started to grow in the mid-nineties and in some cases (Poland and Slovenia) surpassed the pre-transition levels, employment levels have not followed the trend. In other words, the correlation between employment and growth, although positive, has been weak, and employment continues to lag behind output recovery (figure 23.7).

FIGURE 23.7 CORRELATION BETWEEN GDP AND AGGREGATE EMPLOYMENT GROWTH RATES IN EU ACCESSION COUNTRIES
(percent)

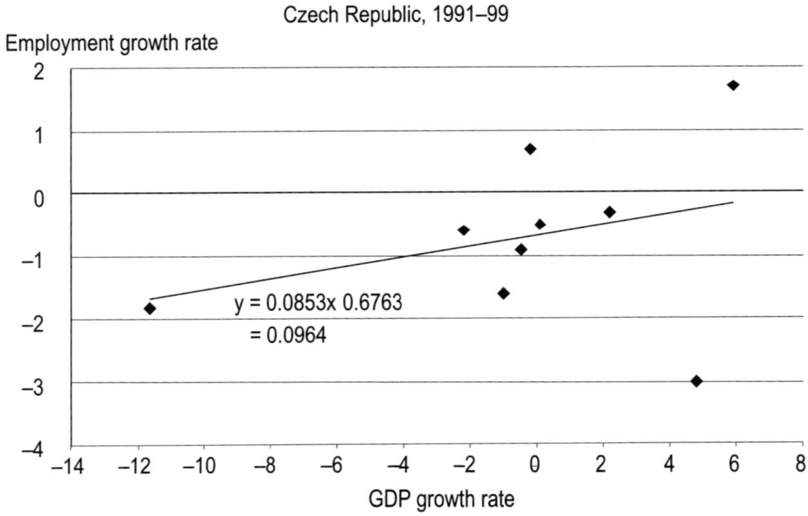

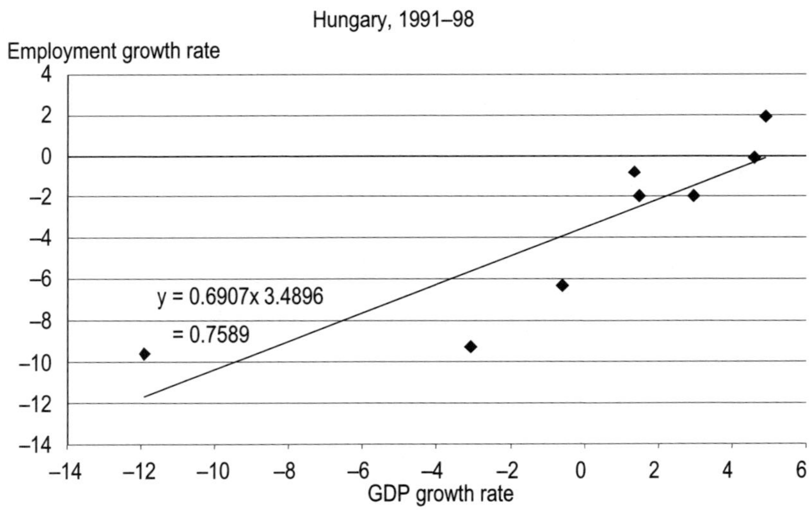

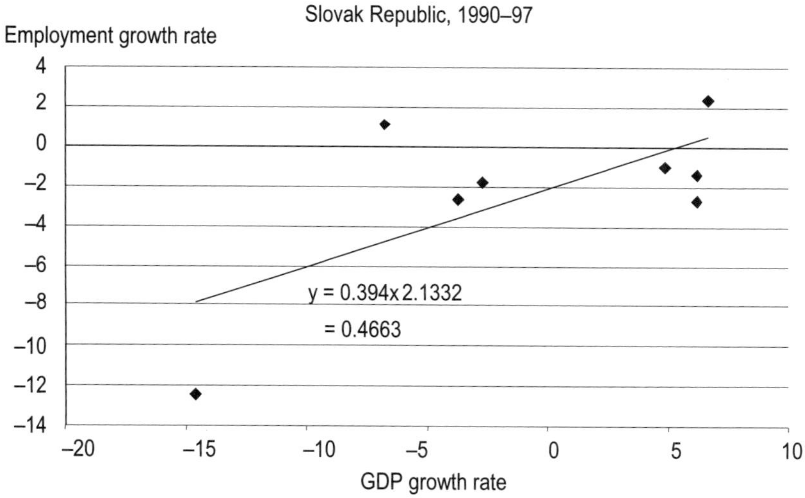

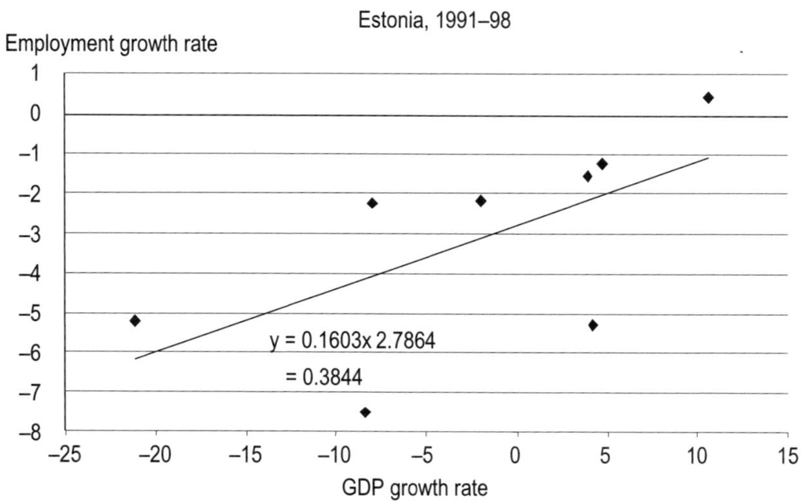

(Figure continues on the following page.)

FIGURE 23.7 (*continued*)

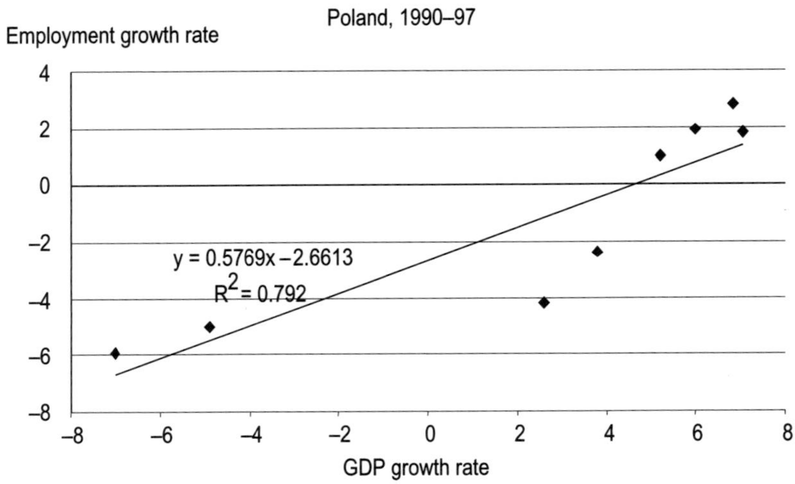

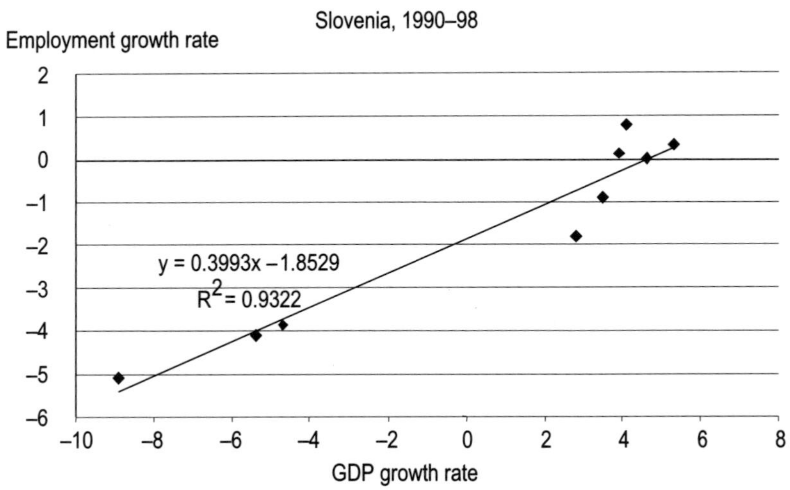

This is obviously a source of concern since employment-to-population ratios in CEECs are lower than those of EU and OECD countries (table 23.A8). Theory and past research do suggest that employment levels may be affected negatively by job security provisions (Lazear 1990; Bertola 1990; Hopenhayn and Rogerson 1993). Using data from 22 countries (from Europe and OECD) over a period of 29 years, Lazear (1990) shows that job security provisions, by increasing the costs of both hiring and laying off workers, reduce the employment-to-population ratio and increase unemployment. A similar conclusion is reached by Heckman and Pages (2000) who analyzed data from Latin America and the Caribbean. Although the view that regulations have no substantial impact also prevails in the literature (Blank and Freeman 1994; Freeman 1999), one cannot dismiss the possible negative impact of regulations on total employment.

Second, in CEECs long-term unemployment is high, another feature associated with stricter employment protection (Bentolila and Bertola 1990; Nickell 1997; Nickell and Layard 1998). The unemployment pool of Central and Eastern European economies has remained a fairly stagnant one, with low worker turnover and increasing numbers of long-term unemployed individuals. Unemployment inflows and outflows (that is, workers moving in and out of unemployment) represented on average less than 10 percent of the overall stock of unemployed individuals. This lack of dynamism meant that the average unemployed individual probably did not leave the unemployment pool. Over time, more and more individuals become unemployed for more than a year. In fact, in most countries in the sample, the share of long-term unemployed grew throughout the 1990s (table 23.12). In this respect, CEECs do resemble other European countries. In contrast, long-term unemployed do not represent more than 7 percent of the pool of unemployed in the United States, which has by far the most flexible labor market.

In sum, although no firm conclusion can be reached, these two features—low job creation and high long-term unemployment—are often associated with inflexible labor markets. Both may become the source of social tensions, and they increasingly weigh on public budgets.

Third, it is hard to imagine that changes in the age and sex composition of the labor force have not been—at least partly—the result of institutional changes (introduction of unemployment benefits, early retirement schemes, reduction of child care support). Indeed, the overall decline in labor force participation rates that we have described (table 23.7) masks significant differences across demographic groups. Participation rates fell the most among women and older workers. The reduction in the amount of child care support provided by the state and the subsequent increase in child care prices, combined with a decline in the number of child care centers and the tightening of social assistance for mothers with small children, led numerous women to exit the labor force to care for their children. Similarly, the existence of support for the unemployed made it easier for employers to dismiss workers, and early retirement schemes made it more attractive for older workers to

TABLE 23.12 SHORT- AND LONG-TERM UNEMPLOYMENT IN EU ACCESSION COUNTRIES

Country	*Indicator*	*1993*	*1994*	*1995*	*1996*	*1997*	*1998*	*1999*	*1993–98*
Czech Republic	STU	3.2	3.0	2.8	2.7	3.3	4.5	5.5	3.3
	LTU	0.7	0.8	1.3	1.2	1.5	2.0	3.3	1.2
	% LTU	18.3	21.5	30.6	31.3	30.5	31.2	37.1	27.2
Estonia	STU	4.7	4.6	6.6	4.5	5.2	5.2	—	5.1
	LTU	1.8	3.0	3.1	5.5	4.4	4.6	—	3.8
	% LTU	27.6	39.5	31.9	55.0	45.8	46.9	—	42.7
Hungary	STU	8.1	6.3	5.5	5.0	4.7	4.3	3.6	5.6
	LTU	3.8	4.4	4.7	4.9	4.0	3.5	3.5	4.2
	% LTU	32.2	41.3	45.6	49.8	46.5	44.3	49.5	43.3
Poland	STU	9.9	10.1	9.0	8.6	7.0	6.6	—	8.5
	LTU	5.0	6.4	6.2	5.7	4.5	4.0	—	5.3
	% LTU	33.5	38.6	40.5	40.0	39.1	37.9	—	38.3
Slovak Republic	STU	8.5	8.0	6.1	5.3	5.7	6.0	8.7	6.6
	LTU	3.7	5.7	7.0	5.8	5.9	5.9	8.4	5.7
	% LTU	30.2	41.6	53.1	52.7	51.5	49.7	49.1	46.4
Slovenia	STU	2.9	2.3	1.8	2.4	2.1	1.8	—	2.2
	LTU	6.2	6.8	5.6	4.9	5.3	6.1	—	5.8
	% LTU	68.5	75.0	75.5	67.3	71.5	77.8	—	72.6
CEE average	% LTU	35.0	42.9	46.2	49.3	47.5	47.9	45.2[a]	45.1
EU average	% LTU	41.4[b]	42.8[c]	45.8	45.3	45.6	43.9[d]	41.2[d]	44.1
OECD average	% LTU	39.1[b]	40.4[c]	43.2	42.7	43.0	41.1[d]	39.0[d]	41.6
United States	% LTU	11.5	12.2	9.7	9.5	8.7	8.0	6.8	9.5

— Not available.
STU: Short-term unemployment.
LTU: Long-term unemployment.
%LTU: Percentage of total unemployment due to long-term unemployment.
a. Includes only the Czech Republic, Hungary, and Slovak Republic.
b. Does not include Austria.
c. Does not include Finland.
d. Does not include Ireland.
Sources: OECD-CCET Labor Market Database 1990–97, Slovene Labor Force Survey, and Estonian Labor Force Survey (1995 and 1997).

exit the labor force. In many countries those schemes were used as a device to control unemployment among this particular group of workers.

High exit rates among certain groups of workers thus helped keep the unemployment rate below potentially higher levels. For example, in Hungary the labor force participation rate fell to 11 percent for women ages 55 to 64 and to 30.8 percent for men in 1999 (compared to an EU average of 30.5 percent and 52.7 percent, respectively) Moreover, "selected exit," combined with the labor market entry of large numbers of young, more educated workers, substantially altered the overall composition of the labor force in the CEECs. Whether labor force participation rates can remain at low levels for long periods of time without hindering the sustainability of benefit systems may become an issue in some of these countries.

Fourth, CEECs stand out relative to EU countries with respect to payroll taxes (and overall tax burden on labor), which are at the high end of the range (table 23.5). While past research has not shown clear evidence of the impact of high labor taxes on the level of employment, there is the presumption that high taxes on labor create incentives for self-employment and an increase in the informal sector. In this regard, the effect of high payroll taxes may add to the effect of employment protection legislation.[15] Available data for CEECs are scanty and subject to measurement errors, but they suggest that this hypothesis may be relevant since the size of the informal sector in CEECs is not insignificant (table 23.13).

It is important to emphasize that there is significant variation across the EU accession countries in terms of the kinds of labor market institutions adopted and in terms of labor market outcomes, and that significant patterns emerge relating the two. In general, those countries that have undertaken more radical and liberal reforms appear to have more fluid and dynamic markets, with larger job and worker flows (Vodopivec 1999; Haltiwanger and Vodopivec 1999; Bilsen and Konings 1998). For example, Terrell (1999) compares employment accession and separation rates across countries and finds that Hungary, one of the most reformist countries, exhibits much larger flows than Slovenia, a moderate reformer (table 23.A10). We illustrate this point further by comparing job and worker flows in Estonia and Slovenia (box 23.3).

TABLE 23.13 SHARE OF UNOFFICIAL ECONOMY IN EU ACCESSION COUNTRIES (percent)

Country	*1989*	*1990*	*1991*	*1992*	*1993*	*1994*	*1995*
Czech Republic	6.0	6.7	12.9	16.9	16.9	17.6	11.3
Estonia	12.0	19.9	26.2	25.4	24.1	25.1	11.8
Hungary	27.0	28.0	32.9	30.6	28.5	27.7	29.0
Poland	15.7	19.6	23.5	19.7	18.5	15.2	12.6
Slovak Republic	6.0	7.7	15.1	17.6	16.2	14.6	5.8
Slovenia	—	—	—	—	—	—	—

— Not available.
Source: Johnson and others 1997.

BOX 23.3 THE IMPORTANCE OF INSTITUTIONS: JOB AND WORKER FLOWS DURING TRANSITION IN ESTONIA AND SLOVENIA

Following Haltiwanger and Vodopivec (1999), and Vodopivec (1999), we compare the experiences of Estonia and Slovenia to emphasize the role that labor market institutions played in shaping up labor market outcomes during the transition. The pace of institutional reform followed in both countries differed substantially, and these differences had a significant impact on job creation and destruction, and on worker accession and separation rates. While Estonia pursued extremely liberal, radical reforms, Slovenia retained a considerable degree of employment protection and adopted much more generous income support policies (table B3.1).

TABLE B3.1 COMPARISON OF LABOR POLICIES IN TRANSITION

Policy	*Estonia* *Change relative to pretransition*	*Slovenia* *Change relative to pretransition*
Employment protection	Job security removed Liberal dismissal policies No job preservation subsidies	Job security removed Restrictive dismissal policies Job preservation subsidies
Unemployment benefits	Duration: maximum of 6 to 9 months Replacement ratio: 10%	Duration: maximum of 24 months Replacement ratio: 60–70%
Wage policies	Low minimum wage Low tax wedge	High minimum wage High tax wedge
Collective agreements	Low density and coverage	High density and coverage
Privatization	Individual sale methods	Mixed methods
Foreign trade	No tariffs/quotas on imports	Up to 28% tariff rates
FDI 1989–96	Cumulative inflow per capita: $459	Cumulative inflow per capita: $366
Maternity leave	Increased from 1.5 to 3 years plus 10 weeks pregnancy leave	Remained at 1 year
Public childcare	Price increases 14% decrease in number of centers	— 1% increase in number of centers
Income support	Up to 4-year extension of UI for women with children under 6	No change

— Not available.
Source: Orazem and Vodopivec 1999.

Haltiwanger and Vodopivec show that in Estonia both job destruction and, with a lag, job creation rates increased tremendously during the transition. In contrast, more protectionist and generous policies in Slovenia resulted in much lower rates. For instance, job creation rates—for which differences between both countries are biggest—were at or below 1 percent a year in Slovenia during 1989–94, while they kept increasing up to 10 percent in Estonia. In addition, job destruction rates differed significantly between both countries. In Estonia job destruction grew rapidly from 1989 to 1992, going from almost 0 percent to 14 percent, to decline slightly afterwards. In contrast, the Slovenian rate started to exhibit a declining trend as early as 1991 and always remained below 60 percent of the Estonian rate (figure B3.1).

The comparison with Slovenia does not seem to be a special case. Job flows in Estonia are also much higher than those reported for some other nonradical reformers such as Bulgaria, Hungary, or Romania (Bilsen and Konings, 1998).

The differences in employment accession and separation rates are even more striking. While Estonia underwent a period of tremendous worker turnover (that is, high accession and separation rates) between 1989 and 1994, worker flows remained fairly stable in Slovenia (figure B3.2), exhibiting almost no trend.

FIGURE B3.1 RATE OF JOB DESTRUCTION IN ESTONIA AND SLOVENIA DURING TRANSITION

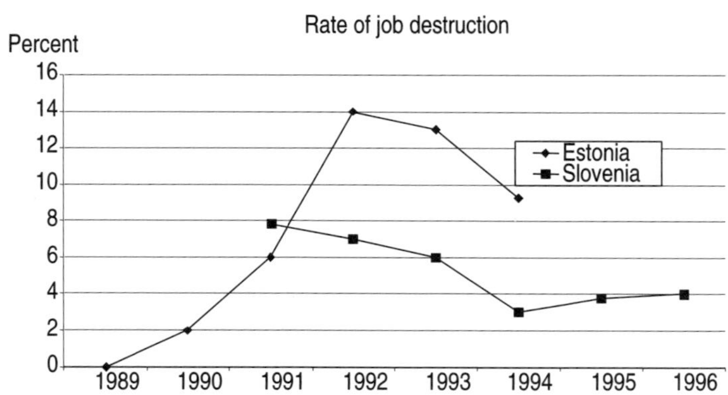

Source: Haltiwanger and Vodopivec 1999.

These differences in job and worker flows between the two countries are attributed by the authors to differences in both labor market institutions and speed of reforms (for instance, substantial differences in their approach to privatization).

(Box continues on the following page.)

BOX 23.3 (*continued*)

FIGURE B3.2 EMPLOYMENT ACCESSION AND SEPARATION IN ESTONIA AND SLOVENIA DURING TRANSITION

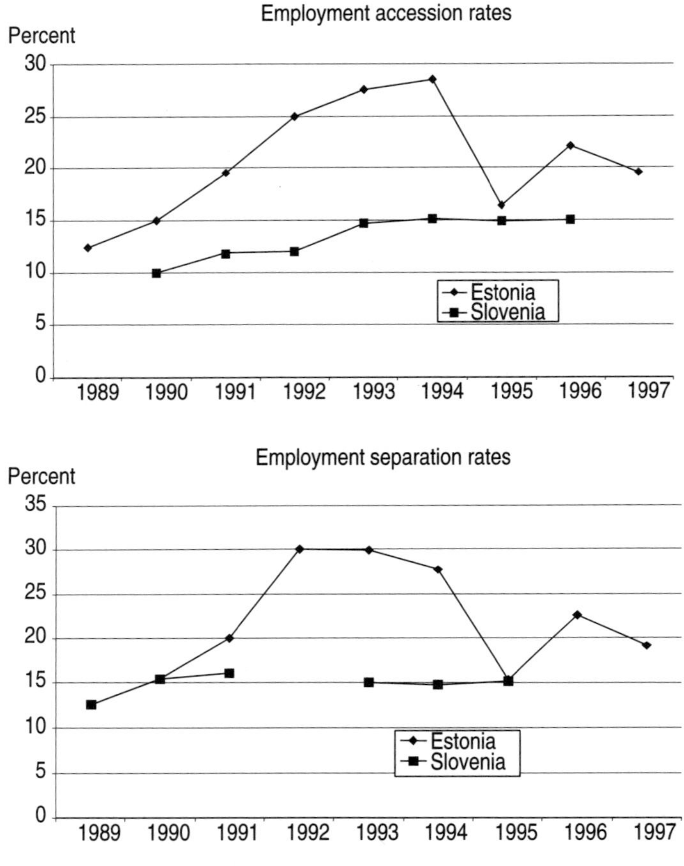

Source: Haltiwanger and Vodopivec 1999; Vodopivec 1999.

Finally, it seems difficult to evaluate at this stage the impact of wage bargaining without further research. Past research has shown that institutions associated with collective bargaining tend to reduce the dispersion of earnings. In CEECs, changes in the bargaining system have been accompanied by a sharp increase in private sector employment and a decompression of the wage structure. It is difficult to assess the extent to which institutions and social norms inherited from the past still play a role in the wage determination process and whether wage inequality—although clearly increasing—has reached levels comparable to other countries.

Conclusions

In this chapter we have studied labor market dynamics in six CEECs over the past 10 years, paying special attention to the nature of the labor market institutions these countries have recently adopted and to their impact on labor market performance. We used the OECD methodology so that we could compare institutions in CEECs seeking EU membership with those in EU and OECD countries. This exercise was motivated by the desire to shed some light on the ongoing debate on the role of institutions in labor market performance, a debate of particular relevance to countries in Europe where unemployment remains high on the list of policy concerns.

The first question we addressed was whether CEECs—candidates for EU accession—had adopted institutions similar to those in the EU and, as a consequence, introduced in their labor markets the same rigidities that exist in EU countries. We found that, indeed, the CEECs have adopted a set of labor market institutions that broadly resemble those in the EU. However, just as labor markets and institutions in Europe exhibit enormous diversity, we find variation across the CEECs in terms of employment protection legislation, support to the unemployed, taxation on labor, and the strength of unions.

Compared to EU members, CEECs fall in the middle of the "flexibility" scale regarding their employment protection legislation. They have not adopted legislation as flexible as that in the United Kingdom or Ireland, nor have they copied the highly rigid Southern European model. They also spend relatively little to support the unemployed, as measured by the share of every dollar generated by a labor force member that is spent on unemployment insurance or active labor market policies. The Central and Eastern European average spending on both passive and active labor market policies falls below the EU and the OECD average, and the behavior of these countries resembles that of the United States, Japan, and Southern Europe, rather than that of Denmark or Sweden in this respect. Where CEECs stand out is in terms of labor taxation: they rank among the highest in all EU and OECD countries.

In assessing the impact of those institutions on labor outcomes, we argued that the dramatic changes observed during the 1990s in employment, unemployment, labor force participation, and wages could not have occurred without the macroeconomic and structural reforms these countries have embraced as part of the transition process. As a result, the effect of institutions may have been masked by the magnitude of these other reform-induced changes.

The effect of institutions, although hard to uncover, should not be disregarded. Although institutions may not have played a substantial role during the first phase of adjustment, they are likely to become more important in the next few years. In particular, we have tried to show, using evidence drawn from other research, that existing labor market institutions, although moderate, may be partly responsible for the lack of recovery of employment and the rising share of long-term unemployment. While the impact on total unemployment remains uncertain, data also suggest that institutions in CEECs may well have an impact on the composition of the labor force and of employment.

Appendix A—Additional Tables

TABLE 23.A1 EMPLOYMENT PROTECTION LEGISLATION IN OECD AND EU ACCESSION COUNTRIES

				EPL Strictness for OECD and CEEC			
				OECD vs. CEEC			
	Regular employment legislation	*Temporary employment legislation*	*Collective dismissals legislation*	*Version 1*[a]		*Version 2*[b]	
Country				*Index*	*Rank*[c]	*Index*	*Rank*[c]
OECD							
Austria	2.6	1.8	3.3	2.2	12	2.3	12
Belgium	1.5	2.8	4.1	2.1	10	2.5	13
Denmark	1.6	0.9	3.1	1.2	8	1.5	8
Finland	2.1	1.9	2.4	2.0	9	2.1	9
France	2.3	3.6	2.1	3.0	17	2.8	17
Germany	2.8	2.3	3.1	2.5	15	2.6	16
Ireland	1.6	0.3	2.1	0.9	4	1.1	5
Italy	2.8	3.8	4.1	3.3	19	3.4	19
Netherlands	3.1	1.2	2.8	2.1	11	2.2	10
Norway	2.4	2.8	2.8	2.6	16	2.6	15
Portugal	4.3	3.0	3.6	3.7	20	3.7	20
Spain	2.6	3.5	3.1	3.1	18	3.1	18
Sweden	2.8	1.6	4.5	2.2	13	2.6	14
Switzerland	1.2	0.9	3.9	1.0	6	1.5	7
United Kingdom	0.8	0.3	2.9	0.5	2	0.9	2
Canada	0.9	0.3	3.4	0.6	3	1.1	4
United States	0.2	0.3	2.9	0.2	1	0.7	1
Japan	2.7	2.1	1.5	2.4	14	2.3	11
Australia	1.0	0.9	2.6	0.9	5	1.2	6
New Zealand	1.7	0.4	0.4	1.0	7	0.9	3
EU average[d]	2.4	2.1	3.2	2.2	n.a.	2.4	n.a.
OECD average[e]	2.0	1.7	2.9	1.9	n.a.	2.0	n.a.
CEEC							
Czech Republic	2.8	0.5	4.3	1.7	3	2.1	3
Estonia	3.1	1.4	4.1	2.3	5	2.6	5
Hungary	2.1	0.6	3.4	1.4	1	1.7	1
Poland	2.2	1.0	3.9	1.6	2	2.0	2
Slovak Republic	2.6	1.4	4.4	2.0	4	2.4	4
Slovenia	3.4	2.4	4.8	2.9	6	3.5	6
Slovenia[f]	(2.9)	(0.6)	(4.9)	(1.8)	(4)	(2.3)	(4)
CEEC average	2.7	1.2	4.1	2.0	n.a.	2.4	n.a.

n.a. Not applicable.
a. Weighted average of indicators for regular contracts and temporary contracts.
b. Weighted average of indicators for regular contracts, temporary contracts, and collective dismissals.
c. All rankings increase with the strictness of employment protection.
d. Does not include Greece and Luxembourg.
e. Average for all OECD countries presented in the table.
f. Based on proposed labor code.
Sources: OECD 1999 and World Bank estimates for Estonia and Slovenia.

TABLE 23.A2 EMPLOYMENT PROTECTION LEGISLATION STRICTNESS FOR OECD AND EU ACCESSION COUNTRIES

	EPL Strictness for OECD and CEEC					
	OECD versus CEEC				*OECD and CEEC*	
	Version 1[a]		*Version 2*[b]		*Version 1*[a]	*Version 2*[b]
Country	*Index*	*Rank*[c]	*Index*	*Rank*[c]	*Rank*[c]	*Rank*[c]
OECD						
Austria	2.2	12	2.3	12	16	15
Belgium	2.1	10	2.5	13	14	17
Denmark	1.2	8	1.5	8	8	8
Finland	2.0	9	2.1	9	13	12
France	3.0	17	2.8	17	22	22
Germany	2.5	15	2.6	16	20	21
Ireland	0.9	4	1.1	5	4	5
Italy	3.3	19	3.4	19	25	24
Netherlands	2.1	11	2.2	10	15	13
Norway	2.6	16	2.6	15	21	20
Portugal	3.7	20	3.7	20	26	26
Spain	3.1	18	3.1	18	23	23
Sweden	2.2	13	2.6	14	17	19
Switzerland	1.0	6	1.5	7	6	7
United Kingdom	0.5	2	0.9	2	2	2
Canada	0.6	3	1.1	4	3	4
United States	0.2	1	0.7	1	1	1
Japan	2.4	14	2.3	11	19	14
Australia	0.9	5	1.2	6	5	6
New Zealand	1.0	7	0.9	3	7	3
EU average[d]	2.2	n.a.	2.4	n.a.	n.a.	n.a.
OECD average[e]	1.9	n.a.	2.0	n.a.	n.a.	n.a.
CEEC						
Czech Republic	1.7	3	2.1	3	11	11
Estonia	2.3	5	2.6	5	18	18
Hungary	1.4	1	1.7	1	9	9
Poland	1.6	2	2.0	2	10	10
Slovak Republic	2.0	4	2.4	4	12	16
Slovenia	2.9	6	3.5	6	24	25
Slovenia[f]	(1.8)	(4)	(2.3)	(4)	(12)	(16)
CEEC average	2.0	n.a.	2.4	n.a.	n.a.	n.a.

n.a. Not applicable.
a. Weighted average of indicators for regular contracts and temporary contracts.
b. Weighted average of indicators for regular contracts, temporary contracts, and collective dismissals.
c. All rankings increase with the strictness of employment protection.
d. Does not include Greece and Luxembourg
e. Average for all OECD countries in the table.
f. Based on proposed labor code.
Sources: OECD 1999 and World Bank estimates for Estonia and Slovenia.

TABLE 23.A3 UNEMPLOYMENT INSURANCE SYSTEM IN SELECTED OECD AND EU ACCESSION COUNTRIES, LATE 1990s

Country	*Benefit replacement ratio (%)*	*Benefit duration (months)*
OECD		
Austria	50	5–12
Belgium	57	12–No limit
Denmark	70	60
Finland	63	24
France	70	27–54
Germany	61	6–32
Ireland	49	15
Italy	42	6
Netherlands	69	6–54
Norway	67	46
Portugal	65	10–30
Spain	73	4–24
Sweden	75	12–18
Switzerland	73	8.5–20
United Kingdom	36	12
Canada	59	12
United States	60	6
Japan	60	6
Australia	36	No limit
New Zealand	30	No limit
EU average[a]	60	n.a.
OECD average[b]	58	n.a.
CEEC[c]		
Czech Republic	50	6
Estonia	10[d]	3–6
Hungary	64	12[e]
Poland	40[f]	12–24[g]
Slovak Republic	60	6–12[h]
Slovenia	63	3–24[h]
CEEC average	48 (55)[i]	n.a.

n.a. Not applicable.

Note: Description of categories: (1) benefit replacement ratio—initial benefit level divided by previous earned income, (2) benefit duration—maximum duration, in months, depending on various criteria (age, family status, employment record/contributive history).

a. Does not include Greece and Luxembourg.

b. Average for all OECD countries in the table.

c. Data for Czech Republic, Estonia, and Slovenia are from 1998; data for Hungary are from 1997; and data for Poland and Slovak Republic are from 1996.

d. Benefits are set at 60 percent of minimum wage. This amounts to approximately 10 percent of the average wage.

e. Requires four years of employment.

f. The replacement ratio is 40 percent of the average wage for the year prior to unemployment.

g. Benefit duration increases with previous employment tenure.

h. Benefit duration is a function of the worker's contributive history.

i. Figure in parentheses does not include Estonia.

Sources: OECD 1995, 1999; IMF 1999; IMF Article IV—Consultation with the Slovak Republic; World Bank estimates for Estonia and the Slovak Republic; World Bank 1998a, 1999.

TABLE 23.A4 SPENDING ON PASSIVE AND ACTIVE LABOR MARKET POLICIES IN SELECTED OECD AND EU ACCESSION COUNTRIES

			Passive policies		*Active policies*	
Country	*Year of data*	*Unemployment rate*	*% GDP*	*Spending per unemployed*[a]	*% GDP*	*Spending per unemployed*[b]
OECD						
Austria	1999	3.7	1.22	0.32	0.52	0.14
Belgium	1998	9.5	2.51	0.26	1.34	0.14
Denmark	1999	5.2	3.12	0.60	1.77	0.34
Finland	1999	10.3	2.33	0.23	1.22	0.12
France	1999	11.3	1.85	0.16	1.33	0.12
Germany	1999	8.7	2.12	0.24	1.30	0.15
Greece	1997	9.8	0.50	0.05	0.35	0.04
Ireland	1996	11.7	2.42	0.21	1.66	0.14
Italy	1999	11.4	0.64	0.06	1.10	0.10
Netherlands	1999	3.3	2.81	0.85	1.80	0.55
Norway	1999	3.3	0.47	0.14	0.82	0.25
Portugal	1996/98	5.2	0.83	0.16	0.87	0.12
Spain	1999	15.9	1.41	0.09	0.81	0.05
Sweden	1999	7.2	1.70	0.24	1.84	0.26
Switzerland	1997/98	4.2	1.03	0.25	0.41	0.10
United Kingdom	1997/98	7.0	0.82	0.12	0.37	0.05
Canada	1998/99	8.3	0.99	0.12	0.51	0.06
United States	1998/99	4.5	0.25	0.06	0.18	0.04
Japan	1998/99	4.1	0.52	0.13	0.09	0.02
Australia	1998/99	8.0	1.06	0.13	0.52	0.07
New Zealand	1998/99	7.4	1.57	0.21	0.62	0.08
EU average[c]	—	—	1.73	0.26	1.16	0.16
OECD average[d]	—	—	1.43	0.23	0.92	0.14
CEEC						
Czech Republic	1999	8.8	0.31	0.04	0.19	0.02
Estonia	1998	9.9	0.08	0.01	0.08	0.01
Hungary	1997	8.7	0.56	0.06	0.40	0.04
Poland	1996	14.3	1.71	0.12	0.49	0.03
Slovak Republic	1996	11.1	0.54	0.05	0.56	0.05
Slovenia	1998	7.9	0.89	0.11	0.83	0.11
CEEC average	—	—	0.68	0.06	0.42	0.04

— Not applicable.
a. Ratio of GDP spending on UI to unemployment rate (both in percentage terms).
b. Spending per unemployed individual as a percentage of GDP per labor force participant.
c. Does not include Luxembourg.
d. Average for all OECD countries in the table.
Sources: OECD 1997, 1999; CEM Slovak Republic, ELFS 1998.

TABLE 23.A5 THE ROLE OF UNIONS AND PAYROLL TAXES IN SELECTED OECD AND EU ACCESSION COUNTRIES

Country	*1*[a] *Union density (%)*[b]	*2 Union coverage index*[c]	*3 Coordination*		*4 Payroll tax rate (%)*	*5 Total tax rat (%)*
			Union	*Employer*		
OECD						
Austria	41.2	3	3	3	22.6	53.7
Belgium	51.9	3	2	2	21.5	49.8
Denmark	80.1	2	3	3	0.6	46.3
Finland	79.3	3	2	3	25.5	65.9
France	9.1	3	2	2	38.8	63.8
Germany	28.9	3	2	3	23.0	53.0
Ireland	48.9	3	1	1	7.1	34.3
Italy	44.1	3	2	2	40.2	62.9
Netherlands	25.6	3	2	2	27.5	56.5
Norway	57.7	2	3	3	17.5	48.6
Portugal	25.6	3	2	2	14.5	37.6
Spain	18.6	3	2	1	33.2	54.2
Sweden	91.1	3	3	3	37.7	70.7
Switzerland	22.5	2	1	3	14.5	28.6
United Kingdom	32.9	2	1	1	13.8	40.8
Canada	37.4	2	1	1	13.0	42.7
United States	14.2	1	1	1	20.9	43.8
Japan	24.0	2	2	2	16.5	36.3
Australia	35.2	3	2	1	2.5	28.7
New Zealand	24.3	1	1	1	—	34.8
EU average[d]	44.4	—	—	—	23.5	53.0
OECD average[e]	39.6	—	—	—	19.5	45.4
CEEC						
Czech Republic	42.8	2	1	1	47.5	73.4
Estonia	36.1	2	2	1	33.0	63.3
Hungary	60.0	3	1	2	44.0	81.5
Poland	33.8	3	2	1	48.2	80.0
Slovak Republic	61.7	3	2	2	50.0	81.0
Slovenia	60.0	3	3	3	38.0	69.1
CEEC average	49.1	—	—	—	43.4	74.7

— Not available.

a. All data for 1995, except for Denmark, Ireland, Italy, Spain, and Sweden (1993), and estimated data for Slovenia.

b. Percentage of salaried workers that belong to a union.

c. 1: less than 25 percent of salaried workers are covered by collective agreements; 2: between 26 and 69 percent are covered; 3: 70 percent or more are covered.

d. Does not include Greece and Luxembourg.

e. Average for all OECD countries in the table.

Sources: Bank of Estonia, Business Eastern Europe, Deloitte Touche Tohmatsu International 1997, EIU 1998, ILO 1997, Nickell 1997, OECD 1997, the Polish Agency for Foreign Investment, the World Bank.

TABLE 23.A6 GDP IN EU ACCESSION COUNTRIES: GROWTH RATES AND LEVELS

Country	*Indicator*	*1990*	*1991*	*1992*	*1993*	*1994*	*1995*	*1996*	*1997*	*1998*	*1999*	*2000*
Czech Republic	Growth rate	–1.2	–11.6	–0.5	0.1	2.2	5.9	4.8	–1.0	–2.2	–0.2	2.7
	Level (1990 = 100)	100.0	88.4	88.0	88.0	90.0	95.3	99.9	98.9	96.7	96.5	99.1
Estonia	Growth rate	–7.1	–8.0	–21.2	–8.4	–2.0	4.3	3.9	10.6	4.7	–1.1	5.0
	Level (1990 = 100)	100.0	92.0	72.5	66.4	65.1	67.9	70.5	78.0	81.7	80.8	84.8
Hungary	Growth rate	–3.5	–11.9	–3.1	–0.6	2.9	1.5	1.3	4.6	4.9	4.5	5.6
	Level (1990 = 100)	100.0	88.1	85.4	84.9	87.4	88.7	89.9	94.0	98.6	103.1	114.6
Poland	Growth rate	–4.9	–7.0	2.6	3.8	5.2	7.0	6.0	6.8	4.8	4.1	2.2
	Level (1990 = 100)	100.0	93.0	95.4	99.0	104.2	111.5	118.2	126.3	132.4	137.8	150.5
Slovak Republic	Growth rate	–2.7	–14.6	–6.7	–3.7	4.9	6.7	6.2	6.2	4.1	1.9	1.8
	Level (1990 = 100)	100.0	85.4	79.7	76.7	80.5	85.9	91.2	96.9	100.9	102.8	108.3
Slovenia	Growth rate	–4.7	–8.9	–5.4	2.8	5.3	4.1	3.5	4.6	3.9	4.9	4.5
	Level (1990 = 100)	100.0	91.1	86.2	88.6	93.3	97.1	100.5	105.1	109.2	114.6	124.8

Sources: WDI database and Unified Survey FY01 database, national authorities, IMF, and the World Bank country team estimates.

TABLE 23.A7 EMPLOYMENT IN EU ACCESSION COUNTRIES: GROWTH RATES AND LEVELS

Country	*Indicator*	*1990*	*1991*	*1992*	*1993*	*1994*	*1995*	*1996*	*1997*	*1998*	*1999*	*2000*
Czech Republic	Growth rate		–1.8	–0.9	–0.5	–0.3	1.7	–3.0	–1.6	–1.4	–2.3	–1.5
	Level (1990 = 100)	100.0	98.2	97.3	96.8	96.5	98.2	95.2	93.7	92.4	90.3	88.9
Hungary	Growth rate		–9.6	–9.3	–6.3	–2.0	–1.9	–0.8	–0.1	1.5	3.1	2.7
	Level (1990 = 100)	100.0	90.4	82.0	76.8	75.3	73.9	73.3	73.2	74.6	76.9	79.0
Estonia	Growth rate		–2.3	–5.2	–7.5	–2.2	–5.3	–1.6	0.4	–1.3	—	—
	Level (1990 = 100)	100.0	97.7	92.6	85.7	83.8	79.4	78.1	78.5	77.5	—	—
Poland	Growth rate	–5.0	–5.9	–4.2	–2.4	1.0	1.8	1.9	2.8	1.9	–0.2	–0.5
	Level (1990 = 100)	100.0	94.1	90.1	88.0	88.9	90.5	92.2	94.8	96.6	96.4	95.9
Slovak Republic	Growth rate	–1.8	–12.5	1.1	–2.6	–1.0	2.4	–1.4	–2.3	–1.0	–1.4	–1.1
	Level (1990 = 100)	100.0	87.5	88.5	86.2	85.3	87.3	86.1	83.8	82.9	81.7	80.0
Slovenia	Growth rate	–3.9	–5.1	–4.1	–1.8	0.3	0.8	–0.9	0.0	0.2	1.8	1.3
	Level (1990 = 100)	100.0	94.9	91.0	89.4	89.6	90.4	89.5	89.5	89.6	91.2	92.3

— Not available.
Sources: European Training Foundation 1999 and EBRD 1999.

TABLE 23.A8 EMPLOYMENT-TO-POPULATION RATIOS IN EU ACCESSION COUNTRIES (percent)

Country	*Workers*	*1993*	*1994*	*1995*	*1996*	*1997*	*1998*	*1999*
Czech Republic	All	—	71.5	69.6	69.4	68.7	67.5	65.9
	Female	—	66.2	61.6	60.6	60.0	58.8	57.4
Estonia	All	68.7	68.1	65.5	64.9	65.4	64.7	—
	Female	62.6	62.0	60.5	60.2	60.4	60.4	—
Hungary	All	—	48.2	52.9	52.7	52.7	55.3	55.7
	Female	—	41.9	45.9	45.5	45.5	47.3	49.0
Poland	All	—	58.3	58.1	58.4	58.8	58.9	—
	Female	—	51.9	51.8	51.8	51.8	52.2	—
Slovak Republic	All	—	61.1	62.3	63.2	59.7	58.8	—
	Female	—	56.0	56.8	57.5	53.1	52.6	—
Slovenia	All	60.7	60.3	62.9	61.9	63.4	63.7	—
	Female	56.5	56.0	58.0	57.7	58.9	59.6	—

— Not available.
Note: Ages 15 to 64.
Sources: European Training Foundation 1999, Statistical Office of Estonia, and OECD 1999.

TABLE 23.A9 UNEMPLOYMENT RATES IN EU ACCESSION COUNTRIES

Country	*Data source*	*1990*	*1991*	*1992*	*1993*	*1994*	*1995*	*1996*	*1997*	*1998*	*1999*
Czech Republic	Survey	—	—	—	3.9	3.8	4.1	3.9	4.8	6.5	8.8
	Registered	—	4.1	2.6	3.5	3.2	2.9	3.5	5.2	7.5	9.6
Estonia	Survey[a]	0.6	1.5	3.7	6.5	7.6	9.7	10.0	9.7	9.9	11.7
	Registered	—	—	—	4.4	4.1	4.4	4.0	3.7	5.1	—
Hungary	Survey	—	—	9.8	11.9	10.7	10.2	9.9	8.7	7.8	7.1
	Registered	1.4	7.4	12.3	12.1	10.4	10.4	10.5	10.4	8.8	—
Poland	Survey	—	—	—	14.9	16.5	15.2	14.3	11.5	10.6	12.0
	Registered	6.5	12.2	14.3	16.4	16.0	14.9	13.2	10.3	10.4	11.5
Slovak Republic	Survey	—	—	—	12.2	13.7	13.1	11.1	11.6	12.5	17.1
	Registered[b]	1.5	11.8	10.4	14.2	14.6	13.1	12.8	13.4	16.4	19.2
Slovenia	Survey	—	—	—	9.1	9.0	7.4	7.3	7.1	7.9	—
	Registered	4.7	8.2	11.5	14.4	14.5	14.0	13.9	14.4	14.5	—
EU-15 average	Survey	7.0	7.7	8.9	10.1	10.3	9.8	9.8	9.2	8.3	7.6
EU- Group 1 (North)[b]	Survey	4.9	5.9	7.5	9.2	9.5	8.5	8.3	7.5	6.7	6.0
EU- Group 2 (Central)[c]	Survey	7.6	8.0	8.7	8.5	9.0	8.9	9.4	9.7	9.5	8.8
EU- Group 3 (South)[d]	Survey	10.2	10.6	11.5	13.2	13.6	12.9	12.7	11.8	10.5	12.4[e]
United States	Survey	5.6	6.8	7.5	6.9	6.1	5.6	5.4	4.9	4.5	4.2

— Not available.
a. Data from Ministry of Labor, Family and Social Affairs, 1998.
b. Includes Finland, Sweden, Denmark, United Kingdom, and Benelux.
c. Includes Germany, France, Austria, and Italy.
d. Includes Portugal, Spain, Greece, and Ireland.
e. Only Portugal and Spain.
Sources: Central Bank of Estonia, EBRD 1999, European Training Foundation 1999, and OECD 1999.

TABLE 23.A10 UNEMPLOYMENT INFLOWS AND OUTFLOWS IN EU ACCESSION COUNTRIES
(percent)

Country	*Type of rate*	*1991*	*1992*	*1993*	*1994*	*1995*	*1996*
Czech Republic	Annual average inflow rate[a]	0.9	0.9	0.7	0.6	0.6	0.6
	Annual average outflow rate[b]	17.1	26.6	22.0	21.3	21.3	19.3
Hungary	Annual average inflow rate[a]	—	0.9	1.3	1.1	1.0	1.3
	Annual average outflow rate[b]	—	6.6	7.7	9.1	7.9	9.4
Poland	Annual average inflow rate[a]	—	0.9	1.1	1.2	1.3	1.2
	Annual average outflow rate[b]	—	4.3	4.8	6.2	8.0	8.2
Slovak Republic	Annual average inflow rate[a]	1.3	1.1	1.5	1.3	1.4	1.4
	Annual average outflow rate[b]	4.8	10.2	7.8	7.4	9.5	10.0
Slovenia	Annual average inflow rate[c]	—	—	—	6.7	8.4	9.0
	Annual average outflow rate[c]	—	—	—	9.8	6.9	9.7

— Not available.
Note: Data for Estonia were not available.
a. Average annual rate of the number flowing into unemployment divided by the number employed and multiplied by 100.
b. Average annual rate of the number flowing out of unemployment divided by the number unemployed and multiplied by 100.
c. Average annual rate for the number flowing into and out of unemployment divided by the number unemployed and multiplied by 100 (based on monthly rates).
Sources: Terrell 1999 and the European Training Foundation 1999.

TABLE 23.A11 UNEMPLOYMENT RATES IN SELECTED OECD COUNTRIES
(percent)

Country	*1993*	*1994*	*1995*	*1996*	*1997*	*1998*	*1999*	*1993–98/99*
Austria	4.0	3.8	3.9	4.4	4.5	4.7	3.7	4.1
Belgium	8.9	10.0	9.9	9.7	9.2	8.8	9.0	9.4
Denmark	10.1	8.2	7.3	6.8	5.6	5.1	5.2	6.9
Finland	16.4	16.8	15.3	14.6	12.7	11.4	10.3	13.9
France	11.7	12.3	11.7	12.4	12.3	11.7	11.3	11.9
Germany	7.9	8.4	8.2	8.9	9.9	9.4	8.7	8.8
Greece	8.6	8.9	9.2	9.6	9.6	10.7	—	9.4
Ireland	15.6	14.3	12.3	11.6	9.9	7.8	—	11.9
Italy	10.3	11.4	11.9	12.0	12.1	11.9	11.4	11.6
Luxembourg	2.7	3.2	2.9	3.0	2.8	2.8	2.3	2.8
Netherlands	6.6	7.1	6.9	6.3	5.2	4.0	3.3	5.6
Portugal	5.7	7.0	7.3	7.3	6.8	4.9	4.5	6.2
Spain	22.7	24.1	22.9	22.2	20.8	18.8	15.9	21.0
Sweden	9.1	9.4	8.8	9.6	9.9	8.2	—	9.2
United Kingdom	10.5	9.6	8.7	8.2	7.0	6.3	6.1	8.0
United States	6.9	6.1	5.6	5.4	4.9	4.5	4.2	5.4
EU-15 average	10.1	10.3	9.8	9.8	9.2	8.3	7.6	9.3

— Not available.
Note: The rates are based on survey data.
Source: OECD 1999.

TABLE 23.A12 SHORT- AND LONG-TERM UNEMPLOYMENT RATE IN SELECTED OECD COUNTRIES
(percent)

Country	*Indicator*	*1993*	*1994*	*1995*	*1996*	*1997*	*1998*	*1999*
Austria	STU	—	3.1	2.9	3.3	3.2	3.3	2.5
	LTU	—	0.7	1.0	1.1	1.3	1.4	1.2
	% LTU	—	18.5	25.6	25.6	28.7	30.2	31.7
Belgium	STU	4.2	4.2	3.7	3.8	3.6	3.3	3.6
	LTU	4.7	5.8	6.2	5.9	5.6	5.5	5.4
	% LTU	53.0	58.3	62.4	61.3	60.5	62.6	60.5
Denmark	STU	7.6	5.6	5.3	5.0	4.1	3.6	4.1
	LTU	2.5	2.6	2.0	1.8	1.5	1.5	1.1
	% LTU	25.1	32.1	27.9	26.5	27.2	28.7	20.5
Finland	STU	11.4	—	9.5	9.6	8.9	8.3	7.3
	LTU	5.0	—	5.8	5.0	3.8	3.1	3.0
	% LTU	30.6	—	37.6	34.5	29.8	27.5	29.6
France	STU	7.7	7.6	6.8	7.5	7.2	6.5	6.7
	LTU	4.0	4.7	4.9	4.9	5.1	5.2	4.6
	% LTU	34.2	38.3	42.3	39.5	41.2	44.1	40.3
Germany	STU	4.7	4.7	4.2	4.6	4.9	4.5	4.2
	LTU	3.2	3.7	4.0	4.3	5.0	4.9	4.5
	% LTU	40.0	43.9	48.7	47.8	50.1	52.2	51.7
Ireland	STU	3.8	6.0	4.7	4.6	4.9	—	—
	LTU	11.8	8.3	7.6	6.9	5.6	—	—
	% LTU	75.9	57.8	61.4	59.5	57.0	—	—
Italy	STU	4.4	4.5	4.3	4.1	4.1	4.1	4.4
	LTU	5.9	6.9	7.6	7.9	8.0	8.1	7.0
	% LTU	57.3	60.8	63.6	65.6	66.3	68.1	61.4
Netherlands	STU	3.6	4.0	3.7	3.2	2.6	2.1	1.9
	LTU	3.0	3.1	3.2	3.2	2.6	1.9	1.4
	% LTU	45.4	43.5	46.8	50.0	49.1	47.9	43.5
Portugal	STU	3.7	4.1	3.6	3.4	3.0	2.7	2.6
	LTU	2.0	2.9	3.7	3.9	3.8	2.2	1.9
	% LTU	32.5	41.8	50.9	53.1	55.6	44.6	41.2
Spain	STU	11.3	10.6	9.9	9.8	9.3	8.6	7.7
	LTU	11.4	13.5	13.0	12.4	11.5	10.2	8.2
	% LTU	50.1	56.1	56.9	55.7	55.5	54.1	51.3
Sweden	STU	8.1	7.8	6.4	6.7	6.6	5.5	—
	LTU	1.0	1.6	2.4	2.9	3.3	2.7	—
	% LTU	10.9	17.2	27.8	30.1	33.4	33.5	—
United Kingdom	STU	6.0	5.2	4.9	4.9	4.3	4.2	4.3
	LTU	4.5	4.4	3.8	3.3	2.7	2.1	1.8
	% LTU	42.5	45.4	43.6	39.8	38.6	33.1	29.8
United States	STU	6.1	5.4	5.1	4.9	4.5	4.1	3.9
	LTU	0.8	0.7	0.5	0.5	0.4	0.4	0.3
	% LTU	11.5	12.2	9.7	9.5	8.7	8.0	6.8

— Not available.
STU: Short-term unemployment.
LTU: Long-term unemployment.
% LTU: Percentage of total unemployment due to long-term unemployment.
Sources: OECD-CCET Labor Market Database 1990–97 and OECD 1999 and 2000.

TABLE 23.A13 LABOR FORCE PARTICIPATION RATES IN SELECTED OECD COUNTRIES
(percent)

Country	*Workers*[a]	*1994*	*1995*	*1996*	*1997*	*1998*
EU-15 Average	All	60.1	61.1	61.4	62.0	63.0
	Female	57.1	57.6	58.3	58.7	59.4
Austria	All	—	68.4	67.3	67.2	67.4
	Female	—	62.3	61.8	61.8	62.5
Belgium	All	55.7	56.3	56.3	57.0	57.3
	Female	51.2	51.7	52.0	52.9	53.8
Denmark	All	72.4	73.9	74.0	75.4	75.3
	Female	73.8	73.3	73.6	74.2	75.0
Finland	All	60.7	61.9	62.8	63.6	64.8
	Female	69.1	69.5	69.9	69.5	69.7
France	All	58.3	59.0	59.2	58.8	59.4
	Female	59.2	59.8	60.3	60.1	60.8
Germany	All	64.7	64.7	64.1	63.6	64.1
	Female	61.4	61.3	61.3	61.8	60.9
Greece	All	54.1	54.4	54.9	54.8	54.9
	Female	43.2	44.3	45.8	46.0	48.2
Ireland	All	52.3	53.8	54.8	56.1	59.8
	Female	46.9	47.0	48.8	49.7	52.1
Italy	All	50.9	50.5	50.6	50.5	50.8
	Female	42.2	42.5	43.3	43.6	43.9
Luxembourg	All	60.2	58.5	59.1	59.9	60.2
	Female	47.0	44.1	45.7	47.1	47.6
Netherlands	All	36.0	34.2	66.2	68.1	69.8
	Female	57.3	59.1	60.2	61.9	62.9
Portugal	All	62.9	62.5	62.3	63.4	66.8
	Female	58.8	59.1	59.5	60.3	61.9
Spain	All	46.5	47.4	48.2	49.4	51.2
	Female	45.4	46.2	47.0	48.0	48.7
Sweden	All	71.5	72.2	71.6	70.7	71.5
	Female	77.0	77.2	77.1	76.3	75.5
United States	All	76.7	76.9	77.1	77.4	77.4
	Female	69.4	69.7	70.1	70.7	70.7

— Not available.
a. Ages 15 to 64.
Source: OECD 1999.

Appendix B—Constructing the Employment Protection Legislation Index

Since the late 1980s, the OECD has been interested in analyzing the relationship between employment protection legislation (EPL) and labor market flexibility (and performance). The first round of studies used an EPL index based solely on permanent and temporary employment regulation. This index was later updated to account for regulation concerning collective dismissals. The methodology described here corresponds to the most recent version of the EPL index.

This index is constructed as a weighted average of 22 different indicators describing various aspects of both permanent and temporary employment, as well as collective dismissals. Although some of these indicators are readily available from the country's labor code (notice period, severance payment, maximum duration of temporary contracts), most of them need to be constructed using different sources of information, together with some subjective aggregation method.

Table 23.A1 contains a detailed description of all 22 indicators classified in three groups (level 3): indicators describing legislation for regular or permanent contracts (RC); indicators capturing the nature of temporary employment legislation (TC); and indicators for the strictness of collective dismissal procedures (CD). These broad groups can then be broken up into more narrowly defined subgroups (level 2). For instance, when looking at temporary employment legislation, we consider separately the indicators for the nature and characteristics of fixed-term contracts (TC1) and temporary work agencies (TC2). Finally, each subgroup may contain one or more individual indicators, such as "Valid cases other than objective" (TC1A) and "Maximum number of successive contracts" (TC1B) in the case of fixed-term contracts legislation (level 1).

This classification is rather important, since the EPL methodology relies heavily on it to move from the individual indicators to the overall index. In particular, the EPL calculation is organized in three steps, each of them aggregating information from one level to the next (level 1 to level 2, level 2 to level 3, and so on) and using a different set of weights (in parentheses in table 23.B1 in appendix B).

It is important to notice that different indicators are expressed in different units, making standardization necessary in order to aggregate them in a comprehensive manner. For this purpose, all indicators are rescaled using a common ranking, from 0 (very flexible legislation) to 6 (very strict legislation), in the way described in table 23.B2.

In sum, the EPL index is constructed as follows:

- Calculation of individual indicators (tables 23.B3, 23.B4, and 23.B5)
- Rescaling of individual indicators using the conversion presented in table 23.B2

- Aggregation in three steps from levels 1 to 4 using the weights described in table 23.B1.

As a result of this methodology, the countries with very flexible employment protection regulation have a low overall EPL index (close to 0 or 1), and those with very strict legislation will have a high index (close to 5 or 6).

TABLE 23.B1 EMPLOYMENT PROTECTION INDEX: SELECTION OF INDICATORS AND WEIGHTING SCHEME

Level 4	*Level 3*	*Level 2*	*Level 1*		
EPL overall summary indicator	RC Regular contracts (5/12)	RC1 Procedural inconveniences (1/3)	Procedures		(1/2)
			Delay to start of notice		(1/2)
		RC2 Notice and severance pay for no-fault individual dismissals (1/3)	Notice period after	9 months	(1/7)
				4 years	(1/7)
				20 years	(1/7)
			Severance pay after	9 months	(4/21)
				4 years	(4/21)
				20 years	(4/21)
		RC3 Difficulty of dismissal (1/3)	Definition of unfair dismissal		(1/4)
			Trial period		(1/4)
			Compensation		(1/4)
			Reinstatement		(1/4)
	TC Temporary contracts (5/12)	TC1 Fixed-term contracts (1/2)	Valid cases other than objective		(1/2)
			Max number of successive contracts		(1/4)
			Max cumulated duration		(1/4)
		TC2 Temporary work agency (1/2)	Types of work for which is legal		(1/2)
			Restrictions on number of renewal		(1/4)
			Max cumulated duration		(1/4)
	CD Collective dismissals (2/12)		Definition of collective dismissal		(1/4)
			Additional notification requirements		(1/4)
			Additional delays involved		(1/4)
			Other special costs to employers		(1/4)

TABLE 23.B2 EMPLOYMENT PROTECTION INDEX: CONVERSION INTO A COMMON SCALE

Code	*Original unit*	*0*	*1*	*2*	*3*	*4*	*5*	*6*
Individual dismissals								
RC1A	Scale 0–3	—	—	—	Scale (0–3)*2	—	—	—
RC1B	Days	0–2	< 10	< 18	< 26	< 35	< 45	≥ 45
RC2A1	Months	0	≤ 0.4	≤ 0.8	≤ 1.2	< 1.6	< 2	≥ 2
RC2A2	Months	0	≤ 0.75	≤ 1.25	< 2	< 2.5	< 3.5	≥ 3.5
RC2A3	Months	< 3	≤ 2.75	≤ 5	≤ 7	≤ 9	> 11	< 11
RCB1	Months	0	≤ 0.5	≤ 1	≤ 1.75	≤ 2.5	< 3	≥ 3
RCB2	Months	0	≤ 0.5	≤ 1	≤ 2	≤ 3	< 4	≥ 4
RCB3	Months	0	≤ 3	≤ 6	≤ 10	≤ 12	≤ 18	> 18
RC3A	Scale 0–3	—	—	—	Scale (0–3)*2	—	—	—
RC3B	Months	≥ 24	> 12	> 9	> 5	> 2.5	> 1.5	< 1.5
RC3C	Months	≤ 13	≤ 8	≤ 12	≤ 18	≤ 24	£ 30	> 30
RC3D	Scale 0–3	—	—	—	Scale (0–3)*2	—	—	—
Temporary dismissals								
TC1A	Scale 0–3	—	—	—	Scale (0–3)*2	—	—	—
TC1B	Number	No limit	≥ 5	≥ 4	≥ 3	≥ 2	≥ 1.5	< 1.5
TC1C	Months	No limit	≥ 36	≥ 30	≥ 24	≥ 18	≥ 12	< 12
TC2A	Scale 0–4	—	—	—	Scale (0–4)*6/4	—	—	—
TC2B	Yes/no	—	—	No	—	Yes or TC2A=0	—	—
TC2C	Months	No limit	≥ 36	≥ 24	≥ 18	≥ 12	> 6	≤ 6 or TC2A = 0
Collective dismissals								
CD1	Scale 0–4	—	—	—	Scale (0–4)*6/4	—	—	—
CD2	Scale 0–2	—	—	—	Scale (0–2)*3	—	—	—
CD3	Days	0	< 25	< 30	< 50	< 70	< 90	> 90
CD4	Scale 0–2	—	—	—	Scale (0–2)*3	—	—	—

— Not applicable.

TABLE 23.B3 EMPLOYMENT PROTECTION LEGISLATION INDEX: DISMISSAL REGULATION FOR PERMANENT EMPLOYEES

	Regular procedures		*Notice and severance pay for "no-fault" individuals*						*Difficulty of dismissal*			
			Notice period (months) after			*Severance pay (months) after*						
Country	*Scale 0 to 3*	*Delay to start of notice (days)*	*9m*	*4y*	*20y*	*9m*	*4y*	*20y*	*Definition of unfair dismissal*	*Trial period before eligibility (months)*	*Compensation at 20 years of tenure (months)*	*Extent of re-admission (months)*
Czech Republic	2.0	7.0	2.0	2.5	2.5	1.0	1.0	1.0	2.0	3.0	8.0	2.0
Estonia	2.0	1.0	2.0	2.0	4.0	2.0	2.0	4.0	1.5	1.0	6.0	3.0
Hungary	1.0	13.0	1.0	1.2	3.0	0.0	1.0	5.0	0.0	3.0	10.0	2.0
Poland	2.0	13.0	1.0	3.0	3.0	0.0	0.0	0.0	0.0	1.8	3.0	2.0
Slovak Republic	1.0	2.0	2.0	2.0	2.0	2.0	2.0	2.0	1.0	1.0	6.0	3.0
Slovenia	2.0	9.0	6.0	6.0	6.0	0.0	2.0	10.0	2.5	2.0	10.0	3.0
Slovenia[a]	2.0	9.0	1.0	2.0	4.0	0.0	0.8	6.7	2.0	1.3	12.0	2.0

Note: Index is based on 12 indicators.

a. All indicators are based on proposed Labor Code.

Sources: OECD 1999, Labor Code of Estonia, Labor Code of Slovenia (current and proposed), and Labor Code of Slovakia.

TABLE 23.B4 EMPLOYMENT PROTECTION LEGISLATION INDEX: REGULATION OF TEMPORARY FORMS OF EMPLOYMENT

	Fixed-term contracts			*Temporary work agencies*		
Country	*Valid reasons for use other than "temporary activity"*[a] *(scale 0–3)*	*Maximum number of consecutive contracts (number)*	*Maximum accumulated duration (months)*	*Types of activities for which agency can be hired (scale 0–4)*	*Restriction on renewals (yes/no)*	*Maximum accumulated duration of contracts (months)*
Czech Republic	2.5	no limit	no limit	4	No	No limit
Estonia	1.0	no limit	60	4	No	No limit
Hungary	2.5	no limit	60	4	No	No limit
Poland	3.0	2	no limit	4	Yes	No limit
Slovak Republic	1.0	no limit	36	4	No	No limit
Slovenia	1.0	no limit	no limit	1	No	2 months
Slovenia[b]	2.5	no limit	36	4	No	No limit

Note: Index is based on six indicators.

a. Temporary activities include specific projects, seasonal work, replacement of temporarily absent permanent workers (on sickness and maternity leave), and exceptional workload.

b. Based on proposed law.

Sources: OECD 1999, Estonian Labor Code, Slovenian Labor Codes (current and proposed), and Slovak Republic Labor Code.

TABLE 23.B5 EMPLOYMENT PROTECTION LEGISLATION INDEX: PROCEDURES AND STANDARDS FOR COLLECTIVE DISMISSALS

Country	*Definition of collective dismissal (scale 0–4)*	*Additional notification requirements (scale 0–2)*	*Additional delays involved (days)*	*Other special costs to employers (scale 0–2)*
Czech Republic	4	2	83	0.0
Estonia	3	2	46	1.0
Hungary	3	2	47	0.0
Poland	3	1	32	2.0
Slovak Republic	2	2	60	1.5
Slovenia	3	2	60	1.5
Slovenia[a]	4	2	45	1.5

Note: There are four indicators.

a. Based on proposed code.

Sources: OECD 1999, Estonian Labor Code, Slovenian Labor Codes (current and proposed), and Slovak Labor Code.

Appendix C—Trade Unions and Collective Bargaining in the EU Accession Countries

The Czech Republic

There are currently two main trade unions and two main employer associations in the Czech Republic. All of them operate on the basis of free association; that is, agreements signed between unions and employer associations are only binding for union workers and firms belonging to the employer association. (If a firm disagrees with a certain industry-level agreement, it is free to leave the employer association and ignore such agreement.)

Labor unions in the Czech Republic are very weak, with the exception of those in sectors where the presence of public enterprises is still substantial. As a consequence, union coverage is limited, with only 30 percent of the work force covered by the 1,222 collective agreements signed in 1998, and the number of new unions in privatized and new companies is low.

Wage bargaining occurs at multiple levels. First, a tripartite body, composed of representatives from trade unions, employer associations, and the Ministry of Labor and Social Affairs, determines aggregate wage growth and basic working conditions (provided the government is willing to participate in the negotiations). Second, there are industry-level and firm-level negotiations between employers and unions. During these negotiations, however, wages are *de facto* set by employers, with the exception of the public where negotiations must comply with a pre-set wage grid.

Although initially the tripartite body was responsible for the determination of the minimum wage, since the mid-1990s adjustments have been made unilaterally by the Ministry of Labor when considered necessary.

Estonia

During the 1990s, union membership declined in Estonia from almost 100 percent to 30 percent. This decrease was due to the privatization process and to the increasing importance of small and foreign firms, where union presence is generally weak. In addition, the bulk of economic activity shifted from manufacturing, where traditionally unions were strong, to services.

The level of coordination among employers is not high. Employers are represented, only on a voluntary basis, by a single employers' association that covers around 6,000 firms or 200,000 employees (out of a total of approximately 640,200). As a consequence of the weakness of social partners, the government plays a major role in shaping industrial relations, the basis of which are then laws rather than agreements.

Both unions and employers are invited to participate in the design of such laws through tripartite negotiations. Discussions, however, focus on working conditions rather than wages. These are generally determined unilaterally by the employers, at the firm level, or by the government in the case of public sector workers.

Hungary

After transition, trade unions in Hungary have been mainly relegated to newly privatized state firms, since they have gained little representation in new companies. This implies that unions are strong in heavy industries and weak in the expanding service sector.

General economic policy issues and labor matters are discussed in two different forums. The first is the Economic Council, a consultative body composed of different organizations including trade unions and employer organizations, multinational investors, the Hungarian National Bank, and the Hungarian government. The second forum is the National Labor Council, a tripartite council for consultation and negotiation on labor issues including employment legislation, industrial relations and social policy, training, wages, and work-place safety regulations.

Although the National Labor Council is also empowered to set the national minimum wage and recommend wage increases, centralized collective bargaining has never been very important in Hungary. Wage deregulation began before the transition, and during the privatization period most private sector wages became freely negotiable at the industry and firm levels. Hence, it is only in the public sector, regulated through a strict wage tariff system, that some form of collective bargaining is still binding.

Poland

One of the main features of the labor market in Poland, unlike its Central European neighbors, is the large number of labor organizations that operate in it. Trade unions and other employee organizations, which started and accelerated the transition process, still play an important role. Currently, the two most important trade union confederations are Solidarity and the Organization of Post-Communist Trade Unions (OPZZ). In addition, there are nine smaller nationwide union confederations, 273 national trade union organizations, and about 24,000 local trade unions, organized by enterprise, industry, or region. Similarly, there are more than 1,000 employer organizations across the country.

Unions enjoy by law extensive power in the areas of worker rights, wage policy, and social benefits. In contrast, they have no control over managerial decisions regarding company strategy and ownership transformations—a fact that in the past led them to initiate numerous strikes to express dissatisfaction with the privatization process. In the last few years, union power has been eroded by constant growth in the number of small and medium enterprises. (For example, 90 percent of all firms outside the agriculture sector have five or fewer employees, and 89 percent of these are sole proprietorships.) Most of the current activity of unions, therefore, is concentrated in large, heavy industry firms yet to be privatized. This has led many to blame unions for the inefficiencies that plague these large enterprises.

Since 1995 industrial relations have been organized through the Tripartite Commission, which includes representatives of the government, employers' associations, and trade unions. Other smaller, more localized organizations—composed of trade unions, local government officials, employers' associations, and groups of unemployed workers—serve as consultative and advisory bodies to the heads of general administrative organs.

Wage negotiations between employers and workers can take place at the industry and the firm levels. However, collective agreements can be adopted only when a union is present. This implies that, in practice, collective agreements cover mostly state-owned companies or big privatized companies rather than newly created private firms. As a consequence, the average pay in the public sector has remained significantly higher than that in the private sector during the last decade.

Slovak Republic

Union coverage is fairly extensive in the Slovak Republic. Moreover, unions play an important role in the design of industrial relations since the Employment Act (1997) stipulates that they be represented as a social partner at all levels of the National Labor Office and its organs. The Confederation of Trade Unions, composed of 42 independent groups, is the largest union, while the two most important employer organizations are the Association of Employers and the Association of the Slovak Republic, with 27 member organizations in total.

The Slovak Republic adopted a tripartite system to regulate labor and industrial affairs in 1990. For this purpose, the Council of Economic and Social Agreement was created. It has a total of 21 representatives from trade unions, employers' associations, and the government. Among other functions, the Council decides on the minimum wage and the Minimum Living Standard (that is, the poverty line), and further wage negotiations are conducted at the industry and firm levels. Such negotiations, as well as the organization of strikes, are regulated through the Act on Collective Bargaining.

Slovenia

There are 130 national trade unions in Slovenia operating along industrial and occupational lines. Although there are no official figures on membership, 21 out of these 130 unions are considered "representative." In other words, membership represents at least 15 percent of all employees in the particular industry or occupation the union operates in. Employers, on the other hand, are organized in three different associations, and their interests are also represented by the Chamber of Commerce, to which membership is compulsory.

According to the current labor legislation, collective agreements are a main instrument for determining specific rights and duties between employers and employees.[16] Consultations occur first at the national level, resulting in (1) a collective agreement for the private sector that determines base wages and adjustment factors for 26 industries and nine educational levels, and (2) a collective agreement for the nonmarket sector. Both agreements constitute the basis for all other contracts, thus limiting wage variation across industries and firms.

In addition, social dialogue is organized around the Economic and Social Council, founded in 1994. This is a national tripartite consultative body of 15 representatives, five from each of its three members (the government, trade unions, and employers). The Council provides recommendations concerning legislation, such as compulsory insurance schemes (old-age and disability pensions, social welfare, allowances), employment, labor relations, collective bargaining, prices and taxes, and economic policy, and these recommendations are then submitted to the Parliament. The Council also plays an important role as a facilitator of negotiations between unions and employers' associations, helping them reach the agreements described earlier.

Notes

1. Due mainly to lack of accurate data, we do not examine in detail the role of minimum wages. However, the available evidence seems to suggest that they are not binding in most of the countries studied here.

2. Version 1 can be found in tables 23.A1 and 23.A2 in appendix A.

3. See appendix B for a detailed methodological description of the EPL index.

4. Slovenia is about to adopt a new, much more flexible labor code. We have included in all tables EPL values corresponding to this new legislation for the reader to appreciate the magnitude of the potential changes.

5. The thorough reader may consult table 23.A3 in appendix A.

6. The thorough reader may consult table 23.B4 in appendix B.

7. A collective dismissal is dismissal of more than 10 employees.

8. All tables containing data for OECD and EU countries can be found in appendix A.

9. Unemployment benefits are a function of the minimum wage rather than of previous earned income. As a result, the level of protection, measured by the replacement ratio, is very low, especially for those with high salaries.

10. For example, assume country A and country B have the same unemployment insurance system, but the unemployment rate in country A is double that in country B. Then spending will appear to be higher in country B, even though both systems are equally generous.

11. Appendix C discusses these issues for each one of the EU accession countries considered in this chapter.

12. See also table 23.A5 for EU and OECD data.

13. In spite of these developments, unemployment remained low in Slovenia as a result of the privatization process that generated low dynamics in the labor market.

14. Another caveat is the impossibility to evaluate the degree of enforcement of regulations and policies.

15. Recent literature (Marquez 1998; OECD 1999; Kugler 2000) suggests that job security provisions provide incentives for self-employment and operation in the informal sector.

16. The new labor legislation that is proposed will determine most of the rights of employees at a minimum level. Thus the conclusion of collective agreements will no longer be obligatory. The Law on Collective Agreements is in the process of being adopted. The division into commercial and noncommercial sectors will be replaced by a division of profit and nonprofit sectors.

References

Bentolina, S., and G. Bertola. 1990. "Firing Costs and Labor Demand: How Bad Is Eurosclerosis?" *Review of Economic Studies* 57:381–402.

Bertola, G. 1990. "Job Security, Employment and Wages." *European Economic Review* 34:851–86.

Bilsen, V., and J. Konings. 1998. "Job Creation, Job Destruction and Growth of Newly-Established, Privatized, and State-Owned Enterprises in Transition Economies: Survey Evidence from Bulgaria, Hungary and Romania." *Journal of Comparative Economics* 26:429–45.

Blanchard, O., and J. Wolfers. 1999. "The Role of Shocks and Institutions in the Rise of European Unemployment: The Aggregate Evidence." Working Paper 7282. National Bureau of Economic Research, Cambridge, Mass.

Blank, R., and R. Freeman. 1994. "Does a Larger Social Safety Net Mean Less Economic Flexibility?" In R. Blank and R. Freeman, eds., *Working under Different Rules.* New York: Russell Sage.

Business Eastern Europe. *Labour Regulations in Eastern Europe.*

Deloitte Touche Tohmatsu. 1998. *Taxation in Central Europe*. New York.

Eamets, R. and others. 1999. "Background Study on Labor Markets and Employment in Estonia." Brussels: European Training Foundation.

EBRD (European Bank for Reconstruction and Development). 2000. *Transition Report 2000: Employment, Skills and Transition.* London.

———. 1999. *Transition Report.* London.

Economist Intelligence Unit. 1998. *The Economist.* London.

European Training Foundation. 1999. Employment and labor market country reports. Brussels.

Forteza, A., and M. Rama. 2000. "Labor Market Rigidity and the Success of Economic Reforms across More Than a Hundred Countries." Policy Research Working Paper 2521. World Bank, Washington, D.C.

Freeman, R. 1999. "Wages, Employment and Unemployment: An Overview. Can the EU Pass the Jobs Test?" Wages and Employment Seminar. European Communities, Brussels.

Haltiwanger, J. C., and M. Vodopivec. 1999. "Gross Worker and Job Flows in a Transition Economy: An Analysis of Estonia." Policy Research Working Paper S2082. World Bank, Washington, D.C.

Heckman, J., and C. Pages. 2000. "The Cost of Job Security Regulation: Evidence from Latin American Labor Markets." Working Paper 7773. National Bureau of Economic Research, Cambridge, Mass.

Hopenhayn, H., and R. Rogerson. 1993. "Job Turnover and Policy Evaluation: A General Equilibrium Analysis." *Journal of Political Economy* 101(5):915–38.

Horváth, R., and others. 1999. "Background Study on Labor Markets and Employment in Hungary." Torino, Italy: European Training Foundation.

ILO (International Labour Organization). 1997. *World Labor Report, 1997–98.* Geneva.

International Monetary Fund. 1999. *World Economic Outlook.* Washington, D.C.

Johnson, S., and others. 1997. "Politics and Entrepreneurship in Transition Economies." Working Paper 57. The Williamson Davison Institute at the University of Michigan, Ann Arbor, Mich.

Kugler, A. 2000. "The Incidence of Job Security Regulations on Labor Market Flexibility and Compliance in Colombia: Evidence from the 1990 Reform." Research Network Working Paper R-393. Inter-American Development Bank, Washington, D.C.

Lazear, E. 1990. "Job Security Provisions and Employment." *Quarterly Journal of Economics* 105:699–726.

Lubyova, M. 1999. "Background Study on Labor Markets and Employment in the Slovak Republic." Torino, Italy: European Training Foundation.

Marquez, M. 1998. "Protección de Empleo y Funcionamiento del Mercado de Trabajo: Un Aproximación Comparativa." Washington, D.C.: Inter-American Development Bank.

Munich, D., and others. 1999. "Background Study on Labor Markets and Employment in the Czech Republic." Torino, Italy: European Training Foundation.

Nickell, S. 1997. "Unemployment and Labor Market Rigidities: Europe versus North America." *Journal of Economic Perspectives* 11(3):55–74.

Nickell, S., and R. Layard. 1998. "Labor Market Institutions and Economic Performance." Discussion Paper 407. London School of Economics, Center for Economic Performance, London.

OECD (Organisation for Economic Co-operation and Development). 1994, 1995, 1997, 1999, 2000. *Employment Outlook.* Paris.

———. 1994, 1995. *Jobs Study.* Paris.

Orazem, P. F., and M. Vodopivec. 1999. "Male-Female Differences in Labor Market Outcomes During the Early Transition to Market: The Case of Estonia and Slovenia." Policy Research Working Paper S2087. World Bank, Washington, D.C.:

Pirher, S., and others. 1999. "Background Study for the Employment Policy Review for Slovenia." Ljubljana: National VET Observatory Slovenia and the European Training Foundation.

Rama, M., and R. Artecona. 2001. "A Database of Labor Market Indicators across Countries." Unpublished. Washington, D.C.: World Bank.

Statistical Office of Estonia. 1997. *Estonian Labor Force Survey.* Tallinn.

———. 1998. *Estonian Labor Force Survey.* Tallinn.

Statistical Office of the Republic of Slovenia. 1995. *Slovene Labor Force Survey.* Ljubljana.

Statistical Office of the Slovak Republic. Various years. *Slovak Labor Force Survey.* Bratislava.

Statistical Office of Spain. Various years. *Spanish Labor Force Survey.* Madrid.

Sztanderska, U., and B. Piotrowski. 1999. "Background Study on Labor Markets and Employment in Poland." Torino, Italy: European Training Foundation.

Terrell, K. 1999. "Czech Republic: Labor Market Study." Technical Paper Series. Washington, D.C.: World Bank.

Vodopivec, M. 1999. "Worker Reallocation during Estonia's Transition to Market." World Bank, Washington, D.C. Processed.

World Bank. 1998a. *Slovak Republic: A Strategy for Growth and Economic Integration.* Country Economic Memorandum. Washington, D.C.

———. 1998b. *Slovenia: Labor Market Issues.* Washington, D.C.

———. 1999. *Czech Republic: Towards EU Accession.* Washington, D.C.

———. 2000. *Progress toward the Unification of Europe.* Washington, D.C.

———. 2001. *Poland: Labor Market Study. The Challenge of Job Creation and Destruction*. Washington, D.C.

CHAPTER 24

Comparative Experience with Labor Market Reform

Maria Helena André

The process of EU enlargement is the most challenging process the European Union has ever faced. It will underpin democracy, peace, and stability for the whole continent, and it has the potential to foster economic and social progress for all Europe. Enlargement will broaden the internal market; it will reinforce the role of the European Union in the world, both in economic and political terms. It must be a win-win situation, with no winners and no losers. In any case the cost of nonenlargement would be much higher.

Enlargement of the European Union: A New Challenge for Europe

The efforts that will be asked from both sides must be matched by clear objectives in terms of economic growth, the improvement of living and working conditions for all, environmental protection, the functioning of labor markets, equal opportunities, and the free movement of persons. The starting point for each accession country is varied, and the situation is rather heterogeneous. But this is also the situation in the present Member States of the European Union, and this has not been an obstacle in the past: we are confronted in the EU and in the accession countries with deep differences, not only between countries but also between regions inside the same country. The *Second Report on Economic and Social Cohesion* published by the European Commission early in 2001 has confirmed this fact. Such regional disparities have a direct impact on unemployment and job opportunities, and they may be a push factor in migratory terms, namely, in those regions that have a border with accession countries.

A number of policies will have to work together during both the preaccession and the postaccession periods. There is clearly the need to implement targeted structural and employment policies; however, these policies must be combined with democratization of the institutions and processes, macroeconomic policies leading to stability in terms of inflation and fiscal policies as well as to growth in Central and Eastern European countries, social policies (namely, those linked to social protection systems, the fight against unemployment, poverty, and social exclusion), education and vocational training policies leading to the development of human capital, active labor marker policies, and strong cooperation among the social partners. The involvement of the social partners in the management of this process of change and in the accession negotiating process is fundamental in order for enlargement to gain effective public support.

High levels of unemployment with a clear impact on welfare services, increased poverty and social exclusion (affecting women, elderly people, children, and young people), high inequalities between women and men, low wages, huge sectors confronted with economic restructuring and privatization, and a considerable informal sector are serious social problems that need to be addressed with determination. The full transposition of the social *acquis* by applicant countries is certainly the first step in the right direction.

The European Social Model

Throughout the 1990s, unemployment levels rose considerably in the European Union. By the end of 1991, all gains in employment obtained between 1985 and 1991 had been lost. This was the result of tight monetary and fiscal policies with the sole objective of fighting against inflation and lowering budgetary deficits in order to attain the nominal convergence criteria established by the Maastricht Treaty, in view of Economic and Monetary Union.

The impact of such policies on employment was not taken seriously and blame was put on labor market rigidities. However, one must look back into history. Over the past 50 years Europe became one of the most advanced societies in the world because economic and social progress went hand in hand and thus were mutually reinforcing. This link is the core of the European Social Model. It is true that this model has taken different forms from country to country, but, at the same time, it reflects the same set of values and produces comparable policies and institutions. The actual vision of the European Member States as "welfare states," the recognition of social rights and the role of social partners, the existence of public services and the social protection systems are all elements that together form the European Social Model. The principles enshrined in the EU Charter of Fundamental Rights, in the Council of Europe revised Charters, and in the 1989 Charter of Workers' Rights are also an integral part of this model.

The European integration process took shape against this common background, and thus the European Social Model remains the kingpin of the European integration process, especially concerning the enlargement of the European Union. During the past two decades, the European Social Model was brought into question, considered an obstacle for competitiveness and job creation. This has created a weakening of social protection and redistribution policies. Unemployment in Europe has reached historic figures; inequality has grown; poverty and social exclusion have increased.

The European Social Model needs to be revitalized, but this has to be done on the basis of an active role by governments and on their capacity to steer the economy, on effective redistribution policies and social protection, on high quality and fully accessible public services, and on comprehensive systems of collective bargaining. In this respect the Treaty of Amsterdam—its integration of the social protocol, allowing social partners to negotiate European framework agreements and the right of codecision of the European Parliament in the fields of social policy—offers a good basis of action.

At the same time consideration must be given to the deep changes that are taking place in our societies. These changes reflect demographic factors, such as the aging of the population, as well as the impact of new technologies and globalization. They are felt in the economic environment, in the organization of work, and in the nature of the work force, especially in view of the higher participation of women in the labor market, the incorporation of disabled persons and black and ethnic minority workers, and the growing number of workers in small enterprises and workers with nonstandard employment contracts. Taking account of the need to adapt and to modernize social regulations and provisions in the light of these factors, the European Trade Union Confederation developed a plan for action.

Reform must be negotiated at all the appropriate levels. At this stage of European integration, the process must be put into a European perspective that guarantees social harmonization and upward convergence in the integrated economic area. The aim is to construct a reordered and updated European Social Model that reinforces the basic link and balance between economic efficiency and external competitiveness on the one hand, and basic rights and social justice on the other.

The European Employment Strategy: The Need for the Right Policy Mix

The establishment of the Employment Policy at the European level has seen considerable progress since the 1997 Inter-Governmental Conference (IGC), where a title on employment was included in the Amsterdam Treaty, recognizing the gravity of the

European unemployment problem. The Luxembourg Jobs Summit in November 1997, which put into practice the principles of the employment title before the ratification of the Amsterdam Treaty, is a proof of the urgency of the problem.

However, by itself, the European Employment Strategy is inadequate to solve the unemployment problem and the need to create more and better jobs. It is necessary to develop an integrated policy approach. The introduction of the Euro is a landmark in the building of Europe. The single currency must be the basis for launching a coordinated strategy for sustainable economic growth and development, which respects the needs of the environment and which has the objective of ending unemployment and providing improved employment prospects as well as raising the living standards for all in Europe.

In order to achieve the objective of full employment, it is necessary to have better coordination of the different policies as well as a mutually supportive policy mix: macroeconomic policies (monetary, budgetary, and fiscal policies), structural policies (promoting adaptable labor markets, innovation, and competitiveness), and social policies (an active welfare state promoting human resource development, participation, inclusion, and solidarity). But it is also necessary to improve the substance of these policies as well as the consistency between the Employment Guidelines and the Broad Economic Policy Guidelines.

Achieving a successful policy mix under Economic and Monetary Union must be a shared undertaking, although one that respects the autonomy of the parties. The participation of the social partners in the Cologne macroeconomic dialogue, together with the European Central Bank and the European Commission, is an important step in the right direction.

Structural as well as macroeconomic policies have an important role to play in promoting a fully employed, dynamic, and cohesive economy. The EU's two structural policy processes are the Luxembourg process for employment and the Cardiff process for goods, services, and financial markets. There must be good coordination between these two processes as well as with the Cologne process in order to achieve the required objectives.

The Lisbon Council on Employment, Economic Reform and Social Cohesion, held in March 2000, represents for the European Trade Union Confederation (ETUC) the start of a new phase in the European policy: after the single market and EMU, Europe must give priority to the objective of full employment, based on stronger and sustainable growth, social cohesion, and the creation of a knowledge-based society (ETUC 2000). The time has come to put people back at the heart of the development process.

Stability is no longer the only priority of the EU; growth and employment are also taken on board. Full employment, based on a more efficient economy, innovation, knowledge, and social cohesion, is an objective of the European Union.

One of the important conclusions of the Lisbon conference is the setting of targets in relation to economic growth and employment rates. For these to be efficient, national targets must be set, and it is necessary to further develop comparable indicators as well as national and European targets in order to make it possible to assess the impact of the employment strategy and to facilitate identification and exchange of good practices.

The Employment Guidelines

Since 1998 the Employment Guidelines, translated into National Action Plans and a peer review in order to analyze the implementation of the strategy at the national level as well as recommendations addressed to each Member State, have contributed to the improvement of the employment situation. The Employment Guidelines, through a four-pillar structure, address the issues of employability, entrepreneurship, adaptability, and equal opportunities for women and men (EC 2000a).

Expressed in a different way, they address:

- The skills gap: the need for people to be able to constantly upgrade their skills so they can adjust to economic and social change; the anticipation of skilled labor demands in order to prevent bottlenecks, the improvement of digital literacy of the work force

- The jobs gap: the need for good entrepreneurship to save and create high-quality jobs, the specific role of SMEs in job creation

- The partnership gap: the need for all relevant partners to find innovative ways of working together to master the process of change and to implement new forms of work organization leading to the improvement of job security, the quality of work, productivity, and competitiveness

- The gender gap: the need to expand the gender approach in all employment and social policies in order to end the scandalous discrimination against women and achieve better conciliation between work and family life as well as equal pay.

The European Employment Strategy focuses on employment, not just unemployment problems; it highlights the importance of active as opposed to passive policies and of lifelong learning in particular. It stresses the need to prevent problems rather than just try to solve them. It takes into account the future importance of services, the jobs and environment interface, and the need to prepare for demographic changes, modernize work organization, strengthen cooperation between social partners, and promote equal opportunities between women and men. At the same time it attempts to tackle problems at different levels of intervention, including the regional level, which is very important in terms of enlargement of the EU.

The European Employment Strategy has an agenda of positive, negotiated flexibility, where structural and macroeconomic policies have to be integrated and coherent. The promotion of access to lifelong learning for all is certainly one of the most important policies of this strategy, although progress has been slow and Member States have not yet fixed national objectives, as agreed by the Lisbon European Council.

Good quality education and initial vocational training must be available to all young people. This education and training must be based on sound foundations and on clear guidance and counseling, including apprenticeships and other programs that lead to recognized qualifications. The aim should be to to reduce to zero the number of school dropouts, thus avoiding the inevitable fall into exclusion of those who leave school without qualifications. Education and vocational training systems must take into consideration social, technological, and economic changes and at the same time answer to the needs of the people.

Adult workers, employed or unemployed, must be able to upgrade and extend their skills and acquire recognized qualifications throughout their working lives. This implies that those who are working, not just the unemployed, have the chance to receive training. For this reason more European targets should be set. The goal should be to increase from 3.4 to 5 percent the share of the employed labor force receiving training. A time limit also is needed (four years, for example) for ensuring that at least 20 percent of the unemployed are offered training.

In addition to the education and training policies, counseling and placement policies, other proactive labor market and employment policies should be strengthened, such as equality and nondiscrimination policies, work experience and job creation policies. Employment services have a key role to play in the implementation of such policies.

New forms of work organization, the reorganization and reduction of working time, a better share of the work available—via the reduction of structural overtime, for instance—will help raise Europe's employment level and include more persons now excluded from the labor market. The social partners must take up their responsibilities and negotiate new forms of positive flexibility, resulting in more secure and more motivated workers. The right balance between flexibility and security is needed.

The precarious character of the European labor markets—the use of atypical forms of work—must be matched by a clear engagement from social partners and public authorities in order to provide occupational security, career development, and continuing vocational training opportunities as well as decent wages for atypical workers. There is a clear need to analyze the types of jobs that are being created and the growing income dispersion in order to have a clear picture of wage levels, income distribution, and the new balance between income from wages and from other sources (new forms of remuneration, tax cuts, or welfare).

There is also potential for job creation in sectors not exposed to the demands of worldwide competition, such as the territorial or local employment initiatives.

Systematically fostering the strengths of regional and local economies; developing local, cultural, and personal services; and promoting local products can create new employment opportunities. Social economy organizations can play an important role in making the link between real, unmet needs and those seeking employment.

The provision of work and training incentives to those excluded from the labor market must not jeopardize the general right of unemployed women and men to receive fair unemployment benefits. As said before, a number of different actors will have to give their contribution, according to their levels of responsibility, in order to put these policies into practice. The social partners have a key role to play in the development of new rights and obligations at different levels and through varied actions (intersectoral, sectoral, and company level), via collective bargaining and joint agreements. Although we note some progress at the national level in some countries, at the European level progress has not been significant, due to the lack of commitment of employers' organizations. But the social partners also need to develop partnerships with public authorities at all levels, including public employment agencies.

Governments must ensure that the resources required are available: active policies to reduce unemployment and to prevent further increases will involve considerable resources. But so would inaction. In most Member States there is scope for a redistribution of public expenditures to reflect the current serious situation. This should be seen in terms of employment policies constituting genuine investments that have high returns both in economic and social terms.

The implementation of the European Employment Strategy should be an integral part of the enlargement process of the European Union. Accession countries should devise active labor market mechanisms adapted to their needs and leading to the promotion of structural change through the elaboration of their own national action plans. To a certain extent, this is already happening within the framework of the joint assessment papers and of the employment policy reviews that are being carried out in candidate countries. The objective of these papers is to review recent trends and prospects for the economy and for the labor market and to identify the main priorities for employment policy, allowing for a more targeted use of preaccession support. The full association of the social partners with this process is extremely important, not just in terms of their knowledge about the labor market situation, but also as an impetus for the development of social dialogue and for the emergence of credible social partner organizations (especially from the side of employers).

The Role of Social Partners

Social dialogue is a central element of the European Social Model. In a knowledge-based economy—in a brain-based not muscle-based economy—the involvement of all relevant actors and the use of opportunities offered by the new forms of work organization are essential. Thus the traditional "European" way forward is to work together, the partnership approach. Social dialogue is an important instrument to support reform. It is economically efficient and socially acceptable. Besides, it is part of the community *acquis*, both in legal and institutional terms.

There are several phases in the development of the European Social Dialogue. It started in 1957 with the signing of the Treaty of Rome and the setting up of a social partnership between the European Commission and the social partners. It was strengthened with the "Val Duchesse Social Dialogue," launched by Jacques Delors in 1985, when the European social partners (ETUC, the Union of Industrial and Employers' Confederations of Europe [UNICE], and the European Centre of Enterprises with Public Participation and of Enterprises of General Economic Interest [CEEP]) met for a bipartite meeting for the first time. This was a period when the social partners jointly learned about the different industrial relations systems and cultures, and they prepared for what is today the European Social Dialogue. They cooperated on economic and social matters as well as on the implementation of the social action program resulting from the Social Charter of Fundamental Workers' Rights (1989).

As a result of the "Val Duchesse Social Dialogue," the social partners reached an agreement on October 31, 1991. It was incorporated in the Maastricht Treaty as the Social Protocol and later in the Amsterdam Treaty. With this new procedure, social partners have become "legislators," although we regret, from a trade union perspective, that the social partners have not yet been able to negotiate voluntary agreements without the "legislative menace" of the European Commission. In any case, three interprofessional agreements have been concluded: on parental leave (December 1995), on part-time employment contracts (June 1997), and on fixed-term employment contracts (March 1999). These agreements have been converted into EU directives (EC 2000b). Other attempts to negotiate have not worked. Examples include the European Works Councils Directive or more recently the proposed directive on information and consultation. Negotiations regarding temporary agencies also failed.

At the sectoral level intensive social dialogue is occurring in 27 sectoral social dialogue committees. The results have been positive—the framework agreement on working conditions in agriculture (1997) and three agreements on the organization of working time in maritime transportation, railways, and civil aviation. Candidate countries are confronted with the difficult task of managing economic, industrial, and technological changes; only a strong social dialogue will enable them to come to terms with these changes. Lessons from the 600 European work councils should not be forgotten. On these councils the candidate countries are often integrated.

The European social partners must play an active role to support strong social partner organizations in candidate countries, bearing in mind the fact that there is no single model and no ready-made formula. At this specific moment in time there may be some confusion about autonomous social dialogue between the social partners and the public authorities.

The European social partners have jointly organized two conferences on the promotion of social dialogue in Central and Eastern European countries. As a result, they have agreed to deepen exchanges on specific themes of relevance to them, such as management of industrial and technological change; analysis of different collective bargaining systems; the handling of specific issues related to SMEs; and promotion of the role of the social partners in developing quality services essential for social cohesion.

The European social partners have enlarged participation in meetings of the Social Dialogue Committee (which brings together the social partners at the European level) in order to include representatives from candidate countries. Other points require further analysis, such as the participation of social partner representatives from candidate countries as observers in the EU advisory committees in which the European social partners take part. The full participation of social partners from candidate countries in all EU programs directly concerning education, vocational training, and employment policies, including the European Social Fund, is of the utmost importance. Transnational cooperation, exchange of information and experiences, and the development of networks and partnerships are also relevant in this respect.

At the national level, social partners from candidate countries must be fully involved in the accession negotiations, not only on matters directly linked to the social dimension, but on all other matters.

The Need for Specific Cross-Border Policies

The implementation of specific cross-border measures is an important part of the preaccession process. Cross-border areas are those where tensions and migratory pressures are most likely. The differences in living standards and income levels certainly contribute to tensions. This gap will take a certain number of years to bridge.

The experience acquired by the ETUC through the Interregional Trade Union Councils is very important. In the Member States of the European Union there are 39 Interregional Trade Union Councils (ITUCs) composed of representatives of the trade union regional offices, which are members of the ETUC. The first one was established in 1976 as a trilateral initiative in the border regions of Saarland, Lorraine, and Luxembourg. ITUCs have a direct regional impact since they operate in all cases in the immediate border area of two or three neighboring countries.

The defense of interests and rights of cross-border workers, the promotion of mobility, the development of cross-border social dialogue, and the definition of an integrated European labor market within the framework of the European Employment Strategy are the most important features of the work of ITUCs. At the same time, ITUC representatives are represented at the European Employment Services (EURES)–T (cross-border EURES) as Euro-advisers.

Since 1993 we have developed specific activities in the seven ITUCs that cover Italy, Slovenia, Croatia (not yet a candidate country), Germany, Poland, the Czech Republic, Austria, and Hungary. These ITUCs allow for a permanent exchange of information, the institutionalization of cross-border contacts, and the creation of trade union networks. Some examples of these activities are the constitution of a data bank on work contracts for different professions between Italy and Slovenia (Friuli-Venezia-Guilia/Slovenia); the training of cross-border workers on topics related to the European Works Councils in the German, Polish, and Czech Republic region (Elbe/Neisse); and issues related to social, economic, and trade union policy development, like pay and working time policy, collective bargaining, equal opportunities, youth questions, and regional structural and labor market policies. With these structures the ETUC plans to launch information campaigns on the enlargement process, on the advantages of EU accession, and on possible consequences for the labor market and industrial relations.

Interreg and the "cross-border" Phare projects also have a very important role to play, and the social partners should be able to participate fully in the implementation of these instruments. The same applies to the need to enlarge the EURES network to the applicant countries; cross-border EURES should be established in the borders with applicant countries. Such instruments will facilitate the exchange of information on the labor market situation, and on living and working conditions on both sides of the border, while contributing to a better understanding of possible migratory flows. The same applies to the creation of Employment Observatories, which analyze the specific situation of employment in these regions, and serve as early warning systems for structural and labor market policies.

Such actions will positively influence the accession process. Most probably they will not be enough to eliminate migratory pressures, a source of worry for some sectors of the European society. The free movement of persons is one of the four fundamental freedoms of the Internal Market. The position of the ETUC on this is very clear: if transitional periods are unavoidable, they should be as flexible as possible and fit the economic and social situation (ETUC 1999). The ETUC opposes the selective introduction of free movement for highly skilled workers, which would undermine the economic potential of applicant countries.

Recent studies show that migration is primarily the result of short-term stays, time-limited work, or worker secondment. They also show that the risks to the labor markets of the current Member States are limited and "controllable." These studies recognize that more pressure will be felt in the border regions. (One should not forget that these regions will certainly benefit the most from trade relations with accession countries.) There is certainly a need to control flows and labor supply in order to avoid distortions on the labor market and social conditions in the host countries that could lead to social dumping.

The need to reduce the income gap is of the utmost importance. But wide income disparities between and within EU Member States have not disrupted the labor markets of Member States with the highest income: the richest 10 percent of the population has an income 9.2 times higher than the poorest 10 percent, on average, in the EU. Although the richest 10 percent earn 24 percent of the total income, the poorest 10 percent earn only 2.6 percent of the total income.

Citizens and workers of the European Union Member States and of candidate countries must be fully informed on the benefits of enlargement. Trade union organizations are ready to play an active role in this respect and to develop information campaigns in close cooperation with the European institutions.

Conclusion

The enlargement of the European Union and the progress toward European integration entailed by this process are the most historically significant development to take place in Europe since the end of World War II. Enlargement means investing in the common future of the European peoples.

For the process to succeed, both the EU and applicant countries must be prepared to adapt their policies and structures. Applicant countries must consolidate democratic standards and transform and develop their economies. The EU must reform internal policies and tackle institutional reform to prepare for a larger and more diverse membership.

The European Union's social *acquis* represents an essential core to the process of enlargement. Success in integrating the social *acquis* can be guaranteed only if there is the full involvement of trade unions in the candidate countries and recognition by governments of their role as legitimate partners in the process. Trade unions must be involved in all stages of the accession process.

Incorporating the European Union's social *acquis,* which entails considerable social reorganization, will produce a successful outcome only if based on a firm social consensus. The development of genuine social dialogue and of authentic industrial relations in the accession countries is therefore a key element for a successful enlargement process. Only in these ways will it be possible to achieve a win-win situation.

References

ETUC (European Trade Union Confederation). 1999. *Ninth Congress: General Resolution*. 9th Congress. Helsinki.

———. 2000. *Executive Committee Resolution: Post-Nice Enlargement of the European Union*. Helsinki.

European Commission. 2000a. *Employment Guidelines.* Brussels.

———. 2000b. *Industrial Relations in Europe, 2000.* Directorate General for Employment and Social Affaires. Brussels.

———. 2001. *Second Report on Economic and Social Cohesion.* Brussels.

CHAPTER 25

Discussant Notes

Georg Fischer

I would like to comment on four issues: first, the role of active labor market policies; second, employment and product market liberalization; third, the role of social partners; and finally, the European Social Model.

Let me start by commenting on the categorical sort of judgments on active labor market policies. Some seem to think that active labor market policies are totally useless, and they refer to evaluation studies that do not show strong effects on employment. Other studies may show different results, but the point I would like to make here is different. Active labor market policies are one element in a policy package (and in a system of employment), and their impact depends strongly on the overall policy package (and the system of employment). We do, however, observe distinctive differences in the way unemployment has responded to more favorable employment prospects. In some Member States unemployment remained high for a prolonged period, while in others unemployment responded quickly. Among these countries are those with well-developed active labor market policies including Sweden and Denmark. I think one would have difficulty finding good answers if one totally disregarded active labor market policies. Active labor market policies have contributed to maintaining the employability of the unemployed, which has in turn facilitated a rapid return to work when opportunities become available.

The second comment relates to the strong linkage of market liberalization, in particular product markets, and employment. It is indeed a very important point, this part of the single market. Endorsing the single market in context should have a similar beneficial effect in candidate countries in the field of product market liberalization, at least in the medium and long term. How somebody coming from a country with well-implemented product market liberalization would judge the linkage to employment would be interesting to hear since prima facie the effect of liberalization on employment is uncertain. Anyhow, a question on capital market liberalization should be added in this case.

The third point relates to Maria Helena André's paper and the role of social partners with regard to employment policies. Outside observers sometimes underestimate the seriousness of Europe's commitment to the reform agenda—very well summarized in her paper—and not only in terms of how easy it will be to reach the 70, over 60, and 50 percent employment rate targets. All the Council announcements on Europe becoming the most competitive economy, on modernizing the European Social Model, and on restoring the conditions for full employment are essentially about changing economic structures, not preserving them.

Social partners are key actors in achieving this change. It was good to hear how much the social partners see themselves as committed to this reform agenda. In my view there are two questions with respect to social partners. First, do they support the broad reform agenda and facilitate government action? Second, what do social partners achieve, in the fields where they act autonomously (an autonomy that is a precondition for a well-developed labor market)? Indeed, it is to a large extent in the hands of social partners to bring about labor market and also product market reform: modernizing work organization, making working time arrangements more flexible, ensuring broad access to training in enterprises and lifelong learning. In this second area governments need to support and facilitate, but social partners need to act. An interesting question for policy debate and research is the extent to which social partners already meet these expectations and what the future trends are in this respect.

My final comments go back to the discussion of the European Social Model, because I think there is some misunderstanding on this. Some commentators expressed doubts about the concept, given the great diversity of social and economic institutions in the European Union. I would like to quote something that all prime ministers adopted in 2001. Under the heading "Modernising the European Social Model," they said, "A dynamic union should consist of active welfare states. Well-designed and functioning welfare systems should be seen as productive factors by offering security and change. This requires continuous modernisation of the European social model on the basis of the European social agenda adopted at Nice [this is the previous European Council] which constitutes a framework for social policies."

And then there are five headings:

- Improving the quality of work

- Promoting social inclusion

- The role of social partners in managing change
- Corporate social responsibility
- Safe and sustainable social protection systems.

One could summarize policy thinking coming from these European Councils in four messages. First, commonly shared social values are now explicitly recognized at the European level. Since these values refer to rights, quality, equity, social cohesion, and solidarity, they go beyond what the EU shares with the United States or with other OECD countries. Second, and more important, there is a political willingness expressed at the highest level to affirm and develop these shared values at the EU level and to put them into practice within different societal structures and welfare systems, including different ways of involving the social partners (see, in this respect, the Amsterdam Treaty provisions). The third message is that there is a need for an appropriate policy mix to promote economic performance (competitiveness and growth) and social performance (employment and social cohesion) in a balanced and mutually reinforcing way. Of course, this optimal, balanced policy mix must always be refined and improved or consolidated because we live in a changing world. Fourth, in order to sustain this integrated approach combining commonly shared social values with economic and market forces, our institutions and policies must change to respond to the new common challenges that we face, in particular economic restructuring and aging. These four dynamic elements define what is called the European Social Model.

CHAPTER 26

Discussant Notes

Mária Ladó

The current eastward enlargement is not "just another expansion" of the European Union. Although this statement is a commonplace, it is useful to remember when assessing the future of the European Social Model.

In discussions of the distinct nature of the current enlargement process, reference is usually made to the unprecedented high number of candidate countries and to their great diversity. Discussions regarding the European Social Model, however, seem to emphasize that the majority of the applicants are Central and Eastern European countries (CEECs) that have been or still are in the process of transformation: from centrally planned economies to market economies and from totalitarian regimes to democracies. These applicants face a "double challenge": while still struggling with the process of transformation, they have to adjust themselves to the community *acquis*. These are two overlapping but still distinct processes. The extent of overlapping varies according to the starting position of the countries and the progress made by them in each area.

Accession to the EU is very much influenced by the transition and vice versa. The preparation for EU membership, however, sometimes requires measures that conflict with the economic transformation (and vice versa). This makes managing "the double challenge" rather complicated and politically risky. Let me refer to some key differences.

The economic transition can be described in terms of macroeconomic stabilization, structural reforms, privatization, and trade and price liberalization. The accession process has a somewhat different agenda: to adopt the entire *acquis communautaire;* to modify the domestic legislation accordingly; to establish new institutions that facilitate, monitor, and enforce the implementation of the *acquis;* to take part in the European Employment Strategy and other coordinated policies; and to observe the basic values of the European Social Model.

While CEECs have been focusing on the historic tasks of transforming their economies, they have not made the social dimension a priority. In fact, this issue has often been pushed to the background. Most CEECs, as investigations already have proved, have paid a much higher social price for the economic transition than was necessary. The transition to the market economy has been accompanied by deteriorating living standards for many groups and by rising income inequalities in all CEECs. Attempts to cure these negative effects usually were confined to the preaccession period. Social differentiation, however, is likely to continue after accession and may worsen. The losers are likely to be the same social groups as the victims of the transition: elderly (retired) people, less skilled workers, the unemployed, minorities, residents of rural settlements, and large families. The social problems of CEECs, therefore, must addressed both in the pre- and postaccession periods.

This leads me to my second observation. I would urge a more future-oriented approach when discussing employment and social policies in the context of enlargement. Much has been written about the current labor market and employment situation of the candidate countries. Research findings compare the standing of the candidate countries to the EU average or to individual Member States. We know, more or less, the historic reasons that have led to different trajectories and different outcomes in economic and social terms.

Having accumulated this knowledge, we have reached the point when the vision of the enlarged Europe can be the reference. The European Union, with 28 or more Member States and more than 500 million people, is the place to start. Policy options could be deducted from this perspective. Such an approach would lead us to basic issues not yet examined.

Let me cite two examples. Almost all of the CEECs must accelerate their real GDP growth rates substantially in order to close the income gap with the EU. According to the World Bank (2000, p. 3), "to achieve real convergence in 20 years (assuming the EU average grows at 2 percent per annum in per capita terms, which is the growth rate of the oldest members of the EU), all the CEECs except for Slovenia and the Czech Republic will have to grow at an average of over 5 percent per capita per annum in real terms for the next 20 years. In fact, Bulgaria, Latvia, Lithuania and Romania will need to grow at an average of 8 percent per annum in real terms, or even higher."

A series of questions arises immediately: what does it mean to achieve 5 to 8 percent GDP growth year after year without any slowdown? Is it realistic at all? What are the policy implications of this dynamic growth? What kind of employment policy can boost the economy to that extent? How can the shortage of skilled labor be managed? How can the increasing economic and social disparities within the EU be tackled if the envisaged dynamic catch-up process does not take place?

My other example relates to the ambitious goal for the European Union that was adopted by the Lisbon European Council in March 2000: to achieve full employment by 2010. Other objectives were to increase the overall employment rate in the EU to 70 percent and to increase the employment rate of women in the EU to more than 60 percent. In 1999 the employment rate in some candidate countries was significantly lower: in Hungary, 55.4 percent; in Poland, 57.5 percent; and in Latvia, 58.5 percent.

The questions are numerous: How can these countries rapidly increase their employment rates? What are the relevant policies? What are the measures? What institutions can support these targets? How can the declining tendencies in employment, still present in some candidate countries due to the ongoing transformation process, be halted and turned into job creation? How can the quality of employment be ensured amid the conditions of accelerated growth?

Regarding the enlarged Europe, the Second Report on Economic and Social Cohesion by the European Commission envisages "a doubling of the income gaps between countries and regions. A doubling in the sense that if a Union of 27 existed tomorrow: i) at national level, over one-third of the population would live in countries with an income per head less than 90% of the Union average—the current threshold for eligibility for aid under the Cohesion Fund—compared to one-sixth in the present EU15; ii) at regional level, the average income per head for the bottom 10% of population, living in the least prosperous regions in EU27, would be only 31% of the EU27 average. In the EU15 today, the income per head of the bottom 10% of population equates to 61% of the average." The document concludes that "given existing levels of income per head in the candidate countries, convergence between regions in the enlarged Union would take at least two generations if it occurred at the same pace" (European Commission 2001, pp. xi and xii).

A lasting cohesion problem of that magnitude cannot be effectively tackled by a system based on fiscal transfers alone. It can seriously be addressed only if economic and social convergence is placed at the top of the European Community's political agenda. I would, therefore, welcome a similar conference in the future that places the vision of the enlarged Europe in the center and discusses the perspectives of and policy options for convergence.

My final remark relates directly to the paper by Maria Helena André on the European Social Model. She has focused on the European Employment Strategy and emphasized the role of social dialogue and of social partners in designing, implementing, and monitoring this strategy as well as the appropriate national guidelines. For the social partners of candidate countries, the challenge is twofold. On the one hand, social partners have to be involved in national policy formulation; they must be consulted, seemingly a traditional practice in all candidate countries.

The involvement of social partners, however, has to be realized on a wider scale and in a meaningful, efficient way, which has not always been the case so far. On the other hand, regarding the implementation of the jointly formulated employment policy, collective agreements and joint initiatives are key instruments. The weakness of autonomous social dialogue, the lack of sectoral collective agreements, and the low coverage ratio in most candidate countries are sources for serious concern in this context. These difficulties will be addressed in detail by the report on industrial relations in candidate countries, which will be published, for the first time, as part of the Commission's annual report on industrial relations in the EU.

Although it is remarkable that the social partners have been significantly empowered in the European Union in the employment field (among others), the success of this development will very much depend in the long run on the capacities of the social partners coming from the new Member States. Therefore, one thing is certain: for social partners of candidate countries, it is high time to prepare themselves for their new roles in the enlarged Europe and for their changing responsibilities in their domestic environment.

References

European Commission. 2001. *Unity, Solidarity, Diversity for Europe, Its People and Its Territory*. Second Report on Economic and Social Cohesion. Brussels.

World Bank. 2000. *Progress toward the Unification of Europe*. Washington, D.C.

CHAPTER 27

Discussant Notes

Elena Iankova

These remarks on the contributions of Katherine Terrell, Michelle Riboud et al., and Zdenka Kovac et al. focus on a variety of challenges that the Central and Eastern European countries (CEECs) seeking European Union (EU) membership have faced in their labor markets. A common message is that *institutions matter*. In contrast to the United States and Asia, Europe as a regional entity developed exclusively on the basis of a dense institutional web, ever since the foundation of the European Communities in the 1950s. In the area of labor markets, the EU expansion to the East is subject to important institutional constraints as well as facilitating factors.

Katherine Terrell's paper outlines the institutional determinants of labor reallocation in the CEE transition economies. The author argues that some labor market institutions (such as unemployment benefits) have played a significant role in the overall transition, while others (such as union presence, minimum wages, income policies to control wage growth, and employment protection legislation) have been less important. The paper by Michelle Riboud, Carlos Silva-Jauregui, and Carolina Sánchez-Páramo also concludes that the impact of labor market institutions is significant although hard to uncover. Finally, based on Slovenia's case, the paper by Zdenka Kovac, Franci Kluzer, and Alenka Kaizer emphasizes the crucial role of social partnerships in the years to come.

In addition, all papers emphasize important differences in the labor market policies and institutional arrangements across Central and Eastern Europe. Riboud and her colleagues reveal that the CEECs adopt the set of policies and institutions common to the European Communities but are not a monolithic group: some have more flexible labor markets than others. Terrell also emphasizes cross-country institutional differences that explain many puzzles of postcommunist labor reallocation.

All papers raise a couple of questions that need further explanation: (1) Why is the impact of labor market institutions modest? and (2) Why are there significant differences among the CEE applicants in their labor market policies and institutional arrangements?

As far as challenges for the labor markets of the CEECs stemming in particular from the Eastern enlargement of the EU are concerned, I would like to emphasize, as a starting point for discussion, three broad issues. The first is the issue of legal-institutional reform. All CEE applicants face this issue in their race for EU membership, including in the area of labor markets. No country so far has succeeded in rapidly developing a legal system and institutions that would be highly conducive to the functioning of a market economy. In retrospect, this appears to have been the Achilles heel of the first 12 years of transition. Overall, the importance of a well-functioning legal system has been largely underestimated across the region. But Europe is a legal-institutional entity, and in order to become EU members, the CEE countries must not only harmonize their legislation with the EU common law, but also implement and apply that legislation in practice. So far this has proved to be a very difficult and even a tricky task for Central and Eastern European policymakers. The "tricky" part aside, it is important to note that the task of implementing 100,000 pages of the European common law, the *acquis communautaire*, is not an easy task for any public administration. There are additional high financial costs of implementing the new legislation, especially in the areas of health and safety and environmental protection.

The second issue is the role of civil society and the social partners in formulating labor market policies. The paper by Zdenka Kovac, Franci Kluzer, and Alenka Kaizer brings an important message to policymakers across the region. The social partners have to be included in the accession process, especially in the restructuring of the social and employment policies because at the end of the day the society at large has to vote in referendums for or against EU accession. Right now accession is developing as a highly elitist process, with governments doing most of the work, while civil society and even parliaments stay to the side. None of the policymakers in CEE applicant countries want the Norwegian scenario of accession: in referendums the people twice rejected accession to the European Union.

Perhaps the biggest issue to be explored is the fragile linkages between labor market rigidities, East and West, and the free movement of labor in an enlarged Europe. This third issue is the most sensitive one in the on-going accession negotiations in the area of labor markets. Would enlargement increase or decrease labor market rigidities? Would transition periods for the free movement of labor from the newly accepted CEE members increase or decrease labor market rigidities? Neither policymakers nor academic researchers have yet found compelling answers to these difficult questions. Riboud and her colleagues lay the basis for further exploration in that regard.

CHAPTER 28

Discussant Notes

Andreas Woergoetter

What I have prepared is an introduction with numerous questions, a number of useful comments, and a few personal remarks.[1] I cannot refrain from discussing social partnerships—what we can expect from this concept for Central and Eastern European countries during the accession process and afterwards.

When we look at social partnerships in Austria and in the Netherlands, we must keep one thing in mind. They were extremely successful, especially in Austria, under special circumstances. That set of circumstances made it possible for Austria to have one of the most successful catch-up experiences after the war. Social partnerships reduced conflict costs in the society. Strikes could be avoided, wage price spirals could be eliminated, and things of that kind.

It was clear to the top representatives of the social partners what the right policy was. Now we must keep in mind Austria's very low need for restructuring. In a manner of speaking, Austria's postwar experience was something like blowing up a balloon: it became greater and greater but the shape more or less remained intact.

I think you have to be a bit suspicious when applying such a model to the accession countries. Consider, for instance, the Dutch experience with so-called flex security. At the moment the Netherlands is extremely troubled by a system in which about 10 percent of the population is officially disabled in an age group where one normally would expect persons to work. One million Dutch are receiving a full disability pension, and that means they are out of the labor force. That is, of course, something extremely expensive, and that is something that you have to be able to afford. One should study experiences with such models very carefully and then see what the successful features are, of the social partnership model, for example, that could be applied.

Preceding chapters have mentioned the success or failure of active labor market policy. I would say the most interesting case is what is going on in Germany. More or less without any budget constraints, Germany has offered active labor market policies to new lenders to help them help their populations become integrated into the labor market. And 10 years after we only have to look below the line and see that the success of this is more or less zero. We still have huge unemployment rates. Active labor market policy is shifting a considerable part of the labor force from one program to another, into public employment programs, and back into unemployment. Active labor market policy is no substitute for job creation. It can be successful when it facilitates the job-matching process, when it matches the labor force that is there with the jobs that are there. But creating jobs, that is costly. The Germans obviously decided that they were able to afford that, and in the accession countries this decision seems to have been going the other way.

I would like to end with a few puzzles. One really puzzling issue concerns Slovenia. By all indicators it is the country with the most tidy transition. It has the highest per capita income. It has greatly restructured its economy from an industry focus to a service focus. Nevertheless, it is one of the countries with the lowest foreign direct investment per capita. That is puzzling because foreign direct investment is so small. Normally, in some countries you have higher levels of foreign direct investment. For instance, that is how the Irish economic wonder has been organized—by attracting foreign direct investment. So what is going "wrong" in Slovenia?

The other question one cannot help ask is why are the Central and Eastern European countries not more competitive? Why are they not flooding Western Europe with all of their goods and services? They have such phenomenally low wage levels. All of the employment protection legislation indicators show a very flexible labor market, and still most of them have huge current account deficits that are going far beyond what one could explain with a higher investment share.

Finally, what are the necessary conditions to make enlargement of the European Union a success? This is a nontrivial issue. Even when we look at this from the Austrian experience, we see the Austrian economy falling behind EU average levels since Austria joined the European Union. So I think one should concentrate on this issue. That is the area where the possible conclusions can have the most benefits for policymakers in the accession countries.

Note

1. The author has expressed his personal opinion, which does not necessarily reflect the opinions of the OECD.

PART V

When Markets Fail: Preventing Social Exclusion

CHAPTER 29

Unemployment, Poverty, and Social Exclusion in Central and Eastern Europe

Ana Revenga

I would like to focus my comments on four issues that have been mentioned but deserve further attention in the context of how to prevent social exclusion. First, long-term unemployment, poverty, and social exclusion are strongly linked. Second, there are signs that persistent, or permanent, poverty is emerging in Central and Eastern Europe. Third, certain groups (not always those discussed the most) are particularly vulnerable. Finally, I would like to offer some reflections on what these trends may imply for the design of social policy and social safety nets.

Let me start by emphasizing a phenomenon that has been amply discussed: the rise in long-term unemployment. Figure 29.1 presents long-term unemployment (unemployment for more than one year) as a percentage of total unemployment for selected EU accession countries. This percentage has increased steadily. In 1998 long-term unemployment ranged from a "low" of over 30 percent in the Czech Republic to about 50 percent in the Slovak Republic, to over 70 percent in Slovenia. For most countries the incidence of long-term unemployment is above the EU average.

Obviously, these are very worrisome trends. Now why are they so worrisome? First of all, these are individuals, often in their prime productive years, who could be productively employed and yet are not working—individuals who over time become increasingly disconnected from the labor market and possibly from social and economic life as well. But a second reason for concern about long-term unemployment is precisely because in all the countries of the region there is a very strong association between unemployment and the risk of being poor.

FIGURE 29.1 LONG-TERM UNEMPLOYMENT AS A PERCENTAGE OF TOTAL UNEMPLOYMENT IN CENTRAL AND EASTERN EUROPEAN COUNTRIES, 1993 AND 1998

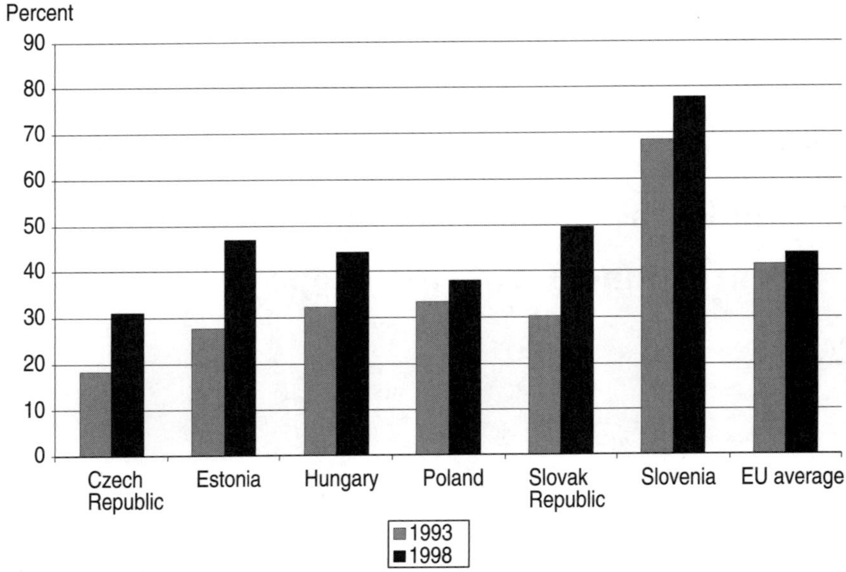

Note: Long-term unemployment is unemployment for more than 12 months.
Source: World Bank 2000 and 2001.

Figure 29.2 presents recent data on poverty (World Bank 2000). The graph plots the poverty risk, or poverty rate, for a subset of countries from Europe and Central Asia, and it differentiates between poverty rates for households where the head is unemployed and those where the head is employed. These poverty rates are based on a relative poverty line, equal to 50 percent of mean expenditures or income. So in some sense the poverty line is not the same in all countries. You cannot compare them in an absolute sense in terms of poverty rates. But what is important is to look at what it tells about who is at risk of poverty in each of these countries.

The first column for each country is the risk of poverty for a family where the head, the main income earner, is unemployed. The second (more darkly shaded) column is the poverty risk or poverty rate for the average family (household) in the country. Figure 29.2 clearly shows that the risk of poverty increases dramatically with unemployment. Take, for example, a country like the Czech Republic, where the risk of poverty is actually very low—about 3 percent at that relative

FIGURE 29.2 RELATIVE POVERTY INCIDENCE FOR HOUSEHOLDS WITH UNEMPLOYED HEAD IN CENTRAL AND EASTERN EUROPEAN COUNTRIES

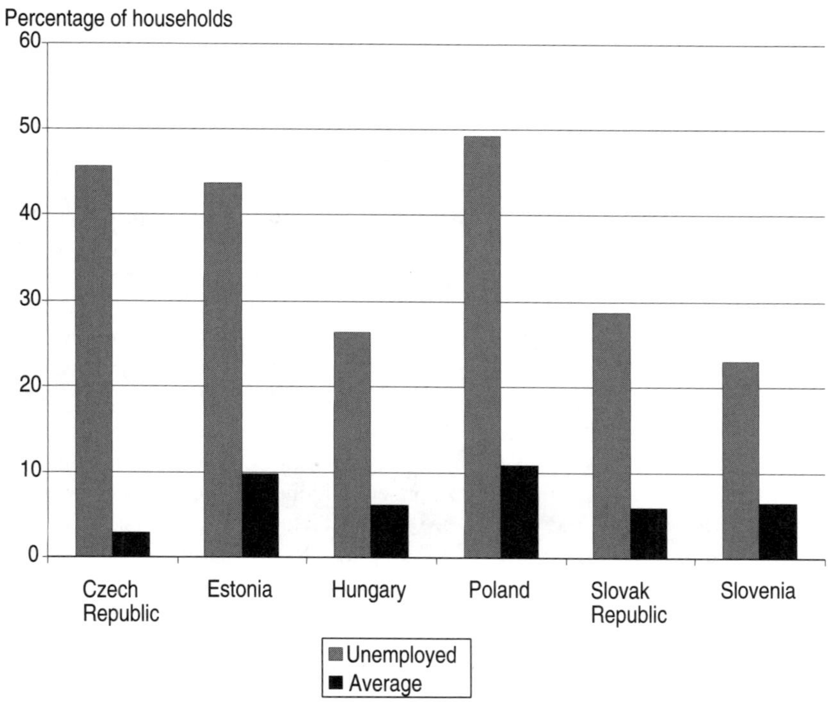

Source: World Bank 2000 and 2001.

line. Despite low average poverty rates, the risk of poverty for a Czech household where the head is unemployed is very high, more than 10 times that of the average family. This is a pattern that repeats itself in all countries and the same pattern for households for individuals.

These two trends—the increasing trend in long-term unemployment and the strong correlation between unemployment and poverty—raise a very worrisome question: Are we seeing a trend toward the emergence of much more persistent poverty? Unfortunately, the answer is absolutely yes.

The same World Bank study (World Bank 2000) examined the dynamics of poverty. We followed households over time and examined whether poor households were able to exit poverty on a sustained basis. Results for Poland and

Hungary—two countries for which we had longitudinal data that allowed us to perform this kind of analysis—are shown in table 29.1. In Poland we found that 80 percent of households that started off as poor were still poor a year later. Similarly, among the nonpoor, there was relatively little descent into poverty. The same experiment on Hungary gave us very similar results.

The sense that we got from this work is that we are seeing the formation of a class of "structurally" poor households—an underclass. This is likely to feed rising social exclusion, as we have seen in many of the OECD countries.

As Michal Vašečka pointed out in his paper, minorities, and especially the Roma, are at particularly high risk of falling into this poverty-unemployment trap. But I would defer on one point: I do not think the Roma are the only group at high risk of falling into a poverty-unemployment trap, nor are they the only group at high risk of social exclusion.

When we ask what groups are at risk, we find that perceptions and reality often diverge. Some have referred to the feminization of poverty and to the precarious situation of the elderly. And yet when we look at the information that we do have, we see a different reality. Some groups, such as single mothers with children, are at high risk of poverty, but, on average, women are not at a higher risk of poverty than men in these countries, and we do not see evidence supporting the feminization of poverty. Similarly, the elderly, are not, in fact, at a higher risk of poverty than anybody else. If anything, they tend to be at a lower risk of poverty because pension systems have functioned very effectively to protect them from poverty (World Bank 2000).

But other groups are very vulnerable, and often they do not get mentioned. One such group is rural households, especially in isolated areas. Another is children. When we look at individuals by age group, we find that the risk of poverty for children is much higher than that for other age groups (World Bank 2000). This is partly because families with three or more children are at a much higher risk of

TABLE 29.1 FLOWS INTO AND OUT OF POVERTY IN POLAND AND HUNGARY (percent)

	This month's poverty status	
Poverty status 12 months ago	*Poor*	*Nonpoor*
Poland (1994–95)		
Poor	80.2	19.8
Nonpoor	4.9	95.1
Hungary (1995–96)		
Poor	78.5	21.6
Nonpoor	5.4	94.6

Source: World Bank 2000.

poverty than families with no children or with fewer than three. And there is clearly an interaction between ethnicity and the number of children. But that is not the only explanation. One thing that seems to be very important is that in families with young children, or many children, the mother often must stay out of the labor force. Therefore, more people are dependent on a single income.

Again I would like to stress the fact that the low poverty rates among the elderly should be seen as an achievement. It is a sign that social policy in that dimension has functioned very effectively. But the lesson I would take away from these figures is that social policy has not been very effective in protecting children from poverty. Child poverty is especially worrisome because it can affect the ability of those children to get an education, and it will affect their ability to move themselves out of poverty in the future, setting the basis for intergenerational transmission of poverty.

These trends raise some questions about the role of social policy in preventing social exclusion and fighting poverty. It is clear that safety nets have played a very important role in protecting large parts of the population from falling into poverty, and the contrast that has been made between the countries of the former Soviet Union and those of Central Europe is very striking in that regard. Safety nets in Central Europe have been very effective in preventing the bottom from falling out.

But the problem is that safety nets are designed to protect households from shocks that are in some sense *temporary*. There is a question as to whether, with the current design, these safety nets are adequate for dealing with the problem of *permanent* poverty or *long-term* unemployment.

When poverty becomes permanent, traditional safety nets risk creating a culture of welfare dependency and do not provide a way out of the problem (nor protection against social exclusion). For example, in a recent study on the Slovak Republic, we followed individuals over time while they were receiving benefits and examined how their behavior changed when they stopped receiving benefits. We found a clear negative impact of the benefits on the effort that individuals put into looking for a job. While receiving benefits, people looked much less for a job; the moment the benefits ran out, they searched and usually found a job. The exception among the latter was the Roma. Among isolated Roma communities, unemployment rates oscillated in the 90 to 100 percent range, and long-term dependency on social assistance—not unemployment benefits, which have long run out—was found to be the norm

Part of the problem of incentives has to do with faulty design: in many countries, such as the Slovak Republic, some benefits have been designed so that the moment a person gets a job he or she loses all entitlements, even if that job pays a very low wage (for example, child allowances). For families where the adult is unskilled, and market wages are low, it may simply not be rational to accept a job. The result is that people stay unemployed and dependent, creating a vicious cycle of growing dependency. This degrades skills and diminishes ability to integrate into the labor market, ultimately leading to social exclusion.

Some of these problems can be tackled through reforming the design of many of these systems and making the transition from welfare to work easier. And, paradoxically, that may imply at the margin making benefit systems slightly more generous so that when people start to work, they do not immediately lose their entitlements. But it requires some thinking about the design of that transition and mechanisms to support families moving from welfare dependency to work.

Safety nets that are directed at cushioning the impact of shocks cannot solve the problem of permanent poverty or prevent social exclusion. The key is in reintegrating people into the labor market and in enhancing their opportunities to earn income. Sometimes this will require investments in education and training. Sometimes what is needed is an antidiscrimination policy. However, for any of these measures to pay off, you also need to foster increased labor demand for people with relatively low skills. As Michal Boni mentioned in his paper, strong, stable growth is a key component of labor demand and job creation. It is also a very important element of any strategy to reduce persistent poverty.

References

World Bank. 2000. *Making Transition Work for Everyone: Poverty and Inequality in Europe and Central Asia*. Washington, D.C.

———. 2001. "Slovak Republic: Living Standards, Employment and Labor Market Study." Report No. 22351-SK. Washington, D.C.

CHAPTER 30

Searching for Solutions to Reduce Social Exclusion in Latvia

Ruta Zilvere

Following the restoration of independence, Latvia has undergone progressive changes in its transition from a planned economy to a market economy. These changes have greatly affected everyone's everyday life, individual welfare, and material situation. Strict fiscal and monetary measures have had a stabilizing effect on the economy; inflation has decreased considerably, but the living standards of part of the population have deteriorated. Some profited from the advantages of the new economic system, but many faced social problems that had been ignored earlier—unemployment, poverty, social exclusion. Personal responsibility for economic and social well-being was stressed in the new social policy that was less "paternalistic." The same economic and social changes that took almost the whole previous century in Western countries—like developing social security systems and laws step by step—have been implemented at an increased pace in Latvia. The transition period was hard because nobody was prepared for such long-lasting moral and material sacrifices.

Reforming the Social Protection System

Social welfare reform was already at the top of the political agenda in 1995. The Government of the Republic of Latvia issued a concept paper in which the implementation of a comprehensive social welfare reform program was among the top priorities. In order to provide the legislative framework for this, the Saeima

(Parliament) at the end of 1995 approved legislation for a completely new social welfare system. Other legislation introduced a three-tier pension scheme, a compulsory unemployment insurance scheme, and a compulsory occupational health and injury insurance scheme. The reform was targeted at creating a national social security system.

The welfare sector is of great importance in eliminating the risk of social exclusion. Even if the Latvian social security system in not precisely targeted at social exclusion, it plays a role of the utmost importance by keeping people away from poverty and exclusion through financial benefits, labor market measures, and services activating integration and inclusion.

Funding in the welfare sector, which covers social insurance, social assistance, health care, and employment, tends to grow (table 30.1). This makes it possible to improve the quality of services provided and to increase the size of the material benefit and the number of beneficiaries of services and assistance. However, this increase in funding should not be viewed only as positive. The growth of allocations for specific expenditure categories testifies to the change for the worse in the social situation.

The number of people who find themselves in a situation of social risk requiring public and local government support is constantly growing. The project "Support for the Development of Strategy for the Prevention of Poverty," implemented jointly by the United Nations Development Programme (UNDP) and the Ministry of Welfare, conducted research showing that poverty is not only expanding but also deepening for a population that already is quite poor. Thus the challenge of the government is to set up a stable and efficient social security system with the restricted resources allocated for social purposes to reduce the risk of poverty.

TABLE 30.1 WELFARE SECTOR EXPENDITURES AS A PERCENTAGE OF GDP, 1995–2000

	1995	*1996*	*1997*	*1998*	*1999*	*2000*
Gross domestic product (Latvian Lats mln)	2,349.2	2,829.1	3,275.5	3,773.5	3,838.1	4,090.0
Spending category (percent of GDP)						
Social insurance	11.7	11.3	11.9	11.4	12.3	11.4
Social assistance	0.3	1.9	2.0	1.8	1.9	1.9
Health care	4.5	4.2	4.2	3.7	3.8	3.5
Employment	0.5	0.5	0.5	0.8	1.2	1.0
Total	16.6	17.5	17.9	17.6	19.3	17.8

Note: Total expenditure of the central government basic budget and the special budget.
Source: Central Statistical Bureau of Latvia.

Addressing Poverty Issues

The report *Living Conditions in Latvia* recognizes that Latvian society is characterized by material conditions that are multidimensional and contradictory. Therefore, the assessment of welfare should be made using different methods and indicators (for example, GDP per capita, monthly average income per household member, Gini coefficients, and household analysis by quintiles). Since the risk of social exclusion is closely linked to poverty, the government's attention has been focused on the integration of society and poverty reduction.

Several domestic and foreign developments created this focus on poverty. Mass media and press publications contained controversial data on poverty levels in Latvia. Some maintained that more than 80 percent of the population were poor, some that the number of the poor did not exceed 20 percent. There was no uniform approach to what poverty was. Was it the shortage of money alone, or should the absence of opportunities for people to improve their living conditions be treated as poverty as well?

In view of the insufficient resources of the national budget, various groups of the population—families with children, pensioners, the politically repressed, and the disabled—competed with each other for funding. Each of these groups had its own special arguments and needs, which, alas, could be satisfied neither by the existing system of social protection nor by the funds of the national budget. The government has acknowledged the need to assess the extent, distribution, and characteristics of poverty, unemployment, social tensions, and social exclusion, and it is taking measures to eradicate poverty, increase productive employment, and enhance social integration.

In order to evaluate the first results of the social security reform, the Central Statistical Bureau of Latvia (CSB) in cooperation with the World Bank began developing a reoriented Household Budget Survey (HBS). In April 1996 the CSB published its first HBS, undertaken in the last quarter of 1995. The survey is continuous and aims to provide internationally comparable information on the composition of the household, its income and expenditure (consumption) on durable goods, health care, and culture, as well as the opinion of the household on its welfare situation. In the context of the social insurance and assistance reform, the survey is intended to analyze the level of living standards in Latvia and the effectiveness of the social protection system.

Because the Ministry of Welfare expressed the need for a comprehensive poverty assessment in Latvia and development of policy recommendations for a National Poverty Eradication Strategy, studies were commissioned in cooperation with UNDP for the examination of the poverty situation. Data were gathered on the spread and depth of poverty, poverty risk factors, the subjective assessment of the population of their living conditions, and survival strategies practiced. In addition, the impact of the labor market on poverty, as well as ethnic aspects of poverty, was studied. The findings, published in 1999, are now accessible to all interested parties.

Poverty assessment research reveals insufficient income (low wages, unemployment, loss of savings) as one of the poverty dimensions in Latvia. Like other transition economies, Latvia has extensive "low wage poverty." Incomes from salaried work are too low to ensure the subsistence even for one person. The level of wages in the national economy is affected by the low labor productivity, in particular in agriculture, the high competition in the labor market, and the wage level in institutions financed by the national budget. The overall wage level is influenced also by the established amount of the minimum wage, which is comparatively low.

Latvia has a quite high level of unemployment. As a result of the economic crisis in Russia, the rate of Latvian registered unemployment in April of 1999 reached 10.2 percent. By the end of the year, it had decreased to 9.1 percent. There are large numbers of people who desire full-time employment but cannot find this type of work. The young adults with no previous work experience, women with children, and old people have a particularly difficult time finding decent work. Between 26 and 27 percent of the registered unemployed are persons with blue-collar skills. More than half of the total registered unemployed are women. In the middle of 1999, women constituted 58 percent of the sum total unemployed.

Considerable problems are caused by the so-called "black or gray" labor market. Some employers do not make social insurance contributions. As a result, upon workers' retirement or in the event of incapacity for work or unemployment, employers encounter problems. Tax evasion and failure to make social contributions reduce funds that would be used for benefits and pensions and thus have a negative impact on the welfare of other social groups. Besides, the shadow economy stimulates unproductive employment and is not beneficial for the economy in general.

Regional Disparities

There is evidence of significant regional differences in Latvia. Some regions in the eastern part of the country have an underdeveloped infrastructure; it is difficult for them to attract investments, and this results in an exceptionally high unemployment rate—about 25 percent. The chances of residents of various regions to acquire high-quality education differ. Talented intellectuals often leave economically underdeveloped regions to move to regions developing more dynamically. This results in the continued consolidation of economic backwardness.

Differences in Urban and Rural Livelihoods

World Bank (1999) and other studies show that poverty is more widespread in rural areas. The Riga region has a significantly lower poverty rate than other regions. The capital, Riga, has the lowest poverty rate. Rural areas have higher poverty rates than urban areas. In the World Bank study the poverty line is equivalent to about $3 per person per day at 1993 international prices. The poverty headcount varies by location (Riga city, other urban areas, rural areas): using per capita measurement, less than 11 percent of people in Riga are poor, while poverty in rural areas exceeds 28 percent.

Infrastructure and the Limited Mobility of the Population

Low-income inhabitants are significantly restricted in their opportunities to search for employment or to work at a distance from their present residence. The infrastructure and the market availability of affordable housing are insufficient, the infrastructure of roads is not sufficiently developed, and services by public transportation are quite expensive and not always accessible. Wages are too low to cover the transportation costs or the expenses of housing. In addition, the social values, stereotypes, and way of living of low-income inhabitants become an obstacle to their mobility as regards access to jobs in their profession. This results in their inability to adapt to the rapid structural changes and new technologies of the national economy.

Stratification and Inequality

Research findings showed that the risk of poverty in Latvia is considerably higher in:

- households where there are children (households with three or more children are especially subject to the risk of poverty)
- Single parent households (especially if it is a single mother)
- Households of the unemployed (especially unemployed of preretirement age)
- Households where the breadwinner is employed in agriculture
- Households where the provider lacks professional education or work experience
- Households where the provider has low general education
- Households with one or more seriously ill or disabled family members
- Households where one or more family members are alcoholics.

Families with three or more children are most affected by changes in society. The risk is said to increase not only with additional children, but with additional adults as well.

During recent years average personal income has increased (table 30.2). But this growth has not been uniform countrywide. Average personal income has increased mostly in cities, particularly in the Riga region. The income gap between persons in rural and urban areas is growing. It testifies to the increase in material inequality in the society.

Social inequality in society is one of the reasons for poverty. Inequality of income or consumption can be measured by the Gini coefficient. It varies from 0 to 1. The Gini coefficient per se does not measure poverty or the spread of poverty. But its increase testifies to conditions for growth in poverty, particularly when the income level in society is low or income changes in low-income households are inadequate compared to the average increase in income in the country.

The data show a growth in the Gini coefficient, notably in rural areas (table 30.3). The inequality in income of the population grows faster in rural areas. The average income per household member per month in the whole country increased by 6.8 percent from 1999 to 2000. During the same period the average income per one household member in quintile 1 decreased by 5.9 percent. In 2000 the average income of households in quintile 1 was 34 percent lower than the average income in the country.

Data from the Household Budget Survey show that in 2000 the support of municipalities' social benefits is at 0.3 percent from average income per household

TABLE 30.2 AVERAGE MONTHLY PERSONAL INCOME PER MEMBER OF HOUSEHOLD, 1996–2000
(Latvian Lats)

Type of household	*1996*	*1997*	*1998*	*1999*	*2000*
All households	51.50	55.45	62.33	64.73	69.19
Households in urban areas	53.11	57.80	67.26	70.93	76.69
Households in rural areas	47.71	49.86	51.40	50.93	52.13

Source: Central Statistical Bureau of Latvia.

TABLE 30.3 EVOLUTION OF GINI COEFFICIENT IN LATVIA, 1996–2000

Type of household	*1996*	*1997*	*1998*	*1999*	*2000*
All households	0.30	0.31	0.32	0.33	0.34
Households in urban areas	0.30	0.31	0.32	0.32	0.33
Households in rural areas	0.27	0.30	0.30	0.33	0.33

Source: Central Statistical Bureau of Latvia.

member. In households in quintile 1 this support was even lower. The average income for the most vulnerable group—lone parent families with children—unlike other demographic types of households did not increase between 1999 and 2000.

These alarming data indicate that the social assistance benefit system is not targeted enough to the most vulnerable groups and that serious improvements are needed. To achieve this goal the central government and municipalities are negotiating legislation to establish a uniform Guaranteed Minimum Income (GMI) Benefit. Both the central government and local governments are in agreement on the main principles of GMI, but they have not yet reached consensus on the financial mechanisms of the new scheme.

HBS data show that in comparison with consumption in the first quintile, the consumption level in the second, third, and fourth quintiles is higher—1.8, 2.4, and 3.2 times higher, respectively (figure 30.1). Even comparison of the relatively better off part of society (the fourth quintile) with the richest (the fifth quintile) shows that the consumption level is twice as low. Thus households where consumption is close to the average consumption level are closer on the whole to the consumption of the poorest households than to the consumption of affluent households.

FIGURE 30.1 MONTHLY HOUSEHOLD EXPENDITURE PER HOUSEHOLD MEMBER BY QUINTILE, 1999

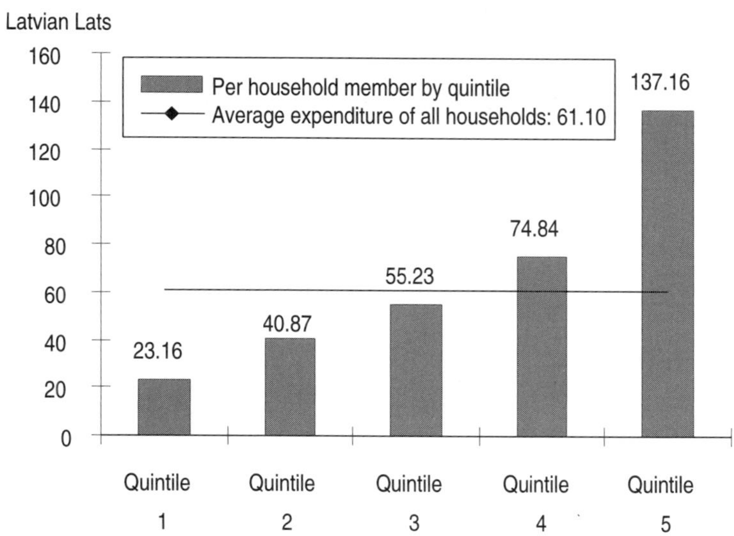

Source: Central Statistical Bureau of Latvia.

Data of the Central Statistical Bureau show that social and economic inequalities exist from the gender perspective as well. In general terms, women in Latvia hold lower paid jobs than do men. Women are paid about 80 percent of men's earnings.

Table 30.4 presents the ethnic composition of the population of Latvia. Ethnicity is not of major relevance when poverty in the country is described and explained (Aasland 2000). The transition has winners and losers among all ethnic communities living in the country. Background characteristics other than ethnicity (educational level, urban and rural settlements, regional variation) are much more important than ethnicity in explaining differences in poverty levels.

There are some areas where there are notable differences between the ethnic groups, however. The first concerns the evaluation of present conditions when seen through the lens of the past. Russians tend to be more negative in their evaluation of current economic conditions than are other ethnic groups. There are several possible explanations. Russians may have been privileged in the past, and even if they now are on an even footing with ethnic Latvians, their situation may have deteriorated comparatively more; or Russians may see the changes in less positive terms and have a more pessimistic view of social and economic developments in Latvia in general (political reasons).

Long-Term Unemployment

The unemployed constitute another social group with very high poverty and a high risk of social exclusion. As table 30.5 shows, the long-term unemployed represent an increasing share of unemployed persons in Latvia. In 1999 the increase was attributable to the crises in the Russian market. The decline in 2000 shows the adaptability of the Latvian labor force to structural changes in the economy. It was mostly caused by the involvement of unemployed people in retraining courses.

Regional disparities exist in long-term unemployment. The highest share of long-term unemployed out of the total number unemployed (around 50 percent) is

TABLE 30.4 POPULATION OF LATVIA BY ETHNIC GROUP, 2000

Ethnic group	*Percent*
Latvians	55.8
Russians	32.3
Belarussians	3.9
Ukrainians	2.9
Poles	2.2
Others	2.9

Source: Central Statistical Bureau of Latvia.

TABLE 30.5 LONG-TERM UNEMPLOYMENT

	1995	*1996*	*1997*	*1998*	*1999*	*2000*
Unemployment rate (percent)	6.5	7.2	6.7	9.2	9.1	7.8
Unemployed (in thousands)	83.2	90.8	84.9	111.4	109.5	93.3
Long-term unemployed (in thousands)	21.2	28.3	32.4	29.3	34.0	27.1
Long-term unemployed (as a percentage of total unemployed)	25.5	31.2	38.1	26.3	31.1	29.0

Source: Central Statistical Bureau of Latvia.

in the regions with a high overall level of unemployment. The low level of overall economic activities increases the risk that the unemployed will fall into long-term unemployment. About two-thirds of the long-term unemployed have been out of work more than 10 years. Some groups of people face more difficulties adapting to the structural changes in the economy because they are not flexible enough to change their qualifications. This leads to the long period of job seeking in the profession. At the same time these people are in the age group (30 to 49 years of age) that covers around 60 percent of total long-term unemployed. Another group likely to fall into long-term unemployment is women after child care leave because they have lost their professional skills and relations with their previous employer.

Efforts of the Latvian State Employment Service

The Latvian State Employment Service (LSES) has assisted the risk groups of unemployed, particularly long-term unemployed, by involving them in active labor market measures. Most long-term unemployed are persons with little education. Therefore, the LSES involved 8.5 percent of the long-term unemployed in professional education and requalification courses in 2000. The efficiency of this active labor market measure is proved by the job placement of 52 percent after attendance in these courses. Assistance in looking for jobs also was provided; because of this effort, 39.6 percent of long-term unemployed have been placed in jobs.

LSES is working to (1) reduce the share of long-term unemployed in total unemployment and (2) reduce the time persons must wait before they can be involved in any active labor market measures. To achieve the above-mentioned targets, LSES can (1) offer individual action plans for the unemployed to help them find out the most suitable and effective way of becoming integrated in the labor market and (2) promote the involvement of the long-term unemployed in active labor market measures.

In accordance with the provisions of the Accession Partnership, the Government of the Republic of Latvia and the European Commission will prepare a Joint Assessment of Latvia's employment policy priorities. This document will present the education and training, employment, and labor market objectives necessary to advance the country's labor market transformation. The Joint Assessment is necessary for Latvia to be able to implement the Employment Strategy and to prepare for accession to the EU. The Joint Assessment was finalized during the summer of 2001. In conformity with the EU Employment Guidelines, Latvia set the following priorities for 2001: promotion of youth employment, reduction of long-term unemployment, and improvement of the labor force quality.

The public employment services play an important role at the local level in the implementation of the Employment Strategy. Given recent developments in the labor market, it is essential to redefine the role of the public employment services and their priorities and methods of operation in the implementation of the Employment Strategy. The Latvian State Employment Service must develop new information and communication technologies in order to offer more efficient assistance to the unemployed and to enhance the quality of services provided to clients (job-seekers and employers).

National Poverty Prevention Strategy

The acquisition of research findings was accompanied by discussions about poverty in Latvia. These discussions involved researchers, representatives of nongovernmental organizations, and the staff of various ministries. In order to formulate the National Poverty Prevention Strategy, a work group was established by the decree of the prime minister in 1999. Its task was to reach specific solutions for the prevention and alleviation of poverty. The work group encountered problems because of the considerable scale and scope of poverty, insufficient targeting of current social assistance measures, weak intersectoral cooperation, and unclear division of responsibilities between the national and subnational levels.

The Cabinet of Ministers accepted the Strategy for Poverty Reduction on August 29, 2000. The next step is the development of an action plan for the implementation of the strategy. A system of monitoring and evaluation will assess the effectiveness of the implementation of the policy measures and their impact on the community in general. Awareness of poverty reduction measures needs to be raised at the highest political levels in order for the action plan to be successfully implemented. We believe the involvement of all stakeholders (governmental institutions, nongovernmental organizations, private businesses, and academics) and the involvement of all administrative levels (national, regional, and local) will be beneficial.

National Program on Social and Regional Integration

On February 6, 2001, the Cabinet of Ministers approved the National Program on "The Integration of Society in Latvia." This program pays special attention to the need to diminish the risk of social exclusion. In particular, it focuses on demographically endangered groups in society.

The aims of social integration are:

- To create a society with equal opportunities for all
- To extend the possibilities for social participation to all individuals and groups of residents
- To secure equal opportunities for members of society to gain access to resources of the society and to live life to the fullest
- To promote formation of a middle class.

Social integration is constrained by poverty, unemployment, inadequate education and lack of information, insufficient social mobility, and shortcomings in the social security system. In this context the program addresses the following problems of social development:

- An increase in social polarization caused mainly by gaps in income levels and by widespread poverty
- The prevalence of unnatural and violent deaths
- Marginalization of individuals, families, and social groups
- The spread of violence (in society and in the mass media)
- An increase in the number of beggars, homeless persons, and "street" children
- The spread of alcoholism as "an escape" from long-term stress, as well as an increasing incidence of drug and substance abuse.

For several social groups, the risk of social exclusion is usually higher. Increased attention should be paid to this fact in considering social integration. These groups include orphans; "risk" families and families in crisis, including large families; the unemployed; the homeless; people living in poverty; persons discharged from prison; people with mental disabilities; people with special needs; and elderly people near retirement age.

Conclusions

During the past 10 years Latvia experienced progressive changes toward a market economy—stabilization of the economic situation, lower inflation, improved living standards. Social welfare reform has been implemented to create a national social security system. Yet empirical data show that the risk of social exclusion has not disappeared, especially for those in poverty. An analysis of the dimensions of poverty allowed the government to elaborate a comprehensive Poverty Reduction Strategy. Long-term unemployed people are one of the target groups for both the poverty reduction policy and the National Employment Plan. The approved National Program on "The Integration of Society in Latvia" addresses the increased social polarization mostly caused by gaps in income levels and the marginalization of individuals, families, and social groups. The program aims to support activities that help adults and children overcome homelessness.

References

Aasland, Aadne. 2000. "Ethnicity and Poverty in Latvia." Riga: Ministry of Welfare and the United Nations Development Programme (UNDP).

Central Statistical Bureau. 1999. *Annual Report for 1999.* State Labour Inspection. Riga.

———. 1999. *Report on Household Budget Survey 1999.* Riga.

———. 2000. *Annual Report for 2000.* State Labour Inspection. Riga.

———. 2000. *Report on Household Budget Survey 2000.* Riga.

Central Statistical Bureau and Norwegian Institute for Applied Social Science (FAFO). 1999. *Living Conditions in Latvia.* Norbalt II Living Conditions Project. Riga.

Gassmann, Franzisca. 2000. "Who and Where Are the Poor in Latvia?" Riga: Ministry of Welfare of Latvia and UNDP.

Gassmann, Franzisca, and Chris de Neubourg. 2000. "Coping with Little Means in Latvia?" Riga: Ministry of Welfare and UNDP.

Keune, Martin. 2000. "Poverty and the Labour Market in Latvia." Riga: Ministry of Welfare and UNDP.

Trapenciere, Ilze, and others. 2000. "Listening to the Poor: Social Assessment of Poverty in Latvia." Riga: Ministry of Welfare and UNDP.

World Bank. 1999. *Latvia—Poverty Assessment: A World Bank Country Study.* Main report. Washington, D.C.

CHAPTER 31

Social Exclusion and Double Marginalization of the Roma in the Slovak Republic after 1989

Michal Vašečka and Iveta Radičová

The Roma issue has been the hottest topic in the Slovak Republic since 1989 when the communist regime fell. Politicians and celebrities have invested considerable time, money, social capital, and especially political will in solving the so-called Roma issue. This is a remarkable shift from the past. The Slovak Republic's political and social elite, regardless of their motives, have begun to understand the complexity of the issue and the urgent need to deal with it.

A New Understanding of the Roma Issue

Interest in addressing the Roma issue peaked during the past few years for the following three reasons. The first concerns morality and the importance of human rights. Some began to realize their obligation to help the Roma, and that the inappropriate, misguided, or directly discriminatory methods and policies that had been applied to Slovaks in the past should no longer be tolerated on Slovak soil. This conviction, however, is limited to a relatively small group of people who call themselves liberal democrats. The second reason for the shift in thinking concerns integration and pragmatism. A significant number of Slovak representatives are eager to find a solution to the Romany issue, because the country's integration ambitions and efforts to join the European Union (EU) and North Atlantic Treaty Organization (NATO) depend on it. Finally, there is the issue of self-defense. Many in the majority of the Roma population, represented mainly by the parliamentary opposition, have admitted the necessity of solving the issue because of fears that stem from Romany demographic developments and the practically uncontrollable birth rates in Romany settlements (Vašečka 2001).

The Roma are the second largest ethnic minority in the Slovak Republic. The census in 1991 showed a total of 75,802 citizens claiming Roma nationality, or 1.4 percent of the population. However, various estimates put the Roma population at exponentially higher figures. Head counts conducted in 1989 by local and municipal administrations showed that there were 253,943 Roma (4.8 percent of the population); however, these statistics registered only socially dependent citizens. Therefore, it can be assumed that the number of Roma in the Slovak Republic is today even higher. Current estimates by experts put the total number between 420,000 and 500,000, a number continuously on the rise due to the high Roma birth rate (Statistical Office of the Slovak Republic).

According to experts, there are approximately 12 million Roma worldwide, 8 million of whom live in Europe. Many European countries have more Roma communities than the Slovak Republic has. The largest Roma community in the world lives in Romania (estimated population between 1.8 million and 2.8 million). Relatively speaking, however, the Slovak Republic, Bulgaria, and the former Yugoslav Republic of Macedonia have the largest per capita Roma community in the world (8 to 9 percent of each country's population [Statistical Office of the Slovak Republic]).

The deteriorating socioeconomic status of the Roma and the majority population's strongly negative perception of the Roma are becoming the most important challenges the Slovak Republic faces on its way to the EU. The Slovak Republic has the largest Roma minority of all EU-hopeful countries, and the one with the worst social status. The European Commission (EC) has repeatedly stressed that the situation of ethnic minorities in candidate countries aspiring to join the EU was acceptable, with the exception of that of the Roma.

The Roma constitute a truly distinct minority, and solution of the Romany issue therefore requires a rather complex approach. The unsatisfactory socioeconomic situation of most Roma in the Slovak Republic raises the question of whether they are becoming a social, as well as a purely ethnic, minority. Expert and professional circles see the Roma becoming an underclass, a word that perhaps best describes Roma settlements.

The basic characteristics of the members of an "underclass" are the following: long-term unemployment, fragmentary work history, permanent success on the secondary labor market only, and dependence on social welfare benefits or on activities that have to do with the shadow economy. The underclass environment is characterized by general resignation, low respect for authorities, a low level of social self-control, reliance on welfare, and poor labor ethics. These general characteristics of the underclass environment perfectly describe the situation of those Roma who dwell in Roma settlements and, increasingly, those who reside elsewhere.

Discussion of the underclass issue, which has been going on for several decades in some other countries, is perceived in the Slovak Republic as having an ideological basis; many people seem to erroneously interchange the terms "underclass" and *lumpen proletariat*. Nevertheless, opening such a discussion in the Slovak Republic is vital for the country to prevent further negative consequences of the transformation from a modern industrial society to a postmodern, postindustrial one. Otherwise, the gap between the majority and the Roma will continue to widen, and ethnic poverty will intensify.

The Roma community has many different subgroups. The most common are colonies of settled Roma (Rumungres) and nomadic Vlachika Roma; the remnants of the Germanic Sints represent a separate group. The Roma also differ by the language and dialects they use. In a Slovak environment, they use some Slovak language words and dialects, while in the Hungarian environment in the southern part of the Slovak Republic, they use Hungarian. Like the majority population, the Slovak Roma can also be distinguished by their place of origin (that is, whether they are influenced by an urban or rural environment) as well as by their affinity to a particular region of the Slovak Republic.

Regarding such differences, some Roma experts observe that the old caste system continues inside the Romany community, determining in advance a person's role within the social system. (In the case of the Slovak Republic, we may speak of clans and groups.) The distinctiveness of the Roma minority is also illustrated by questions of whether the Roma are a nation or merely an ethnic group. As recently as 1991, the Slovak Roma ceased to be perceived merely as an ethnic group and were treated by the country's legislation as a full-fledged ethnic minority, equal to other ethnic minorities living on Slovak territory (Vašečka 2001).

Pre-1989 Policies: The Roma and Social Exclusion

The social, economic, and political changes in 1989 brought an unprecedented transformation to the Slovak Republic. The communist regime distorted the general understanding and observance of civic and political rights, while developing social rights that have been significantly expanded. In contrast to other totalitarian regimes, this one changed the system that determined the course of the economy, making it unable to compete by disregarding the rules of supply and demand. But the most significant intervention into the functioning of the society was the forcible effort to change the organization of the society, altering its natural stratification. Systematic favoritism was shown toward the lower social stratum of the society at the expense of the higher stratum, and several segments of the precommunism elite and intelligentsia were directly discriminated against.

The majority of the Roma belonged to the lower layers of the society, and they were the targets of different experiments by the communist regime to improve their social status. The change that came in 1989 caught the Roma by surprise; most agree that no stratum of the Roma population was prepared for these changes.

The communist regime counted on the assumption that if the living standard of the Roma and the average living standard were equalized, the reason for the differences between them and the majority population would be eliminated. In order to achieve this, different measures have been employed, which could be characterized as acts of social engineering. Examples follow:

- The diffusion of the Roma (within the Slovak Republic but also from the Slovak Republic to the Czech Republic), directed and supported by the state policy
- The disintegration of natural Roma communities
- The movement of the rural Roma population from Roma settlements to cities and industrial areas
- The destruction of natural binding between the Roma community and the majority population
- Insensitive and administrative (forcible) allocation of flats to the Roma from a socially disadvantaged environment
- Forced compliance with the general compulsory labor service, under the threat of imprisonment
- Statutory enforced obligation of school attendance by children
- Obligatory participation of the Roma in health prevention.

These seemingly positive results have been achieved by forcible means that imposed external pressure on the Roma without their active participation and acceptance. This, in turn, affected the views of some Roma toward the property allocated to them.

Why are these measures considered to be forcible without active internal participation of the Roma? Although the government managed to achieve a much higher standard of living for most Roma in comparison to the past decades, many of the forms of behavior typical for a traditional Roma family remained. The process of modernization of the Roma community during the era of the communist regime was predominantly one-dimensional, taking place only on the level of material improvement.

The characteristic attributes of a traditional Roma family include the following:

- Life in a broader family, thus lacking the motion toward the nuclear family
- Community-oriented life style
- An absence of boarders between what is private and what is public (privacy is nonexistent because of the way of life but also because of the relationship to property)
- A view of their current housing as temporary or provisional
- A clear division of roles in the Roma family (man as the provider, woman responsible for household maintenance)
- Multiple family members as a persistent demographic characteristic of Roma families.

The Roma community can be characterized as a nonagrarian society that is not able to sustain itself with its own resources and thus traditionally has entered into relationships with agrarian cultures. Agrarian cultures, with their private ownership relationship to land and through land to the territory, have contributed to the establishment of institutional and customary norms in the non-Roma population. Since the Roma have never been an agrarian culture, and their relationship to land has always been rather tepid, they have not established mechanisms and institutions related to the agrarian type of private ownership relationships. Thus the Roma have never belonged to a territory and have never attributed importance to the acquisition of property. On the contrary, their geographic mobility did not adversely affect demand for their craftsmanship.

The Roma's view of ownership and housing is related to their social structures, which are based on kinship ties. These specific cultural norms of the Roma can be described as a permanent provisional strategy. Education in its institutional forms (formal and contextual) puts limits on the Roma's provisional strategy. The educational institutions of the majority population thus lack an equivalent with the institutional structure of the Roma community. This is the cause of conflict between two types of organization and social function. The participation of Roma in two important activities, work and education, confronts them with a different world. Their incorporation into these two spheres is an asymmetric process: the Roma are asked to play the game although they did not contribute in any way to its rules and regulations. They are marginal, and their only choice is to adjust.

Many of the measures undertaken by the communist regime have undoubtedly improved the living standard of the Roma population. But these measures also can be evaluated as disadvantageous for the Roma. Placing a Roma family that has adapted to the backward environment of a settlement among the majority population often causes unsolvable problems in city housing estates and has fueled hatred on both sides. This tension is at the root of recent outbursts of violence and racism.

Through the policy of resettling, diffusion, and employment, the Roma community became a part of the social provision policy, which helped them to escape total material need reflected in hunger and malnourishment. The result was that the Roma gradually got used to state paternalism, which replaced the traditional family solidarity. This process led to the establishment of a new culture of dependence on state institutions.

In the preindustrial era (until the beginning of the twentieth century), the most important jobs of the Roma included forging as smiths and musical production; many also processed raw materials. Since the Roma did not own land, they had to purchase basic food from the peasants. The peasants, in turn, needed cheap labor to collect potatoes, harvest grain, take in hay, build homes, sink wells, or prepare wood for the winter. The Roma usually demanded pay in food, used clothing, old furniture, or household items. The convenience of this system of coexistence for both sides has been reflected in the relationships between families of the Roma and peasants. With the arrival of industrialization, these relationships have been gradually broken, and the Roma have been forced to become a resource of labor for heavy industry. After 1989 the majority of them became useless in the new economy, mainly due to their poor qualifications, and the former relationships between the Roma and the majority have almost disappeared.

Their nonexistent relationship to ownership and provisional strategy influenced the access of the Roma community to opportunities. The gradual closure of Roma communities was taking place, leading to their social exclusion. The process of social closure has taken place in two ways: through marginalization and through incorporation. Marginalization limits choices and often produces poverty. During the communist regime, the government tried to solve the problem of marginalization within the state-organized economy by incorporating citizens living in rural areas in newly created zones of heavy industry. They were placed mainly into jobs for unqualified workers. This incorporation had the form of illusionary integration, since it did not lead to the improvement of social status.

The determining influence on the social situation of communist country inhabitants was the second economy. Only those who based their living strategies on participation in both economies had a chance to improve their social status. The second economy required the existence of financial household management and production (own land and own means of production). But this still is not the case of the Roma. Their exclusive dependence on the formal economy was the main factor contributing to their deeper fall into poverty than was observed in the majority population.

The poverty of the Roma during the communist era thus reached more significant forms than the poverty of the majority population with similar education and qualifications. The Roma were much more dependent on income from social assistance, which made up a greater proportion of their income than did the income generated by work. Another significant factor contributing to the living standard of the majority population and their incorporation into the society was the participation of both partners in the work force, a so-called two-income family. Many Roma families had only one source of income (the Roma women stayed at home with their children), and most families had many children.

The income differentiation and living standard during communist rule were not suited to the achieved degree of education. Certain branches of industry, mainly in the manufacturing sector, were preferred as a means of achieving a certain social status. There was a principle of collective not individual mobility. Education was not exclusively understood as a means of reaching a certain living standard and social position. The overall educational structure in the Slovak Republic reflects this principle. The majority of citizens have only a primary or secondary education without the certificate of apprenticeship (figure 31.1). This orientation toward education became a trap after 1989.

The Roma's views on education and work have been determined by two basic factors. The mechanism of closure of the Roma community, which led to life on the edge of society, ultimately produced behavioral patterns in the areas of education and the labor market. The new generation of Roma from the closed communities does not feel the need to choose an educational strategy different from the one chosen by their

FIGURE 31.1 SHARE OF ROMA AMONG REGISTERED UNEMPLOYED BY LEVEL OF EDUCATION, 1999

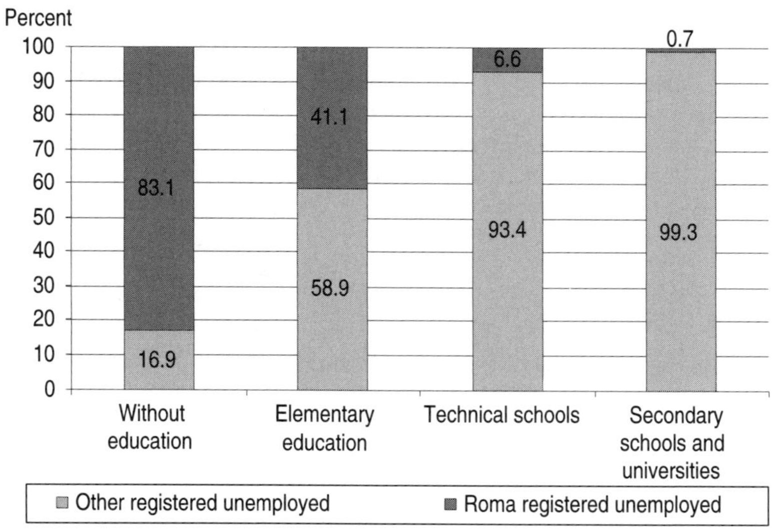

Source: Ministry of Work, Social Affairs and Family of the Slovak Republic, 1999.

fathers and mothers. In this area the behavior of the Roma minority significantly differs from the behavior of other minorities, for example, the Jewish minority. The Roma continue to follow approved patterns that are oriented to the present, but education depends on an orientation to the future. This reproduction of patterns was supported by the majority population, which knowingly or unknowingly failed to create the conditions that would improve the education and qualifications of the Roma ethnic group. The communist form of economy required a large, unqualified work force, and so the Roma did not need to improve their education or qualifications.

The historic experience of the Roma resulted in specific types of reactions and behaviors toward the majority population. Their withdrawal to the borders of society and strategy of escape (readiness to leave) resulted in the Roma behaving like an endangered group—multiplying the cohesiveness of the community. This broadens the degree of seclusion and marginalization of the Roma.

The family has always played a very significant role in the life of the Roma. The head of the family was always the father. When it came to raising children, the Roma usually paid attention to the older ones, who then took care of the younger children. Roma children are very reluctant to leave their parents, even once they reach adulthood and establish their own families. In general, the Roma family represents the traditional type of multigenerational family. This is also the most important difference between the Roma and the majority population family. The traditional Roma household is only beginning to divide into its nuclear forms, while the same phenomenon took place in the non-Roma population during the first half of the twentieth century.

Today the Roma family represents a different type of family, but the difference is not determined by ethnicity but by a drift in time. This is the reason why it is possible to talk of a phase drift in regard to this area, rather than of ethnic-specific behavior of the Roma. The data on the demographic behavior of the Roma population in the Slovak Republic strongly resemble data describing the demographic behavior of the non-Roma population several decades ago, or statistics comparable with the data from developing countries. One example is data on child mortality. In the Roma population during the 1980s child mortality data were very similar to the data from the whole of Czechoslovakia in the 1950s. The medium length of life span of the Roma minority between 1970 and 1980 was similar to that of the entire Czechoslovakia between 1929 and 1933 (for Roma men) and to the era after the Second World War (for Roma women). It is realistic to assume that the present Roma population will reach the demographic characteristics of the majority in one generation (Statistical Office of the Slovak Republic).

The demographic boom did not occur among the Roma until 1945 because of the high mortality of Roma children and inadequate health care. With a certain degree of simplification it is possible to conclude that the health of the majority of Roma citizens is still worse than that of the non-Roma population in the Slovak Republic (World Bank 2000). The communist regime has achieved significant success in the elimination of certain diseases and in the overall improvement of the health state of the Roma—lowering the child mortality, increasing the medium life span, and eliminating certain diseases. Mandatory preventive health care, improved living conditions, and better quality food contributed to the significant growth of the Roma population during the communist regime. The demographic behavior of the Roma was probably influenced by the population policy of the communist state (economy of full employment, social policy). This did not cause the people to re-evaluate their own reproductive behavior.

Although health care improved during the communist regime, the estimated medium life span of the Roma population has been and still is lagging behind the estimated medium life span of the majority population. This is due mainly to the Roma's unhealthy life style, socially disadvantaged environment, high incidence of alcoholism, and (most important of all) low quality and cheap food. The basic ingredient of the Roma diet has traditionally been entrails, prepared in different ways. The food considered to be the most typical Roma dish is called "goja," washed pork large intestine, turned with the fat side inside and filled with potatoes, corn meal, grits, or rice. In addition, floury pastry dishes dominate the diet in Roma families, and consumption of vegetables is low.

Changes after 1989: From Social Exclusion to Social Isolation

The social, economic, and political transformation after 1989 began at a time when relations between the majority population and the Roma were tense, originating from feelings of unjust redistribution of resources. Various factors contributed to the situation. First, the Roma had fully adjusted by 1989 to the conditions introduced by the communist regime and its rules of the game. Second, the state approached the Roma on the basis of its conclusions about their behavior patterns, which some viewed as socially pathological. The state considered differences between the Roma and the majority population as manifestations of social pathology. Social policy was targeted to eliminate these differences. Third, the Roma entered the transformation period with considerably lower qualifications than the majority population had and with working habits unsuited to the requirements of the transforming economy.

The gradual reconstruction of economic, political, cultural, and social life of the society has taken from the Roma all of the securities they obtained during the communist regime. And the Roma have not been prepared for any of these changes.

The number of absences and truancy by Roma children increased with the liberalization of constraining rules related to education, the schooling system, and the placement of children in children's homes. During the communist regime situations were solved with the assistance of police, through the help of parents, with the removal of children into institutional care, and with the reduction of social benefits.

The Roma children from separated or segregated settlements are handicapped upon their arrival in the primary school and later at the entrance exams for higher education. If they decide to continue their education, they usually choose apprenticeship schools. (This choice is mainly determined by accessibility—the distance of the schools from home.) Later the Roma are trapped in the position of unemployed graduates of apprenticeship schools, without a chance of finding employment, within the official formal economy, in the close surroundings of their home. If they finish their education, they go back to their original environment, where they reproduce the behavior of their parents. They fall into the social safety net, and the young generation begins to perceive this as the normal way to behave. If they do get employed, it is mainly in informal jobs, illegal work, or short-term jobs. Opportunities for them diminish with growing segregation.

The change in the area of health care to an insurance system with emphasis on personal responsibility for health is worsening the health state of the Roma population. Mandatory preventive health care was canceled, and the orientation of the Roma to the present leads them to neglect preventive health care. The bad socioeconomic situation and, related to that, the inadequate housing and infrastructure conditions in the place of residency are the reasons behind the worsening health status of the Roma in the Slovak Republic after 1989.

All available data reflect the worsening health state, mainly in the constantly growing isolated Roma settlements. Since 1989 the incidence of upper respiratory disease has been on the rise, and in some settlements there have been repeated outbreaks of tuberculosis. Because of the above-mentioned facts, the risk of epidemics exists. Skin diseases and venereal diseases are common, as are accidental injuries. Among the Roma children infectious and parasitic diseases are being observed, diseases no longer found among the majority population. Another big danger is the spreading of the infection of brain membranes. The socially disadvantaged environment is associated with the high incidence of different levels of mental retardation. Despite the elimination of epidemics of typhoid and typhus, and the efforts to gain control over respiratory diseases, intestinal diseases, and syphilis on the national level, many of these and other diseases are still found in the Roma settlements.

Housing policy (as it relates to flats and houses as well as to adjoining real estate) changed dramatically after 1989. Ninety percent of rental flats have been privatized; the real estate has new owners. The lands that were in the so-called private holding could be given to their tenants free of charge if the following two basic conditions were fulfilled. First, the house standing in the real estate had a valid building permit or had been awarded the appropriate approval in the term given by law. Second, the real estate was registered in the land-register, and no application had been filed for its restitution.

If these conditions were met, the tenant was free to apply for property transfer to his or her name. While a majority of the population did not know about these procedures, the lack of understanding among the Roma was even more complete. The issue of legal or illegal ownership of land was nonexistent during communism. Thus the changes after 1989 uncovered a large group of Roma living illegally on someone else's land. The conditions for the legalization of a property have become very complicated, with increased demands and preconditions for the issuance of the building permit (it requires 32 individual permits), as well as the adequate approval. The houses of many Roma do not fulfill the norm given by the law, and the Roma lack financial resources for the reconstruction of their houses. If they have the resources, they often cannot use them because they do not legally own the real estate.

After 1989 the government system of several types of loans for housing acquisition was canceled, as well as the building of new houses by the state. Housing issues were transferred to the jurisdiction of communal municipalities and city councils. They began to behave just like any other economic unit. The present situation of high demand has led to an increase in the prices of flats and homes. Housing costs are extreme from the point of view of citizens with an average income. The chance of gaining and maintaining housing thus became minimal for the Roma, because they are unable to succeed in this competition.

The building of housing estates in the Slovak Republic after 1989 has been inadequate when compared to the demand. Despite saving programs and limited loans from the state, a citizen with an average income has little chance to get a flat. The public reacts very sensitively to unfair decisions regarding housing policy, the allocation of flats, and provision of profitable loans. Social housing as a solution to the market situation does not begin to cover the demands and needs of families in social and material need. The Roma are not alone in this situation, but unquestionably they are the least successful at solving it. The rental price liberalization and privatization of flats brought significant increases in housing-related expenses. Rent increased by 200 percent in response to higher costs of water, gas, garbage removal, and other services. And these higher prices pushed the Roma to cheaper flats or lodging-houses. The lack of a realistic policy of social housing is dealt with by the Roma by withdrawal strategies: they go back to the settlements and revitalize them. The reason for this is simple. Housing in settlements has minimal or no expenses related to it.

The unemployment rate among the Roma skyrocketed after 1989, reaching 100 percent in some Roma settlements. Exact statistics for Romany unemployment do not exist, and one can only make estimates on the basis of the overall situation in the Slovak Republic's most troubled regions. Districts with the highest share of Roma are the ones most severely hit by unemployment.

The only data available on Romany unemployment are the unofficial data of the Ministry of Work, Social Affairs and Family. These data, which cannot be considered fully representative, were recorded by district labor bureau officers who wrote the letter "R" in the dossiers of Romany job applicants. Since this practice was illegal and discriminatory, it was discontinued after the 1998 elections. Unfortunately, one negative effect of the decision is that the Slovak Republic now lacks a database on Roma unemployment. Nevertheless, unofficial data from the previous period show that the number of unemployed Roma in the Slovak Republic is increasing (figure 31.2) and that the Roma represent a significant majority of the long-term unemployed in the country. The main factors influencing the high unemployment rate among the Roma are the following: their low level of qualifications, the lack of interest among employers in hiring Roma due to the large supply of workers in the labor market, the poor work ethic of some Roma, the lack of interest among some Roma to find a job on public benefit work projects, and the general scarcity of job opportunities, especially in regions with a large Roma population (Statistical Office of the Slovak Republic).

According to expert estimates, approximately 10 percent of Slovak citizens are dependent on social security benefits. The Roma represent a significant share of these citizens. The disbursement of social security benefits to the Roma has become one of the main causes for the growing tension between the minority and the majority populations. The majority argues that the Roma do nothing, yet they receive large sums of money, which they waste on alcohol. The government's inability to better plan the disbursement of welfare benefits, and widespread usury among the Roma, argue for the development of a supervisory mechanism through which the government could control the Roma's spending of their social benefits. The most serious objection to the two approaches was that they were implemented across the board, without applying individual criteria. The scheme was tested during the first half of 1999, and the Ministry of Work, Social Affairs and Family is not now considering a broader application (Statistical Office of the Slovak Republic).

FIGURE 31.2 NUMBER OF UNEMPLOYED ROMA IN THE SLOVAK REPUBLIC, 1992–99

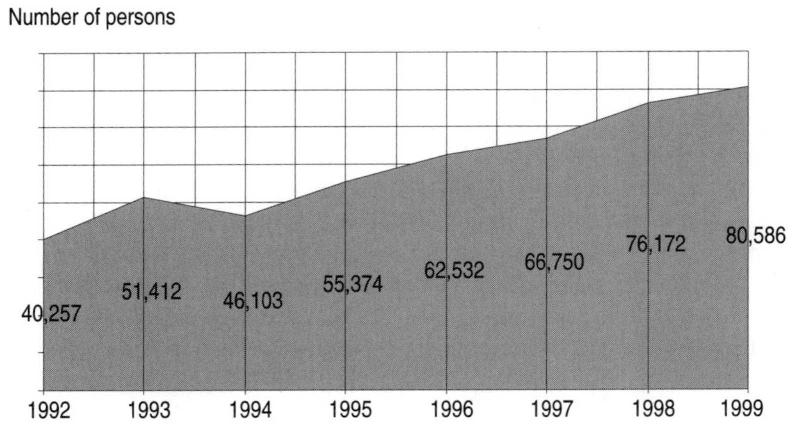

Note: For 1992–98, as of December 31; for 1999, as of August 31.
Source: Ministry of Work, Social Affairs and Family of the Slovak Republic, 1999.

Unemployment, especially the long-term and permanent unemployment so common among the Roma, perpetuates the cycle of poverty and the unemployment trap. The Roma become dependent on social security benefits, resulting in a high rate of long-term unemployment (table 31.1 and figure 31.3). The situation is then passed from one generation to the next. Consequently, the number of families in which both parents and children are permanently unemployed is also increasing; moreover, children have no experience of stable and permanent employment. Hence, all current conditions support a subculture of unemployed Romany youth (Statistical Office of the Slovak Republic).

TABLE 31.1 STRUCTURE OF UNEMPLOYMENT BY DURATION, 1999

Period of registration	*Number of all registered unemployed*	*Number of registered unemployed Roma*	*Roma registered unemployed as a percentage of all registered unemployed*
Up to 6 months	194,737	10,380	5.33
More than 12 months	194,657	59,176	30.40
More than 24 months	100,020	40,922	40.91
More than 48 months	42,861	22,399	52.26

Source: Ministry of Work, Social Affairs and Family of the Slovak Republic, 1999.

FIGURE 31.3 SHARE OF ROMA AMONG UNEMPLOYED BY DURATION, 1999

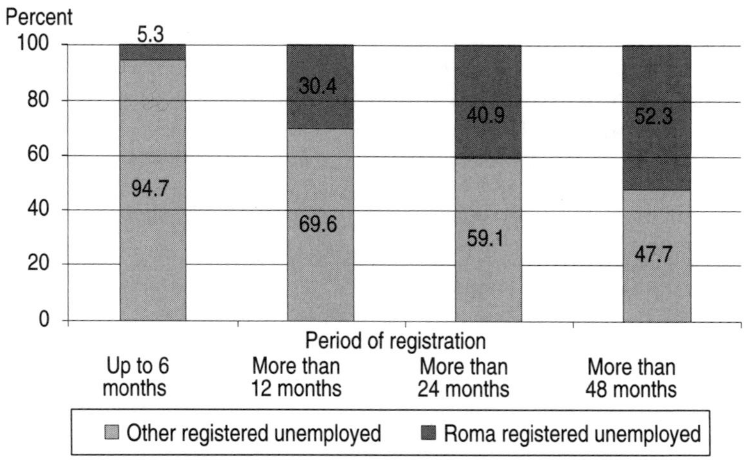

Source: Ministry of Work, Social Affairs and Family of the Slovak Republic, 1999.

Strategies to Cope with Poverty

The changes we have mentioned reflect a new type of social stratification. Two stratification pyramids formed during communism: the pyramid of establishment (social capital) and the pyramid of second economy (private capital). These pyramids have been merging, with the social capital creating opportunities for access to material capital. The Roma do not belong to either of the pyramids that provide a way to be integrated into a higher class of society. They cannot manage to fulfill the requirements for integration into the new market relationships nor successfully master the new rules of the game governing the labor market and the market for privatized property.

Poverty existed during the communist regime, and the Roma represented a large share of poor citizens. After 1989 the term *poverty* gained a new meaning based on the inequality between individuals on the one hand and whole social categories on the other. The individual criteria involve the old demographic definition of poverty: the basic determinant of poverty is the number of children in a household. This type of poverty can be escaped by individual strategies, mainly changes in reproductive behavior. (Indeed, this strategy was implemented by the majority population in the middle of the twentieth century.) Under this concept of poverty the communist regime transformed poverty from a public issue to a personal problem. Poverty lost its social status and became understood as personal failure. The state regulated this poverty with means based on strong redistribution, subventions into the infrastructure, prices of basic foods, and incomes.

The group characteristic is being described as the new vertical poverty. Changes in the structure of employment move a whole social category into social dependence. The main factor is not the number of children but the low degree of education in fields that are vanishing. Whole branches of industry are disappearing, resulting in long-term unemployment. The Roma minority combines the old demographic poverty with the new vertical poverty. In the case of a group's vertical poverty, it is not enough to change individual living strategies. The chances for a successful solution are determined by the system of social provisions and rights. The state of vertical poverty is the result of systemic conditions, not individual failures. The poverty of the Roma reflects the degree of their disintegration; their income and property inequality is the direct result of this disintegration.

When it comes to social class and qualifications, the Roma in the Slovak Republic are largely a homogeneous group. From the point of view of their socio-professional status, most Roma are nonqualified workers, which is the reason why they have such high representation among the low-income groups of the Slovak population. From the point of view of employment, a certain "monotype" of the Roma family could already be observed during the communist regime: unqualified building workers or agrarian workers without professional or general higher education, low average income per family member, with a prevailing majority of men working away from the place of their residence. Since 1989 the unemployment of Roma men has been on the rise, as well as the number of Roma families with both partners unemployed.

The state reacted after 1989 by creating a system of social assistance, a social safety net. But it narrowed the meaning of poverty to so-called material and social need. The state did not recognize poverty as a social status. The absence of entitlements and emphasis on procurement reflect the comprehension of poverty as individual responsibility and individual failure, and predetermine the provision of social assistance by testing, measuring, and monitoring individual behavior and strategies. This strengthens the culture of dependence, with all the signs of reproduced poverty: feelings of marginality, being in danger, fatalism, desperation, passivity, and aggression; communal closure; impulsiveness; absence of planning and saving; and distrust of the authorities.

The basic strategy for solving life situations, in the majority as well as in the Roma population, is family cooperation, mutual help within families, and broader family belonging. Differences are in the type of help provided by the family, and whether it is actually able to provide any help at all. Family strategies are determined mainly by the cultural and historical background and living conditions of individual families. The family strategy that becomes prevalent in a settlement or village depends more on the sociocultural character of the family and the microclimate in the settlement than on demographic characteristics of the family. The sociocultural character of separated but mainly segregated settlements is a type of collective marginalization and social exclusion without a potential for mutual help. The living strategy oriented to family networks is ineffective in these circumstances. The more homogeneous a settlement is, the smaller are the chances for the effectiveness of supporting family networks. In segregated settlements these living strategies have zero effectiveness. Some nongovernmental organizations are trying to replace the absence of supportive family networks and mutual help with their own activities (creating community centers).

In the new social conditions, it is mainly well-known and time-proven family strategies that are implemented as coping mechanisms. The traditional family in the majority population revitalizes through changes in in-house consumption (self-catering) and the departure of family members to find work abroad. But self-catering has never been practiced in segregated Roma communities. The majority population considers the Roma's nonacceptance of this self-catering strategy, not as a traditional and typical behavior pattern of the Roma but rather as proof of their laziness and tendency to steal, their preference for choosing the easy way, and their unwillingness to change their living situation. The more open a Roma community is, the more heterogeneous the environment is and the greater the chance of reproduction of the self-catering strategy.

The Roma are left with only one active strategy—departure. This strategy cannot be implemented in marginalized, segregated settlements because a departure requires resources. A specific phenomenon for the Roma is collective departure, the departure of entire families from a certain locality; in the majority population it is usually one member of a family who leaves to work. The collective departure of the Roma creates and multiplies the existing tension in the society. The majority population is being "punished" by other countries' visa requirements (defensive measures to stop the inflow of Roma).

It is not easy to establish a clear profile of the typical Romany asylum seeker from the Slovak Republic according to classic demographic categories. Most asylum seekers came from the Košice and Michalovce districts, especially from the town of Michalovce and the villages of Pavlovce nad Uhom and Malčice. The typical Romany asylum seeker:

- Hails from the eastern part of the Slovak Republic (the western Slovak territories have remained virtually unaffected by Romany migrations)
- Speaks Slovak (Hungarian-speaking Roma do not often migrate)
- Resides in towns and large villages (smaller villages and settlements have also remained virtually unaffected)
- Enjoys an above-average social status (most migrants are recruited especially from among members of the Romany middle class)
- Has an above-average education (most migrating Roma have completed primary education and some of them even secondary education)
- Has experience of work outside his own region (among migrants, a significant number of Roma have worked in remote regions of the Slovak Republic or abroad in Prague or in the mining region of northern Moravia).

As far as Romany subethnic differentiation is concerned, most migrants are Rumungres and not Vlachika Roma. (Although in terms of their habits and traditions, Vlachika Roma are much closer to the nomadic way of life than are Rumungres.)

All of the above-mentioned strategies have the character of short-term and fast solutions, lacking the perspective of significant long-term improvements in the living situation. The revitalization of strategies with long-term effects, typical for the rural areas in the precommunist era like the development of agrarian small-scale production, animal farming, or retail handicraft, is rather sporadic and uncommon. In addition to lack of experience, there is a lack of government support. These activities are the only possibilities of job creation in many villages after the disappearance of the "Collective Farming Cooperatives" and State farms, which employed an overwhelming part of the majority and Roma population in agriculture. The extinction of agricultural production led to the departure of the majority population—either shuttle migration to working places or the abandonment of rural homes. The typical Roma handicraft, supplementary production or services adjoined to these types of productions, thus lost demand in these villages. Some NGOs are trying to fill the void left by government by running several projects for the support of revitalization of "classical" handicraft, several of them successfully.

In some Roma settlements unemployment is as high as 100 percent. Thus a situation has been created that has been described as "the valley of hunger" with visible "islands of poverty." The "hunger valley" is endangered by total social disorganization, and the culture of poverty is the only possible form of adaptation to the situation. Its results include the formation of the so-called underclass, rural and urban. Besides the structural dimension, the transformation after 1989 had a territorial, regional, and microregional dimension. Some territories have been shifted to the margin of socioeconomic development. Marginalization has its roots in the so-called socialist industrialization and industrial urbanization of the Slovak Republic. After 1989 the socioeconomic marginality of the inherited regions deepened, continually spreading to other territories. The marginalization that has taken place within the economic transformation has created larger compact entities within marginal territories in borderland regions of the northern, eastern, and southern parts of the country. These territories are inhabited by minorities, and that is why the issue also has an ethnic dimension.

The regions have in common increasing or "stabilized" levels of unemployment as well as other problematic qualities. These common characteristics refer especially to the human potential as well as to the infrastructure, spatial position of the region, and the persistence of imbalance inherited from the past. There are concentrations of the old demographic poverty and the new vertical type of poverty, low entrepreneurial spirit, and small influx of capital. Marginal regions are characterized by a decline of civilization and cultural standards of its settlements and life conditions. Problems with access to education and to social and cultural activities have been observed, as well as limited potential for social and civilization development. These regions have problems adapting to the current transformation, and they lack persons able and willing to take the initiative and responsibility for rejuvenation of the region. Marginal regions are seldom entirely marginal. Marginality is a problem, especially in some villages. These regions are ethnically mixed, which adds political meaning to this feature of marginal territories.

The Roma living in segregated settlements of marginalized regions thus find themselves in a situation of double marginalization. The weakened and very limited possibilities of a marginalized region in combination with the absence of potential for self-help, self-organization, and activation require targeted support and developmental social programs. Any concrete program cannot achieve long-term success without systemic changes, especially in the areas of employment policy and housing policy (social housing). It is not possible to overcome double marginalization with an individual living strategy (unless it means moving).

The multiplied effects of disintegration and marginalization are reflected among the Roma in their long-term lack of material security and the lives they live in absolute poverty. Material security means the availability of food, drink, clothing, housing, and shelter, enabling biological survival and the fulfillment of primary needs. Material security is a precondition for social security and the fulfillment of secondary needs such as self-identity and self-affirmation, education, and culture.

The most basic requirements for the achievement of social security are social contacts. Contacts are the only way of incorporation into the social organization of the society. The segregated Roma live under the pressure of material insecurity, which leaves them without the potential for other activities, for the benefit of themselves or others. So they themselves cannot ensure their participation in informal social networks. Creation of these informal social networks for the Roma and with the Roma is the most basic task for all social activists. The strategies of segregated Roma oriented to survival make them dependent. This dependency is of a material character, because their survival depends on the state social assistance benefits and other institutions. The same risk of dependency hangs over the creation of social dependency on other people. The double marginalization of the Roma is accompanied by a double dependency effect—material and social dependency. Double dependency brings with it a loss of self-confidence and self-respect.

References

Ministry of Work, Social Affairs and Family of the Slovak Republic. 1999.

Statistical Office of the Slovak Republic.

Úrad vlády SR. 1999. *Strategy of the Slovak Government to Solve the Problems of the Romany Ethnic Minority, and the Set of Implementation Measures—First Stage.* A document approved at the Cabinet session of September 27, 1999. Bratislava.

Úrad vlády SR. 2000. *Strategy of the Slovak Government to Solve the Problems of the Romany Ethnic Minority as a Set of Concrete Measures for 2000—Second Stage.* A document approved at the Cabinet session of May 3, 2000. Bratislava.

Vašečka, Michal. 2001. "Roma." In Grigorij Mesežnikov, Miroslav Kollár, and Tom Nicholson, eds., *Slovakia 2000: A Global Report on the State of Society.* Bratislava: Inštitút pre verejné otázky.

Vašečka, Michal, and Roman Džambazovič. 2000. *Sociálno-ekonomická situácia Rómov na Slovensku ako potenciálnych migrantov a žiadateľov o azyl v krajinách EÚ* (*The Socioeconomic Situation of the Roma in the Slovak Republic as Potential Migrants and Asylum Seekers in EU Member States*). Bratislava: International Organization for Migration.

World Bank. 2000. *The Health Needs of the Roma Population in the Czech and Slovak Republics.* Washington, D.C.

World Bank and others. 2001. *Poverty and Welfare of Roma in the Slovak Republic.* A Joint Report of the World Bank, the Open Society Institute, the Institute for Economic and Social Reforms; Washington, D.C. Processed.

CHAPTER 32

Discussant Notes

Tom Mulherin

Excellent papers were presented by Ruta Zilvere on Latvia's search for solutions to reduce social exclusion and by Michal Vašečka on the social exclusion of Roma people in the Slovak Republic. Rather than responding in detail to the issues they have raised, I think it may be useful to provide a framework for considering their papers by outlining the approach being taken within the European Union to social exclusion. Candidate countries would no doubt be aware that this issue is of widespread concern in all Member States and that it is now firmly on the agenda of significant matters to be addressed during the coming years.

There have been significant efforts at the EU level over several decades to promote the social dimension of development and to maintain regional cohesion by redistribution of resources through the structural funds and the common agricultural policy (CAP). Despite this, there has been a growing popular perception that the European Union is somewhat remote from ordinary people and their day-to-day concerns throughout the Member States. Partly in response to this, the heads of state and government at successive European Councils in recent years have recognized the need to pay greater attention to the social implications of the very significant economic decisions being taken in the course of creating the single market. Even if competence is primarily at the national level in relation to social protection and social inclusion matters, the EU needed to reflect a balanced concern for the economic, employment, and social dimensions.

In the 1980s and 1990s, three successive EU poverty programs led to many innovative social inclusion initiatives at the national level. For example, Ireland's ongoing local community development projects draw heavily on the experience gained from pilot initiatives that were directly supported by these programs. In the context of the European Commission proposal for a fourth poverty program, a small number of Member States questioned the legal basis for Commission initiatives, insisted that this was a matter purely of national competence, and effectively blocked the proposal. However, following an Irish proposal at the 1996–97 Inter-Governmental Conference, the Treaty of Amsterdam in 1997 incorporated a legal basis for modest future initiatives by the Commission in the area of social inclusion, and since the mid-1990s the Commission has been conducting an extensive dialogue with Member States on the question of modernizing and improving their social protection systems. A series of communications culminating in the 1999 Commission document "Modernising Social Protection" reflected a general consensus on the main topics requiring attention: the long-term sustainability of social protection systems (especially pensions), making work pay, promoting social inclusion, and access to good and sustainable health care.

Following a European Council decision at the end of the Finnish presidency in December 1999, a high-level working group on social protection was set up to pursue these topics. This group decided to prioritize two of them—pension reform and social inclusion—and in close cooperation with the Commission has focused on these themes during the recent Portuguese, French, Swedish, and now Belgian presidencies. The group was replaced by the Social Protection Committee (SPC) in December 2000 following a formal Council decision the previous June. Its members, who are senior officials nominated by social protection ministers, are expected to provide a politically informed view of issues while the Commission provides the Secretariat. The committee works increasingly closely with two other key committees involved in this area: the Economic Policy Committee (EPC), which reports to ECOFIN ministers, and the Employment Committee (EMCO), which reports to the same council formation as the SPC, the Employment and Social Policy Council. As a result of an Irish proposal to the Inter-Governmental Conference, a provision was included in the Nice Treaty to put the SPC on a similar legal basis as the EMCO.

The Lisbon European Council in March 2000 provided a new political context for promoting social inclusion. Heads of state and government agreed on an ambitious 10-year goal that Europe should become the most competitive and dynamic knowledge-based economy in the world, capable of sustained economic growth with more and better jobs and greater social cohesion. In particular, they provided a mandate to set social inclusion objectives: "The European Council invites the Council and the Commission to promote a better understanding of social exclusion through continuous dialogue and exchanges of information and best practice on the basis of commonly agreed indicators." Furthermore, the SPC would be involved in establishing these indicators.

In this new economic and social context, the challenge for Member States within the EU is to reduce the number of people who are at risk of being poor, address the barriers to social inclusion, and prevent new forms of social exclusion. In 1996 about 17 percent of people (65 million) had incomes below 60 percent of their national median incomes; this threshold is approximately equivalent to 50 percent of average income. The way forward, a successful transition to a knowledge-based society, brings new opportunities but also new risks. The opportunity for more prosperity, jobs, and participation carries the risk of new potential exclusion for those without skills. The opportunity to improve competitiveness through technological change may lead to skills becoming obsolete more quickly. Social protection systems undoubtedly help strengthen social cohesion, but they face financial strains due to aging and low employment participation. The outlook for economic growth and falling unemployment is good, but development may leave deprived urban and rural areas in its wake.

It was agreed that Member States would work together using an open coordination method to address social exclusion as envisaged in the Amsterdam Treaty. This involves, first, setting a number of agreed objectives. In line with the principle of subsidiarity, decisions on strategies and actions to meet these objectives are a matter for national governments. These would be set out in individual National Action Plans for inclusion (NAPincl) and submitted to the Commission. They would then be the subject of peer review and Commission analysis that would result in mutual learning on how best to combat social exclusion. This exercise is designed to assist Member States in improving their strategies and actions for their next NAPincl. Active partnership is considered to be an important dimension of the process; local and regional partners as well as social partners and nongovernmental organizations (NGOs) would be involved at the national and European levels. Essential close coordination between the Council and the Commission is already manifest in SPC operations.

Pursuing the Lisbon mandate, the SPC proposed to the Employment and Social Policy Council the following key objectives in the fight against social exclusion:

- To facilitate participation in employment and access by all to resources, rights, goods, and services
- To prevent risks of exclusion
- To help the most vulnerable
- To mobilize all the relevant actors.

These objectives were endorsed at the Nice European Council in December 2000. It was also agreed at Nice that a NAPincl containing a balanced and integrated set of proposals addressing the four objectives and covering a two-year period would be submitted by each Member State to the Commission by June 1, 2001. As envisaged, these plans are undergoing peer review at the SPC and analysis by the Commission.

From the outset it was recognized that social exclusion is a multidimensional phenomenon and that a wide range of different policy measures are required to address it. There was firm agreement that good-quality employment provides the best safeguard against exclusion, so measures to develop employability are very appropriate. These include initial skills development as well as lifelong learning. Active and modern social protection systems also can be a key tool (for example, in promoting access to employment and in providing adequate retirement incomes). Other key measures are needed to ensure access for all to health care, housing, education, justice, information and communications technology, culture, and leisure. A broad range of relevant measures reflecting the particular situation and priorities of each Member State would therefore be set down in its NAPincl.

Other aspects of scope of the proposed NAPincl that were considered important include:

- Gender equality in all measures
- A strong emphasis on prevention measures
- Measures promoting the inclusion of vulnerable people
- Promotion of a stronger partnership approach
- Indicators to monitor progress
- Use of innovative measures to facilitate mutual learning.

There are many practical challenges involved for Member States in preparing their NAPincl. Since social inclusion is a multidimensional issue, there are many ministries and agencies involved, probably at several levels—national, regional, and local. An effective NAPincl requires coordination within each Member State and appropriate consultation with the social partners and NGOs. A second challenge is measuring the impact of the proposed actions. This is all the more difficult because social inclusion indicators are, at this stage, so underdeveloped. Even if indicators are agreed on and available, setting targets for them remains a sensitive matter.

There was an evident need for better social inclusion indicators. This would involve a range of more sophisticated measurements based on more timely data.

The four-year time lags at present in some key areas must be addressed. The SPC recognized that detailed technical work was needed, so in February 2001 it established an Indicators Sub-Group with experts from each Member State to address the problem. It is planned that the outcome of their initial work will be reflected in the Laeken European Council and in the Spring Council at Barcelona in 2002 in relation to both social inclusion and pensions. The Belgian presidency will focus on social indicators; it commissioned an important academic study as a basis for a conference in September 2001. The Organisation for Economic Co-operation and Development (OECD), which has been working in this area, will also be publishing a report on social indicators.

The Indicators Sub-Group, in conjunction with the Commission which provides it with a supporting secretariat, has been examining the structural social indicators underlying the Commission's synthesis report to the European Council at Stockholm early in 2001. These covered the following areas:

- Distribution of income (income quintile ratios)
- Poverty risk before and after social transfers
- The persistence of poverty
- Jobless households
- Regional cohesion (variations in unemployment rates)
- Early school-leavers not in further education or training
- Long-term unemployment.

The aim of the Indicators Sub-Group has been to arrive at a set of commonly agreed indicators that take account of differing national standards and problems of data comparability. The emphasis is on measuring outcomes rather than inputs. The Sub-Group's recent interim report to the SPC reflected good progress. At the European level, the SPC has had discussions on its work with the social partners, the European Anti-Poverty Network (EAPN), and the European Parliament. All have expressed a keen interest in the matter of social indicators.

Both papers mentioned at the beginning refer to social inclusion issues that, while differing in degree, are common to existing Member States (and probably to candidate countries in general). Ruta Zilvere's wide-ranging paper on the Latvian situation is quite consistent with the Commission and SPC analyses that led to the four agreed objectives for a social inclusion strategy. The groups most at risk of poverty in Latvia are strikingly similar to those elsewhere. The focus on tackling unemployment and particularly long-term unemployment, the ongoing alignment of the social protection system with current needs, the regional disparities, the difficulties faced by minority groups for whatever reasons, the need for a preventive strategy, and the challenges of raising political awareness and involving all the stakeholders are all echoes of the issues being grappled with by existing Member States.

Judging by Michal Vašečka's analysis, the Roma issue in the Slovak Republic appears to have much in common with similar minorities in other states throughout the European Union. The open coordination process now in place in the EU is designed to enable Members to learn from each other. Most of the outputs from that process are in the public domain, and it may be immediately useful for candidate countries in advance of accession to keep an eye on the wide range of strategies being tried by existing Member States in the common fight against social exclusion.

CHAPTER 33

Discussant Notes

Janis A. Emmanouilidis

The efforts of the candidate countries to become members of the European Union (EU) and the imposed conditionality linked to this process have influenced the formulation of social policies and the design of social institutions in the accession states. Direct and indirect EU conditionality has promoted social development in Central and Eastern Europe (CEE) and thereby affected the respective social inclusion policies.

Financial aid and technical assistance by the EU and its Member States are directly applied to combat social exclusion in Central and Eastern Europe. EU aid programs provide funding for national programs to adopt the Union's social policy *acquis*. Their aim is to promote the development of adequate institutions, strengthen social protection systems, and improve dialogue between governments, social partners, nongovernmental organizations (NGOs), and the general public. Moreover, the EU provides financial aid for rural development in the candidate countries and technical assistance, especially with respect to policy advice concerning the reform of social institutions (for example, twinning projects aimed to adapt administrative and democratic institutions in CEE to comply with membership requirements).

But the EU does not restrict itself to financial aid and technical assistance. The Union supports the implementation of international legal norms that promote social inclusion by making them part of accession conditionality. Thus, in order to join the EU, applicants must have ratified various human rights conventions such as the European Social Charter, the Framework Convention for National Minorities, the

Convention on the Elimination of All Forms of Racial Discrimination, or the Convention on the Elimination of All Forms of Discrimination against Women.

Moreover, the European Union and in particular the European Commission have expressed strong concerns about the treatment of minorities in a number of applicant countries. The EU has emphasized the implementation of measures that combat the social and political exclusion of minorities, especially the Hungarian minorities in Romania and the Slovak Republic, the Russian-speaking minorities in Estonia and Latvia, and the Roma minority across Central and Eastern Europe that is in need of better protection. In this regard the Union has publicly criticized the insufficiency of certain policies and put pressure on individual countries (for example, on Romania concerning the treatment of the large number of children in state childcare).

The institutional transformation and increase in organizational capacity in the candidate countries in response to EU accession demands have promoted social inclusion. But how can one evaluate the extent to which the Union has promoted social inclusion (Grabbe and Nicolaidis 2000)? The institutional models adopted by the accession countries were not the ones that would have been chosen by policymakers in Central and Eastern Europe in the absence of EU influence. The European model was not, after all, an obvious choice. The candidates might have opted for an American model or some other type. However, EU-driven institutional change has produced two major benefits: (1) it has helped to overcome inertia and avoid a lengthy search for a domestic political consensus, and (2) the accession process provides a set of incentives for rapid institutional change (Grabbe and Nicolaidis 2000, p. 21).

In that sense, the European Union's model can be said to have exercised a positive influence on social inclusion policies in Central and Eastern Europe. To this assessment I must add three other observations.

First, the current process of enlarging the EU has profited from the experience of previous rounds of enlargement. Now, concerning social measures, this has not proven to be solely an advantage. Due to a reliance on previous models, the European Union has not promoted a consistent and coherent social development agenda designed to meet the requirements of the accession countries. As a consequence, the impact of the Union's efforts to promote social inclusion has been less impressive than it might have been if there had been a consistent approach.

Second, the EU's blueprint for promoting social inclusion in the candidate countries sets constraints on social policies in Central and Eastern Europe. In particular, it imposes financial constraints by requiring applicants to devote funds to a large EU agenda, of which social exclusion is only one relatively small part. As a consequence, tight national budgets concerning social transfers are restricted even more.

Third, EU conditionality has promoted the restructuring of the agricultural sector in the accession states. This will, however, prove to be highly problematic, since the number of those employed on the land will massively diminish. As a consequence, most of the candidates will witness an increase in the number of poor in rural areas in the short run and an acceleration of urbanization in the long run. The EU, however, lacks a clear strategy for helping applicants to cope with the socioeconomic upheavals and unwanted social effects of migration from the countryside to the cities. In sum, the European Union has been a factor in promoting social inclusion, but measures could have been more successful.

Beyond this general assessment, one might raise the question whether the EU dimension should play a role in promoting social inclusion at all. Is there really a need to promote social inclusion at the EU level? And is there one single "European Social Model" to be adopted? Some argue that there is. Others claim that no single model exists in either the EU-15 or the candidate countries. However, this is not a clear matter of yes or no. At issue is the extent of common social standards at the EU level. The current approach is for countries to seek the lowest common denominator among themselves. The degree of social standards is largely perceived as a factor of economic competition. As a result, we witness fierce competition among the EU Member States with regard to their social policies. Proposals from the European Commission to strengthen common social standards are not supported by a majority of Member States in the European Council.

But does the EU require a higher degree of common social standards, thereby creating something like a European Social Model worth its name and recognized as a positive element of European integration by citizens in the EU-15 and in future Member States? There are strong arguments both against and in favor of higher standards. On the one hand, low standards provide for flexibility in defining national social standards. From the candidates' perspective, this might be an advantage, since they could profit in economic terms from lower social standards by keeping additional wage costs low. Low common European social standards and a high degree of flexibility in choosing a particular model might give future members a comparative advantage. On the other hand, higher social standards defined at the European level could help combat the risk of social polarization in an enlarged EU, especially in those Member States with economies that still lag behind the average.

The promotion of social cohesion and social inclusion by the European Union requires adequate funding. It is an obvious truth that money cannot compensate for insufficient policies at both the national and European levels. Nevertheless, measures to promote and implement social policies, especially in the candidate countries, which already face budgetary constraints, need to be adequately funded from the common EU budget. But are Member States—especially the net contributors—willing to extensively promote EU programs against social exclusion? The answer to this question does not solely depend on whether the contributors to the EU budget are ready to increase their national contributions. The real question is whether the Member States will be ready to reform those policies that currently absorb the highest proportion of the budget—namely, the Common Agricultural Policy (CAP) and structural policies. Both the CAP and structural policies need to be reformed to allow for a necessary redefinition of solidarity in an enlarged EU.

The current EU-15 are beginning to consider the future distribution of financial means following the end of the financial framework period in 2006. In the last intergovernmental conference, the cohesion countries (especially Spain supported by Portugal and Greece) opposed the immediate and general introduction of qualified majority voting with respect to decisions in the area of structural policies. In addition, Spain attempted to link the EU's common negotiating position on the free movement of labor to the future allocation of regional and structural funds. These are only the most obvious examples indicating the strong controversies we will witness in the years to come.

An enormous welfare gap between Western and Eastern Europe will persist after the next round of EU enlargement. Most likely, the new Member States will not profit in financial terms from EU support as much as Ireland, Greece, Spain, or Portugal did. However, even after enlargement, the European Union must remain a financial-distributive Union and not become merely a normative Union that sets the norms and goals but does not provide the necessary financial means at the EU level. It is in the interest of current and future Member States that the European Union become a *developmental community* that attaches great importance to achieving socioeconomic cohesion between its members. Transfers provided by the EU to its members should not reflect the hierarchic dependence between donors and beneficiaries that often underlies the support programs of international development agencies or bilateral assistance frameworks. Rather, financing should be characterized by equality, solidarity, and community-oriented behavior (Working Group 2001).

Insufficient social cohesion would affect the future of a European Union of, say, 25 members. Should the EU therefore develop into a genuine Social Union to achieve "an ever closer Union," whatever its final quality and institutional structure? No. In order, however, to deepen integration it seems necessary to abort the principle of a lowest common denominator concerning social policy and define a common denominator on a higher level, without disrespecting cost-efficiency criteria. The promotion of social cohesion and the fight against social exclusion will affect how people feel about the EU. And the degree of approval or disapproval concerning the EU in both the current and future Member States will be decisive for any necessary attempt to reform the European Union in the years to come.

References

Grabbe, Heather, and Kalypso Nicolaidis. 2000. "Fostering Social Inclusion in Central and Eastern Europe: The Role of EU Accession Conditionality." World Bank, Washington, D.C.

Working Group on Issues and Consequences of Enlargement. 2001. "Thinking Enlarged: The Accession Countries and the Future of the European Union." Paper of the Villa Faber Group, jointly organized by the Bertelsmann Foundation, Guetersloh, and the Center for Applied Policy Research. Munich.

Index

Note: b with page number refers to boxes, *f* refers to figures, *m* refers to maps, and *t* refers to tables.

V